Foundations of American Education

Ten Questions for New Teachers

Christian P. Wilkens

Cover Credit: Shutterstock.

Published by State University of New York Press, Albany

© 2025 State University of New York

All rights reserved

Printed in the United States of America

No part of this book may be used or reproduced in any manner without written permission. No part of this book may be stored in a retrieval system or transmitted in any form or by any means including electronic, electrostatic, magnetic tape, mechanical, photocopying, recording, or otherwise without the prior permission in writing of the publisher.

Links to third-party websites are provided as a convenience and for informational purposes only. They do not constitute an endorsement or an approval of any of the products, services, or opinions of the organization, companies, or individuals. SUNY Press bears no responsibility for the accuracy, legality, or content of a URL, the external website, or for that of subsequent websites.

For information, contact State University of New York Press, Albany, NY
www.sunypress.edu

Library of Congress Cataloging-in-Publication Data

Name: Wilkens, Christian P., 1975– author.
Title: Foundations of American education : ten questions for new teachers / Christian P. Wilkens.
Description: Albany : State University of New York Press, [2025] | Includes bibliographical references.
Identifiers: LCCN 2024025616 | ISBN 9798855801019 (pbk. : alk. paper) | ISBN 9798855801026 (ebook)
Subjects: LCSH: First year teachers—United States—Handbooks, manuals, etc. | Teaching—Vocational guidance—United States | Public schools—United States.
Classification: LCC LB2844.1.N4 W544 2025 | DDC 371.10023/73—dc23/eng/20241107
LC record available at https://lccn.loc.gov/2024025616

*To Julie, who saw me make most of the
bad teaching decisions I'm about to tell you to avoid*

CONTENTS

List of Illustrations — v

Introduction: Why Should Anyone Read a Book about Foundations of Education? — 1

Chapter 1: Teachers and Schools: What Is It Like to Be a Teacher? — 3

Chapter 2: History: What's the History of Public Schools in the United States? — 21

Chapter 3: Governance and Finance: Why Does It Matter that Public Schools Have Local Control? — 52

Chapter 4: Communities: What Should I Learn about My Students, Their Families, and Their Communities? — 78

Chapter 5: Curriculum: How Will I Know What to Teach? — 103

Chapter 6: Instruction: What Should I Do in Class My First Year? — 123

Chapter 7: Classroom Management: How Should I Manage My Classroom? — 155

Chapter 8: Assessment: How Will I Know If Students Are Learning What They Should? — 180

Chapter 9: Law and Ethics: How Can I Get Fired? — 207

Chapter 10: What Comes Next: How Can I Make Things Better for Students? — 235

Bibliography — 252

Index — 295

ILLUSTRATIONS

Figure 2.1	"Colored" scholars excluded from schools.	24
Figure 2.2	The first-grade class of Mary Louise Mitchell at the Blackwell School in Marfa, Texas.	29
Figure 2.3	Black student Elizabeth Eckford is jeered by white student Hazel Bryan as she attempts to enter Central High School in Little Rock, Arkansas.	30
Figure 2.4	K–12 public school enrollment, by race and ethnicity.	32
Figure 2.5	Percentage distribution of public elementary and secondary school students, by student's race/ethnicity and percentage of own racial/ethnic group enrolled in the school.	33
Figures 2.6a and b	Henry Standing Bear, Wounded Yellow Robe and Chauncy Yellow Robe at Carlisle Indian School, Carlisle, Pennsylvania.	37
Figure 2.7	School children, Manzanar Relocation Center, California.	38
Figure 2.8	Children and their parents demonstrate against English-only Proposition 227, Oakland, California.	39
Figure 2.9	Exterior of the Montana State Training School, Boulder, Montana.	41
Figure 2.10	Devyn Pereira with service dogs Rubin and Hannah, Rochester, New York.	43
Figure 3.1	Students line up outside a dorm at Hunters Point Boarding School, St. Michaels, Arizona.	56
Figure 3.2	Sample school district organizational chart.	60
Figure 3.3	The Whiskey Rebellion.	62
Figure 3.4	A demonstrator at a "Tax Day" demonstration in Cincinnati, Ohio, holds a sign reading "taxation is theft."	63

Figure 3.5	Revenue for U.S. public elementary and secondary schools, by source of funds.	64
Figure 3.6	Expenditures per student, U.S. public elementary and secondary schools, by type of expenditure.	66
Figure 3.7	Demetrio Rodríguez with his sons (left to right) Carlos, Alexander, and James outside Edgewood Elementary School, San Antonio, Texas.	74
Figure 4.1	President Barack Obama visits a pre-kindergarten classroom at the College Heights Early Childhood Learning Center, Decatur, Georgia.	80
Figure 4.2	Two Navajo women talk to each other during a Gourd Dance, Gallup, New Mexico.	84
Figure 4.3	Chris Agragiiq Apassingok, with Ina Koonooka on a Honda outside his family's home, Gambell, Alaska.	94
Figure 6.1	Maslow's hierarchy of motivation.	127
Figure 6.2	Elementary classroom with stations, Sally Ride Elementary School, Orlando, Florida.	129
Figure 6.3	Shuyukan High School classroom, Fukuoka, Japan.	130
Figure 6.4	Takanawadai Elementary School, Tokyo, Japan.	131
Figure 6.5	Skyline High School science classroom, Lake Frederick, Virginia.	132
Figure 6.6	Reading at Bardon Infant's School, Queensland, Australia.	132
Figure 6.7	Elementary classroom, Alaska.	133
Figure 7.1	Students at Hogarth Kingeekuk Sr. Memorial School, Sivunga (Savoonga), Alaska.	158
Figure 7.2	Students at Nanyou Primary School at the end of class, Shenzen, Guangdong, China.	158
Figure 7.3	Abe Wheeler, forester, visits Buckman Elementary School, Portland, Oregon.	173
Figure 8.1	Cartoon illustration.	180
Figure 8.2	Item from New York State Grade 8 Intermediate-Level Science Test, June 2022.	183

Illustrations   vii

Figure 8.3	A biologist examining a sample of brown algae (*Fucus spp.*), Gulf of Alaska.	185
Figure 8.4	Life cycle of assessment.	190
Figure 8.5	We need air support (meme)!	193
Figure 8.6	Item adapted from New York State Regents Living Environment Test, January, 2023.	197
Figure 8.7	Differing interpretations of a numerical grade.	199
Figure 9.1	Inclusive restrooms, St. Anthony Park Elementary School, St. Paul, Minnesota.	208
Figure 9.2	Cain, after killing his brother Abel. Statue by Henri Vidal, Paris, France.	231
Figure 10.1	Super-tired teacher sitting at his desk.	236
Figure 10.2	Three students reading in a classroom.	247

INTRODUCTION

Why Should Anyone Read a Book about Foundations of Education?

Without foundations, teaching is technical work probably best left to robots. It is the decisions teachers make, hour by hour, that makes us good, bad, or somewhere in between. Decisions in teaching are complex and uncertain (*How should I address that student with his head down? What should I do when students don't do their homework? How do I handle fourth period . . . which is a depressing mess?*). Foundations give you a base for making good decisions.

The point of this book is to outline major areas you need to consider as you prepare to teach. A consistent criticism of teacher education programs is that they don't do a good job preparing teachers for the real world of schools. You may read a bunch of books (like this one), write papers, and have excellent discussions of schools, of teaching, and of students. And then . . . out in a field placement or in student teaching, you might find yourself wondering . . . *why didn't my classes help me with this? Why didn't anyone ask me to practice a phone call home, or what to do when someone throws up in class?* This is a known problem in our work: a divide between theory and practice. In my own work, I view the divide as a problem, something we need to take seriously and fix.

Not everyone sees the theory/practice divide as a problem. John Dewey, one of the most influential theorists of American public education in the early twentieth century, claimed that a divide between teacher education and public schools was a good thing. Dewey was disappointed in our public schools. He encouraged teacher education programs to concern themselves with teaching and learning as they should be, rather than as they were: "To place the emphasis upon the securing of proficiency in teaching and discipline," Dewey wrote, "*puts the attention of the student teacher in the wrong place, and tends to fix it in the wrong direction*" (Dewey, 1904, 13, emphasis in the original). He disparaged a "lack of intellectual independence among teachers, their tendency to intellectual subserviency" and claimed that "[t]eachers, actual and intending, flock to those persons who give them clear-cut and definite instructions as to just how to teach this or that" (16). Dewey wanted teachers like you prepared not for "proficiency in teaching and discipline"—but for challenging the status quo.

I'm not convinced. I think gaining "proficiency in teaching and discipline" is a necessary and worthwhile goal for you, and for any new teacher. That's the job. You will be expected to help students learn. You will be expected to manage your classroom effectively. Do those two things well, and you'll be a long way down the road toward becoming a good teacher.

This book is organized around questions. Each question clarifies the purpose of the chapter and provides built-in accountability. If I ask a question, I owe you a coherent answer. Sometimes the answers are admittedly squishy, variations on "it depends." They'll all be *true* answers, as far as I know. But few of the most important questions in teaching have answers beyond specific contexts. It matters where, what, and who you teach. You'll want to keep your own teaching goals central as you read. *How does this answer work for kindergarteners? Or for a middle school math class featuring Josiah who keeps falling out of his chair?*

You'll have questions all the time as a new teacher. Uncertainty will be a constant companion. Teaching, as you'll learn, isn't anything like being a P–12 student. Teachers work within a huge number of constraints (schedule, curriculum, policies, laws, which kids are in your classes); teachers are responsible for students who have variable interests, skills, and needs; and teachers face hour-by-hour questions about what to do (*Spend more time on this? Move on? Tell Jolen to quit drawing Sonic the Hedgehog on his arm?*). You'll need to answer hundreds of questions a day, often quickly and with limited information. How you approach questions and make decisions will be foundational for the kind of teacher you will become. I think there's real value in asking questions even if we can't find certainty in some of the answers. A good question helps us identify what we don't know and what we should try to learn. I hope you find the questions that open each chapter useful as you prepare to teach.

At the end of each chapter, you'll see three things. First, a brief answer. Second, a major court case, intended to provide a real-life example of issues raised in the chapter. Third, a set of additional readings intended to reinforce or extend points made in the chapter.

I hope you find the questions interesting. I hope the answers provided make sense, even if they're incomplete or otherwise flawed. And I hope that this book provides some "clear-cut and definite instructions," even if John Dewey objects.

Why Should Anyone Read a Book about Foundations of Education?

Because the decisions you will make in the classroom will shape your success as a teacher. Because you'll have to make decisions in complex and uncertain contexts. And because foundations can help your decisions improve.

1

Teachers and Schools
What Is It Like to Be a Teacher?

Back in 1974, professional philosopher Thomas Nagel asked his philosopher friends, rivals, and whoever else may have picked up a copy of *The Philosophical Review*: "What is it like to be a bat?" (Nagel, 1974). His point in asking wasn't really to try to get others to describe what it was like to echolocate, chase moths, or poop upside-down. His paper was instead aimed at the nature of consciousness and experience—whether we (humans) can ever really understand what it is like to experience some other consciousness, such as that of a bat. Ultimately, Nagel seemed dubious, concluding, "[a]t present we are completely unequipped to think about the subjective character of experience without relying on the imagination" (Nagel, 1974, 449). Who knows what it's like to be a bat? Not Thomas Nagel. And not us—because we aren't bats.[1]

If Nagel's right, then the question, "What is it like to be a teacher?" is probably not answerable (yet) because it revolves around experiences you haven't had. There may be no way for you to truly understand what it's like to be a teacher (generally), nor what it's like to be any of the specific teachers who may have inspired you to become one yourself. Even if we adopt a more precise wording of the question—something like: *What will it be like for YOU to be a teacher?* . . . the short answer is some version of: no idea. There are millions of public school teachers in the United States, but you aren't one of them yet. And it's not like teaching is the same everywhere. You might be teaching combined grades 2–3 in rural Alaska; you might be teaching high school geometry in Houston, Texas. Those are very different jobs. In a real sense, you won't be able to answer our opening question, even in part, until you start teaching. Nor will your experiences of teaching be static; unless you fail to learn anything whatsoever along the way, your first years and your last years of teaching will be different experiences as well.

The intent of this chapter, then, isn't to tell you what teaching will or won't be like for you personally. It is instead to outline some of the basics of the profession, and what we know about public schools, teachers, and students in the United States. I'm not going to tell you teaching is awesome, the best work ever. You may love it. You may find out that working with young people is not for you. No judgment either way. You are owed (I think) an early and accurate sense of what we know about the work at this particular moment. Just keep in mind, per Nagel and his bats, that the most critical experiences can and will only be known by one person: you.

NOTES ON OBVIOUS THINGS

- You will work with young people. Every year this seems to surprise some of my student teachers, so I'll be explicit: *teaching involves spending most of every single day with young people. In groups.* Most of the plans you prepare, most of the problems you'll solve, and most of the interactions you'll have every day will be with . . . you guessed it . . . young people. If you teach in the rural South, you're going to spend a lot of time with rural Southern kids. If you teach in Alaska, you're going to spend a lot of time with kids who want to play basketball outside in shorts, even when it's freezing. Teaching is not about you. It is not about how much you love reading, or French, or history, or quadratic equations (although your loves are necessary and important). It is about whether you enjoy spending time with young people. If so, you'll succeed and stay. If not—look, it's the *job*. You should figure out your feelings here as soon as you can. Every kid who has ever existed knows whether an adult wants to be with them. You cannot fake this aspect of teaching.

- Your students are not you. This too surprises some new teachers. One non-obvious problem with teachers (you) is that, for the most part, teachers are academically successful. You graduated from high school, you're going to graduate from college, or already did. This alone makes you different from a majority of Americans (38% of U.S. adults graduated from college, 62% did not; Schaeffer, 2021). The issue here: *can you can understand and address student struggles?* If you are preparing to teach math, for example, you were probably good at math. Why is this a problem? By itself, it isn't. I'm glad you know math. You should be able to do math successfully with your students, duh. Here's a true thing that happens, though:

Kid in algebra class: I don't get it.

Algebra teacher: Which part?

Kid: All of it.

Teacher: Um.

Obviously you can't just re-say the math louder. Something in the lesson didn't work for that student. Your beautiful perfect math lesson, brilliantly explained . . . didn't stick. What next? Your job as a teacher is not (only) explaining things well. It is, more accurately, anticipating challenges for your students and organizing your lessons so that most or all can successfully navigate those challenges. It's to help students understand things that they find difficult, even or especially when you find them simple. It can be very hard for people who are good at things to know why others struggle. Heads up: your students are not you.

- Individual relationships are huge. This is why we don't simply record our most brilliant 2nd-grade teachers in the United States (or 3rd-grade, etc.), post the videos, and tell our kids to watch. You and your students are at the center of teaching work. It may take you time to develop relationships with your students—that's OK. Be ready to connect with students who are not like you (see above). Your ability to form strong relationships with each of your students, especially the ones who may be harder to reach or love, is a career-defining skill. You don't need to be good at it yet, but you will need to learn how in the years ahead.

- Good things: coffee, comfortable shoes, compartmentalization. You are going to start your days early. You are going to turn into a person who gets tired at 10 p.m. You are not going to be the most elegantly dressed person in school every day. It's OK: teachers are not required to be cool. We *are* required to be ready for class tomorrow morning, and we *are* required to take good enough care of ourselves to be there every day. This is something I want you to take seriously: we need to be *up* for our students. When we are sleepy, our classes are sleepy. If we are crabby, things do not go well. You need to get some sleep; you need to eat your vegetables and call your mother back. Of course you will remain a human being with an outside life. Teachers struggle with finances, have difficult relationships, and experience real hurt and anger and stress, just like everyone else. You cannot, cannot bring all that mess into your classroom. Whatever else is going on in your outside life: Keep. It. There. When you teach, you need to have energy, you need to smile, crack jokes, and be there fully with your students. Every day, every lesson. Students do not need your stress and worry. I won't lie—this can be one of the hardest things for new teachers to learn. *You need to be what your students need*—not whatever else you feel like. Every day.

The above is not a set of precise answers to *What is it like to be a teacher?*—but I hope it's clear there are a few universals. Be ready to spend a lot of time with young people, many of whom are not like you. Be ready to work hard on relationships. And be ready to be good and positive and affirming even when you're feeling other things inside.

Below I'll outline some aspects of schools, teachers, and students that are useful for teachers to know. My hope is not to overwhelm with numbers but to give you a sense for the work you're about to join. As always, averages are not particulars—your own school, teaching job, and students will have their own shape and feel each year.

U.S. PUBLIC SCHOOLS

In 2022–2023, almost 100,000 public schools were operating in the United States, educating roughly fifty million students (National Center for Education Statistics, 2022a; National Center for Education Statistics, 2022b). That same year, our public schools employed three million teachers, about half in elementary grades (K–6) and half in secondary grades (7–12; National Center for Education Statistics, 2022c). Most public schools in the United States (92%) were classified as "traditional" (governed by a local school board); the remainder (8%) were classified as "charter" (governed by a private board under a charter, or contract; National Center for Education Statistics, 2022d). Although not a major subject in this book, the United States also had an estimated 30,000 private schools in 2019–2020 (most recent data, National Center for Education Statistics, 2022e), educating 4.7 million students, or 9% of school-aged children. Finally, an estimated 2.6 million students in the United States were homeschooled in 2020–2021, about 5% of school-aged children (most recent data, National Center for Education Statistics, 2022f).

Table 1.1. U.S. Public schools, 2019–2020

Average enrollment	529
Location: City	25%
Location: Suburban	32%
Location: Town	14%
Location: Rural	29%
Average number of teachers	30
Average student-to-teacher radio	17:1
Average expenditure per student	$13,701
White–Black racial segregation index	0.49
Economic segregation index	0.30

Sources: Enrollment: Riser-Kositsky (2023); location: National Center for Education Statistics, Table 214.40 (2021a), teachers: Table 2 (2022g); number of schools: NCES Table 216.10 (2021b); number of students: NCES Table 203.40 (2022g); expenditures: "Public School Expenditures" (2023a); segregation indices: University of Southern California (2022).

Overall, about 90 percent of school-aged children in the United States attend public schools, most in "traditional" schools run by public authorities and open to all students within a defined geography. Although there's really no such thing as an "average" public school, Table 1.1 offers a quick look at some descriptive statistics for public schools in the United States as they were in 2019–2020. A few things in these averages are worth noticing. Schools are in every community in the United States, employ lots of teachers, and spend a lot of money. A quick back-of-the envelope calculation (529 students times $13,701/year) suggests the "average" public school has an operating budget of over $7 million each year. That money largely goes into salaries. The economic impact of public school spending can be especially pronounced in rural communities, where teaching is a comparatively well-paid profession (National Center for Education Statistics, 2023a). It's also worth noticing the student-to-teacher ratio of 17:1, which suggests that class sizes in U.S. public schools need not be huge. U.S. public schools employ a lot of specialists (literacy specialists, special education teachers, and others who work with small groups), hence don't all have exactly seventeen students per class. Some teachers may have large classes while others work with small groups or individuals.

Note the two "segregation indices." Segregation by race, ethnicity, money, and other variables is foundational for U.S. public schools—there from the beginning in almost every jurisdiction, still shaping schools and communities today. These indices were calculated by researchers at Stanford and the University of Southern California (https://segindex.org), with a scale of 0 to 1 (0 = complete integration; 1 = complete segregation). The "segregation index" numbers provide one way to understand how segregated students from various backgrounds are from others at school. The White–Black racial segregation index of 0.49 means that the proportion of white students in a given white student's school is roughly 50% higher than the proportion of white students in a given Black student's school.[2]

The economic segregation index provides a measure of concentrated poverty in schools, using the federal free lunch program as a marker, again with a scale of 0 to 1 (0 = no concentrated poverty; 1 = completely concentrated poverty). An economic segregation index of 0.30 means that the percentage of students eligible for free lunch was 30 percentage points higher in the average free-lunch-eligible student's school than in the average ineligible (wealthier) student's school.

Most of the racial and economic segregation we see in U.S. public schools exists between *districts* rather than between *schools*. This means that entire school districts in the United States—not just schools—are often identifiable by race or income (such as "predominantly Black" or "predominantly low-income"). Although some segregation happens between and within schools (for example, honors or AP tracks within a high school may draw disproportionately wealthy students), the hard lines of segregation in U.S. public schools are typically those drawn along school district boundaries. I'll explore some of the history behind the development (and hardening) of school district boundaries in the next chapter—just know that racial and economic segregation are major features of public schools in the United States and will shape your experiences as a classroom teacher in the years ahead.

U.S. PUBLIC SCHOOL TEACHERS

Any group of three million people includes a range of humanity, but public school teachers in the United States aren't a simple cross-section of the American public. For example, a disproportionately small percentage of teachers in U.S. public schools are men, compared to the general population (see Table 1.2, opposite page).

Some notes on Table 1.2:

- % male teachers: This could just as easily be % female teachers. I'm highlighting male teachers because the field has been disproportionately female since the late nineteenth century; the trend in the last several decades has been even more women teaching, and fewer men entering the profession. It's now 3:1 women-to-men teaching in U.S. public schools (Wong, 2019). This may be non-optimal for a student body that's roughly

Table 1.2. U.S. Public School Teachers

% certified teachers	94%
% male teachers	24%
% Black teachers	7%
Average (modal) years of teaching experience	14
Average teacher age	42
Average annual salary for first-year teachers	$41,770
Odds of staying in the same teaching job next year	84%

Notes and sources: "Certified teachers" includes those who held a regular or standard state teaching certificate or advanced professional certificate, National Center for Education Statistics, 2017; % men: Wong, 2019; % Black: National Center for Education Statistics, 2020; experience: National Center for Education Statistics, 2019a; age: National Center for Education Statistics, 2018; salary: National Center for Education Statistics, 2021c; odds of staying: National Center for Education Statistics, 2014.

half young men, though the evidence base is mixed on effects (Hansen & Quintero, 2018).

- % Black teachers: This could just as easily be Indigenous teachers, Latinx teachers, etc. I'm highlighting Black teachers as an important benchmark because of a long history of dismissals, forced resignations, and demotions fueled by racism and white supremacy in the United States (Tillman, 2004), including post-*Brown v. Board* school closures and consolidations of schools that specifically harmed our ranks of Black teachers (Givens, 2021). Identify a group subject to racism, discrimination, and fear in broader American society—and you will find a reduced supply of teacher talent. There's a lot to discuss here; just know that public schools in the United States are not yet representative of the young people they serve.

- Average (modal) years of teaching experience: these are averages among teachers who were currently teaching when surveyed; these averages don't count everyone who started teaching but left. Be advised: we've got a turnover problem in teaching—back in 2015–2016, roughly 8% left the profession annually (National Center for Education Statistics, 2015); Ingersoll et al. (2018) estimated that 44% of new teachers leave within five years.

- Average annual salary for first-year teachers: teacher salaries vary a lot by states and districts. As of 2023, the lowest starting annual salary for teachers with a bachelor's degree was in Montana ($33,568), and the highest in Washington, DC ($56,313). Here's a table so you can find salaries in states where you might work: www.nea.org/resource-library/educator-pay-and-student-spending-how-does-your-state-rank.

- Odds of staying in the same teaching job next year: these National Center for Education Statistics (2014) data are aging; it's unclear whether these odds have changed in more recent years, though most reports suggest the impact of the COVID-19 pandemic (2020–2022) may increase teacher attrition for years (see Goldhaber & Theobald, 2022).

You may or may not match the teacher demographics above—no matter what, you'll want to build connections with teachers already doing the work, especially teachers with experience. During your first year, you will make hundreds of decisions every day—about lesson plans, management, family contacts, seating charts, homework, and much, much more. It can be hard to know which details are most important, which is where experienced colleagues can help. A good goal for any new teacher is to find a mentor you trust. They can help you learn what the job requires, how to respond successfully to some of the early challenges, and how to be successful enough in the work that you want to come back next year.

Table 1.3. U.S. Adults, Teachers, and Students: Race, Ethnicity, and Gender

	Percentage U.S. Public (age 18+)	Percentage U.S. Public School Teachers	Percentage U.S. Public School Students (age 3–21)
American Indian / Alaska Native, non-Hispanic	1.3	0.5	1.0
Asian, non-Hispanic	6.1	2.1	5.2
Black or African American, non-Hispanic	13.6	6.7	15.2
Hispanic, regardless of race	18.9	9.3	26.8
Native Hawaiian / Pacific Islander, non-Hispanic	0.3	0.2	0.4
Two or more races, non-Hispanic	2.9	1.8	3.9
White, non-Hispanic	75.8	79.3	47.6
Male	49.5	23.5	50.5
Female	50.5	76.5	49.5
Non-binary or other	0.3	Not collected / reported	Not collected / reported

Notes and sources: U.S. adult population: U.S. Census Bureau, 2022; teachers: National Center for Education Statistics, 2019b; student race and ethnicity: National Center for Education Statistics, 2022h; student gender: U.S. Census Bureau, 2019.

Let's explore demography in some detail. As shown in Table 1.3, teachers, students, and the U.S. public beyond schools have notably different backgrounds (terminology from U.S. Census Bureau). Public school teachers are less diverse than the adult U.S. population as a whole, and far less diverse than the students they teach. We clearly have a supply problem: not everyone heads into teaching. Why not? What makes teaching more attractive or doable for white women than those from other backgrounds? We also have a clear demographic mismatch between teachers and their students. For example, in 2021, over 40% of our school-age students in the United States, but just 16% of teachers, identified as Black or Hispanic. Nor is the difference neutral for students; racial and ethnic mismatches are implicated in a range of less-than-good outcomes for young people, including disproportionately harsh discipline (Bristol, Shirrell, & Britton, 2021; Lindsay & Hart, 2017), lowered expectations (Gershenson, Holt, & Papageorge, 2016), lowered achievement (Dee, 2004; Quiocho & Rios, 2000), and reduced attainment in schools (Gershenson et al., 2022), among others. Conclusion: *we need to diversify and improve teacher pipelines virtually everywhere.*

There's growing evidence that teacher backgrounds matter. For example, a recent study concluded that Black students who had at least one Black teacher were more likely to graduate from high school and go to college than Black students who had never had a Black teacher (Gershenson, 2022). It's not that white women shouldn't go into teaching. Racial, gender, and ethnicity gaps between teachers and students aren't insurmountable—all of us can learn to teach and be effective with students who share, and who don't share, our backgrounds. Rather, it's clear that we need to expand the teacher supply everywhere, *and* we need everyone who teaches to dedicate themselves to getting to know their students as well as they possibly can so they can teach (and students can learn) effectively.

U.S. PUBLIC SCHOOL STUDENTS

Table 1.4 (next page) offers a look at our fifty million U.S. public school students:

Notes on Table 1.4:

- Students with disabilities (SWDs): Students eligible for services under the Individuals with Disabilities Education Act (IDEA); typically offered an Individualized Education Program (IEP).

- Students learning English as a new language: Also identified as English Learners (ELs), English Language Learners (ELLs), or English as a New Language (ENL) students; these are students not yet proficient in spoken and/or written academic English.

Table 1.4. U.S. Public School Students: Grade Levels, Demography, and Outcomes

	Number	Percentage
All students	49,375,467	100%
Grades Pre-K–8	34,059,364	69%
Grades 9–12	15,316,103	31%
Highest parent attainment = no college degree		43%
Eligible for free and/or reduced-price lunch	26,000,645	52%
Students with disabilities (SWDs)	7,200,000	15%
Students learning English as a new language	5,100,000	10%
4th-grade NAEP reading "proficient" (238)		33%
4th-grade NAEP math "proficient" (249)		36%
4-year cohort graduation rate		86%

Notes and sources: Grade levels, parent attainment, free and reduced-price lunch, disability, and English learner status from National Center for Education Statistics, 2023a; 4-year cohort graduation rate from National Center for Education Statistics, 2019c; NAEP data from National Assessment of Educational Progress, 2022.

- 4th-grade NAEP Reading: Students who are "proficient" (score of 238 or higher out of 500) should be able to "integrate and interpret texts and apply their understanding of the text to draw conclusions and make evaluations."

- 4th-grade NAEP Mathematics: Students who are "proficient" (score of 249 or higher out of 500) should "consistently apply integrated procedural knowledge and conceptual understanding to problem solving in the five NAEP content areas."

- 4-year cohort graduation rate: "[T]he number of students who graduate from high school in four years with a regular high school diploma" based on the number of students entering grade 9 four years prior. Technical guidance in U.S. Department of Education (2017).

Plenty to unpack here. First, 43% of U.S. public school students do not have a parent or guardian in the household who earned a college degree. Sit with that for a second. Almost half of your students go home to a household where no one graduated from college. This isn't *bad*, but it matters . . . because you, and all your teacher friends, and your school principal, and the guidance counselor down the hall, and the nurse and the social worker and all those specialists who work with your students—they *all* graduated from college. Every single one of them. Be advised: the "college degree" statistic itself is not terribly important—but it may signal important differences between your background and that of the families you serve, including communication styles, discipline at home, earnings, employment, health, housing and food security, and the academic and work expectations held for children. It will be on you to find out what families expect from their own children, from you, and how best to teach and communicate without disrespect.

It's also worth noting one basic truth: virtually all of your students' parents, guardians, and grandparents went to school themselves. They have histories with schools and teachers that have nothing to do with you. Some of them were lucky enough to attend schools with skilled and joyful teachers. Some went to schools that were miserable. And every one of these parents and guardians carries their experiences with them when their own children go to school. They may or may not trust and love teachers or schools. And if you teach anything other than Pre-K or kindergarten, their children have had other teachers and experiences at school before you. As a teacher, you're stepping into narratives that existed before you got there. You may be held responsible for things that are not articulated and events to which you bore no witness. I'm not telling you it's *fair*—I'm telling you it *is*. Some of your best early work with parents and families will be to listen to what they tell you. They may share a story that sounds a lot like "The Horrible Thing This Awful Teacher Did to My Other Child Four Years Ago," but here's another way to hear it: "This Thing That Happened Was No Good. I Hope You Do Better."

Back to those student numbers, above. More than half the U.S. public school student population is eligible for food subsidies at school (typically, breakfast and lunch). In many schools, the entire student body is eligible. This matters for two reasons. First, hungry kids don't learn well—so it is a truly good thing that students have access to nutrition at school (Hecht et al., 2020). Second—a high proportion of students eligible for free or reduced price meals in your classroom means that a high proportion of your students go home to families that do not earn a lot of money, and who may face food insecurity on a regular basis. If you know, for example, that the only regular meals your students access are at school, what might that mean for the volume and type of homework you assign? Can you provide snacks for after-school activities? Or just keep a box of granola bars in your classroom for your students?[3]

Let's put the percentages of students with disabilities (15% of students in U.S. public schools) and those learning English (10% of students in U.S. public schools) into context. If you have twenty-five students in your classroom, that means your class will likely include three or four students with disabilities, and two or three students who are learning academic English. That should be true of every class in your school, not just yours. Three important notes:

1. As a public school teacher in the United States, you don't get to pick and choose students. Every student deserves access to skilled teachers.

2. Public school teachers owe every student who comes to class acceptance, welcome, and effort to meet their learning needs.

3. Segregation is bad.

One caution: there's a code among teachers who are trying to avoid certain kinds of students. It goes something like this: "Well . . . I just don't feel *qualified* or *trained* to provide the kinds of supports that student needs. They're better off with a specialist." Don't fall into this trap. You're the teacher, kids need you, figure it out. Imagine doctors who only wanted to see healthy patients, or lawyers who only helped perfect people. It's never your role to decide that a student is better off elsewhere (because of excuse X or Y or Z).

On a related note: hyper-specialization and exclusion does not help kids. Schools often do foolish things like pulling students with language-based disabilities out of . . . wait for it . . . English class. Perhaps the most language-rich class in school. To get services. About language. It's never a good idea to treat students as if they are (only) their disability, or as if they are (only) their language proficiency status. Doing so harms learning. Want evidence? Compare the four-year graduation rates among students with disabilities (75.9%; National Center for Education Statistics, 2021b) and English Learners (68.4%; U.S. Department of Education, 2022) to the overall four-year graduation rate of 86%. Many students with disabilities and English Learners are awash in specialists providing services—and they're still not doing well. We can do better.

With respect to terminology, I'm using the term "segregation" as a label for what many schools do with students with disabilities and students learning English. They separate them into special classes or special programs with specialist teachers, excluding them from general education classes, teachers, and peers. I'm not convinced the intent is always nefarious—but the effect most certainly is. Separating students from each other, and from skilled teachers, invariably causes worse outcomes for those who are removed. We've known this for generations. Yet we keep trying to do it because . . . well, that's what we know how to do. The irony here is that the Individuals with Disabilities Education Act (IDEA, 1975) requires all students to be placed in the "Least Restrictive Environment (LRE)." Even back in 1975, we knew that if we allowed schools to educate students with disabilities however they wished, many would do the easiest thing: warehouse them in a separate class, down the hall by the boiler room.

Last notes from the table above—on graduation rates and achievement. In 2018–2019, just 86% of seniors who started 9th grade four years earlier graduated (most recent data available; National Center for Education Statistics, 2023b).Even if that rate seems decent, it still means *millions* of U.S. public school students did not finish high school. Not graduating from high school is permanently bad. Students who don't finish face (on average) lower earnings, higher unemployment, worse health, a higher risk of drug and alcohol abuse, higher risks of criminal activity and incarceration, lower tax contributions, higher dependency on public benefits like Medicaid and Medicare and welfare, and shorter lifespans (National Dropout Prevention Center, n.d.). So one challenge all teachers face—not just those who teach 12th grade or 9th grade—*all teachers*—is making sure we teach well enough that students *stay engaged* long enough to want to graduate. That's on all of us. And most of the narrative for students who drop out is established long before high school. Don't make school miserable for your students.

With respect to learning and achievement, our best evidence on U.S. public school students comes from the National Assessment of Educational Progress (NAEP), a series of exams given to samples of students all over the nation on a regular basis since 1969. It carries no stakes (no one needs to pass it to graduate), it isn't linked to funding or scholarships (so there's little incentive to cheat), and it's the same test given across the country and in all U.S. territories (so we can compare student performance across states and territories).[4]

What the NAEP tells us is that *most U.S. students aren't proficient* at reading, math, science, or history in grades 4, 8, or 12 (see Table 1.5). Bleak, right? We're handing high school diplomas out to 86% of our high school students . . . but NAEP data suggest only about a third of those high school seniors can actually read and do math proficiently. If you're thinking: "Hey, maybe the NAEP is just super hard or something . . . ?" No. You can see sample questions here: https://nces.ed.gov/nationsreportcard/nqt. Following Table 1.5 (next page) is a question from an 8th-grade U.S. History test (with a 15% proficiency rate):

Table 1.5. U.S. Public School Students: NAEP Proficiency in Various Subject Areas

NAEP Subject Area: Reading	
Grade Level	Percentage Proficient
4th grade	33%
8th grade	31%
12th grade	37%
NAEP Subject Area: Mathematics	
Grade Level	Percentage Proficient
4th grade	36%
8th grade	26%
12th grade	24%
NAEP Subject Area: Science	
Grade Level	Percentage Proficient
4th grade	36%
8th grade	35%
12th grade	22%
NAEP Subject Area: Geography	
Grade Level	Percentage Proficient
8th grade	25%
NAEP Subject Area: U.S. History	
Grade Level	Percentage Proficient
8th grade	13%

Notes: Reading and mathematics results in 4th and 8th grades from the 2022 NAEP. Reading and mathematics results in the 12th grade and science results from 2019 NAEP. U.S. History results from the 2022 NAEP. Geography results from the 2018 NAEP. www.nationsreportcard.gov.

Which group of Americans followed what has become known as the "Trail of Tears" when they were forced to leave their homes?

    A. Japanese Americans

    B. Irish Americans

    C. Cherokee Indians

    D. Mormons

Other questions ask about the purpose of the Underground Railroad and how inventions like telephones and automobiles changed people's lives. The NAEP is not rocket science.

You may be tempted to shrug off the NAEP with anti-testing refrains common among (some) teachers: "Some kids just don't test well!" Or: "Tests can't measure everything!" Or: "Imagination is more important than knowledge!"[5] Don't. National-level tests like the NAEP are well designed and provide meaningful information about student knowledge and skills. More on this in the assessment chapter. If we ignore the information assessments provide, who pays the price? Not us. Our students.

NAEP averages mask variability in student achievement across the country. In New York State, for example, there are 700+ public school districts educating 2.5 million P–12 students. Some of New York's school districts are stellar—with near-universal graduation rates, high test scores on the New York Regents examinations, and well-dressed pep bands at every home football game (U.S. News & World Report, 2023). At the same time, some of New York's school districts are among the worst in the country (Felton, 2016). We have decided, all of us collectively, that this variability is an acceptable consequence of local control (more on this in the history and governance chapters ahead).

This too is part of the story of what it is like to be a teacher in U.S. public schools: the work varies, a lot, depending on where you are and who you teach. We've generally agreed that every student deserves a qualified teacher, and that schools should pay attention to nutritional, emotional, physical, and mental health needs. But . . . we tolerate circumstances that don't provide those things. We've found ways to graduate most students from high school across the country. But . . . we also don't graduate millions of students from high school. And we tolerate remarkably low overall student achievement. Our work is by the numbers a decidedly uneven project.

I hope it's clear at this point that what teaching is like in U.S. public schools depends on circumstance as much as anything else. Our 100,000 schools (and the three million teaching jobs in them) aren't really a single thing we can point to and say: *This is it. This is what it will be like.* There are some general outlines. Public schools in the United States have origins that are deep, rooted in ethnic and racial discrimination (read the next chapter for a few origin stories), and continue through the present to reflect the values and fears of those who built them. Public schools are full of contradictions; they remain among the few institutions in American society that a very high percentage of the population uses (National Center for Education Statistics, 2022c); they are consistently well regarded by the parents and families who use them (Brenan, 2021); they also remain profoundly segregated (U.S. Government Accountability Office, 2022) and academically disappointing (National Assessment of Educational Progress, 2022). Clearly, U.S. public schools haven't yet figured out how to do all things well, reliably over time, for each and every student.

The major takeaway? Your students are going to need you. This chapter has outlined, very briefly, how important the work of teaching is, and how much room for improvement exists in our public schools. Wherever you teach, it matters deeply how you spend your days. You will need to prepare, to be patient, to have a sense of humor, to be constant. You can do all of these things, even if they don't feel natural yet. Some days will be better than others. Hold on to the good ones, and when you're ready, process and learn from the bad ones.

Your students will bring their problems to your class, and they will also bring their joys. They are kids; that's what kids do. You are going to be one of the major adults in their lives. And this is your major charge as a teacher: *be your best self with them*. Because there's one absolutely true thing about our work: your kids will need you. Thanks for joining what I am convinced is the most important work we can do.

What Is it Like to Be a Teacher?

Teaching means working with people who aren't you, and who probably aren't like you. Teaching means working with kids who are diverse on multiple measures, and who are on the whole struggling. Good news: you're *necessary*. Related news: the one way to find out what it's like to be a teacher is to go do it.

SUPREME COURT CASE FOR DISCUSSION

Case: *Kennedy v. Bremerton School District*, 597 U.S. ___ (2022)
Link: www.supremecourt.gov/opinions/21pdf/21-418_i425.pdf

In October 2015, high school football coach Joseph Kennedy was fired from the Bremerton (WA) School District after he repeatedly knelt to pray at midfield following games. Mr. Kennedy's prayers began in 2008 as quiet, brief, individual prayers. Over the course of seven years he invited his players and those from opposing football teams to join him on a "voluntary" basis. Many did. Mr. Kennedy eventually started giving motivational speeches to those who gathered for the prayers, often invoking religious content.

Bremerton School District first suspended and then fired Mr. Kennedy because (they explained) the prayers presented a "risk of constitutional liability" under the Establishment Clause of the First Amendment to the U.S. Constitution. The Supreme Court outlined what "constitutional liability" means in the 1971 *Lemon v. Kurtzman* (403 U. S. 602) decision. Specifically, the Court previously held that, to be permissible protected speech, all actions of teachers (or any public servants):

- Must have a legitimate secular purpose.
- Must not have the primary effect of either advancing or inhibiting religion.
- Must not result in an excessive entanglement of government and religion.

On June 27, 2022, the U.S. Supreme Court found in favor of Coach Kennedy, reasoning that the Bremerton School District had prevented him from exercising his rights to free speech and free exercise of religion. The Court found that, while praying, Coach Kennedy "was not instructing players, discussing strategy, encouraging better on-field performance, or engaged in any other speech the District paid him to produce as a coach." Because the prayers were not part of his job, the Court found no violation, and ordered the school district to re-hire Coach Kennedy. They did so; Coach Kennedy returned to coach one game in 2023, and then resigned (Medina, 2023).

QUESTIONS

1. How fair is it for a coach to invite their players (or students) to pray with them, even if voluntary?

2. To what extent do you see important differences between quiet, individual prayer (in 2008) and what eventually became Coach Kennedy's large-group prayer with speeches (in 2015)? Why do those differences matter?

3. Imagine Mr. Kennedy wasn't praying after games but instead giving speeches accusing the Bremerton School District of being a bunch of clowns. Or selling bars of Coach Kennedy Scented Soap. Should he be fired? Why, or why not?

4. To what extent should the beliefs teachers hold—religion, politics, anything—be shared with students?

FURTHER READINGS AND RESOURCES

Data on U.S. student achievement:
National Assessment of Educational Progress (the NAEP Data Explorer tool is particularly useful). https://nces.ed.gov/nationsreportcard

Learning about students:
Schwartz, K. (2016). *I wish my teacher knew: How one question can change everything for our kids*. Lebanon, IN: Da Capo Books.

Teaching memoirs:

Codell, E. (2009). *Educating Esmé: Diary of a teacher's first year.* Chapel Hill, NC: Algonquin Books.

Harris II, P. (2022). *The first five: A love letter to teachers.* Portsmouth, NH: Heinemann.

Rademacher, T. (2017). *It won't be easy: An exceedingly honest (and slightly unprofessional) love letter to teaching.* Minneapolis: University of Minnesota Press.

NOTES

1. Nagel adorably explained why he chose bats: "I have chosen bats instead of wasps or flounders because if one travels too far down the phylogenetic tree, people gradually shed their faith that there is experience there at all" (Nagel, 1974, 438).

2. It's possible to calculate a "segregation index" for any two groups of interest. The White–Black racial segregation index is of obvious historical and policy interest nationwide—so too are others.

3. I know: you're not Mom. Don't forget what being hungry feels like. There's headaches, fatigue, general grumpiness. You can get mad and send students to the office because they handled themselves poorly. But what's going to promote learning and make class better? Enforcing consequences? Or not being hungry? Just do some due diligence: ask about allergies, avoid nuts, etc.

4. There are sixteen U.S. Territories, five with permanent residents: American Samoa, Guam, the Northern Mariana Islands, Puerto Rico, and the U.S. Virgin Islands.

5. A common classroom poster, attributed to Albert Einstein. Here's what he said in 1929: "I am enough of the artist to draw freely upon my imagination. Imagination is more important than knowledge. Knowledge is limited. Imagination encircles the world" (Nilsson, 2010). Einstein was not slagging on people knowing things. He was working out new physics, which required deep knowledge, mathematical skill, and imagination. What he meant, in context: *the generation of new knowledge requires imagination.* He did not claim that it's fine for schools to graduate ignorant (but imaginative!) teenagers.

2

History

What's the History of Public Schools in the United States?

THE FIRST U.S. PUBLIC SCHOOLS

Many books claim the first public school in the United States was Boston Latin School, founded in 1635. Not true. Closer to true: "the first settler colonial government-funded tuition-free school for white Protestant boys in what we now call the United States" was Boston Latin School, founded in 1635 (Boston Latin School, n.d). And way closer to true: "since time immemorial, various Nations in lands now called the United States have educated young people according to diverse cultures and beliefs, knowledge systems and pedagogies—many of which have shaped the way public schools today operate" (Thomas, 2022).

Before 1635, the area around Totant (now Boston, Massachusetts) was populated by Algonquian peoples (including the Massachusett, the Pawtucket, and the Pokantoket). Those Nations showed their children who they were, how to live, and what was valued via formal and informal teaching and learning experiences. We'd recognize many of their approaches to teaching and learning today—because we do those same things now (Facing History, 2020). Which raises the question: if Totant was all occupied land, how could anyone set up a Western-school-for-Protestant-white-boys in the first place?

Good question. The land *had been* occupied for generations—forests cleared, crops planted, towns flourishing—but a deadly plague (1616–1619) killed off an estimated 90% of the peoples living along the Atlantic coast (Marr & Cathey, 2010). That left roads, fields, and orchards empty and easily occupied. Thomas Morton, an English merchant, pointed out in spectacularly creepy fashion that all those deaths had left the land "much the more fit for the English Nation to inhabit in, and erect in it Temples to the glory of God" (Laskey, 2014).¹ So the origin story of Boston Latin School is that of mass death, stolen land, and a postapocalyptic idea of what the purpose of schools should be. Even today, Boston Latin School is not open to all students but remains a limited-admissions "exam school" facing serious questions about discrimination on the basis of race, disability, ethnicity, and English-learner status. It is notable that a school celebrated as the first "public school" in the United States emerged from horror and still hasn't, four hundred years later, figured out how to serve a representative student body.

In any case, formal schools didn't invent education. People have been teaching and learning since they've been people. Schools just make some kinds of learning more efficient. So, starting our story about public schools in 1635 is bad because it ignores the education of Indigenous youth and adults for millennia prior (Hensley, 1966; Kawagley, 2006). And it's New England–centric in any case, potentially irrelevant to the histories of schools where you'll teach.

If you want to check out the earliest *formal* school (teacher at the front, kids in rows) in the now-United States, it was on Borikén (Puerto Rico, now part of the United States), where the Escuela de Gramática was set up by Catholic Bishop Alonso Manso in 1513 on stolen Taíno lands. The Escuela de Gramática was a grammar school—what we'd now call an elementary school—and it was "free" in that the Catholic Church stole the land, built a Cathedral and school, and then . . . didn't charge the locals for a now obviously ethnocidal curriculum (Latin, Christianity, "history"). To be clear: although the Escuela de Gramática did not charge tuition, it was *not* free. It, and other schools like it, cost Taíno parents and peoples their lives, livelihoods, language, land, traditions, stories, knowledge, and Nationhood. By any account, the Escuela de Gramática was one of the most costly schools anywhere. I'm highlighting it because it was first.

There are *thousands* of origin stories for schools in the United States (Adams, 2020; Churchill, 2008). In what's now called Florida, Franciscans established the Mission Nombre de Dios on the outskirts of St. Augustine in 1587 (purpose: convert local Mocama and Agua Dulce peoples to Catholicism; Florida Museum, n.d.). The first mission school in what's now called Texas, San Francisco de los Tejas, was set up in 1690 (purpose: convert local Nabáydácu [Nabedache] peoples to Catholicism; Berger & Wilborn, 1976). Farther west, on Guåhan (Guam), Jesuits established the Colegio de San Juan de Letrán in 1669 (purpose: convert "specially selected" Chomorro boys to Catholicism; Heath, 1975). Up north, Russian Orthodox priests founded a school at Sun'aq (Kodiak, Alaska) in 1784 (purpose: convert local Alutiiq peoples to Russian Orthodoxy). In Hawai'i, King Kamehameha III established the first publicly funded education system west of the Mississippi in 1840.² You get the idea. There's a lot more than dour-looking Protestants with starched collars setting up schools in New England. And if you're thinking . . . *wait, Puerto Rico and Florida and Guam and Hawai'i and Alaska . . . weren't those not the United States until way later?* You're right! That's colonialism; *none* of the United States was the United States . . . until it was (Immerwahr, 2020).

A question like *What's the history of public schools in the United States?* is huge. We're probably better served asking about specific contexts, like: *What's the history of public schools in Western New York?* Or better: *What's the history of education, including public schools, on the traditional homelands of the Wenrohronon?* (The location of my home institution, SUNY Brockport). I don't know the histories of the place(s) where you're going to teach, but it's important that *you* do. You'll never teach in a vacuum, and one of the most obvious places to start is with place and people. Ask yourself: *Where am I? Who's been here, and is here now? What does that mean for education and schools?* Good places to start include the National Museum of the American Indian's *Native Knowledge 360°* (https://americanindian.si.edu/nk360), Roxanne Dunbar-Ortiz's *An Indigenous Peoples' History of the United States* (2015), and Native Land Digital (https://native-land.ca).

It's important that we know what happened in the places we teach. Histories are always contested and messy. It's easy to learn the wrong thing if we don't seek information from a range of sources. Check out how one popular teacher education book described the earliest schools in the American South: "You wouldn't have attended a public school, because they didn't exist at the time. If your parents weren't wealthy, you probably wouldn't have gone to school at all. Life for most people in the colonial South was hard, and formal education was a luxury reserved for those with money (Pulliam & Van Patten, 2013). Private tutors often lived on plantations, or parents pooled their resources to hire a tutor to teach the children of several families" (Kauchak & Eggen, 2014, 111). Contrast that with a perspective on Southern education from a previously enslaved person: "If they caught you trying to write they would cut your finger off and if they caught you again they would cut your head off" (Unnamed, in Rawick, Ed. [1972], 78–79).

Do you see the difference? One perspective on nineteenth-century education in the South describes it as "a luxury" and mentions how "tutors often lived on plantations" and that "parents pooled their resources." That sounds kind of familiar, right? Like a carpool? Or a tutoring club? The other perspective points out that education could get you maimed or killed.

I'm not telling you to pick one history or another, but . . . we're talking about education during *slavery*. Authors can't fairly talk about "tutors" for the plantation class without pointing out that those tutors served the enslavers only. And that it was *illegal* to teach enslaved persons throughout the South—that anyone doing so faced fines, whipping, disfigurement, or murder (Williams, 2005; Cornell University, 2002). Figure 2.1 shows a white "schoolmaster" (a male teacher) actively blocking a Black woman and two Black children from entering school. Many enslaved peoples pursued education anyway; an estimated 9–20% of those escaping slavery before the Civil War could read and write (Span, 2005, 38).

These histories have long legacies, shaping our work right now. Indigenous students in Puerto Rico, Florida, Texas and all over the United States continue to have unequal access to good teachers and schools—and are often invisible in curricula. Today in the South it is not hard to identify which families generated wealth and privilege from slavery, and which were harmed. The point is that there isn't one history of education in the United States. There are many, and they vary by whose story gets told. When I claim it's important that we know what happened in the places we teach, I don't mean knowing famous battles of long-ago wars. I mean knowing the stories of the students and families we teach. What came before we got there? Who has had access to quality schools, and who has not?

Figure 2.1. "Colored" scholars excluded from schools. *Source:* American Anti-Slavery Society, 1838. Archived by Library Company of Philadelphia. Public domain.

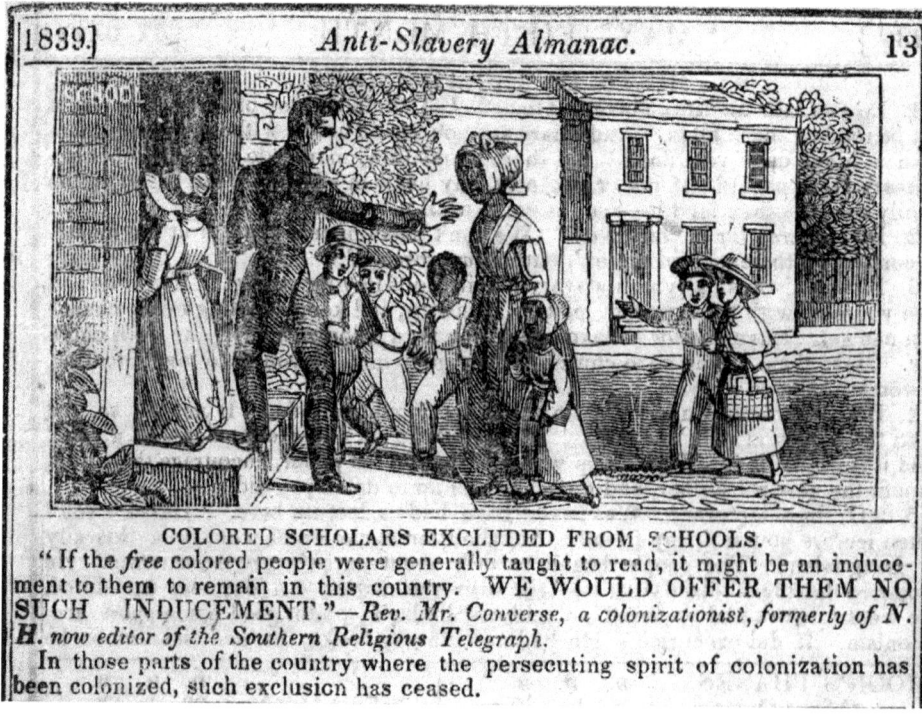

A BRIEF HISTORY OF U.S. PUBLIC SCHOOLS

You should understand two major themes. First: U.S. public schools are locally controlled. Second: U.S. public schools segregate students from each other. Both themes have been in place from day one. Both shape the schools we have today. As a teacher, you're not going to change either on your own—but the more you know about the roots of our schools, the better equipped you'll be to operate within (and sometimes, against) that history.

LOCAL CONTROL

Public schools in the United States are (mostly) local institutions. That first formal school, Escuela de Gramática, was set up in one specific place, for specific (benevolent and nefarious) purposes. Boston Latin was a local school (for elite college-bound white Protestant boys). The school where you'll work? There's probably a local school board running the place. Today we've got more than 13,000 locally controlled public school districts across the United States (NCESa, 2022). One school district has over a million students (New York City Department of Education); one is bigger than Minnesota (North Slope Borough School District in Alaska); one has just three students and one teacher (Bois Blanc Pines School District in Michigan). Almost all public schools in the United States are run by local people. Exceptions make the rule, of course: Hawai'i, Guam, and Puerto Rico have unified school systems operated by the state or territory. The federal Bureau of Indian Education operates schools on Tribal Nation lands; the U.S. Department of Defense operates schools across the globe on or near military installations.

U.S. public schools don't have a single origin story—they have *thousands*. One of the earliest efforts to create a public school *system*—a set of multiple schools—came in the Colony of Massachusetts Bay. In 1647, white Puritan landholding men (the only ones allowed to vote) passed a law known as the Old Deluder Satan Law, which had three major goals for newly created public schools (Commonwealth of Massachusetts, n.d.):

1. Make sure the kids weren't corrupted by Satan.

2. Teach reading and writing.

3. Do college preparation.[3]

Efforts to build school systems varied widely in purpose and access—and evolved over time. The Old Deluder Satan Law in Massachusetts (1647) was intended, first and foremost, to save souls. About 130 years later, Massachusetts approved a state Constitution that explicitly *prohibited* funding religious schools (Commonwealth of Massachusetts, 1780, Article XLVI§2). In Virginia, then Governor Thomas Jefferson proposed a statewide public school system in 1779, clarifying that the schools wouldn't actually be for everyone (just "free children," not those enslaved; Jefferson, 1779). His proposal for a statewide public school system was rejected over concerns about local control and taxes, two issues still relevant today. It would take another century for Virgina to establish a statewide public school system.

Most early federal efforts to promote public schools came cloaked in land theft. Remember the United States Congress of the Confederation (1781–1789)? I did not. It was our first federal government. It was remarkably weak. Among its weaknesses was that it couldn't tax anything (only states could). Yet the federal government had huge war debts after the Revolution (especially to France, Spain, and the Netherlands). How to pay off all that debt? Sell someone else's stuff! From 1784 to 1789, Congress passed three laws (the Northwest Ordinances) that organized new territories to the north and west of the thirteen colonies—in the very-much-still-homelands of multiple Indigenous Nations. The lands taken were surveyed and sold to settlers, raising cash to pay off debt and run the federal government. Tucked into the Northwest Ordinances were two features notable for public schools:

1. Occupied land was divided into square townships six miles by six miles (36 mi²). One square mile of each township (specifically the 16th section out of the 36 available) was set aside *"for the maintainance of public fchools within the faid townfhip"* [*sic*] (U.S. House of Representatives, Committee on Public Lands, 1785); &

2. The Northwest Ordinances banned slavery in the new territories. A big deal in its own right, this set the legal stage for America's eventual reckoning with slavery, the Civil War, Reconstruction, Jim Crow, segregation, now.

One takeaway is that schooling across what became the United States in the eighteenth and nineteenth centuries wasn't any single thing. There were missionary schools, private tutors, private schools, church-sponsored schools, secret tutoring, some state- and town-operated public schools, and a wide range of approaches to funding education. Because schools were already established as a diverse lot, there was little serious discussion of education while the U.S. Constitution was written in 1787. Ultimately, the Constitution was silent on public schools. Or . . . was silent at first. Two later Amendments have had substantial impact on our public schools. You should know them both. Here's the 10th Amendment (1791): "The powers not delegated to the United States by the Constitution, nor prohibited by it to the States, are reserved to the States respectively, or to the people" (U.S. Const., Amend. X, 1791). What the 10th Amendment meant, at least in 1791, was that schools were not a matter for the federal government but for the states, or "the people." During the founding years of the United States, beyond the Northwest Ordinances' land-theft-for-school-funding, there was little role for the federal government when it came to public schools. This was true until the passage of the so-called Civilization Fund Act (P.L. 15-85) in 1819, which provided federal dollars for schools near "frontier settlements." These early federal schools were overseen by the U.S. War Department for the purpose of genocide (or at the very least, ethnocide). The Act was one of the primary legal precedents that produced the horror show of Indigenous boarding schools in the United States in operation through 1969 (Bureau of Indian Affairs, 2022).

The 10th Amendment didn't require states to *do* anything. It just clarified that wherever the Constitution was silent, states and "the people" had power—*not* the federal government. This remains true today: states, territories and local governments are the ones primarily responsible for U.S. public schools, not the federal government.

Local control has produced a highly variable landscape of U.S. public schools. Massachusetts created a public school system in 1780. New York started funding public schools in 1795. Mississippi didn't create a public school system until 1870. Massachusetts passed the first compulsory education law in the nation (requiring all children to attend school) in 1852. Texas didn't require school attendance until 1915. Even after compulsory education laws had been passed, not all children attended school. Districts made exemptions for children who had jobs, who lived far away from schools, whose parents were poor, or who could, for example, already "[r]ead and write simple sentences in English" (Defenbaugh & Keesecker, 1935, 88). About half the states allowed local authorities to exempt children from going to school for the "best interests of child or for good reasons" (ibid., 21). Sometimes those "good reasons" included things like being a girl. For example, if you lived near Boston Latin High School (est. 1635), but happened to be a girl . . . you had to wait until 1972 to get in. It's not difficult to find exclusion after exclusion in the various histories of our public schools. In the United States, while local control has been praised as a means to ensure our schools are responsive to local concerns—it has also allowed our schools to discriminate and exclude based on local fears and prejudices.

The federal government addressed explicit discrimination (in part) following the Civil War via the 14th Amendment (1868), declaring: "No

State shall make or enforce any law which shall abridge the privileges or immunities of citizens of the United States; nor shall any State deprive any person of life, liberty, or property, without due process of law; nor deny to any person within its jurisdiction the equal protection of the laws" (U.S. Const., Amend. XIV, 1868). The 14th Amendment is known as the Equal Protection Clause of the Constitution. The Amendment clarifies that wherever there's a public good—the postal service, national parks, public schools—everyone is supposed to have equal access and equal protection under the law. We're clearly not there yet. Public schools in the United States provide massively unequal opportunities to students depending on where they live and who they are—more on that throughout this book. The 14th Amendment provided law, not guarantees (Pelsue, 2017).

States and "the people" fought the Equal Protection Clause immediately. After Reconstruction was abandoned in 1877, states from Delaware to Texas passed Jim Crow laws (1877–1960s) preventing Black students from attending schools (at all), or requiring them to attend race-segregated, shoddily built, underfunded, crowded schools (Anderson, 1988; Douglas, 2005). It wasn't just anti-Black codes in the South that harmed students and families (and violated the 14th Amendment); *every* state and Territory had its own damaging variation. Alaska, Arizona, Oklahoma, Minnesota, New Mexico, South Dakota, and others (37 states and Territories total) actively removed Indigenous students from their homes and communities, and sent them ethnocidal residential or day schools (Adams, 2020; Newland, 2022). In New Mexico, Texas, California, Arizona, Nevada, and elsewhere in the Southwest, communities built segregated schools for students with Mexican heritage (García, 2018; Gonzalez, 2013). California excluded students identified as Black, Indigenous, and/or Chinese from schools attended by white students, except for "half-breed Indian children, and Indian children who live in white families or under guardianship of white persons" (State of California, 1866, Sec. 57, 265). And so on, across states and territories, for hundreds of years.

All of which may be terribly depressing for people like you preparing to teach. Have public schools replicated many of the inequalities they're supposed to help fix? Yes. But it's worth noting that our public schools remain one of the very few public institutions in the United States with the potential to make large and lasting differences. Public schools are used by 90% of American families, are widely trusted (at least at the local level; Houston et al., 2022), and have large windows of time to do their work. There's reason for hope, and there's reason to understand that we have to do better. A last note on local control, featuring adorable kids. Figure 2.2 shows Mary Louise Mitchell's first-grade class at the Blackwell School in Marfa, Texas, 1947.

Figure 2.2. The first-grade class of Mary Louise Mitchell at the Blackwell School in Marfa, Texas, 1947. *Source:* Blackwell School Alliance. Used with permission.

See those smiles? See that girl covering her mouth with both hands, giggling? There's real joy there. And yet: these first-graders are at a segregated school for students with Mexican ancestry. The school year started with a mock funeral. Everyone wrote words and phrases in Spanish on slips of paper, and then they all watched as the principal buried their Spanish words in the dirt next to the American flagpole (Ortiz Uribe, 2022). Who does that to kids? We do. And sometimes we do it while telling ourselves that local people are in the best position to do right by our kids.

SEGREGATION

You can't know anything useful about American public schools without understanding segregation. We've always segregated students from each other. Public schools are actively doing it right now. How and why we segregate students is arguably the most powerful historical thread connecting our first schools to today's schools. Although public schools have occasionally been portrayed as gathering places where students from all backgrounds come together, learn, and grow—they've never consistently functioned that way in the United States. Below we'll explore different varieties of school segregation in U.S. public schools, including race, wealth, nationality, disability, and sex and gender expression.

None of these operates independently. You'll almost never see *just* racial segregation, or *just* wealth segregation, or segregation by any single characteristic. It's common to see schools segregated by race and wealth. It's common to see students segregated from each other by disability, in patterns identifiable by race and wealth. And so on. Be advised: you will be navigating various and overlapping segregations throughout your teaching life.

RACIAL SEGREGATION

You may be most familiar with racial segregation. It is among America's foundational stains. One example is Black–White school segregation, required by law in seventeen states until the 1954 *Brown v. Board* decision by the U.S. Supreme Court ("We conclude that, in the field of public education, the doctrine of 'separate but equal' has no place. Separate educational facilities are inherently unequal." *Brown v. Board*, 347 U.S. 483 [1954]). Figure 2.3 is an image you may have seen. In the sunglasses is sixteen-year-old Elizabeth Eckford on her way to Central High School in Little Rock, Arkansas, on September 4, 1957. She is surrounded by a jeering, scary mob of students and adults as she walks. What you can't see in this photograph are two things. First, Elizabeth is all by herself. She was supposed to meet up with eight other Black students and walk with them as a group. Somehow Elizabeth missed the meetup and decided to go on her own. Second, when Elizabeth arrives at

Figure 2.3. Black student Elizabeth Eckford is jeered by white student Hazel Bryan as she walks to Central High School, Little Rock, Arkansas. September 4, 1957. Photographer: Will Counts. Public domain.

school, the entrance is blocked by a line of helmeted Arkansas National Guardsmen with rifles. Segregationist governor Orval Faubus had ordered the National Guard to keep Elizabeth and the other Black students out. Elizabeth made it to school that day and was turned away. Three weeks later, on September 24, President Eisenhower ordered federal U.S. Army troops to escort Elizabeth and the others past the Arkansas troops. The Little Rock Nine were ostracized, threatened, attacked, and humiliated. They had to be escorted *inside the school* between classes by the U.S. Army. They couldn't go to football games or be in the drama club or go to the prom. Still, four of the nine graduated from Central High, and the other five from other high schools (National Park Service, n.d).

You might have noticed that Elizabeth Eckford and the others were desegregating Central High in 1957—three years *after* the 1954 *Brown v. Board* decision. *Brown* didn't dismantle school segregation by race overnight. It didn't say *when* schools had to desegregate. States across the South simply didn't comply with *Brown*, instead pursuing "massive resistance" programs that included campaigns of racial terror, cross burnings, and open threats intended to preserve segregated schools (Daugherity, 2016; Lassiter & Lewis, Eds., 1998). Mississippi fought desegregation until 1969, when a U.S. Court of Appeals ordered the state to integrate schools immediately (*Alexander v. Holmes County*, 396 U.S. 19). In response to the court order, Mississippi promptly defunded its public school system and allowed white parents to open a raft of private "segregation academies" (Harris, 2019), many of which remain open today (Carr, 2012). You can still find segregated majority-white private schools operating alongside underfunded majority-Black public schools in Mississippi, Virginia, Arkansas, Louisiana, North and South Carolina, and Texas today.

Nor has the legacy of *Brown* been entirely positive. When formerly segregated systems were dismantled, it was common for districts to simply close the Black schools and fire all the Black teachers and principals (Fenwick, 2022). Nearly overnight, we abandoned the accumulated talents of generations of Black teachers and administrators, along with the curricula and pedagogy they had developed (Givens, 2021; Lutz, 2017; Thompson, 2019).

Nor is the story of resistance to racial desegregation one limited to the U.S. South. In the 1970s, as efforts to desegregate schools expanded across the country, many white families moved their children out of cities and into new, majority-white suburbs with majority-white schools (or majority-white private schools)—a phenomenon known as "white flight" (Fairlie & Resch, 2002; Kruse, 2007). School districts in cities like Boston, Charlotte, Chicago, New York, and Berkeley tried to mitigate racial segregation in housing by busing children across neighborhood lines to racially balanced schools. The busing movement was short-lived; districts faced lawsuits, angry conflicts at school board meetings, and violent protests (Delmont, 2016; Formisano,

2004; Murphy, 2022). Nor was busing popular among Black and Hispanic families, whose children faced long rides and hostility on daily journeys out of their neighborhoods. By 1974, the U.S. Supreme Court decided in *Milliken v. Bradley* that busing students between different school districts to achieve racial balance was unconstitutional (Baugh, 2011). In many U.S. school districts today, there's simply no way to meaningfully desegregate by race without changing housing patterns or district lines (Bramhall, 2021). Public schools today are by some measures more racially segregated now than they were during the 1960s (Frankenberg et al., 2019).

Why has it been, so far, nearly impossible to desegregate schools by race? A major barrier is local control. The thirteen thousand school districts in the United States, with a few exceptions, are independent and have neither incentive nor legal frameworks that could promote change (Gamson & Hodge, Eds., 2018). After *Brown*, white property owners realized that if they didn't want to pay for or have their children attend integrated schools, all they had to do was move to a neighborhood with segregated housing, or cut taxes and send their kids to private schools (Walsh, 2017). To be clear: racial segregation is a feature of every public school system in the United States.

Figure 2.4 offers a look at the racial and ethnic makeup of public schools in the United States. One note on the figure: race and ethnicity are separate social concepts. Race describes people based on physical features (such as hair type or skin color). Ethnicity describes people based on common origins, including religious, language or cultural backgrounds.

Figure 2.4. K–12 public school enrollment, by race and ethnicity, school year 2020–2021. *Source:* U.S. Government Accountability Office, June 2022. GAO-22-104737, Fig. 2. Public domain.

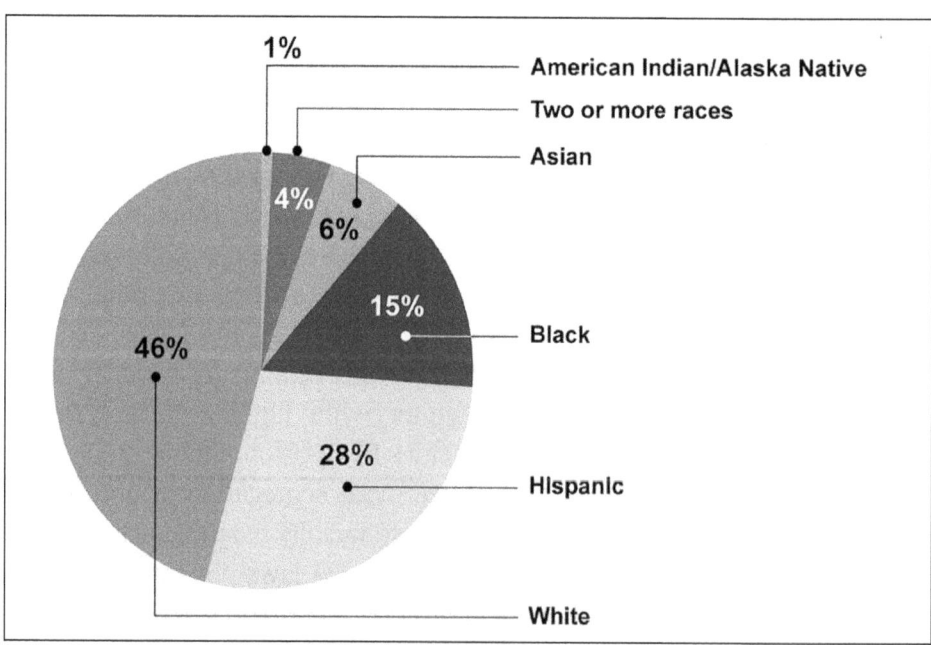

The U.S. Census Bureau recognizes just two ethnicities: "Hispanic or Latino" and "Not Hispanic or Latino" (United States Census Bureau, n.d.). A person identifying as "Hispanic or Latino" can be of any race. Those identified in Figure 2.4 as "Hispanic" are reported only in the "Hispanic" category, not in any of the racial categories.

Looks like a mix of students by race and ethnicity in our schools, right? Not exactly—Figure 2.4 just presents averages. Figure 2.5 shows how those students are distributed in schools. *How to read Figure 2.5:* look at the second column, labeled "White." In Fall 2019, 46% of white students attended a school composed of ≥75% white students. 32% of white students attended a school composed of 50–74% white students. So . . . 78% of white students in Fall 2019 attended majority-white schools. Just 22% of white students attended a school composed of ≤50% white students. The flip side, as the Government Accountability Office noted, was that "students of color disproportionately attended schools in which the combined enrollment of students of color was at least 75 percent of total enrollment." (NCESb, 2022, Fig. 2).

Figure 2.5. Percentage distribution of public elementary and secondary school students, by student's race/ethnicity and percentage of own racial/ethnic group enrolled in the school: Fall 2019. *Note:* Data are for the fifty states and the District of Columbia. The term "students of color" is being used synonymously with "minority students" in Digest table 216.50. Students of color include those who are Black, Hispanic, Asian, Pacific Islander, American Indian/Alaska Native, and of Two or more races. Data reflect racial/ethnic data reported by schools. Race categories exclude persons of Hispanic ethnicity. Detail may not sum to totals because of rounding. Although rounded numbers are displayed, the figures are based on unrounded data. *Source:* National Center for Education Statistics (2022). Racial/Ethnic Enrollment in Public Schools. Condition of Education. U.S. Department of Education, Institute of Education Sciences. https://nces.ed.gov/programs/coe/indicator/cge. Public domain.

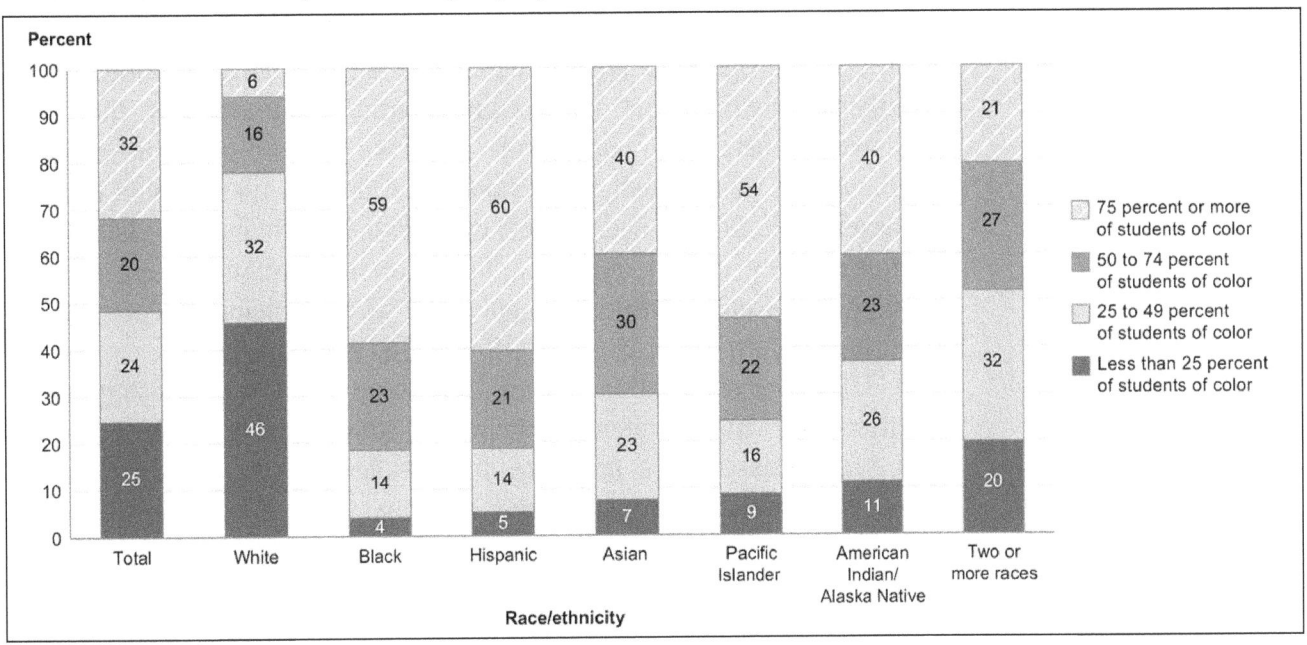

Segregation by race is a feature of U.S. public schools, and has been since day one (NCESc, 2022; Frankenberg et al., 2019). Why does that matter? Here are four major problems with racial segregation, all connected:

1. Racial segregation does psychological damage to students (Kluger, 2004).[4]

2. Racial segregation concentrates students of color in high-poverty schools, which are, on average, less effective than lower-poverty schools (reardon et al., 2022).

3. Segregation produces isolated experiences and harms opportunities as young people become adults (Wells et al., 2016).

4. Segregation produces a cycle of uneven public support, funding, and resources (Rothstein, 2017).

Before *Brown v. Board* (1954), we had school segregation by race. After *Brown,* we had brief moments of desegregation, followed by white flight and resegregation. Today, few policymakers at any level of government are making serious efforts to desegregate public schools by race. I'm not trying to be depressing—I'm just describing what *is:* you are heading into a public school landscape segregated by race, and there's little indication that's going to change in the near future.

WEALTH SEGREGATION

Students whose families are wealthy generally don't attend the same public schools as those whose families are not. This is because wealthy and poor families don't often live in the same neighborhoods, and school districts are geographic. Wealth segregation is particularly prominent in the Northeast, where school districts are geographically small. In the South and West, where large countywide districts are more common, students from various wealth backgrounds are more likely to go to school together (Owens et al., 2016). Segregation by wealth is perhaps less visible than segregation by race or ethnicity, but it corrupts public school systems (and distorts opportunities) in powerful ways (Coleman Report; 1966; Duncan & Murnane, Eds., 2011; Rothstein, 2004).

Like racial segregation, wealth segregation is linked to housing. School districts with high student achievement (that offer a lot of Advanced Placement classes, that graduate most students and send them to college) are surrounded by expensive housing. Why? Economics. There's a lot of demand among families with school-aged children for homes in high-performing school districts. So families with wealth purchase access to good public schools by buying or renting expensive homes. Families without wealth must find housing wherever else they can afford it, whatever the neighborhood school quality. Students from wealthy families go to school together, and students from economically disadvantaged families go to other schools together.

Here's a real-life example. Where I live, in Monroe County (NY), two school districts border each other: the Brighton Central School District and the Rochester City School District. Brighton (est. 1814) is wealthy. Rochester (est. 1817) is not. Rochester has the highest child poverty rate in New York state (Murphy, 2018). You can drive northwest from Brighton High School, up Monroe Avenue 2.7 miles to James Monroe High School in Rochester. It takes five minutes. As you drive, you pass a car repair garage, some restaurants and apartments, a music store, and a beautiful park designed by Frederick Law Olmstead. You cross an (invisible) school district boundary at Highland Avenue. You won't notice anything at the boundary. It's green and pretty, there's a reservoir, some tennis courts. But Table 2.1 shows what you'd experience academically if you were a *student* who moved 2.7 miles from Brighton High School to James Monroe High School.

Table 2.1. Brighton High School and James Monroe High School, Rochester, New York

2020–2021 school year	Brighton High School	James Monroe High School
Median home sales price	$280,000	$150,000
% economically disadvantaged	20%	93%
% white students	70%	3%
Graduation rate	97%	73%
Chronic absenteeism	20%	49%
English, % proficient	96%	30%
Math, % proficient	81%	15%
Science, % proficient	95%	14%
Social studies, % proficient	95%	37%
Number of AP courses offered	21	4
AP exams, % scoring 3 or higher (passing)	80%	0%
U.S. News HS Rank (Rochester)	#4 (of 78)	#65 (of 78)

Notes: Median home sale price from realtor.com, aggregated from Multiple Listing Services. Student data from New York State Education Department, data.nysed.gov (school year 2020–2021). *U.S. News & World Report* rankings: www.usnews.com/education/best-high-schools. % passing means % of students attempting and passing a required-for-graduation NYS Regents exam in an appropriate subject area. English is English Language Arts; math is Algebra I; science is Living Environment (biology); social studies is Global History & Geography II.

First, notice the difference in housing cost. It's expensive to live in Brighton. It's cheaper to live in Rochester. Expensive housing generates high tax revenue for school districts—which in turn enables things like AP courses, music and arts programming, science labs with actual science equipment, and certified teachers (Kenyon et al., 2022). Spending money on students and teachers can increase achievement (Kirabo Jackson, 2020; Kirabo Jackson & Mackevicius, 2021; Lafortune et al., 2016), though probably not if it's just spent on fancy buildings (Martorell et al., 2015).

Next, look at demography: these schools are segregated by wealth *and* race. Students at Brighton High are predominantly white and wealthy. Students at James Monroe High are predominantly non-white and non-wealthy. Now consider academics: students at Brighton High attend one of the best high schools in the area. Students at James Monroe High School, one of the worst.

Brighton and Rochester are on the *same street*. The two high schools are 2.7 miles apart. They're *connected*. People from Brighton and Rochester are part of the same county, use the same roads, and shop at the same grocery stores.[5] It's not like there's a wall or anything. But there *is* an invisible line, the school district border, running along Highland Avenue. One side has wealth and educational opportunity. The other does not.

I don't mean to beat up on either district. They're not the bad guys here. Wealth-based school segregation is not their fault. Monroe County has eighteen school districts, including Brighton and Rochester; they're *all* implicated in how opportunity is or isn't available. So too is the government of New York, who bears ultimate responsibility for public schools in the state. What I'm pointing out is that it's not difficult to figure out where the highest-performing and lowest-performing schools are: look at real estate listings.

You should understand what wealth does (and does not do) for schools. It's not like rich parents insert dollars into children and achievement goes up. Wealth, first and foremost, enables families to provide predictable and sufficient food, clothing, shelter, health care, and enriched learning environments (books in the home, regular sleep, high-quality childcare or preschool). These direct investments promote lifelong academic achievement among students (Borman & Dowling, 2010; Duncan et al. 2011; Jones, Milligan, and Stabile 2015; Milligan and Stabile 2011; Owens et al., 2019). Wealth also enables the purchase or rental of housing in high-performing school districts (Kane et al., 2006; Taylor, 2013; Thieboult, 1956). The aggregation of wealth within school districts (as in Brighton) also creates a large tax base for public schools (more on this in Chapter 3). High-wealth districts have more resources than others; it will not surprise you that they have, on average, better student outcomes than low-wealth districts (Dumont & Ready, 2020; Kahlenberg, 2007; Palardy, 2020; Schwartz, 2010; Willms, 2010).

SEGREGATION BY NATIONALITY, ENGLISH PROFICIENCY, DISABILITY, SEX AND GENDER

In addition to race and wealth, public schools in the United States segregate students from each other by a range of other attributes. The basic idea of all school segregation has a common flawed logic:

1. Students from (*insert group*) are a threat to the education of students generally; and/or
2. Students from (*insert group*) have educational needs that are unique and therefore require segregation into specialized classes to be effective.

Rather than describe in great detail each of the various segregationist approaches public schools have taken over the centuries, I'll share a few pictures. My hope is that you will remember them. They all represent a challenge for us to do better.

SEGREGATION BY NATIONALITY

The photos in Figure 2.6 were taken at the United States Indian Industrial School (often called Carlisle Indian School), which operated from

Figures 2.6a and b. Henry Standing Bear, Wounded Yellow Robe, and Chauncy Yellow Robe at Carlisle Indian School, Carlisle, Pennsylvania. *Source:* John N. Choate (1884). Archives & Special Collections, Dickinson College. Used with permission.

1879 to 1918 in Carlisle, Pennsylvania. In before-and-after format are Henry Standing Bear, Wounded Yellow Robe, and Chauncy Yellow Robe, Lakota Nation citizens kidnapped or orphaned during the Sioux Wars (1854–1890) and shipped to the Carlisle Indian School. At Carlisle, the mission was to "kill the Indian, save the man" by erasing Indigenous languages and cultures, replacing them with English, short hair, and shop class (Adams, 1995).[6] This is segregation by *nationality*. Indian Tribes are sovereign governments: Nations, with citizens. Like Canada. There is misunderstanding on this point, traceable to the (federal) Dawes Act (1884) and the Indian Reorganization Act (1934), which confused Indigenous identity with race. Tribes are Nations, not races.

Segregation by nationality continues today via schools operated by the United States Bureau of Indian Education (BIE; www.bie.edu). I'm *not* arguing that the Bureau of Indian Education is a bad thing, though it has a number of critics (Woods & Phillip, 2021). I am just noting that the BIE operates 183 schools on 64 reservations in 23 states for Indigenous students, separate and apart from public school districts operated by local governments. BIE schools can be awesome—as when Tribally-operated schools teach language and cultural knowledge no one else can. And they can be awful, as small, under-resourced schools serving vulnerable students anywhere can be (Juneau, 2018; Woods, 2020). On the theme of vulnerable students, look at Figure 2.7, from 1943.

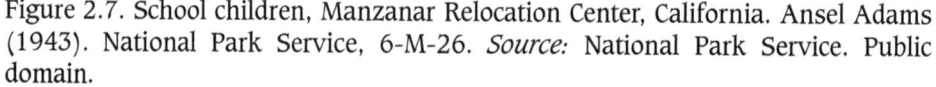

Figure 2.7. School children, Manzanar Relocation Center, California. Ansel Adams (1943). National Park Service, 6-M-26. *Source:* National Park Service. Public domain.

See those girls? Those smiles? Those girls are federal prisoners at Manzanar Relocation Center in California, 1943. Manzanar was one of ten internment camps for Japanese Americans from 1942–1945 (National Park Service, n.d.). Why are these girls prisoners? Because they and their families were seen as threats during wartime. And also because they were thought to need specific instruction—for example, to ensure loyalty or patriotism of a particular sort. Manzanar closed in 1945. I don't know what happened to those three girls. I don't know if they had good teachers at Manzanar or after. But I've seen that kids can be powerful and resilient even in the worst circumstances. Wherever you teach, don't forget that your job is to be good with young people, to help nurture joy and learning no matter what.

SEGREGATION BY ENGLISH PROFICIENCY

See the kid with the kitten t-shirt (Figure 2.8)? She's holding a sign that says: "VOTE NO ON 227." Proposition 227 was a ballot initiative in California in 1998 that eliminated bilingual education in California in favor of English-only classes (State of California, 1998). The proposition was led by millionaire software developer Ron Unz, and was law in California until 2016 (State of California, 2016). Proposition 227 wasn't intended to segregate students, exactly. It was a thinly veiled jab at immigrant

Figure 2.8. Children and their parents demonstrate against English-only Proposition 227, Oakland, California, 1998. *Source:* Photo by David Bacon, http://dbacon.igc.org. Used with permission.

families and English Learners under the guise of improved English instruction. Unz tried to explain that eliminating bilingual instruction wasn't anti-immigrant or racist or anything by contrasting Spanish speakers in California with his Jewish grandparents: "[They] came to California in the 1920s and 1930s as poor European immigrants. They came to WORK and become successful . . . not to sit back and be a burden on those who were already here!" (Barabak, 1997).

Unz: yuck. Immigrants as burdens is a common false trope (Beyer, 2021). Two things teachers should know about students learning English:

1. All students, including undocumented students and English learners, have the right to an education in U.S. public schools (U.S. Department of Education, 2015).

2. A majority of English learners in the United States are born in the United States, hence are United States citizens (Zong and Batalova, 2015).

When asked, families of English learners have near-universal goals for their children: to work hard and to have opportunities (Arellanes et al., 2019; Chavira et al., 2016; Langenkamp, 2019; Zill, 2020). Yet hostility toward immigrants and English learners—who make up about 10% of public school students in the United States (National Center for Education Statistics, 2022g)—is common throughout the United States. Some politicians in the United States openly advocate for *not allowing immigrant or refugee students to go to school at all* (Lee, 2023). There's ample irony here for a nation of immigrants.

Segregation by English proficiency is common and often substantial. Roughly 20% of U.S. public schools enroll 75% of the nation's English learners. English learners are, broadly speaking, concentrated in districts and schools that are urban, low-income, and lower-achieving (Quintero & Hansen, 2021). More than half of the English learners in the United States attend school in just five states—Texas, California, Florida, New York, and Illinois (NCES, 2021a, Table 204.20). Most English learners in the United States attend school with large numbers of other English learners. Like wealth, the segregation of English learners from peers across U.S. schools isn't necessarily due to teacher or school decisions about how they learn best; it's an artifact of immigration policy, geography, jobs, wealth, and housing (U.S. Department of Education, 2017).

We also segregate English learners *within* schools. Why? They need tailored instruction in reading, writing, and speaking English along with instruction in all the other things schools try to teach (math, science, health, dodgeball, cafeteria food). Learning any new language takes time and teaching. Within schools, there can be reasonable arguments for some separate classes for those learning English (Markos & Himmel, 2016). What's harmful is segregating students from each other for reasons that have nothing to do with English-language reading, writing, or speaking instruction. Key for English learners is a continuum of supports over time. This is why Unz and Proposition 227 were wrong: one size definitely does not fit all for learning English at school.

SEGREGATION BY DISABILITY

Figure 2.9 shows the now-closed Montana State Training School in Boulder, Montana. It's hard to see, but there are two buildings: up front, a modern wing-shaped administrative building, and in the back, a big brick building, originally the Montana Deaf and Dumb Asylum (est. 1897). Before it opened, it was a given that d/Deaf students in Montana couldn't attend public schools.[7] Being d/Deaf meant being excluded. The Montana State Training School, despite the name, wasn't really a school. It was a center for eugenics. Rather than teaching students, it warehoused and often *sterilized* them, usually without consent, and with full legal support from authorities. As the U.S. Supreme Court reasoned in its *Buck v. Bell* decision (274 U.S. 200 [1927]), disability alone was sufficient cause for sterilization. In the Court's words: "three generations of imbeciles are

Figure 2.9. Exterior of the Montana State Training School, Boulder, Montana. *Source:* Photo by Kate Hampton, from the National Register of Historic Places. National Park Service. Public domain.

enough." This reasoning held sway for generations. As late as the 1970s, the Northern Cheyenne Nation brought lawsuits against the federal Indian Health Service (IHS) to stop forced sterilization of Tribal members; records showed that teenage girls had come in to have their tonsils removed and left without their ovaries (Montana Historical Society, 2014; O'Sullivan, 2019; Pegoraro, 2015).

For most of the history of U.S. public schools, students with disabilities had no access to public schools. Eventually, in the late nineteenth and early twentieth centuries, communities and states *did* get around to providing an option or two . . . but as with the Montana State Training School, they were explicitly segregated, and often horror shows of neglect, violence, and inhumanity.

Things changed in 1975, when Congress passed a law now reauthorized as the Individuals with Disabilities Education Act (IDEA) (20 U.S.C. § 1400, *et. seq.*, 1975; Neilson, 2013). Basic concepts of IDEA:

1. All students with disabilities in the United States have the right to attend public schools.

2. Students with disabilities should not be arbitrarily segregated from nondisabled peers.

3. Parents can individually sue school districts who do bad things.

In 2020–2021, 7.2 million students with disabilities attended U.S. public schools, roughly 15% of the student population. One part of this story is positive: two-thirds of those students spent more than 80% of every school day in general education classrooms (National Center for Education Statistics, 2023). That's some serious (and relatively rapid) progress. However, as with the *Brown* decisions, which didn't end racial segregation overnight, IDEA didn't quickly or magically end the segregation and miseducation of students with disabilities. It did get us started. Whatever and wherever you teach, odds are your classroom will include multiple students with various disabilities. We're doing better at desegregating students with disabilities in U.S. public schools than we are with just about any other identifiable group. More on this in upcoming chapters—but at least we're collecting data and *trying*. There's a long way to go.

Look at one more picture, Figure 2.10 (opposite page), from a few years ago. That smiling kid with the dogs is eleven-year-old Devyn Pereira, who attended the Gates-Chili School District near Rochester, New York, from 2012 to 2019. Devyn has Angelman Syndrome, which manifests in autism and epilepsy. The medium-sized dog on the left—Rubin—was

Figure 2.10. Devyn Pereira with service dogs Rubin (L) and Hannah (R) in 2019, Rochester, New York. *Source:* Photo by Heather M. Burroughs. Used with permission.

Devyn's service dog in 2019. The big hairy dog on the right—Hannah—was Devyn's prior service dog. One of Rubin's primary services was early detection of life-threatening seizures.

The Gates-Chili School District provided Devyn with various supports at school, including a 1:1 aide. But school officials decided they wouldn't allow school employees (including Devyn's aide) to help with Rubin (e.g., taking him out to pee). The school district told Devyn's family that if she was going to bring the dog to school, her family would have to hire, at their expense, an adult handler to accompany Devyn and the dog at school (WHAM News, 2020). Devyn's family sued, and the U.S. Department of Justice intervened. Gates-Chili eventually settled, paying the family $42,000 for costs and emotional distress. And Devyn's family moved to another area school district who accommodated service dogs more readily (bravo, Hilton Central School District).

What should we learn from Devyn and Rubin? First, school districts are still learning how to include students with disabilities. It's not automatic. Some districts are good with accommodations and modifications, but others are not. Also: school districts are wary of liability and costs—but sometimes in unexpected ways. In Devyn's case, Gates-Chili appeared more concerned about being partially responsible for her dog than about her seizures. Third, parents of students with disabilities have explicit legal rights that are unique and can be useful. Oh, and bonus fourth point: local control matters. In one district, a service dog was seen as a challenge, a risk, and a cost a school district would not pay. A few miles down the road, the same dog was welcome.

SEGREGATION BY SEX AND GENDER

Many U.S. public schools, like Boston Latin School (est. 1635) and Colegio de San Juan de Letran, Guåhan (Guam, est. 1669) educated only boys at first. Yet perhaps surprisingly, public schools in the United States went coeducational relatively early compared to schools worldwide. Many had done so by the early 1800s. It's not entirely clear why, given stringent and deep-rooted sex and gender roles in other spheres. Educational Historians David Tyack and Elizabeth Hansot noted that "Coeducation of the sexes occurred in such a slow and quiet process in thousands of communities that it is, in fact, one of the mysteries of educational history" (1988, 34). By the mid-1800s, roughly equal numbers of boys and girls attended public schools. By 1870, the girls were outperforming the boys academically (Sklar, 1993; Vinovskis & Bernard, 1978). Horace Mann—educational reformer in 1840s Massachusetts—called this period "smuggling in the girls" (Mann, 1853, 5).

Even when coeducational, U.S. public schools have frequently segregated students from each other by sex and gender, typically providing girls worse options than boys. As explained by Edward H. Clarke (Harvard-educated Bostonian, physician, and opinionated Explainer of Things), exclusions and limits were really in girls' best interests. We *could* allow girls to study botany and chemistry in classes with boys, he wrote—but check out what will happen if we do: "[I]t is not true that she can do all this, and retain uninjured health and a future secure from neuralgia, uterine disease, hysteria, and other derangements of the nervous system, if she follows the same method that boys are trained in" (Clarke, 1873, 17–18). Who wants the girls to get uterine disease or hysteria? Not Edward H. Clarke! Legislators, state officials, and school districts listened, and many tracked young women into programs thought more appropriate than botany or chemistry for generations. Throughout the country, no matter their brilliance, motivation, or dedication to academics, young women were often prepared for lives as wives and mothers first . . . and only secondarily for (restricted) opportunities in careers deemed appropriate (such as secretarial, nursing, or teaching work; U.S. Department of Education, 2012).

In 1972, the U.S. Congress passed the Education Amendments of 1972 (Title IX; pronounced "Title Nine") declaring: "No person in the United States shall, on the basis of sex, be excluded from participation in, be denied the benefits of, or be subjected to discrimination under any education program or activity receiving Federal financial assistance[.]" (Education Amendments of 1972). Although Title IX was originally written to ensure opportunities for girls, the specific language prevents discrimination "on the basis of sex." Not "on the basis of being a girl." It turns out that's powerful language for everyone, including boys, transgender, nonbinary, and gender-expansive students.

These days, you're unlikely to teach in a sex-segregated public school—there are only about three hundred nationwide (*Education Week*, 2017). But you'll immediately notice that our profession is disproportionately female: 76% in 2021–2022 (National Center for Education Statistics, 2022f). There's nothing necessarily *wrong* with that. It's just . . . different from our students, who are not 76% girls. Our students are roughly evenly divided between boys and girls, along with an estimated 5% of students who identify as transgender and/or nonbinary (Pew Research Center, 2022). Teaching in the United States has been majority-female for a long time—since the 1880s at least (Wong, 2019). Male teachers in the United States hit a high mark in 1970 at 30% of the field, and have declined to 24% since (Ingersoll et al., 2018).

No one's precisely sure what effect(s) a disproportionately female teacher workforce may have on students. But here's another thing you'll notice in schools: boys are doing *much worse* than girls in school, especially boys from economically disadvantaged backgrounds (Autor & Wasserman, 2013; Reeves, 2022; Whitmire, 2011). At some point over time, our public schools have shifted from providing worse opportunities for girls to worse outcomes for boys. Briefly, boys in U.S. public schools (compared to girls):

1. Get worse scores in reading (reardon et al., 2018).
2. Get punished by teachers more often (Owens, 2016).
3. Are more than twice as likely to get suspended or expelled from school, be arrested at school, or be referred to law enforcement by school officials (NCES, 2019).
4. Are twice as likely to be in special education (NCES, 2021b).
5. Receive more than twice as many grades of D and F in high school (Farrell & Gray, 2018).
6. Are less likely to enjoy school or consider it important (Yarrow, 2018).

7. Graduate from high school at lower rates (Reeves et al., 2021).

8. Are less likely to go to college, and less likely to graduate from college (Reeves & Smith, 2021).

Depressing, right? It's probably even worse for nonbinary, transgender, and gender-expansive students, though data are thin. One possible bright spot is that schools can make a big difference. We don't *have* to be bad at teaching boys to read. We aren't *required* to punish or suspend boys more often. There's no law that says there should be more boys with IEPs than girls, or that boys should enjoy school less. That's *us. We are doing those things to our students.* Those are things we can change.

SEGREGATION BY SCHOOL CHOICE

Schools are also segregated by the choices families make. One example of how segregation by choice can work was the construction of "segregation academies" in the South. As white families chose to leave public schools, the effect was racial segregation. Another example of segregation by choice is when wealthy families choose to purchase homes in expensive neighborhoods. The effect of that choice is segregation by wealth.

Another driver of segregation by choice in the United States is charter schools, which make up about 7% of all public schools in the United States (National Center for Education Statistics, 2022e). Charter schools are public schools of choice. The first charter school opened in Minnesota in 1992. As of 2020–2021, forty-three states, as well as Guam, Puerto Rico, and Washington, DC, operated charter schools (Xu, 2022). There's been a lot of argument over whether charter schools are better or worse than traditional schools—much of it nonproductive, since charter schools vary widely in purpose and outcomes (Wang et al., 2019). Charter schools have been heavily criticized for providing few or no special education services (U.S. Government Accountability Office, 2012), for having discipline policies that quickly remove students with attendance or behavior issues (Losen et al., 2016), and for discouraging or ignoring applications from families with struggling students (Bergman & McFarlin, 2018). One thing that's certain about charter schools is that *families must choose them.* Any family using a charter school must choose not to use their local public school.

Those choices appear to be making already-existing urban school segregation by race, wealth, disability, and English language proficiency worse (National Center for Education Statistics, 2022e). How? In order to attend a charter school, families must:

1. be motivated to find an alternative to their traditional public school,

2. learn about specific available charter school(s),

3. apply by one or more deadlines, and

4. be offered and accept a spot for their child (and figure out transportation, schedule, etc.).

Access to knowledge and the ability to choose is not evenly distributed among families. For example, if all the information a charter school provides about itself is in English, only families with English proficiency will find them. On average, families and children who choose are different in measurable ways from families and children who do not choose (Potter & Nunberg, 2019). It may or may not be intentional, but the effect amplifies segregation in multiple dimensions (race, wealth, disability, language status, family engagement, etc.). It's not at all clear that this is what was intended when charter school laws were originally passed decades ago.

Nor is it clear whether families choose schools (including charter schools) for the reasons we might think (perceived academic quality, a chess club, cool uniforms?). A recent study noted that the top two reasons families chose their charter school were convenience and safety (Jason, 2017). Imagine that flyer: *Academy of Convenience and Safety . . . we're pretty close, and our kids usually don't get hurt at school*. Low bar, right? It's worth asking: why aren't traditional public schools providing that already?

RE: FEAR

One hard lesson of the last several hundred years is that much of our school history has been driven by fear. Fear of a loss of control or advantage, fear of others. We can't understand our public schools without understanding fear. Why have our public schools promoted genocide, the erasure of culture and languages, sterilization, and the many variations of segregation that continue through today? We—officials, families—and yes, teachers—have been *afraid* of our students and their families. We've been afraid that students from (*insert group*) are a threat; we've been afraid that students from (*insert group*) have educational needs that are too complicated for us to address in our classrooms.

You won't often hear the language of fear in schools, save in whispers. What you may hear is that some students are lazy, or disruptive, or unprepared. You may hear that a student "needs a specialist"—invariably not whoever's suggesting it. The way to identify fear among teachers is to identify what they think should be done. Anytime you hear that a student should be removed from a class or school—you're hearing fear. Even when a removal is suggested as "better" for the student (somehow). It might be fear of failure, or fear from not knowing what to do. Fear of incompetence. But it's all fear. And what a tragedy it would be if we continued to make decisions about students in our public schools based on fear.

How can you help our schools get better? One way to start: *welcome every student into your classroom and keep them there*. Then do your best. It's pretty basic: every student has a right to be in your classroom. You've just got to show up and start figuring it out.

What's the History of Public Schools in the United States?

Schools didn't invent education. Education has always happened among peoples where you'll teach. Formal schools in the United States began with land theft and intended cultural erasure in 1513. The most important history of public schools for you isn't national — it's local. How have local control and segregation shaped your school and your community? How can you do better?

SUPREME COURT CASE FOR DISCUSSION

Case: *Milliken v. Bradley,* 418 U.S. 717 (1974)
Link: www.law.cornell.edu/supremecourt/text/418/717

Brown I (1954) and *Brown II (1955)* required school districts across the country to racially desegregate. Desegregation proved difficult in Detroit and many other northern cities. By 1970, discriminatory housing policies, neighborhood intimidation, and white flight had produced a student population in the Detroit Public Schools that was two-thirds Black, while the surrounding fifty-three suburban school districts were all majority-white.

On April 7, 1970, the Detroit Public Schools Board of Education passed a plan to bus nine thousand students within the district to achieve some amount of racial balance in schools. The plan would have bused students out of racially segregated neighborhoods to other schools within the district. A group of white parents formed an anti-busing group, the Concerned Citizens for Better Education (CCBE), and the Michigan State Legislature quickly nullified the plan using its authority as the state educational agency responsible for public education.

The National Association for the Advancement of Colored People (NAACP) sued Michigan Governor William Milliken in federal District Court on behalf of several parents, including Verda Bradley, mother of two school-aged children (Ronald and Richard Bradley) living in Detroit. The aim of the NAACP lawsuit was to force the implementation of the April 7 busing plan to (modestly) desegregate the Detroit Public Schools.

The District Court found that, since school segregation was ultimately the responsibility of the State of Michigan, it didn't make any sense to allow a Detroit-only plan that couldn't substantially desegregate schools. They commented: "School district lines are simply matters of political convenience and may not be used to deny constitutional rights." The District Court ordered the Detroit Board of Education to draw up a much larger desegregation plan—one that included the entire three-county metropolitan area, and fifty-three of the eighty-five outlying school districts.

The Governor of Michigan appealed. The fifty-three suburban districts objected that racial segregation in Detroit schools was Detroit's problem. Ultimately, the case landed in front of the U.S. Supreme Court in 1974, and they ruled 5-4: "School district lines may not be casually ignored or treated as a mere administrative convenience; substantial local control of public education in this country is a deeply rooted tradition." In a nutshell: segregation in the Detroit Public Schools wasn't the fault of the suburban districts—so suburban districts couldn't be ordered to participate in metropolitan desegregation.

QUESTIONS

1. The Supreme Court decided that the basic principle of local control of public education overrode the right Richard and Ronald Bradley may have had to attend desegregated schools. Was the Supreme Court right? Why, or why not?

2. To what extent is it fair to order a Detroit-area desegregation plan that goes beyond Detroit City and requires participation of fifty-three surrounding school districts?

3. Today, school districts are more racially segregated than they were in 1974 (EdBuild, 2019; Nadworny & Tuner, 2019). Should states or the federal government require local school districts to desegregate with each other? Why, or why not?

FURTHER READINGS AND RESOURCES

Data on public education:
National Center for Education Statistics, U.S. Department of Education: nces.ed.gov.

Federal role in schools:
Pelsue, B. (2017). When it comes to education, the federal government is in charge of . . . um, what? *Harvard Ed. Magazine.*

Indigenous education:
Reyhner, J, & Eder, J. (2017). *American Indian education, a history* (2nd ed.). Norman: University of Oklahoma Press.

Indigenous lands map:
native-land.ca. Useful for identifying Indigenous peoples, territorial boundaries, languages, and treaties.

Local control of schools:
Scribner, C. (2016). *The fight for local control: Schools, suburbs, and American democracy.* Ithaca, NY: Cornell University Press.

School segregation (data and research):
Segregation Index. University of Southern California: socialinnovation.usc.edu/segregation; Civil Rights Project, University of California, Los Angeles. www.civilrightsproject.ucla.edu

NOTES

1. *Translation:* We lucked out, everyone's dead. Hey look! Open fields with good drainage!

2. Several cool things going on here. King Kamehamea III was Kānaka Maoli (Native Hawaiian), which makes the Hawaiian school system the only U.S. public school system established by a sovereign monarch *and* the only statewide system established by Indigenous peoples. It also helps explain why Hawai'i to this day has just one statewide school district.

3. I hope it's clear this is my paraphrasing. Also: Towns with at least a hundred households were required to fund a school *"to instruct youth so far as they may be fitted for the Universitie."* The only "Universitie" in Massachusetts in 1647 was Harvard. No two ways around it: an explicit purpose for some of our earliest public schools was sending kids to Harvard. *That* purpose remains alive and well for many public schools today.

4. Black psychologists Mamie Clark and Kenneth Clark's "doll test" in the 1940s showed that children growing up in segregated environments developed warped racial concepts. The test asked three-year-old children to choose dolls to

play with. They could choose white dolls with yellow hair or brown dolls with black hair. A majority of children, including Black children, chose the white dolls, assigning them positive traits, while discarding the brown dolls and assigning them negative traits (McNeill, 2017).

5. Wegmans. *Headquarters*: Rochester, New York. Wegmans is the best grocery store in the nation, dear reader. Just trust me on this.

6. Fun fact: Carlisle alum Wa-Tho-Huk / Jim Thorpe (Sac and Fox and Potawatomi) was and remains the world's greatest athlete of all time. King Gustav V of Sweden will back me up on this (Flatter, 1999). Other fun fact: Thorpe's Carlisle football team (coached by Pop Warner) beat the U.S. Army team at West Point, where future U.S. general Dwight Eisenhower played running back and linebacker (Anderson, 2008). Is there something cool about the Carlisle Indians beating the U.S. Army Cadets on a dark and stormy night? (Yes.)

7. Capital-D "Deaf" = those who identify with Deaf culture and use a signed language (in the U.S., American Sign Language). Lower-case "deaf" = those with hearing loss. Capital-D Deaf individuals often reject the idea that deafness is a disability (Padden & Humphries, 2005).

3

Governance and Finance
Why Does It Matter that Public Schools Have Local Control?

This chapter is about the governance and finance of our public schools. Before your eyes glaze, let me reassure you: *they're fascinating*. Governance and finance shape your life as a teacher every day. Who's your boss? Who pays your salary? Is there any money for markers, or Play-Doh, or band instruments? Let's tackle definitions of governance and finance first, and then explore what each means for you:

- Governance is about *control*. Who gets to make decisions about curriculum, hiring, policies, and operations (including whether we have band)? Knowledge of school governance can help teachers understand who makes decisions within schools, and what kinds of decisions teachers may be able to influence.

- Finance is about *money*. Where does the money come from for public schools? How is it spent? It will not surprise you that money impacts our work as teachers, in ways that can be direct (e.g., *do we have enough money to hire another teacher?*) and indirect (e.g., *when schools accept federal money, what must they do in return?*).

You might be surprised by who's in charge of U.S. public schools. It's not the federal government. The United States didn't have a cabinet-level Department of Education until 1979 (United States Department of Education, 2010); to this day, it's the smallest cabinet in the federal government (U.S. Office of Personnel Management, 2018). In the United States, the federal government has a relatively small role when it comes to our public schools. Far more important are local, state, Tribal, and territorial governments. Why?

ROLE OF THE FEDERAL GOVERNMENT

Public schools in the United States have deep roots and variable origins and purposes. By the time the United States began operating as a constitutional republic in 1789, schools serving different purposes and populations had already been established throughout the states and territories (Graham, 2005; Spady, 2020). Although there was some interest in education among the framers of the Constitution, they couldn't agree about a role for the federal government (Black, 2020a). The U.S. Constitution is silent about "schools" and "education" and "lunch duty." There is, however, a clear *restriction* concerning what the federal government can and can't do spelled out in the 10th Amendment (ratified in 1791): "The powers not delegated to the United States by the Constitution, nor prohibited by it to the States, are reserved to the States respectively, or to the people." Two Constitutional notes here. First, because the Constitution doesn't mention education, it isn't a fundamental, protected right of U.S. citizens (unlike, for example, due process, speech, and religion; Dorsey, 2020). So far, no one has successfully claimed that their Constitutional rights were violated because they got a lousy education (though they have tried; see Wong, 2018; *San Antonio v. Rodríguez* [1972]; *Gary B. v. Whitmer* [2020]). Second, because the 10th Amendment reserves powers not delegated to "States respectively, or to the people," states, Tribes, and other authorities are responsible for public schools in the United States, not the federal government.

But wait! There's one major role for the federal government in education that emerges from a later edit to the Constitution: *equal protection*. In 1868, in the wake of the Civil War, the United States ratified the 14th Amendment, which specified, "No State shall make or enforce any law which shall abridge the privileges or immunities of citizens of the United States; nor shall any State deprive any person of life, liberty, or property, without due process of law; nor deny to any person within its jurisdiction the equal protection of the laws." Rough translation: states can't pass laws or provide services in ways that discriminate. The 14th Amendment (§ 5) also specified that the federal government had enforcement power; any state attempting to deny equal protection would have to answer to the federal government. So, if and when states and territories operate public schools (at this point, they all do), they must provide access to all students on an equal basis (Tyack & Lowe, 1986). The 14th Amendment is a big deal, even if it hasn't worked quickly or universally well. States obviously didn't provide equal protection to all citizens in 1868, or 1869, or in the years following. There's ample reason to think they have yet to do so, ever.[1]

The 14th Amendment provides the federal government the authority to step in to prevent discrimination in public schools. It has rarely done so without being forced. Take racial discrimination, for example. The U.S. Supreme Court's 1954 *Brown v. Board* decision declared that "in the field of public education, the doctrine of 'separate but equal' has no place" (*Brown v. Board* [1954], 495). *Brown v. Board* didn't happen because the federal government decided that segregated schools were bad. *Brown v. Board* happened because Black lawyers filed lawsuits on behalf of Black plaintiffs in South Carolina, Virginia, Delaware, and Kansas. It happened because the legal team of the National Association for the Advancement of Colored People (NAACP), led by Thurgood Marshall, forced the Supreme Court to revisit its own erroneous precedent in *Plessy v. Ferguson* (1896). And even once *Brown v. Board* was decided (unanimously), the federal government took years to enforce it (Patterson, 2002). The original *Brown v. Board* decision (1954) said separate school systems weren't constitutional, but it didn't tell the states how or when to dismantle them. The court then decided in *Brown v. Board II* (1955), that states needed to desegregate with "all deliberate speed"—which wasn't the same as saying "in two years" or anything concrete (Ogletree, 2005). Mississippi did nothing to desegregate until 1969, when the Supreme Court finally ordered "immediate" desegregation (*Alexander v. Holmes County,* 1969; Harris, 2020). As of 2023, thirty-two Mississippi school districts remained under federal desegregation orders (Associated Press, 2023).

You can see a federal government consistently reluctant to intervene, until forced to do so, in the histories of students seeking equal protection on the basis of ethnicity (*Mendez v. Westminster* [1946]), immigration status (*Plyler v. Doe* [1982]), language status (*Lau v. Nichols* [1974]), and disability status (*PARC v. Pennsylvania* [1972]; *Mills v. Board of Education* [1972]). There are more. One playing out as I write is whether transgender students, especially transgender girls, should have equal rights to use the bathroom or join a sports team (*Grimm v. Gloucester,* 2020; Liptak, 2023). I hope by the time you read this you're surprised and disappointed there were ever questions about such things. Just keep in mind that the federal role in public schools has been limited. The federal government isn't in charge of public schools in the United States. Its major role is in the enforcement of laws and court decisions, especially those relating to equal protection.

ROLE OF STATES, TERRITORIES, AND TRIBES[2]

The 10th Amendment to the U.S. Constitution clarified that the authority to establish schools was reserved "to the States respectively, or to the people." The 10th Amendment didn't require anyone to set up schools. Even today, no federal law requires states to operate public schools. Eventually, all states established public school systems—but few states directly operate schools themselves. Instead, states usually direct local entities to operate schools (cities, counties, or newly established school districts). Massachusetts was first to require all children to attend school (1852); Mississippi was last (1918) (Tyack, 1974).

What *is* the role of states, territories, and Tribes when it comes to U.S. public schools? Major roles include (adapted from Aspen Institute, 2015):

- Funding—States provide money for public schools, usually from tax revenue. They also receive money from federal sources and pass it along to local school districts.

- Policy—States establish rules and regulations for operating public schools. These include aspects familiar to teachers (e.g., length of school days and school years, fire drills, etc.), and aspects perhaps less familiar (e.g., what's allowed in school vending machines).[3]

- Oversight—States establish student learning standards (for grade levels or subjects), define proficiency, establish accountability systems, and establish licensure standards for teachers and other school personnel.

- Communications—States communicate priorities in education, clarify how districts and schools should implement laws and regulations, and publish student, teacher, school, and district information (especially demographics and achievement data).

States provide U.S. public schools with a lot of money. That matters for you as a teacher because it determines things like teacher salaries, benefits, and available resources. States also set rules and regulations for teaching and school operations. For example, how you'll get certified to teach is determined by the state where you want to teach. States establish learning standards, define proficiency, and operate accountability systems that involve end-of-year testing. Because states are responsible for setting the rules, regulations, and standards for schools within their borders, they are also the ones ultimately responsible for school quality. If a student or family feels that their local school or district is not doing its job, they can bring their concerns to state education agencies. Although states rarely run schools themselves, they're responsible for a lot of what happens inside them. Figure 3.1 shows students outside Tse'Na'shchiiO'lta' (Hunters Point Boarding School), a Tribally Controlled School operated by the Navajo Nation.

Figure 3.1. Students line up outside a dorm at Tse'Na'shchiiO'lta' (Hunters Point Boarding School), St. Michaels, Arizona. *Source:* © Mark Henle, USA Today Network. Used with permission.

Tribal Schools

Tribes (variously also called Nations, Bands, Pueblos, Communities, and Native Villages) are sovereign nations. Tribes are governments responsible for things like determining citizenship and providing for the health, safety, and welfare of their people. For a good overview of what Tribes are and what they do, see the National Congress of American Indians' *Tribal Nations and the United States* (2019). Tribes have *always* educated children. Tribes have *not* always been able to use their languages and cultures in the context of schools. One defining legacy of many schools forced on Tribes was the attempted eradication of languages and cultures of Tribal citizens (Adams, 2020; Reyhner & Eder, 2017).

The Indian Self-Determination and Education Assistance Act of 1975 (P.L. 93-638) confirmed that Tribes have the right to operate public schools with public resources. Most numerous are Tribally Controlled Schools, operated under contracts with the (federal) U.S. Bureau of Indian Education (as of 2023, there were 97 such schools). In recent years, more Tribes have established charter schools or schools under negotiated compacts with states (e.g., see the Washington Office of Superintendent of Public Instruction [n.d.] and the Alaska Department of Education & Early Development [n.d.]). Tribal schools generally operate with three shared purposes:

- **Sovereignty**: Tribal schools are fundamentally a matter of sovereignty and self-determination rights, including the right to decide how children should be educated.

- **Curriculum & instruction:** Tribal schools provide the opportunity to place Indigenous languages, cultures, histories, and knowledge central to P–12 learning experiences.

- **Effectiveness:** Tribal schools provide the opportunity for Tribes to design and deliver alternative models of teaching and learning that may be more effective with Tribal children than other kinds of P–12 schools.

ROLE OF SCHOOL DISTRICTS

Most U.S. public school teachers are employed by a local school district. A school district is geographically defined (with boundaries on a map) and usually operates multiple schools, save those in remote rural areas. The number of school districts within each state varies widely: Hawai'i has one; Texas has more than a thousand (United States Census Bureau, 2022). School districts (not the federal government, not states, not Bob the principal) are the ones who will hire you, pay you, and provide you with a classroom and students. School districts are responsible for just about everything that makes your life as a teacher good (New books! A stipend for Dungeons & Dragons club!) or not so good (Thirty-eight students in third period? Why can't we fix the screen in my room? The windows?, etc.).

Your teaching life is largely defined by the school district for which you work. It's hard to overstate this. When you teach, you teach in that one school district, in that specific context. It's not rare for teachers to have excellent experiences teaching in one district, and less-excellent experiences in another. One tragedy is that many teachers leave the profession having gained experience in just a single district, thinking they know what teaching is like everywhere. Not true. School districts in the United States aren't one thing—they're thirteen thousand different things (United States Census, 2022). One of the most important decisions you'll make during your first year of teaching will be: do I want to come back next year? I recommend pondering a slight variation: do I want to come back *to this district* next year?

Major roles of school districts include:

- Policy—Districts develop policies, often hundreds of them, from Accounting to Workers' Compensation and everything in between.[4]

- Budget—Districts adopt budgets each year, which specify how available resources will be used.

- Leadership—Districts hire superintendents and other administrators who implement district policies and supervise district employees.

- Curriculum—Districts review and approve or adopt curriculum (materials teachers use to teach).

- Contracts—Districts negotiate labor contracts that establish salaries, benefits, and responsibilities for employees (like teachers). Districts also negotiate contracts with vendors—for example, when remodeling buildings, purchasing technology, or buying tater tots in bulk.

Districts vary widely in what they value and how they do business. Some spend a lot of money, some far less. Some have football stadiums that cost millions of dollars (looking at you, Texas). Others have high schools with fifteen science labs and their own scientific journal (Thomas Jefferson High School for Science and Technology in Fairfax, Virginia; *Teknos*). As you can imagine, relying on local school districts (not states, not Washington, DC) to operate schools as they see fit creates opportunities (*It's ours! We're responsible for it! We can tailor it to best serve our community!*) and risk (*It's ours! We're responsible for it! We can do whatever! Wait . . . where are the keys for this thing, anyway?*). One guarantee of having thousands of separately governed school districts is variability. Public schools in in the United States are not, and never have been, a coherent public school "system."

AUTHORITY WITHIN DISTRICTS

For whom do you work? Here's an overview, top to bottom:

BOARD OF EDUCATION (A.K.A. SCHOOL BOARD OR BOARD OF TRUSTEES)

In charge of school districts. Everyone's boss. Responsible for decisions about policies, budget, leadership, curriculum, contracts, and employment. Usually includes five to nine elected community members (usually not educators) who serve unpaid and part-time. Boards generally meet once per month; meetings are open to the public (Ballotpedia, 2022). The most important decision a Board of Education makes is hiring a superintendent. A Board does not manage daily operations in schools—the superintendent does. A Board seeks recommendations from the superintendent on policies, the budget, employment, etc., and takes their input seriously when making decisions.

SUPERINTENDENT

The day-to-day leader of school district operations, hired by the Board. The superintendent supervises other administrators in the district. Most superintendents (not all) have prior experience as teachers and as principals. A major task of the superintendent is to prepare the district's annual budget. The superintendent also serves as the public face of the district. They are responsible for communications with parents, families, local and state government, and the media. The superintendent is also responsible for advocacy on behalf of the district, especially with state educational agencies (e.g., for state policy changes or additional funding).[5]

PRINCIPAL

The day-to-day leader of school building operations. The principal's primary job is supervising faculty, staff, and students, and developing positive relationships with families. Principals are responsible for directly supervising teachers. Principals also figure out schedules, lead faculty meetings, and handle student discipline when needed. You'll get to know your principal well. They'll spend time in your class. They'll evaluate you. Your principal can have a significant influence on how you teach and whether you keep teaching. Make every effort you can to develop a good working relationship with your principal. Ask questions without being needy, invite them to observe you, take their feedback seriously. One nearly universal truth about principals: *principals love fixing problems, and they hate surprises.* What does this mean? Be ready to communicate bad news, stuff you don't know, and things you're worried about. The only way a principal can fix a problem is if they know about it. Timing is often key. If you lose your cool in class and yell at a student, let your principal know what happened as soon as you can. If you don't turn in your lesson plans on time, send a regrettable email, miss an assigned duty, or don't know how to submit grades . . . let your principal know as soon as you can. If you have a plan to fix your mistake(s), share it. If you don't have a plan, or don't know what to do, ask for help. Just don't try to keep problems or mistakes a secret. In a profession as complex as teaching, principals know you are going to make mistakes. They can usually help you fix them. Often teacher fears are larger than the mistakes themselves. If your principal is upset or disappointed, they'll tell you—and then they'll help. The worst thing you can do is allow a problem to fester to the point that it becomes unfixable. Communicate, communicate, communicate.

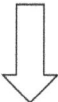

TEACHER

This is you. You're responsible for pedagogy. You're responsible for keeping your students safe, engaged, and learning. And you're responsible for relationships with families and other professionals in the school: counselors, special education teachers and personnel, social workers, mental health professionals, reading specialists, coaches, etc. Although we may occasionally close our classroom doors and work only with our students at times, we don't ever do the work alone. Figure 3.2 shows a sample school district organizational chart, showing who supervises whom—you're down there at the bottom.

Figure 3.2. Sample school district organizational chart. *Source:* Created by the author.

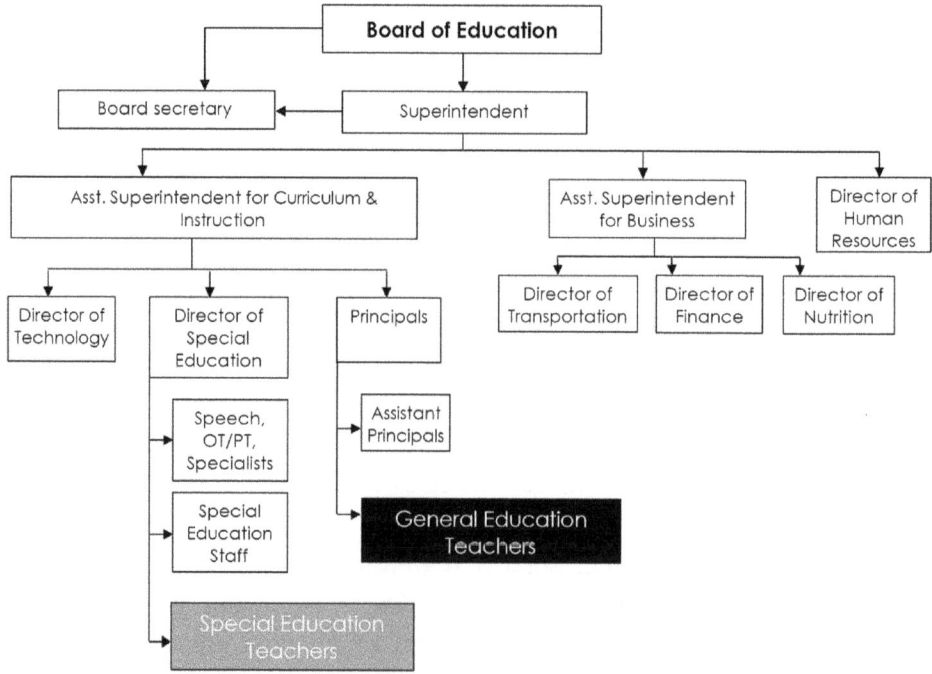

You may have different lines of authority in your district. For example, special education teachers may report to an administrator of special education rather than a principal. Many districts have directors or assistant superintendents who supervise principals or clusters of teachers. Notice that teachers always have several supervisors. Each has the authority to direct our work. In Figure 3.2, teachers have at least four supervisors—a principal or director, an assistant superintendent, the superintendent, and the Board of Education. You may have more.

School Districts: One Size Does Not Fit All

School districts in U.S. states and territories vary widely in enrollment and geography. The smallest school district in the nation operates a single one-room school with three students (Bois Blanc School District in Michigan; National Center for Education Statistics, 2022). The largest operates nearly two thousand schools with about a million students (New York City Public Schools; National Center for Education Statistics, 2021). The largest school district by geography is either the North Slope Borough School District in Alaska (88,700 square miles, bigger than all but the ten largest U.S. states) or maybe the Hawai'i Department of Education (a statewide district that yawns over 1,523 miles of Pacific Ocean). In Northeastern states, where schools were established early and often, districts tend to be geographically compact. Drive half an hour, drive through several school districts (Rhode Island, for example, has sixty-six school districts packed into a semi-rectangle measuring roughly forty-eight miles by thirty-seven miles). Northeastern and Midwestern states commonly have urban (city-center) districts surrounded by separate suburban districts, with sharp demarcations by race, ethnicity, and wealth. Southern states often have countywide school districts, occasionally with separate urban/city-center districts. Midwestern states often have school districts established under land-grant terms with remarkably square geometries (Usher, 2011). Western states tend to have geographically large districts in rural areas, with urban and suburban districts more common as population density increases (Wyoming, for example, has just forty-eight school disticts, many of which are larger than several Rhode Islands). Western states also tend to have more Indian Country, where Tribes or the Bureau of Indian Education operate schools. Hawai'i, Washington, DC, American Samoa, Guam, the Northern Mariana Islands, Puerto Rico, and the U.S. Virgin Islands all have unified districts. There doesn't seem to be a single "ideal" setup for school district governance in the United States. They vary. Look into the origin story of your school district. Where is your district on a map? Who operates it? How will governance there shape your work?

There's probably no ideal governance model in the United States. If, however, your goal is to spend a great deal of money on administration, including lots of superintendents and associate superintendents and directors of human resources and so on, you'd probably do something like our current setup, with its collective 13,000+ public school districts.

Another side effect of having so many school districts, beyond administrative cost, is that districts have become established as political bodies with interests that do not necessarily match broader concepts of the common good (Clotfelter, 2011; Kruse, 2007; Rothstein, 2018). One example of the harm district fragmentation can do is entrenched segregation, explored in Chapter 2. Since the *Milliken v. Bradley* (1974) decision, school district lines have become nearly inviolable in the United States, even when they do active and obvious harm by segregating schools and harming opportunities for vulnerable students.

SCHOOL DISTRICT REVENUES

Where does the money come from for U.S. public schools? Taxes. Not just one tax; there's a mix of local, state, and federal taxes. There's also a mix of opinions in the United States about whether we're paying too many taxes, or using tax revenues properly. Let's start with history. Remember this guy?

Figure 3.3. The Whiskey Rebellion. *Source:* Unknown; attributed to Frederick Kemmelmeyer, circa 1795. Public domain.

That's President George Washington in Figure 3.3, on the white horse. He's riding forth from Fort Cumberland, Maryland, in 1794. Why? To go beat down a rebellion over whiskey taxes in western Pennsylvania that were supposed to help pay off war debt. One foundational theme of the

United States: many Americans don't like paying taxes (for tea, whiskey, or schools). More recently, Figure 3.4 shows us this guy:

Figure 3.4. A demonstrator at a "Tax Day" demonstration in Cincinnati, Ohio, holds a sign reading "taxation is theft," 2017. *Source:* Photo by user 5chw4r7z from Cincinnati, CC BY-SA 2.0.

Anti-tax sentiment remains a powerful force in the United States, even if we've mostly moved away from rebellion-with-guns toward rebellion-with-Sharpies-and-floppy-hats. Anti-tax sentiment matters because it influences the resources public schools have (or don't have). And it matters because educational funding in U.S. public schools varies substantially by state and locale.

As shown in Figure 3.5 (next page), overall, the federal government provided just 7.8% of U.S. public school revenues in 2017–2018. The rest came from state (46.8%) and local sources (45.3%). This distribution may not be surprising, given the histories of U.S. public schools as local institutions. Local funding has been the primary source of funding for public schools for most of their existence. States didn't provide much money for public schools during the eighteenth and nineteenth centuries, because

Figure 3.5. Revenue for U.S. public elementary and secondary schools, by source of funds, 2017–2018. *Source:* Economic Policy Institute (2022). Used with permission.

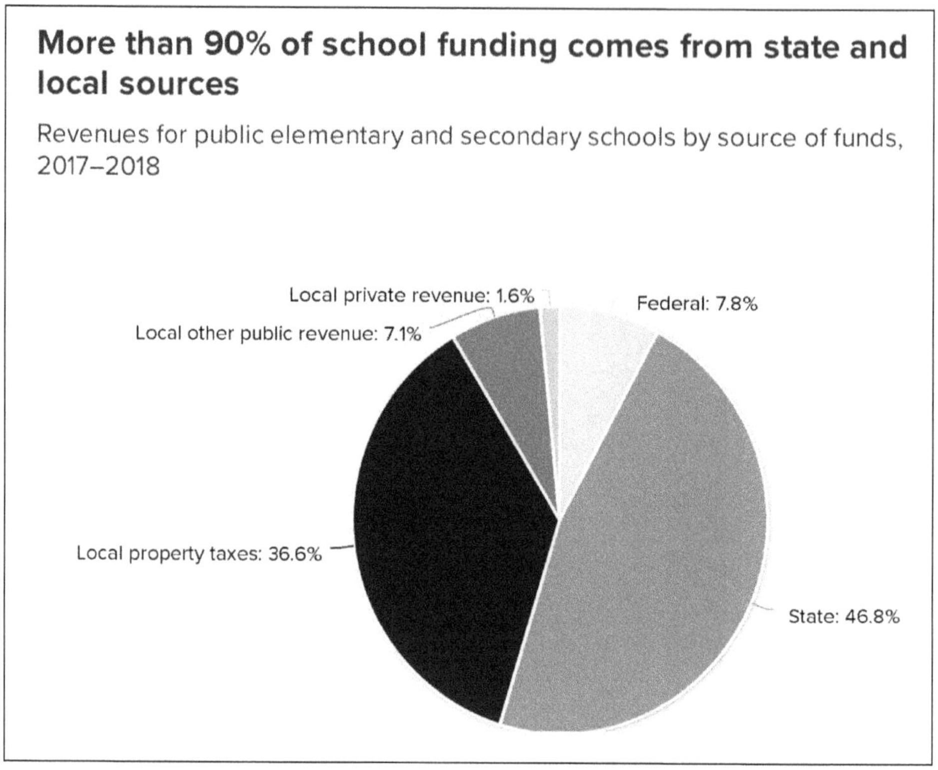

More than 90% of school funding comes from state and local sources

Revenues for public elementary and secondary schools by source of funds, 2017–2018

- Local private revenue: 1.6%
- Local other public revenue: 7.1%
- Federal: 7.8%
- Local property taxes: 36.6%
- State: 46.8%

they generally only raised school revenues from limited property taxes (Paul, 1955). Wisconsin was the first state to pass a modern income tax in 1911 (Stark, 1987); most other states followed and began to generate substantial and predictable revenue for public schools. The proportions of local, state, and federal funding in Figure 3.5 have been largely stable since 1964 (Chantrill, n.d.). There's nothing necessarily right or wrong with those proportions. What's worth paying attention to, though, is how local and state revenue is generated in the U.S. Via taxes, of course, but the specific *kinds* of taxes matter.

Property taxes are a major source of public school revenue, especially local revenue. 36.6% of total public school revenue comes from "Local property taxes"; another 17% of the "State" wedge comes from property taxes levied by states (see Urban Institute, n.d.). Property taxes are taxes on the value of land and real estate, paid every year. Property values vary substantially (try Googling "Four bedroom home in San Francisco, California" and then also "Four bedroom home in Greenwood, Mississippi"). Areas with high property values can raise substantial revenue for schools with relatively low tax rates. You can tax a neighborhood full of million-dollar homes at a low rate and generate lots of revenue.

It would take a much higher tax rate to generate the same revenue in a neighborhood of $100,000 homes. This is notable: *wealthy areas often pay lower tax rates than poor areas, while still generating more revenue for schools.*

States and the federal government often try to balance local revenue disparities by directing funding toward school districts with lower property wealth. In New York, for example, the state collects taxes (on personal income, businesses, property, etc.) and distributes it to school districts by formula, sending more dollars to districts with lower property wealth and higher proportions of economically disadvantaged students (New York State Education Department, 2023b). New York's approach is not universal. A study by the Urban Institute (2017) found that thirty-five states directed extra funding toward districts serving economically disadvantaged students, while fourteen did not. The federal government largely attempts to do the same—directing additional funds toward needier districts—but federal contributions to public schools are modest (7.8%) and don't make up known differences anywhere.

Each year, property owners and politicians across the country are asked: *should we pay higher taxes?* And: *where should that money go?* Answers are influenced by a range of factors, including the health of the local economy, home values, perceptions of local school quality, and local political climates. Remember the Whiskey Rebellion (Figure 3.3) and that TAXATION IS THEFT guy (Figure 3.4)? The United States has a deep history of suspicion about whether the taxes we pay are fair or put to good use (Williamson, 2017). It can be difficult for school districts to successfully convince property owners to pay higher taxes. Some people just hate taxes (generally); others may resent paying for services (like schools) that they don't use.[6]

What about the federal government and its (theoretically) deep pockets? Why aren't the feds providing more than 7.8% of our public school revenues? Good question. The federal government is interested in public schools—but restricted in what it can do. The 10th Amendment leaves education largely up to state, territorial, Tribal, and local authorities. Even federal laws that *do* fund schools are primarily indirect or voluntary, so as to not overstep the 10th Amendment. For example, two of the most significant federal elementary and secondary education laws, the Every Student Succeeds Act (2015) and the Individuals with Disabilities Act (2004), aren't actually Sweeping Laws of the Land Telling Schools What To Do. They're just grant programs. If states or schools want those federal dollars (all of them do), they have to comply with the terms of the grants. It's at least theoretically possible that states could reject the money and do something else. Grant programs are one way the federal government can influence public schools while providing reasonably modest cash. For example, the National School Lunch Program provides money for schools to buy food for free or low-cost meals at school (www.fns.usda.gov/nslp). Schools can't just feed the kids Hot Cheetos and energy drinks, though. They must follow nutrition guidelines adopted by the U.S. Department of Agriculture. If schools take the money, they have to follow the rules. The federal government doesn't spend vast sums on public schools because it never set them up in the first place, because it doesn't have unlimited authority over them . . . and because it's never been necessary to spend a lot to gain influence anyway.

SCHOOL SPENDING

The vast majority of U.S. public school district budgets are spent paying adults. School districts spend roughly 80% of their annual budgets on salaries and benefits for teachers, aides, principals, bus drivers, custodians and administrative assistants. Everything else school districts need—books and buses, computers and crayons, the electric bill and band instruments and football uniforms—must be paid from the remaining 20% (National Center for Education Statistics, 2023a) (see Figure 3.6).

Figure 3.6. Expenditures per student in U.S. public elementary and secondary schools, by type of expenditure: 2003–2004, 2008–2009, 2013–2014, and 2019–2020. Data from U.S. Department of Education, NCES Condition of Education (2023). *Source:* Created by the author.

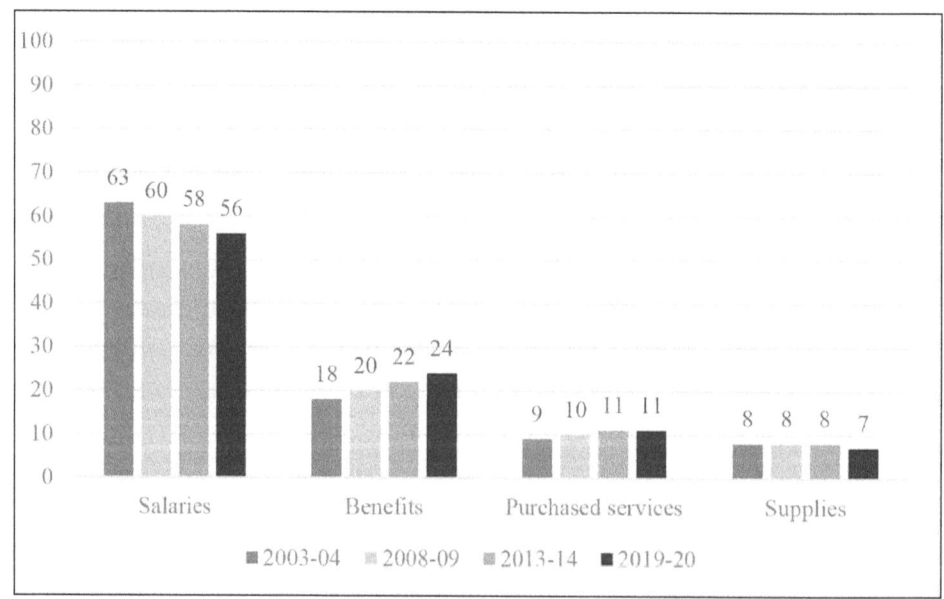

Note: "Salaries" and "benefits" are paid to district employees. "Purchased services" includes expenditures for professional and technical services and renting equipment. "Supplies" typically includes things like books, paper, staples, etc. Totals don't add to 100% due to rounding and excluded expenditure categories totaling less than 2%.

Most public school districts in the United States operate with negotiated, not-really-adjustable salaries, so it's difficult for schools to save money from year to year by doing anything other than cutting jobs (or not replacing people who leave). If tax revenues fall 10% in a year because the local economy is struggling . . . what can get cut? Schools can't turn the lights off. Schools must operate buses and furnaces. Schools need principals. Where are the margins? They can buy cheap toilet paper and cheap crayons and cheap cafeteria food, but those won't save major dollars. Nor can schools re-route dedicated money (federal nutrition dollars can't, for example, get spent on new books). Spending reductions are painful and hated by everyone. They usually impact employment because that's where districts spend the most.

Public school district labor costs vary widely in the United States. Mississippi, for example, paid teachers the lowest average salary in 2021–2022 ($47,902); New York paid the highest ($91,097; National Education Association, 2023). Paying teachers less isn't necessarily evil, nor is paying more a sign of enlightenment. The ability to raise revenue and pay teachers depends on state and local economies and on property wealth. Alaska, for example, has paid teachers higher wages than many other states since the 1970s, not because state government has an elevated commitment to teacher welfare (it does not) but because the state has collected huge piles of revenue from oil taxes. Bragging rights should probably go to states and territories that spend high *percentages* of their budgets on schools, not just high dollar totals . . . pats on the back to Nevada, Vermont, Texas, and Kansas (National Association of State Budget Officers, 2023, Table 5; see also Maciag, 2019).

School district budgets depend on local and state economies and on the choices we make about taxes. No district has unlimited resources—but what's available may factor into where you start teaching, how long you stay in a district, and whether you continue teaching for a career.

SCHOOL CHOICE

Related to any discussion of school governance and finance is school choice. School choice is the ability of families to choose where their children go to school. There are several different choice alternatives to local public schools in most places in the United States—private schools, charter schools, and homeschooling being the three most common. All involve different governance and funding mechanisms. Keep in mind that families with wealth have always had school choice. Wealth lets families purchase housing in preferred public school districts, pay tuition at private schools, or hire private tutors and coaches. Wealth also enables school-related supports like caregivers who can be at home rather than work, or tons of books at home, or SAT prep classes. Wealth enables choice. It's true that wealth isn't an on-off switch; some have more than others. Just keep in mind that access to different public schools depends primarily on the ability of families to purchase or rent housing in different school districts. I'll repeat the idea because it's important: *Families with wealth have always had school choice.*

Private schools are beyond the scope of this book, but you should remember they exist because they often hire certified teachers (like you). They may be a good option for work if openings are limited in your local public schools and you need to gain experience. Private schools educate somewhere around 9% of school-aged children in the United States (National Center for Education Statistics, 2019a), and they may be more diverse in orientation than you'd expect. They are not all *Dead Poets Society* prep school enclaves. About three-quarters of private schools had a religious affiliation in 2019; Catholic schools were the most numerous (National Center for Education Statistics, 2019b). Catholic schools, especially those in urban areas, have often served large numbers of families with low incomes (Murnane & Reardon, 2018). There are day and boarding private schools, private schools for students with disabilities, and private schools with varying academic or athletic emphases (Science and technology! Alpine skiing! Kindergarteners in the forest!).[7]

In the public school arena, "school choice" generally means the ability of families to choose a school at no additional cost (beyond paying property and school taxes, which they have to do no matter what schools they use). Here are the three major means for U.S. families to choose schools without major additional costs:

CHARTER SCHOOLS

These are tuition-free public schools, typically governed by private boards under contract with an authorizer (usually local school districts, local or state governments, universities, or nonprofits). Though charter schools were originally conceived with a range of purposes (such as innovation in teaching and learning or specific academic themes), today they generally exist where communities are dissatisfied with local public schools, especially concerning academic achievement (Lubienski & Weitzel, 2010). Charter schools provide tuition-free options for families who may otherwise not have meaningful school choice. They're popular; in 2021–2022, charter schools educated 3.7 million students, about 7% of all public school students in the United States (National Center for

Education Statistics, 2023b). Some U.S. cities have more than 40% of their students enrolled in charter schools (including New Orleans, San Antonio, Kansas City, Indianapolis, and Washington DC; Xu, 2022, Table 3.5). In 2021–2022, forty-five U.S. states, as well as Guam, Puerto Rico, and Washington, DC, allowed charter schools (National Alliance for Public Charter Schools, 2022).[8]

Charter schools are mostly urban, in part because urban areas have enough students to make parallel school systems (traditional and charter) financially viable (National Center for Education Statistics, 2023c). Charter schools serve, on average, higher percentages of students from low income backgrounds, higher percentages of Black and Latinx students, and lower percentages of students with disabilities and students learning English than traditional district schools (Barshay, 2023; National Center for Education Statistics, 2018; U.S. Government Accountability Office, 2012; Williams, 2019). Charter schools are typically funded by directing per-pupil tax revenues away from the school district of residence and toward the charter school (the money follows the child). As you can imagine, redirecting public tax dollars to fund charter schools has been controversial (Jason, 2017).

Over the years charter schools have been accused of a range of evils. *They're vampires on local school budgets!* (Barnum, 2019). *They're segregated!* (Monarrez et al., 2019; Wilson, 2019) *They're vehicles for the enrichment of corporate fat cats!* (Finn et al., 2016). The label that seems to have stuck most firmly is that charter schools can function as enclaves for engaged families with easier-to-educate children (e.g., by excluding students learning English or those with disabilities). Overall it appears that charter schools have, on average, modest positive effects on academic achievement and graduation rates compared to traditional districts, and there's some evidence that charter schools have improved over time (e.g., see Center for Research on Education Outcomes, 2023; Harris & Chen, 2023).[9]

I'm not going to try to convince you that charter schools are fantastic or terrible. They're not really any single thing at all. As with traditional schools, charter schools are now so numerous (and diverse in mission, context and quality) that it's not terribly useful to discuss them as if they're a coherent group. Three things to keep in mind as you consider where to teach:

- Charter schools exist. They may be a good option for you as a teacher. They can be vibrant, rewarding places to teach.
- Charter schools are free public schools, primarily urban ones at that. They provide meaningful choices for families who

may have limited or bad options for schools near their homes. Many teachers who work in charter schools find a great deal of professional meaning working in them . . . even if they are imperfect. (Remind me where to find a perfect traditional school?)

- Charter schools aren't good or evil. They're public schools, governed and funded differently than traditional schools.

Arguments about charter schools appear to emerge from the different *purposes* we imagine public schools fulfill. Many families want safe schools that do well academically. Some want better opportunities for students with disabilities. Or thriving arts and music programs. Or Therapy Dog Thursdays. The point is, because purposes for what schools should be are not universal, neither charter nor traditional schools will ever be able to claim they're unreservedly good or successful.[10]

One last note about charter schools. Critics have suggested that charter schools are part of various "agendas"—for example, to make money, or to erode public education generally (Black, 2020b; Ravitch, 2016). I don't have a great deal of patience for such ill-defined claims, at least in part because charter schools are not one coherent thing. They're thousands of independent things operating under dozens of different state laws. What I *do* think worthwhile is to ask how students are doing wherever charter schools operate. For example, most of the charter schools in Monroe County (New York) are in the City of Rochester and draw students who would otherwise attend school in the Rochester City School District (RCSD). How's RCSD doing? In 2022–2023, 1,693 RCSD students took the 8th-grade New York State math test. Just 3% (45 students total) of those 8th-graders scored at the top level (Level 4), compared to 29% at the top level statewide. Summary: most students in RCSD are not learning math well. Should RCSD be the only option for families in Rochester who can't afford private school? What we *do* about the struggles of traditional schools lies at the heart of most charter school debates. Can we develop effective alternatives to traditional schools that still serve public purposes? Although charter schools are assuredly not the right answer everywhere, I am convinced that many do excellent work with students traditional schools have failed.[11]

HOMESCHOOLING

Homeschooling is a school choice option throughout the United States. Families who homeschool direct the schooling of their children on their own, rather than using local private, traditional, or charter schools (for a good overview, see Kunzman & Gaither, 2020). Although precise estimates of homeschooling are difficult to obtain, an estimated 3.4% of school-aged children in the United States were homeschooled in in 2019 (National Center for Education Statistics, 2022). There's some evidence that homeschooling percentages rose during and immediately following the COVID-19 pandemic (National Center for Education Statistics, 2022).

"Homeschooling" may be a bit of a misnomer; it's rarely school done (only) at home. Homeschooling *can* involve a parent teaching a child useful things at the kitchen table, but it can also involve homeschooling groups, field trips, activities, and online classes with books, curricula, tests, labs, and (perhaps unexpectedly) teachers providing support. A majority of homeschoolers use formal schools for at least part of their academic or extracurricular experiences (Schafer and Khan; 2017). A lot of what's called homeschooling involves instruction delivered by or with support from professionals. What makes it homeschooling is that families direct it, rather than schools.

Families homeschool for different reasons. A recent study identified these as the top four (National Center for Educational Statistics, 2022, Fig. 4):

- Concern about school environment, such as safety, drugs, or negative peer pressure (80%)

- Desire to provide moral instruction (75%)

- Emphasis on family life together (75%)

- Dissatisfaction with the academic instruction at other schools (73%)

It's not entirely clear how well students who homeschool are doing, academically or otherwise. Homeschooling research has been polarized and problematic. There's little convincing evidence that homeschooling is a coherent set of practices associated with any specific outcomes (good or bad; see Kunzman & Gaither, 2020).

You're unlikely to work with students who homeschool, since . . . well, they're at home. You *are* likely to teach students who previously homeschooled; homeschooling for the entire P–12 grade span is rare. One study estimated that over a third of homeschoolers return to traditional schools after just one year, with attrition rates between 6–27% each year after (Isenberg, 2007, 398). What did they learn while home? Unclear. As with teaching any student, your job will be to find out what they know and can do, and help them take the next steps.

VOUCHERS

Vouchers aren't a type of school—they're a way to pay for a chosen private school. The term "voucher" is shorthand for programs that direct public revenues to families to pay for private school tuition, usually in the form of tax rebates or "scholarships." The idea is old—it was first popularized by economist Milton Friedman in a 1955 essay, "The Role of Government in Education." Friedman suggested that a large-scale system of subsidies (vouchers) could replace the need for traditional "government" (public) schools, and could maximize the responsiveness of schools to parent interests:

> Let the subsidy be made available to parents regardless where they send their children—provided only that it be to schools that satisfy specified minimum standards—and a wide variety of schools will spring up to meet the demand. Parents could express their views about schools directly, by withdrawing their children from one school and sending them to another, to a much greater extent than is now possible. In general, they can now take this step only by simultaneously changing their place of residence. For the rest, they can express their views only through cumbrous political channels. (4)

The idea of vouchers has remained far more popular among people than among the governments that would need to implement them at any kind of scale. There has been little appetite in most states for replacing public schools wholesale with vouchers. The seventeen states and territories that do have voucher programs have largely created them for limited types of students, or capped numbers of participants. The most common voucher programs are limited to students with disabilities (12 programs in 10 states); second most common are voucher programs for students with limited household incomes (5 states plus Washington, DC; Education Commission of the States, 2021). It's not clear how many students in the United States are using vouchers. You won't see anyone using a voucher as a public school teacher, since . . . they're attending private schools. Just know that school vouchers exist, and that like private schools generally, they may influence who does or does not appear in your classroom.

The U.S. public school landscape has a range of models for governance, finance, and choice. Sometimes student paths are linear. Some students start preschool or kindergarten and move along from grade to grade in a local public school district. Sometimes student paths are more complex; students may move between districts, move between schools, move between district and charter schools, or move between public and private and homeschool options. Sometimes students who leave schools come back. U.S. public school students change schools a lot. About 13% of public school students changed schools *four times* before high school (U.S. Government Accountability Office, 2010), including roughly 10% of all students each year. Remember: U.S. public schools are localized. When students change schools, they may face different standards, curriculum, routines, and expectations (Welsh, 2017). Your job as a teacher isn't to worry about what happened during the time before a student arrives in your room. It's to warmly welcome them in, to quickly identify what supports they need, and to carry on with the days and weeks ahead.

> **Why Does It Matter that U.S. Public Schools Have Local Control?**
>
> It matters because it means U.S. public schools vary massively in quality, climate, and resources. The federal government's main role in U.S. public schools is to monitor and promote the equal protection of laws and regulations. States and school districts, in turn, are responsible for most decisions about funding, hiring, supervision, calendars, curriculum, and the many details of your teaching life. School districts vary in wealth, and spend most of their money on salaries. School choice can expand options for families, while potentially reducing enrollment in or support for traditional public schools. The good news about local control? Teachers can quickly have positive impacts on their local schools. Teach well, get involved, make a difference.

SUPREME COURT CASE FOR DISCUSSION

Case: *San Antonio v. Rodríguez*, 411 U.S. 1 (1973).
Link: www.loc.gov/item/usrep411001

In June 1968, Demetrio Rodríguez (Figure 3.7, next page) and three other parents of children attending Edgewood Elementary School in the San Antonio Independent School District filed a class action lawsuit, alleging that Texas' system of school finance was unconstitutional. Their claim was that funding public schools at different levels based on property values (and taxes) harmed children in lower-wealth neighborhoods, violating the Equal Protection Clause (14th Amendment).

Edgewood was (in 1968) a predominantly residential Mexican American neighborhood, with modest property wealth. Homeowners had been paying the highest tax rates in the area for years, yet because their neighborhood had little commercial development, their children's schools

Figure 3.7. Demetrio Rodríguez with his sons (left to right) Carlos, Alexander, and James outside Edgewood Elementary School, San Antonio, Texas. *Source:* Photo provided by Patricia Rodríguez. Used with permission.

were underfunded. Edgewood schools received $37 per student in local tax revenues, compared to schools in predominantly Anglo Alamo Heights, who received $413 per student. Parents in Edgewood asked in court: *How is that fair, or equal protection under the law?*

In 1971, a federal district court agreed with the parents, finding that Texas' public school finance system was discriminatory on the basis of wealth. The district court reasoned that, since education was (in its view) a "fundamental" right (like life and liberty)—a discriminatory funding system violated the Equal Protection Clause of the 14th Amendment. But . . . that wasn't the end of the story. The San Antonio Independent School District appealed to the U.S. Supreme Court. And in 1973, the Court's decision in *San Antonio v. Rodríguez* rejected the claims of the Edgewood parents. The Supreme Court did not agree that education was a "fundamental" right or that schools must be funded equally under the 14th Amendment. Justice Lewis Powell, writing for a narrow 5-4 majority, explained: "[A]t least where wealth is involved, the Equal Protection Clause does not require absolute equality or precisely equal advantages. Nor, indeed, in view of the infinite variables affecting the educational process, can any system assure equal quality of education except in the most relative sense" (411 U. S. 24). Powell and the rest of the majority essentially declared equality in education, with its "infinite variables," an impossible task. The *San Antonio v. Rodríguez* decision has done ongoing damage since 1973 (Price, 2023). It established two precedents that have yet to be seriously reconsidered by the Supreme Court:

- Education is *not* a "fundamental" right (like life or liberty). Educational funding (or opportunity), therefore, doesn't merit "strict scrutiny" under the Equal Protection Clause.

- The use of local property taxes to fund public schools—even when those produce wildly unequal amounts of money—is acceptable.

QUESTIONS

1. The U.S. Supreme Court found in 1973 that education is not a "fundamental" right. Should it be? Why, or why not?

2. Is the existence of inequitable funding for schools discriminatory? Why, or why not?

3. Is it fair to require wealthy districts like Alamo Heights to share property tax revenues with less wealthy districts like Edgewood? Explain.

4. Following the Great Depression, the federal government produced "risk" maps for banks, largely based on race. Areas with high percentages of Black, immigrant, and Jewish residents were coded in red ("redlined"), meaning they were high risk for lenders. Banks often refused to lend money to anyone deemed risky. Redlining forced Black, immigrant, and Jewish homebuyers to crowd into already-redlined areas as the only option (Rothstein, 2017). Redlined neighborhoods today—nearly a century later—have lower home values, lower school funding, higher school segregation, and lower student achievement than other neighborhoods (Lukes & Cleveland, 2021). Is the use of local property taxes to fund public schools a modern-day racist practice like redlining? Explain.

FURTHER READINGS AND RESOURCES

Charter schools:
Finn, C., Manno, B., & Wright, B. (2016). *Charter schools at the crossroads: Predicaments, paradoxes, possibilities*. Cambridge, MA: Harvard Education Press.

Homeschooling:
Kunzman, R., & Gaither, M. (2020). Homeschooling: An updated comprehensive survey of the research. *Other Education: The Journal of Educational Alternatives*, 9(1), 253–336.

School finance:

Allegretto, S., García, E., & Weiss, E. (2022). Public education funding in the U.S. needs an overhaul. Washington, DC: Economic Policy Institute.

School governance:

Reber, S., & Gordon, N. (2023). A primer on elementary and secondary education in the United States: Who does what and how do we pay for it? Washington, DC: Brookings.

NOTES

1. It did not, for example, prevent states from passing Jim Crow laws like this one from Missouri in 1929: "Separate free schools shall be established for the education of children of African descent; and it shall be unlawful for any colored child to attend any white school, or any white child to attend a colored school" (Jim Crow Museum, n.d.). One truth in U.S. history is that *passing* a law is not the same thing as *enforcing* a law. The story of the 14th Amendment to this day is ongoing: When and how do we hold states accountable for equal protection? What do we mean by "equal"?

2. In this chapter, when I use the word "state," I also mean to include territories and Tribes as governments when they serve similar fiscal, policy, and oversight roles for public schools. Each is politically distinct. It's clunky to keep writing "states or territories or Tribes" every other sentence—please forgive the shorthand.

3. In New York (Consolidated Laws, § 915): "*no sweetened soda water, no chewing gum, no candy including hard candy, jellies, gums, marshmallow candies, fondant, licorice, spun candy and candy coated popcorn, and no water ices except those which contain fruit or fruit juices*[.]" Kids in New York: if you want fondant, you're bringing that from home.

4. Fun reading: school district policy handbooks. Everything in those handbooks is or was an issue that needed a policy. There are so very many. For example, the *index* for the policy handbook of the Pittsford Central School District (NY) is *twenty-six pages* long: www.pittsfordschools.org/board-of-education/policy-manual. Pittsford has some awesome policies on anthrax, bus idling, camera phones, "controversial issues," emancipated minors, laser pointers, head lice, pregnant students, and vandalism, among others.

5. Superintendents often become involved with teachers only when bad things happen. It's perfectly fine if you never talk to your superintendent. Like, ever.

6. This is a common feature of taxation—we don't all use everything our tax dollars fund (*have you flown a fighter jet, visited every national park, or read the NIH-funded paper about hamster fights?* [Schwartzer et al., 2013]). It can be difficult to convince those not using a resource that we should raise taxes to pay more for it.

7. Not making this last one up. It's called *Waldkindergarten*, generally for children 3–6 years old, and it's way more popular in Germany than here in the United States (Gregory, 2017). One wonders whether *Waldkindergarten* founders

read any Hans Christian Anderson. What happens to children wandering in the woods, deep and dark?

8. The five that did not: Vermont, Montana, North and South Dakota, and Nebraska.

9. Nuance has not been a constant companion in charter school policy debates. If you need a pop culture break, watch *Abbott Elementary* Season 2 (ABC) . . . then read Winter (2023) discussing *Abbott's* plotline re: charter school conversion.

10. Re: charter schools not being evil. One possible exception to this. There are "virtual" charter schools allowed in thirty states. They appear to have, on average, significantly worse student proficiency, unclear attendance, a high proportion of for-profit operators (42% of all virtual charter schools), and *"heightened financial and programmatic risks to federal funds"* (U.S. Government Accountability Office, 2022). I'm putting "virtual" charter schools in the "dubious and probably bad, if not downright evil" bin.

11. Full disclosure: my wife was a founding ELA teacher at a charter school in Boston (Boston Preparatory Charter School), and I served for several years on the Board of a local charter school in Rochester, New York (Discovery Charter School). It's entirely fair to dismiss my discussion of charter schools as the flag-waving of a toady. I'd still ask any charter school critic: if you were the parent of a school-aged child in the Rochester City School District . . . what kinds of choices would you want, if any?

4

Communities

What Should I Learn about My Students, Their Families, and Their Communities?

Every semester, SUNY Brockport (where I teach) sends a small number of student teachers to rural Alaska. It's exciting for the student teachers, and a good way for Alaska school districts to recruit new teachers. The districts we work with serve primarily Iñupiat, Yup'ik, Alutiiq, and Athabascan students. Before going to Alaska, few of our student teachers have had experience with Indigenous students or families. They're excited about Alaska but know little about the people up there. Somehow—either before and/or during their student teaching semester—they need to learn how to teach (in general), and they need to learn how to do so in the specific contexts of students, families and communities in rural Alaska. Neither is simple.

Almost without exception, what my student teachers in Alaska tell me during the first week of school: *these kids are quiet.* Like: *they almost don't talk in class.* And that's true compared to many students in New York, who are admittedly verbose (Basu, 2016). Ten or twelve weeks later, however, I don't hear about quiet Alaska students anymore. Instead I hear about relationships. Here's what I heard from Maria P. about halfway through student teaching in Nenana, Alaska: *My students come to class expecting to be shown that they can't. That they will fail. That I will find them out, or call them out, or confirm their beliefs with bad grades, harsh words, or unreasonable demands. My teaching needs to show them that they absolutely can.*

Do you see the difference? Early: *these kids are quiet.* Later: *my teaching needs to show them that they absolutely can.* What changed? Not the students; they were mostly whoever they were several weeks prior. What's different was Maria and the relationships in her classroom. Maria got to know her students better. They got to know her better. And Maria stopped seeing them through the lens of her prior experiences. Rather than asking questions like an interrogator (*Who? What? When? Where? Why? Where's your evidence?*), she learned to provide prompts for students to discuss in small groups and then find consensus or confirmation before responding. Maria learned to stop expecting students in rural Alaska to be just like the ones she'd known in New York.

You can't become a decent teacher without getting to know your students, their families, and their communities. Your ability to form good relationships with a lot of people, some of whom won't be anything like you, will be a crucial part of your success.

DIVERSITY AMONG P–12 STUDENTS AND TEACHERS

U.S. public school students and their teachers have different backgrounds (see Chapter 1). Compared to P–12 students, U.S. public school teachers are less racially and ethnically diverse, are disproportionately female, and come from more advantaged backgrounds (Reeves et al., 2018). U.S. public school teachers are also academically and financially successful. We have college degrees, we are capable in ELA and math, and we earn decent salaries ($66,432 in 2021–2022—near the U.S. median of $70,784; National Education Association, 2023; Semege & Kollar, 2022).[1]

Why do these differences matter? We can do damage if we act like our students are just smaller versions of ourselves. They're not. They're themselves, and they need us to learn who they are, and shape our work accordingly. As ever, averages are not particulars. You may have no idea yet who your students will be. But you have to get to know them quickly and in some depth to be able to teach them well. This chapter is primarily about *respect* and *humility*. We show respect when we learn about people who are different from us, and when we treat them well no matter what. We show humility when our actions communicate that our ways aren't the only ways.

HOW TO SHOW RESPECT AND HUMILITY

This may or may not be obvious, but teaching isn't about you. Yes, you're the one writing lesson plans and stopping at Walmart on the way home for two dozen Thingies before class tomorrow. But no, you're not the point. Check out Figure 4.1 (next page). See President Obama, looking at a student with a magnifying glass? That's good modeling for any teacher. *Look* at your students. See who they are, and learn about their families. Teaching is about *them.*

Most early-stage teachers worry about themselves a lot. *Do I know the right answers? What if I say something wrong?* These worries are natural. Lots of teachers worry about knowing stuff and being smart in front of kids.[2] Far more critical is whether you know your students and families and develop strong relationships with them.

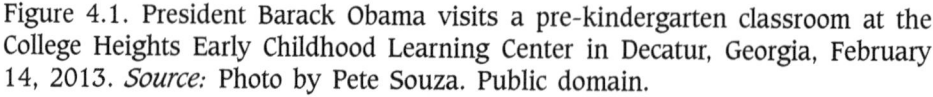

Figure 4.1. President Barack Obama visits a pre-kindergarten classroom at the College Heights Early Childhood Learning Center in Decatur, Georgia, February 14, 2013. *Source:* Photo by Pete Souza. Public domain.

The central nature of relationships in teaching might not be what you expected. I remember starting a career as a teacher because I loved biology. I assumed biology was what I'd spend my days doing (maybe with kids as . . . an audience? Witnesses to my biology-ing?). It turns out life as a high school biology teacher involves spending every day in a room with twenty-five to thirty teenagers who may not automatically assume that biology deserves love. There's a lot of repetition in teaching. And vocabulary. And homework. And slow, steady work on difficult concepts. Teachers can't just jump from cool idea to cool idea the way I imagined. Eventually I figured out that those of us who love teaching *love spending time with students*. Loving a subject area can get you in the door, but you'll *stay* in teaching because of the relationships you build. This is, I think, reassuring. Any of us can get to know others and build good relationships. And making mistakes, which all teachers do, is far less of a big deal when relationships are strong. A big part of your first year needs to include time spent on relationships, including learning about:

- Students—What are their current academic strengths and needs? What interests them? What holds their attention? How do they feel about school? Why? And: What are you going to do about that anyway?

- Parents and families—Who are they? How can you meet them? Are there back-to-school nights, parent/teacher conferences, basketball games, etc.? How will you regularly communicate with families in ways they can access? How will you learn about their goals for the school year ahead?

- Communities—To what communities do your students belong? "Communities" in this sense includes people and places that matter to your students. Maybe they go to a mosque or a church a few times a week, or dance with a group, or play youth football. Those are communities. So too are libraries, rec centers, businesses and housing. Who's in your students' lives? Where do they go after school and on weekends? Some of the most important communities are ones that keep your students safe in and beyond school.

You'll spend 180+ days each year with students. Get to know them. You can just ask them stuff, out loud or in writing. Many teachers do a student interest survey at the beginning of the school year. Keep it to a page and adapt what you're doing to meet your goals (*Are you trying to form groups for instruction? Trying to pick a book to read with the class? Asking about families before open house?*). You can survey multiple times during the year for different purposes. Here's an example of a first-day survey (see also Alber, 2017; Children's Literacy Initiative, 2020); the last question is borrowed from a book by Kyle Schwartz, *I Wish My Teacher Knew: How One Question Can Change Everything for Our Kids* (2016):

Student Interest Survey

My full name is: _____
My pronouns: _____
I prefer to be called (*by teachers*):_____
I live with: _____
How would your family describe you, in three words?_____
What do you enjoy doing when you are not in school? (*hobbies, talents, sports, etc.*) _____
If you could learn more about any subject, what would it be? (*Ryan Gosling, genetic engineering, Yup'ik dancing, Gobi jerboas . . .*) Why that?_____

If you could choose one famous person (*living or not*) to be our substitute teacher for a day, who would you choose? What would you hope to learn from them?_____
In which school subject have you felt that you learned the most? Why do you think this is?_____
Give an example of a class activity where you felt you really learned a lot. Why do you think that was?_____
What is your *least* favorite class or activity in school? Why doesn't it work for you?_____
If I need an adult to talk to at school, I talk to . . . (*Please identify that person by name.*): _____
I wish my teacher knew . . ._____

Parents and families take more time than students to learn about. They're not in class with you. Families are also *busy*. A couple of important truths about families:

1. There are all kinds. Families may be single- or multiple-parent, LGBTQ+, multigenerational, multiple-home, foster, adoptive, refugee, and many others. They can all grow young people into successful adults. They can all be awful.

2. Parents say parenting is both their biggest joy and biggest challenge (Zero to Three, 2016). They love it. It's not easy.

3. Families care more and know more about their children than anyone else. Including you. They're often delighted to share. If you have no idea what to talk about with families, ask about their kids (your students). What are they like at home?

You need to get to know parents and families so that you better understand your students. If you don't know, for example, that your families use a language other than English at home, you won't do enough vocabulary or academic writing support in class. But you can't just send your parents a hundred-question survey. It's not fair to give busy parents homework, especially if there are language barriers involved. What you *can* do is prepare a couple of stock questions for whenever you have a chance to ask (at open house, at the game, in line at the post office). Don't just wing it. Here are some examples:

- How was school for [A] last year? Why?
- What are some things that [A] loves to do?
- Who was [A]'s favorite teacher? Why?
- What do you think I should know about [A]?
- What are you hoping for from [A]'s teachers this year?

One thing to remember is that, while school is *your* job, it's not theirs. They've got lives beyond. However you connect, I'd recommend a few things (see also Adams, 2020; Steen, 2022):

- Offer one or two formal invitations to school each semester. These are usually schoolwide open houses, parent nights, or parent/teacher conferences. If you're not sure what to do with families, consider student-led conferences, where students show their parents what they're doing in class (Cronin, 2016; EL Education, n.d.).

- Share your school email and phone, and when you're available to meet (in person at school, or over the phone or via video). Include these in your first note home.

- Communicate regularly. These are typically one-way (parents are *busy*), like an email or post about what's happening in class or what's coming up at school. Many teachers do weekly or monthly newsletters. The details of what's included are less important than regularity. End each with your contact info and an invitation to connect. Don't expect tons of feedback; send them anyway.

- Be responsive. You can't be on email or texting while you teach. So let parents know what to expect. Something like: "I teach throughout the day, so I'm not on text or email. If there's an emergency or urgent thing, call the school office and they can reach me. For things that can wait, I check email at the beginning and end of every school day and will do my best to respond within 24 hours." Then *do* that, every day.

A note on families using languages other than English: your school *should* provide interpreters and translation services, but many do not. Families would rather have you try (and not be completely intelligible) than not try at all. Besides, communication with families is often brief and specific. If you need to let a parent know Josiah didn't turn in today's homework, you can't wait for a translation that takes three weeks. Try tools like Google Translate for documents or speech if that's the best you can do: https://translate.google.com (bring your laptop or phone to parent conferences). One thing to avoid is relying on students to serve as interpreters for their own parents. That's just not fair.

Learning about communities can be hardest of all, especially when language or cultural backgrounds differ from yours. You need to show interest and respect. You can't be a tourist. Learning that involves others generally requires an invitation. Mostly, you'll need to educate yourself. No fair asking others to assume the burden of removing your ignorance. If you are invited somewhere, *say yes the first time.* Don't say no because you're tired or busy or nervous. When people invite you places, they're taking a risk that you'll be awkward or embarrass them. Say yes, keep your mouth mostly shut, try to be a good sport. After all, if you feel uncomfortable for an hour or two in your students' community or home or wherever . . . consider: What's it like for them in class all day? How might families feel visiting you at school?

Figure 4.2. Two Navajo women talk to each other during a Gourd Dance in Gallup, New Mexico. *Source:* Photo by Donovan Shortey. Used with permission.

Figure 4.2 shows two women chatting during a Gourd Dance. It's a community event, happening in a school gymnasium (see the scoreboard?). I hope the stands are full of teachers. Showing up at community events in your school can be simple and non-intimidating. Showing up out in actual communities can be much harder. It's important that you try. Teachers should be visible to families outside school walls. Why? It communicates that you care about more than just a paycheck. And it communicates that you value the community for its own sake. Encounters you have with parents at the store, in church, or at the game can be brief, positive, and free of pressure to accomplish specific goals. You can crack jokes! Meeting outside school also avoids unpleasant associations families may have with school or other teachers. Consider the following, and plan to do one or more *regularly* (not just once):

- Live near school. This is the most natural way to learn about communities—housing, government, parks, all of it. Living near school also makes after-school participation easier, including coaching or leading clubs and activities. Long commutes discourage after-school stuff. Living near school may not be possible—but consider it, if within reach.

- Coach, lead clubs, or tutor. This lets you see students beyond the formal structure of class *and* puts you in regular contact with parents (picking up their kids, communicating about travel and competitions, etc.).

- Chaperone or attend athletic competitions or other student performances. Find out what your students do, show up. They may come say hello, they may pretend you don't exist. You'll be noticed anyway, it matters. And it's a chance to compliment students directly to their families.

- Shop or eat near your school (coffee, lunch, groceries, new glasses, etc.). You can also use services near your school (the post office, library, mechanic, etc.).[3]

- Go to church or other community events near school. You can also exercise, walk your dog, or ride your bike near school.

- Read the news, listen to the music and/or watch the shows or movies your students and families appreciate. Pay attention to sports and athletes your students love. The point is understanding what kids and families care about. The more you understand, the better your odds of good relationships.

- Visit youth-serving agencies, recreation centers, or nonprofits that work with young people. The goal here isn't necessarily being seen, it's learning what they do so you can connect kids or families with them whenever possible.

You can make small changes to engage more with communities. Maybe skip the Dunkin' drive-through and get coffee at a local spot near school. Maybe change where you work out, what library you visit, where you get cupcakes for the department meeting. Where you volunteer. What kinds of music you pay attention to. The point is *relationships*. They're foundational for good teaching. Plan to work on them all the time.

DIVERSITY IN THE CLASSROOM

Below are some guidelines for teaching in diverse classrooms by a few major themes. This isn't a set of rules, and it's not remotely comprehensive. You haven't met your students yet. The goal is to start thinking now about how to teach in ways that embrace all kinds of different students. Remember that it's natural to be nervous working with new or unknown students and communities. It's also true that you'll make mistakes. We all do. Mistakes that come from *trying* are far better than making the (much larger) mistake of not trying at all. The more we engage, the more we're going to learn.

DISABILITY

Students with disabilities will be in your classroom, whether you work in general or special education. They make up about 15% of our students (National Center for Education Statistics, 2022, Fig. 1). Most students with disabilities spend most of their days (> 80%) in general education classrooms (National Center for Education Statistics, 2022, Fig. 3). It is becoming rare for students with disabilities to be segregated from other students; in 2020, just 13% of students with disabilities spent a majority of their time in separate settings.

The major goal in working with students with disabilities is *inclusion*. Inclusion means providing equal access to teaching and learning opportunities, while providing supports that promote equitable outcomes. It's not enough to just physically have students with disabilities in your classroom; your approach to *teaching and learning* needs to be inclusive. For example, a student who is Deaf and uses American Sign Language isn't truly included in your class if they don't also have access to an ASL interpreter and captioned videos. They might be physically in class, and you might be teaching your pants off, but without the right accommodations, your instruction won't matter. What's the best way to go about being inclusive?

1. Get to know your students. A label alone (such as "specific learning disability") doesn't give you enough information to make teaching decisions. Get to know each student as an individual.

2. Understand overall learning goals. This may seem basic—but it matters what you're trying to teach. For a Deaf student who uses ASL, if you're teaching geography and map skills, a lot of what you're doing is visual and may not need substantial overhaul. If you're teaching listening comprehension, you're facing different questions, like: What's the nature of this skill? Does "listening comprehension" mean I want students to develop short- and long-term memories of the *sounds of speech* (probably not) or . . . to understand the *meaning communicated* (most likely)? And . . . if it's really *meaning* I care about, what other mechanisms besides speech might provide useful learning and practice?

3. Use Universal Design for Learning (UDL) principles to remove barriers. The basic idea of UDL is to change the learning environment for everyone in ways that remove barriers and promote independence (see CAST: https://udlguidelines.cast.org). You are no doubt familiar with elevators, wide doorways, and open captioning; these changes remove barriers for some and are accessible to all. There are three major principles for UDL practices—see Lord (2021) for more detail:

- Provide multiple means of engagement. We need to use our knowledge of students to design engaging lessons. Your 72-slide lecture *may* engage some of your students; it may also not. This principle suggests we vary teaching approaches to increase the odds students will be able to engage with content.

- Provide multiple means of representation. We need to carefully think about what we want students to learn and how it is represented during learning activities. This principle suggests teachers need to pay attention to definitions and language, and to provide multiple means of representing the same content (for example, visuals *and* text).

- Provide multiple means of action and expression. We need to find a variety of ways for students to interact (with content and each other), and to demonstrate their learning. This principle suggests teachers should provide a variety of lesson activities and a range of different approaches to assessment.

Keep in mind that all three aspects of being an inclusive teacher—knowing your students, understanding the learning goals, and implementing UDL principles—are a *process* that you'll be doing continually. We don't *finish* inclusive work; we reflect and improve each year.

GENDER IDENTITY AND EXPRESSION AND SEXUAL ORIENTATION

Students with a wide range of gender identities and expression will be in your classroom. LGBTQ+ students make up an estimated 7–9% of youth aged eight to eighteen (Conron, 2020); it's reasonable to assume similar representation among younger and older students. LGBTQ+ students face, historically and now, elevated risk of exclusion, discrimination, and threat at school (Human Rights Watch, 2016). On the theme of getting to know your students, there are some key ideas you should understand. First, gender identity and expression are not about sex. They're about who our students are. No one is asking us (teachers) to teach about or discuss sex in the classroom. Our responsibility is to recognize our students as humans with equal worth however they identify or dress or wear their hair. Second, language and representation matter. Using respectful language in the classroom is required. Let your students tell you who they are. Students should also see themselves represented positively in curriculum and classroom activities. Third, students have the right to safe classrooms and schools. Teachers need to prevent harassment, bullying, and discrimination at school. Our actions at school matter; while just 37% of LGBTQ youth identified their *homes* as LGBTQ-affirming spaces, 55% of those same youth identified their *schools* as affirming spaces (Trevor Project, 2022). Caring teachers can serve as strong protective factors for LGBTQ+ students (Movement Advancement Project, 2017; Trevor Project, 2022).

GIFTEDNESS

This label is double-edged. Public schools in the United States have a history of calling some students "gifted" or "high ability" and then providing them (sometimes *only* them) with an enriched, high-quality education. The problem isn't with providing a high-quality education. It's that we are terrible at defining and identifying "giftedness" and who gets access to a high-quality education (Gentry et al., 2019).[4] There's no federal definition of giftedness; students may be "gifted" in one school or state, but not in another (Mun et al., 2016, 7). Maryland has the highest percentage of gifted students in the United States (16.1%), and Massachusetts, the lowest (0.7%; Barshay, 2021). Are kids in Maryland really thirty-two times more "gifted" than kids in Massachusetts? No. "Giftedness" in most U.S. public schools is functionally arbitrary (Grissom et al., 2019; Peters & Carter, 2022), which makes it susceptible to bias—against boys, against students of color, against English learners, against students experiencing poverty, and so on (Grissom & Redding, 2016; Grissom et al., 2017; McBee et al., 2016).

The other problem with "giftedness" is what we *do* with students so identified. For the most part, we segregate them from other students (Ford & King, 2014; Pirtle, 2019). And in every instance in U.S. public school history, segregation reinforces privileges already in place (of wealth, class, race, gender, etc.) to the detriment of everyone else. The answer is not killing off enriched or high-quality programs—it's abandoning our efforts to label students as "gifted" and expanding access to rigorous educational opportunities for everyone.

HIGH MOBILITY AND HOMELESSNESS

Some families and students change schools frequently. In U.S. public schools, 13% of students nationwide change schools four or more times in grades K–8 (Government Accountability Office, 2010, 10). That's a lot of movement. You're going to have students who show up after the school year starts, and who leave before it ends. Depending on where you teach, you may see half of your students move in or out during a single academic year (Rumberger, 2003).

High mobility, poverty, and low achievement are connected (Richards, 2018; Spencer, 2017). Families with low incomes are more likely than other families to change residences during the year (National Center for Homeless Education, 2018, 3; Popp et al., 2018), which often means their children change schools. Changing schools is disruptive to teaching and learning. This is another way in which the localized U.S. public school system specifically harms students from low-income backgrounds. Because local schools make their own decisions about placement, credits, curriculum, grades and so on—students who move a lot often face major hurdles in completing school. Highly mobile students may face the prospect of repeating and re-repeating courses they've taken elsewhere; many get discouraged and drop out (National Center for Homeless Education, 2022; U.S. Government Accountability Office, 2010, 16).

Along with students moving in and out of school, you may have students who are experiencing homelessness. Under federal law, homelessness means lacking a "fixed, regular, and adequate night-time residence" (42 U.S.C. § 11434A(2)(A)). One point of clarity: students experiencing homelessness are not usually sleeping outside or in cars (what's called "unsheltered"). Much more common is sleeping "doubled-up," for example, on a relative's couch in a too-crowded apartment. In 2020–2021, students experiencing homelessness made up 2.2% of all students in U.S. public schools (NCHE, 2022). These students and families may be spending nights with friends or relatives or in hotels or shelters. Common experiences among students experiencing homelessness are frequent moves, crowded living conditions, a lack of privacy, financial uncertainty, and stress. Uncertainty is hard on kids and families. A good resource for teachers working with students experiencing homelessness is the New York State Technical Assistance Center for Homeless Students, www.nysteachs.org.

Things to keep in mind with students who are mobile or experiencing homelessness:

- Students who change schools or are experiencing homelessness are our students. It is their right under federal law to be provided equal access to education. Schools may need to provide supports for students and families, such as tutoring, free meals, places to keep school supplies, after-school supervision, access to a social worker, or use of showers or washers and dryers at school.

- Students experiencing homelessness have the right to remain in their school of origin no matter how many times they move, and even if/when they move outside the school district. Students also have the right to transportation from wherever they've found temporary housing to and from school every day (McKinney-Vento, 42 U.S.C. § 11431 *et seq.*).

- The National Center for Homeless Education (NCHE) publishes good resources for teachers and schools (https://nche.ed.gov), including trainings for those who want to learn more. NCHE suggests that teachers can help meet three specific kinds of student needs (adapted from Popp et al., 2018, 5–6):

  o Affective needs: Students may experience frustration, isolation, or a lack of motivation. For secondary students, this can include a sense of helplessness and of being behind their peers in a range of ways due to disruptions. Teachers can help by providing a sense of belonging, attending to emotional needs, and helping students develop intrinsic motivation.

  o Academic needs: Students take time to adjust to new school environments. They must learn new routines, make new friends, and engage with different curricula. The most important thing you can do is teach effectively, and help students learn quickly and well. Get to know new students, help them socialize and make friends, and work 1:1 with students who need individual academic support. Be organized; students who move a lot also tend to miss school frequently. They may need to catch up not just once, but repeatedly over time.

  o Technical needs: Students and families may need services such as assistance with enrollment paperwork, grade or class placement, and/or counseling or social work supports. A priority for any family is meeting basic needs—safety, shelter, food—all of which must be in place for successful academic learning. If schools don't provide these things directly, they need to find ways to connect families with those who do.

In secondary grades, teenagers experiencing homelessness may be on their own. This can happen when students are scared to be home or have been kicked out (risk factors include pregnancy, LGBTQ+ status, and victimization such as physical or sexual abuse; Grant et al., 2018, 6). Such teenagers are known as "unaccompanied youth" (NCHE, 2018). Unaccompanied youth are at elevated risk of neglect, abuse, academic struggles, and dropping out. If you have any reason to think a student is on their own, bring that to the attention of a school counselor, social worker, or administrator. They need to know.

LANGUAGES OTHER THAN ENGLISH

No matter where or what you teach, you're going to have English learners in your classroom. Roughly 10% of students in U.S. public schools are identified as English learners. You should be able to find data from your state here: https://nces.ed.gov/programs/coe/indicator/cgf. English learners have two major goals at school: attaining English proficiency *and* meeting the same academic standards expected of all students. The number of English learners in schools varies by state and community; if you teach in Texas or California, the percentage is close to 20%; if you teach in West Virginia or Vermont, less than 3% (National Center for Education Statistics, 2022, Fig. 1). English learners also make up larger percentages in urban school districts, and in early grades, especially K–3 (National Center for Education Statistics, 2022, Figs. 2–3). Spanish is the most common additional language background in U.S. public schools (roughly 75% of English learners in U.S. public schools in 2019–2020; other common language backgrounds include Arabic, Chinese, and Vietnamese; National Center for Education Statistics, 2022, Table 1). Two facts that may surprise you:

- Most English learners aged five to seventeen (77%) were born in the United States and are American citizens (Zong & Batalova, 2015).
- Most families who use a language other than English at home are *also* fluent in English (60%; Batalova & Zong, 2016, Table 1).

Here are a few classroom guidelines for teaching English learners, adapted from Takanishi and Le Menestrel (2017):

- Provide access to grade-level course content. English learners need to learn the same content everyone else is learning—not just English language skills. If English learners aren't in grade-level classes with skilled teachers like you (because, for example, they're off working with specialists all day), they'll develop academic knowledge and skills gaps schools will need to fix later. English learners are first and foremost second graders, sixth graders, tenth graders . . . and they need to know what you teach as they move up through the grades.

- Effective practices for English-proficient students generally work with English learners. You don't need to become a radically different teacher to meet the needs of English learners. For example, in early reading instruction, it is helpful to teach English learners the same skills as anyone else (phonemic awareness, phonics, fluency, vocabulary, and comprehension). When teaching vocabulary, it's effective to do so for all students by teaching individual words, word-learning strategies, and using words in writing. For many English learners, you may not need to fundamentally change your teaching, but are likely to need to change or add supports.

- Provide specific supports. If you were learning in a language-unfamiliar context, what would help you? Visual, verbal, and cultural supports. Pictures, videos and graphic organizers are useful for English learners, also for students generally. Good language supports include glossaries, tables or charts of key concepts, explicit vocabulary instruction, and any bilingual instruction your school can provide. Modest but effective supports also include bilingual glossaries, translation software, and background materials in heritage language(s).

- Encourage peer-to-peer learning. Students learning English need practice using English, and you shouldn't be the only language model. They'll learn more by speaking, listening, reading, and writing with others. A major asset you have in your classroom is your students. Design lessons to include listening, speaking, and writing in pairs or small groups—another practice that's broadly effective with all learners.

- Be patient. It takes time to develop English proficiency, especially in school. Recent work suggests it takes four to seven years for most students (Thompson, 2017). Anyone learning a new language usually goes through a so-called "silent period" while they develop receptive skills (Robertson & Ford, n.d.). You'll need to adapt what you do—and how students respond—depending on the stage of language acquisition.

Parents and guardians of English learners may also use languages other than English or have cultural backgrounds different from yours. They deserve and appreciate regular communication from school. You may need to adjust *what* you communicate—for example, you may want to emphasize that families have the right to translation and translators (don't forget to explain how they can request either). You may need to adjust *how* you communicate, including using software or human translation. You may need to vary the *means* (emails, texts, phone, etc.), *timing* (before or after various work schedules), or *norms* of communication (for example, to respect different family or gender roles, or ways of addressing school personnel [Breiseth, 2021]). No matter what you do, the goal is respect and the development of good relationships. Good resources for teachers working with English learners:

- Migration Policy Institute: www.migrationpolicy.org/programs/ell-information-center

- Colorín Colorado: www.colorincolorado.org

- *English Learners in American Classrooms: 101 Questions, 101 Answers* (Crawford & Krashen, 2015)

RACE, ETHNICITY, CULTURE

You are likely to teach students from a range of different racial, ethnic, and cultural identities. These identities can be major sources of strength and community for your students. Keep in mind that there's no such thing as a universal experience within any group. Racial, ethnic, and cultural identities matter—they're a key part of who we are—but *how* they matter is individually experienced. Bettina Love, author of *We Want to Do More than Survive*, notes that "no one person is equipped or has the right to speak for millions, particularly on the issues of race and racism" (2019, 1). One of the most absolutely necessary things you will do as a new teacher is to get to know your students as individuals. Here's a true story—read it for what can happen when our students are misunderstood:

> Sivuqaq (Gambell), Alaska, is a predominantly Siberian Yup'ik village on St. Lawrence Island. Every fall and spring for thousands of years, whaling captains in Sivuqaq have organized crews and hunted. Whaling is a big deal: it connects Elders, young people, ancestors, subsistence, language, community, and Yup'ik identity. It is a source of joy. In April 2017, sixteen-year-old Chris Agragiiq Apassingok went whaling with his father's crew. About two miles offshore, Chris fired a harpoon

and struck a 57-foot-long bowhead whale that would feed dozens in the village for months. Chris was celebrated in the village. His mother posted a picture of him with the whale on Facebook. She wrote: "There's my handsome striker son, who blesses us over and over through God almighty, who learned from the best dad, Daniel Apassingok, whale captain" (in Hopper, 2017). Figure 4.3 shows Chris on a Honda, with the Bering Sea behind:

Figure 4.3. Chris Agragiiq Apassingok, with Ina Koonooka on a Honda outside his family's home in Sivuqaq (Gambell), Alaska. *Source:* Photo by Peter Chelkowski. Used with permission.

Then came the internet. Specifically: Paul Watson, self-styled environmental activist. Paul saw Chris's mom's Facebook post and responded: "WTF, You 16-Year Old Murdering Little Bastard! [. . .] [S]ome 16-year old kid is a frigging 'hero' for snuffing out the life of this unique self aware, intelligent, social, sentient being, but hey, it's okay because murdering whales is a part of his culture, part of his tradition." Soon after came hundreds of posts from all over the world: "You little c*nt." "I hope you choke on blubber." "You need to harpoon your mom." And death threats. Eventually, Chis—trying to navigate fear, humiliation, shock, and anger—left school (O'Malley, 2017).

Why share that story? There's no teacher there. Consider the structure, though: a Siberian Yup'ik community is successful at one of its most central cultural traditions. It celebrates. Those outside the culture offer vitriol and shame. And the harm falls on . . . a sixteen-year-old kid. On Chris. Teachers and schools do this kind of thing all the time. Did you read about the white school official who cut off a Black and Puerto Rican student's hair in front of an entire wrestling tournament? (Washington, 2019). Did you see the homework a 6th-grade teacher gave her students: *Translate this sentence into Spanish: "You are Mexican and ugly"*(Steinbuch, 2022)? Although adults rarely call students "murdering little bastards," we can do all kinds of damage if we fail to learn about, connect to, and teach in ways aligned with the strengths of our students, families, and communities.

You'll need to get to know your students as individuals. This means seeing their racial, ethnic, and cultural identities as part of the complex individuals they are. You do not need to wait until you feel like an expert to make a difference. One resource I appreciate is the New York State Culturally Responsive-Sustaining Education Framework (2018), which suggests a few things we can all do:

- Create a welcoming and affirming environment. Pay attention to the physical layout (Are there posters that represent the diversity of my students? Would my ten-year-old self want to spend time in my room?), and also to relationships (How do I build rapport with my students? What are my classroom rules? How and when do I communicate with families?)

- Foster high expectations and rigorous instruction. Pay attention to the engagement and achievement of your students (How are they doing? Are they meeting standards? Are there patterns—by race, by ethnicity—that suggest I need to make changes?). Provide learning opportunities that engage with (rather than avoid) identities (What am I asking students to do? Is it appropriate? Does it allow them to demonstrate their strengths?)

- Identify inclusive curriculum and assessment. Review the curriculum you're using, and ensure positive representation of the diversity of students in your classroom and school (Can my students see themselves in the curriculum? Are the models they see positive and successful?). Use interesting, engaging materials (Is any of this current, or interesting to my students?

If not—where can I supplement or replace?). And when you assess (and assign grades), provide multiple ways for students to respond so you can recognize diverse strengths.

- Engaging in ongoing professional learning and support. We all need to keep learning. (Why is this student doing *that* right now? Why do I keep falling behind on grading? Why do my groups seem so chatty and unfocused?). One of the best long-term investments you can make in your teaching career is to keep learning, especially in an area as rich as teaching in racially, ethnically and culturally diverse classrooms. Stay humble, go to the workshop, read the book, ask what others are doing.

It's important to understand the multiple roles race, ethnicity, and culture play in schools. It's important to understand these identities as strengths.

WEALTH / ANNUAL INCOME

U.S. public schools serve students from the full range of wealth and income backgrounds. One large subset of students you're likely to teach are those eligible for free and reduced-price meals (commonly referred to as Free and Reduced Lunch, or FRL). FRL is one widely used proxy for poverty; in 2022–2023, a family of four could earn up to $36,075 and be eligible for free meals, or up to $51,338 for reduced-price meals (U.S. Department of Agriculture, 2022; National Center for Education Statistics, 2015). About 52% of P–12 students in the United States were eligible for free and reduced-price meals in 2018–2019, up from 38% in 2000–2001 (National Center for Education Statistics, 2022c, Table 204.10). That's over half of our students. New teachers (like you) are also more likely than experienced teachers to work in schools serving communities with lower incomes (Goldhaber et al., 2022; Isenberg, 2021). Although family income itself tells you nothing about how individual students learn, there are actions you can take that can help all of your students, especially those experiencing poverty:

- Have students speak, listen, read and write. One of the most influential studies in education, Betty Hart and Todd Risley's "Meaningful differences in the everyday experience of young American children" (1995) examined language use at home with preschool children. Hart and Risley visited dozens of families identified with high, middle, and low incomes, and recorded an hour of spoken language each month while the kids were awake. They did this for two and a half years. What they found was that children in families with lower incomes were exposed to far less language than children in families with higher incomes. Hart and Risley famously calculated that over the course of four years (before kindergarten starts), children in homes with high incomes would hear almost forty-five million words, while children in homes with low incomes would hear just thirteen million words—a thirty million word gap. Over the decades since their study, evidence has accumulated that students experiencing poverty enter school with language gaps and do poorly on measures of reading and writing. Worse, without good teaching, those gaps persist (Barshay, 2019; García & Weiss, 2017).

- Provide reading and writing supports. All teachers can and should support reading and writing skills, no matter what we teach. This includes foundational reading skills, comprehension strategies, time for writing practice, and lots of feedback about writing. Regularly teach skills, give students clear purposes for reading or writing, and spend time in class on practice. See the U.S. Department of Education's *What Works Clearinghouse* for practice guides focusing on literacy support across grade levels: https://ies.ed.gov/ncee/wwc/PracticeGuides.

- Expect high achievement. In teaching and life, there's truth to the saying that you get what you expect. Expect a lot? Students do well. Expect little? Students do poorly. This is known as the "Pygmalion Effect," also sometimes called a self-fulfilling prophecy (Rosenthal & Jacobsen, 1968). Although mechanisms remain unclear (we don't understand how teacher expectations translate to changed practices that yield achievement differences), there is evidence that teacher expectations concerning students matter (Gershenson, 2020; Hill & Jones, 2021; Jussim & Harber, 2005, 2016; Papageorge et al., 2018). There's also troubling evidence that teachers who expect little from their students—due to racial, class, or other biases, for example—are less effective with students (Cherng, 2017; Gershenson et al, 2015). In practice, one good thing you can do is clearly define what you expect students to learn and do. Then, you can require each and every student to learn and do just that.

- Be flexible on means. Poverty doesn't somehow make families experiencing it the same. There are, however, some common experiences among families experiencing poverty, including:

- Spending a greater proportion of income than other families on housing, utilities, transportation, healthcare and food (Pew Charitable Trusts, 2016).

- Greater odds of living in substandard or crowded housing, which influences frequent household moves (Barnum, 2022) and harms educational outcomes (Solari & Mare, 2013).

- Having zero or negative wealth, which limits options when emergencies arise (Nabi, 2022). About one-third of U.S. households reported that they could not pay an unexpected $400 expense in 2022 (*think*: car repair or other bill) without going into debt (U.S. Federal Reserve, 2022).

- Spending substantial percentages of their incomes on their children for things such as early learning materials and school supplies (Gennetian et al., 2021).

One of our best teaching tools is flexibility in how our students meet learning goals. We know, for example, that students from low-income families are more likely than others to miss school—so an attendance policy that reduces grades for missing school is a structural penalty for poverty. One of the best tips I've learned is to be organized. Have folders (physical or electronic) with all lesson materials, organized by date, available to all students at all times. Have clear makeup work routines so students coming back from absences know what to do. And be involved and available. When parents work multiple jobs, they face constraints in coming to school for meetings, attending sports and activities, or supervising and assisting with homework. *You* can be there. I'm not telling you to be anyone's substitute parent. I'm saying: go to the game when you can. Keep your classroom open before and after school for homework club. Take the call from a parent when it comes, even if it's not a great time. Invite students to eat lunch quietly in your classroom whenever you're there. You don't need to tell the kids to eat their broccoli—just be there.

We all have learning to do when we start new work with new people. You're going to have to stay patient and stay curious. Maybe the best advice I can offer is: plan to stay. Since learning to teach takes time, and since developing relationships takes time, the longer you stay where you are, the better you'll do. And there's nothing like the feeling of coming back the next year. One of the gifts of teaching is that it renews itself. Stay, and see how much better the next year can be.

What Should I Learn about My Students, their Families, and Communities?

Relationships are at the core of our work. If you know who likes Starburst and whose grandmother plays pickleball, you're getting there. All of your students will identify with multiple communities. Anyone you don't get to know, you will fail. Listen; support; stay.

SUPREME COURT CASE FOR DISCUSSION

Case: *Wisconsin v. Yoder*, 406 U.S. 205 (1972).
Link: www.law.cornell.edu/supremecourt/text/406/205

Jonas Yoder, Wallace Miller, and Adin Yutzy were parents of fourteen- and fifteen-year-old students who lived in Green County, Wisconsin. Yoder and Miller were members of the Old Order Amish; Yutzy was a member of the Conservative Mennonite church. After their children finished 8th grade, Yoder, Wallace and Yutzy refused to send them to high school. They claimed that doing so would be contrary to their religious beliefs. Green County school district officials argued that all children were required to attend school through age sixteen under Wisconsin's compulsory education law. Eventually Yoder, Miller, and Yutzy were charged, tried, and convicted in Green County Court, and fined $5 each.

Yoder and the other fathers appealed all the way up to the U.S. Supreme Court. They argued that the requirement to send their children to high school violated their 1st Amendment rights (including free exercise of religion) and their 14th Amendment rights (including equal protection). They pointed out that their communities held a "fundamental belief that salvation requires life in a church community separate and apart from the world and worldly influence" (*Wisconsin v. Yoder*, 4). And they objected to high school specifically because, as Chief Justice Burger summarized in the Court's opinion:

> the values they teach are in marked variance with Amish values and the Amish way of life; they view secondary school education as an impermissible exposure of their children to a "worldly" influence in conflict with their beliefs. The high school tends to emphasize intellectual and scientific accomplishments, self-distinction, competitiveness, worldly success, and social life with other students. Amish society emphasizes informal

learning-through-doing; a life of "goodness," rather than a life of intellect; wisdom, rather than technical knowledge, community welfare, rather than competition; and separation from, rather than integration with, contemporary worldly society. (406 U.S. 205, 6)

The State of Wisconsin argued before the Supreme Court that it had good reasons to require school attendance for all children through age sixteen. Wisconsin had an interest in promoting a literate population, in preparing residents for further education and work, in promoting citizenship, and in avoiding undereducated adults becoming a burden to the state.

The Court ruled 8-1 in favor of Yoder, Miller, and Yutzy. Burger's opinion noted: "The State's interest in universal education is not totally free from a balancing process when it impinges on other fundamental rights, such as those specifically protected by the Free Exercise Clause of the First Amendment and the traditional interest in parents with respect to the religious upbringing of their children" (406 U.S. 205, 1).

QUESTIONS

1. The Supreme Court decided that the goal of universal education, even if well-intentioned, cannot require parents to violate sincerely held religious beliefs. Was the Court right? Why or why not?

2. The Court decided that compulsory education laws cannot violate 1st Amendment rights concerning religion. Consider *secular* (non-religious) objections. For example, Henry David Thoreau famously rejected the social values of his time and moved to a small cabin on Walden Pond. Thoreau stopped paying federal taxes as a protest against slavery (and was arrested for not doing so in 1846). What if a modern Henry David Thoreau refused to send his kids to high school? Are there any non-religious reasons families should be able to exempt themselves from compulsory attendance laws?

3. Justice William O. Douglas dissented from the Court's decision. He worried that the Court's decision considered only the *parent's* religious interests and did not take seriously the *children's* religious interests. Although the children (Frieda Yoder, Barbara Miller, and Vernon Yutzy) all appeared to share the religious beliefs of their parents, Douglas considered

the possibility they did not. He wrote: "I think the children should be entitled to be heard. While the parents, absent dissent, normally speak for the entire family, the education of the child is a matter on which the child will often have decided views. He may want to be a pianist or an astronaut or an oceanographer. To do so he will have to break from the Amish tradition" (406 U.S. 205, 80). Should the Supreme Court have asked the children whether they wanted to go to high school? What should the court have done if the children disagreed with their parents?

FURTHER READINGS AND RESOURCES

Community information:
Demography of U.S. Public School Students and Teachers: National Center for Education Statistics. https://nces.ed.gov/fastfacts

Culturally responsive-sustaining education:
Learning for Justice, www.learningforjustice.org; NYS Culturally Responsive-Sustaining Education Framework, www.nysed.gov/common/nysed/files/programs/crs/culturally-responsive-sustaining-education-framework.pdf

English learners:
Migration Policy Institute, www.migrationpolicy.org/programs/ell-information-center; Colorín Colorado, www.colorincolorado.org

High mobility and homeless students:
National Center for Homeless Education. https://nche.ed.gov

LGBTQ+ students:
Trevor Project, www.thetrevorproject.org; GLSEN, www.glsen.org; PFLAG, https://pflag.org

Universal design for learning:
CAST. https://udlguidelines.cast.org
United States Census Bureau. https://data.census.gov

NOTES

1. Many argue that teachers are underpaid. True. FYI, though: you'll probably earn more than many of your students' families. The average salary for a first-year teacher in 2022 was $41,770 (National Education Association, 2022).

The income cutoff for free and reduced lunch at school—which over half our students get—was $25,142 (U.S. Department of Agriculture, 2022).

2. Yes, you should be smart in front of kids. No, you don't have to be all-knowing. Students benefit from classrooms that normalize error and use it as feedback for learning (Hough, 2016; Schulz, 2011). Engineers know this intuitively. How many failed lightbulbs did Edison go through?

3. Seeing teachers outside school is distinctly fun and weird for kids. Their *teacher*? Buying *toilet paper* and *beer*? Ew!

4. OK, it's also problematic that the origins of "gifted" education lie in the work of eugenicist Lewis Terman, who gave us both IQ tests and the idea that the "feebleminded" ought to be sterilized (Leslie, 2000; Maldonato, 2019).

5

Curriculum
How Will I Know What to Teach?

Your school district will tell you. Or at least, it *should*. Teachers can't just teach whatever we feel like teaching. We teach what our district decides. We're employees—that's the job. We have more influence on *how* we teach than on *what* we teach. Before we get into too much detail, some notes on terminology:

- Standards—What students should know or be able to do. These are usually set by states or territories. We teach to standards. Our success is largely defined by the extent to which our students are able to meet those standards. Here's an example of a standard (a New York State writing standard for 6th grade; New York State Education Department, 2017, 75):

    - 6W1a: *Introduce a precise claim, acknowledge and distinguish the claim from a counterclaim, and organize the reasons and evidence logically.*

- Curriculum—The materials we use to teach. Curriculum may include books, software, workbooks, laboratory or other equipment, or the worksheets we printed out last night.[1] Curriculum may also include hidden or coded messages like "conform socially" or "do what authority figures tell you."[2] Most school districts don't want teachers choosing curriculum on their own, instead adopting (selecting and approving) the curriculum that must be used.

- Pedagogy—How we teach. This may include reading, discussion, lectures, viewing videos, doing labs, etc. Pedagogy is where we have the most latitude as a teacher. Few states or districts require specific pedagogy; most leave it up to teachers. The logic here is that students are diverse, and decisions about pedagogy should be made by teachers who know them best.

STANDARDS

Standards define the goals of teaching. They say what we want our students to know or be able to do. They're central to our work. States and territories are responsible for writing most standards, though some school districts adopt additional local standards as well. Teachers must start planning lessons by reviewing standards, because everything else follows. For example, if meeting New York State standard 6W1a (the writing standard above) is the goal, you're going to have to figure out how to assess whether students have made a "precise" claim in writing (*What is and isn't "precise"? How do I teach that?*). You're also going to have to give students practice writing counterclaims (*In class? In groups? For homework?*). You'll probably have to spend some time in class showing students what "logical" organization looks like (*A diagram? Different examples?*). And so on. Teaching work starts with standards.

The United States does not have national standards (other countries do). One of your first tasks as a new teacher will be to identify the standards that you'll be expected to teach. Go find them now, at your state or territory's department of education. This section will make more sense if you're looking at the actual standards. What you should know as you review:

- States and territories adopt standards. The most fundamental job of teachers is to help students master standards. Districts sometimes add their own local standards.

- There's broad agreement about standards across states and territories. Although the United States does not have national standards, and each state or territory *can* define standards however they wish, they're more alike than not. If you teach math in Mississippi and then move to Alaska, the algebra standards will be familiar.

- Standards are usually organized by grade level (2nd grade, 3rd grade, etc.) and by subject area (e.g., "English Language Arts" or "Social Studies"). You might have just one set of standards to teach, or you might have several (elementary teachers often teach ELA, math, science and social studies—so have many sets of standards). Some states also have standards intended for a range of classes or subjects—such as cultural, career, or technology standards. One example is the Alaska cultural standards (Alaska Department of Education & Early Development, 1998).

- Standards are usually written for students to master during one academic year. States may also establish standards for single-semester courses.

- Each standard usually takes more than one lesson to teach and learn. It may take students a few days, a few weeks, or all year to master a standard.

- There are often a lot of standards. And substandards. Standards are supposed to describe *all the things a student should know or do* in a class or grade. They're supposed to be comprehensive. A good example is the Common Core State Standards, which have been adopted or adapted by over forty-five states and territories (Council of Chief State School Officers, 2022). In 6th grade, for example, there are ten Common Core ELA standards and twenty-eight math standards (or forty-two, depending on how you count substandards).

- Standards are not usually prioritized. They're just a list. It's up to you and your district to make judgments about which standards merit the most emphasis and time, and which merit less. Some of the decisions you make about prioritizing standards will shape later choices about curriculum and pedagogy.

- Standards are often accompanied by performance level descriptions. A "performance level description" (sometimes also called an "achievement level" or a "performance descriptor") is supposed to help you decide whether a student has met a standard. For example, in 2022–2023, New York State described four levels of performance for each standard (Level 4 being good, Level 1 being not good). Here are the performance level descriptions for New York State 6th-grade writing standard 6W1 (from above):

Table 5.1. New York State English Language Arts Anchor Standard 6W1 (New York State Education Department, 2017)

Anchor Standard: Write arguments to support claims in an analysis of substantive topics or texts, using valid reasoning and relevant and sufficient evidence. (W1)

Standard: 6W1: *Write arguments to support claims with clear reasons and relevant evidence.*

Performance Level 4	Performance Level 3	Performance Level 2	Performance Level 1
Write organized arguments, using key textual evidence to support claims and/or counterclaims that demonstrate an insightful understanding of the topic or text; use sophisticated and content-specific vocabulary and purposeful and varied transitions to connect ideas while maintaining sophisticated style and tone; concluding statement or section that explains the argument presented.	Write organized arguments, using relevant textual evidence to support claims and/or counterclaims that demonstrate an understanding of the topic or text; use precise and content-specific vocabulary and appropriate and varied transitions to connect ideas while maintaining appropriate style and tone; concluding statement or section that explains the argument presented.	Write arguments, using textual evidence, some of which may be irrelevant, to support claims and/or counterclaims that demonstrate a limited understanding of the topic or text; writing may lack coherence and/or organization; use content-specific vocabulary and transitions to connect ideas; concluding statement that partially explains the argument presented.	Write arguments, using irrelevant or inaccurate claims and/or textual evidence, that demonstrate little-to no understanding of the topic or texts.

See the differences between levels? At Level 4, a student is "using key textual evidence to support claims," while at Level 1, a student is "using irrelevant or inaccurate claims." In New York, the guidance for teachers is that students at Levels 3 or 4 are "proficient" and have met the standard. Performance level descriptions are helpful in answering the question: *did my students meet the standard?* If they have—great! Move on. If not, you'll need to re-teach (probably in a different way) and get students more practice. In the example above, if your students wrote arguments that were random or wrong (even if grammatically and structurally sound), they're at Level 1 and need more instruction, more practice, or both. Go find your state standards and performance level descriptions, and read them. Whatever else your district and school expect from you, one universal expectation is that you will help your students meet standards.

CURRICULUM

Standards are the starting point, but they leave out a lot. *What materials should you use? How much time should you spend on each standard? How should you assess learning?* Curriculum provides important answers to each. States and territories set standards; school districts adopt (approve and purchase) curriculum (Underwood, 2019). Curriculum adoption is typically a formal process. Committees (of teachers, school leaders, and district personnel) explore options from various publishers, and then make recommendations to administrators. School boards ultimately decide what to approve and purchase. If you stay in the same school district for several years, you might help choose what gets adopted next.

Often new teachers are handed purchased curriculum or materials from other teachers in the same department or grade level. If that's the case for you: awesome. *Use other people's curriculum during your first year(s)*. Doing so buys you time and bandwidth to focus on other aspects of teaching, like figuring out how to be warm and funny with kids even when you have a headache. Just be advised that if you are provided with already-developed curriculum, you're going to skip key parts of the assessment/instruction cycle (discussed in an upcoming chapter). You'll need to expand your work to include all of these steps eventually, or your teaching will suffer.

Who has the authority to choose curriculum? Teachers sometimes assume they have the freedom to choose whatever materials they'd like. They do not. Such authority rests firmly with districts. Teachers *do* retain private free-speech rights outside school (*Pickering v. Board of Education*,

Other People's Stuff Is Better than Your Stuff (For Now)

If an experienced teacher down the hall hands you materials and says: *here you go*, your life just got better. During your first year(s), shared or borrowed or purchased curriculum is better than whatever you might develop from scratch. You're not trained to write curriculum. Maybe you got some practice in a methods course or two, but that's nothing compared to developing a year-long, coherent, standards-based curriculum on the fly while you're figuring out how to teach. You. Will. Not. Have. Time. Even if imperfect, borrowed or purchased curriculum gives you something to work with.

But . . . wait. The downside of using other people's curriculum is that you'll skip the process of translating standards to objectives, skip decisions about how to assess, and skip decisions about how to structure and adjust lessons accordingly. Obviously, those decisions require judgment, which takes time and practice to develop. When you're new, I think it's best to rely on judgments about curriculum and assessment made by others. At first. Not forever. I'd recommend using borrowed or purchased materials for your first year or two, while trying to understand how they were made. Why do they emphasize this standard, and not that? How do they translate standards into objectives? How are objectives assessed? How could lessons be edited to work better for your students? Over time, you can start adapting or generating materials, including assessments, that are more tailored for your students, classroom, and pedagogy. You don't need to teach entirely from scratch on day one.

---

391 U.S. 563 [1968]), but those rights are not absolute. Public school teachers are government employees, and curricular speech is "pursuant to" our official duties, hence subject to district authority (*Garcetti v. Ceballos*, 547 U.S. 410 [2006]). You can see this principle at work in the decision of the U.S. Court of Appeals for the 6th Circuit in their decision about 9th-grade English curriculum in Tipp City, Ohio:

> During the 2001–2002 school year, Shelly Evans-Marshall, an English teacher at Tippecanoe High School, taught a unit about censorship in her 9th-grade class. Her students read *Fahrenheit 451* by Ray Bradbury, and then reviewed a list of the "100 Most Frequently Challenged Books" published by the American Library Association (American Library Association, n.d.). Evans-Marshall directed groups of students to pick a book and investigate why the book was challenged. Two groups picked *Heather Has Two Mommies* by Lesléa Newman. One parent complained. Evans-Marshall's principal directed her to pick a

different book, and Evans-Marshall complied. Later in the same unit on censorship, Evans-Marshall assigned her class *Siddhartha* by Hermann Hesse. After additional parental complaints, which spilled into multiple public school board meetings, the Tipp City school board decided to not renew Evans-Marshall's contract for the following school year. Evans-Marshall sued. The 6th Circuit decided the school board had sufficient cause for her nonrenewal, reasoning:

> When a teacher teaches, "the school system does not 'regulate' [that] speech as much as it hires that speech. Expression is a teacher's stock in trade, the commodity she sells to her employer in exchange for a salary." *Mayer v. Monroe County*, 474 F.3d 477, 479 (7th Cir. 2007). [. . .] Only the school board has ultimate responsibility for what goes on in the classroom, legitimately giving it a say over what teachers may (or may not) teach in the classroom. It is true that teachers, like students, do not "shed their constitutional rights to freedom of speech or expression at the schoolhouse gate." *Tinker v. Des Moines*, 393 U.S. 503, 506 (1969). But that does not transform them into the employee and employer when it comes to deciding what, when and how English is taught to fifteen-year-old students. (*Evans-Marshall v. Board of Education*, 624 F.3d 332 [6th Cir. 2010])

The point isn't to spook you; it's to tell you that you can't and won't choose curriculum on your own. Go ahead and teach *Fahrenheit 451* or *Siddhartha* if they're approved; many districts would be fine with both. Whatever curriculum your district provides, one of your early tasks will be to learn what's there. Doing so can be intimidating; you may be reviewing a full year's worth of lessons, texts, activities, assessments, and supplemental materials. Curriculum for one subject or grade can run thousands of pages and include hours of video or other content. I don't recommend trying to digest all of it at once. Skim the curriculum to get a sense for what's there. Ask a colleague who's used it previously how it works. Later, you'll read every word and complete each assignment in advance as you prepare for lessons. Two notes before more specific guidance on reviewing curriculum:

1. You are trying to learn what's there. You're not trying to identify "good" or "bad" parts. Curriculum isn't usually "good"

or "bad" on its own.³ Some of the most important decisions you'll make will be about how well the curriculum fits your students. For example, a science curriculum that requires a well-equipped classroom laboratory may seem "good" on paper, yet may prove impossible to use if your classroom has no lab equipment. I'll also note that curriculum is a product sold for profit to districts—not teachers, not kids. This is, again, neither good nor bad. You should simply reserve the right to make reasonable judgments about when, whether, and for whom materials need to be adapted or replaced.

2. Don't try to write an entire curriculum yourself. You are not trained in curriculum design. You're a teacher, not a curriculum developer. You are trained to *use* curriculum. You are not ready in your first year(s) to teach all day, and then go home and write a coherent set of standards-linked learning activities, assessments, enrichments, and supports for every day of the entire school year. You will lose focus on your students. If you spend all your time generating new materials (*This worksheet format is super perfect! With the right font!*), you won't spend time reflecting or troubleshooting, providing feedback, connecting with families, etc. Here's a quote that scares me, from Wexler (2019): "[T]he overwhelming majority of teachers turn to the internet to supplement [reading] materials, despite not having been trained in curriculum design. One Rand Corporation survey of teachers found that 95 percent of elementary-school teachers resort to Google for materials and lesson plans; 86 percent turn to Pinterest" (Opfer et al., 2016). Please no. Use existing curriculum your first few years. You need teaching practice, and you need experience learning what's effective with students.

WHAT TO LOOK FOR WHEN REVIEWING CURRICULUM

HOW DOES THIS COVER THE STANDARDS I NEED TO TEACH?

Most curriculum is published for a national audience, not tailored for your state or district (even if there's a sticker on the cover claiming to be). When you look over materials for the first time, try to get a sense for breadth (does it cover all the standards?) and depth (how much time is spent on each?). Don't get hung up on specific lessons or materials yet—just get a sense for how much curriculum is devoted to key standards during the school year (roughly 180 days). This can vary substantially. For example, Table 5.2 (below) outlines two different scope and sequence documents for the same high school biology class (what New York calls "Living Environment") leading to the same statewide test (the NYS Regents Exam).

First is from the New York City (NYC) Public Schools (2020), second is from New Visions for Public Schools (n.d.), a school reform network

Table 5.2. New York City Public Schools (2020) and New Visions (n.d.) Biology Scope and Sequence

Unit	NYC Public Schools Unit	NYC Public Schools Suggested Days	New Visions Unit	New Visions Suggested Days
1	Scientific inquiry	10 days	Characteristics of living things	15–20 days
2	Ecology	25 days	Nutrients, energy, and biochemical processes	22–28 days
3	Organization and patterns in life	20 days	Homeostasis in human body systems	20–25 days
4	Homeostasis and immunity	25 days	Disease and disruption of homeostasis	20–23 days
5	Reproduction and development	25 days	Comparative reproduction	15–20 days
6	Genetics and biotechnology	25 days	Genetics, biotech and decision making	19–24 days
7	Evolution	15 days	Ecosystems and invasive species	22–25 days
8	Human influence on the environment	10 days	Climate change and human impact: Extinction v. evolution	14–18 days
		Total: 155 days		Total: 147–183 days

that operates multiple charter schools in New York City. Notice a few things in Table 5.2. First is that the NYC scope and sequence only maps out 155 days; a school year is usually 180 days (or more). Why doesn't NYC map out 180 days? I have no idea. Are those missing twenty-five days to be spent on test prep or testing? Is there an assumption that teachers will need to review concepts students should know but do not? Again: no idea. Notice too that the units are *different*, even though (in theory) they're written to meet the same standards, and lead to the same test. In NYC public schools, students will spend the first two weeks on "Scientific inquiry." There's no analogue in the New Visions curriculum. NYC has separate "Ecology" and "Evolution" units . . . while New Visions focuses on "Ecosystems & invasive species" and nests discussion of evolution within discussion of climate change and human impact. These curricula are . . . different. Your job as a biology teacher would be different in these two systems.

WHAT KINDS OF STUDENT WORK ARE EXPECTED?

This is the most important thing in any curriculum. It's more important than beautiful lesson plans, detailed scripts for teachers, or links to a million resources. Saying this again, with italics: *Student work is the most important thing in any curriculum.* What students do is what they think about, and what they learn (City et al., 2009; Willingham, 2021). What students do also serves as evidence concerning their knowledge and skills. Look for examples of:

- In-class work—What will students do most days? Are there routines you can identify (for example, at the beginning or end of every class, or whenever there's a text to read)? Are you seeing lots of worksheets? Hands-on activities? How much reading, writing, calculating, note-taking, speaking, listening or other kinds of student work do you see? What kind of learning space(s) might be needed for students to do the curriculum?

- Formal assessments—If it's worth teaching, it's worth finding out whether students learned it. Assessments are more than just quizzes or tests, although those are important. When you look through curriculum, anything with an answer key or rubric can be an assessment. You might see note-taking, projects, labs, essays, or other student work. What will students turn in? How will you decide whether every student has met every learning objective every day?

- Supports, differentiation, and enrichment—Most classrooms include students with a wide range of knowledge, skills, and interests. Your room may include students working below, at, or beyond grade level; it may include students with disabilities; it may include students learning English as a new language. When you review curriculum, look for supplementary materials that go along with each lesson and unit. Are there alternate activities, assignments, or readings tailored to different student needs?

- Homework—Is homework regularly assigned or suggested in the curriculum? If so, how often, and what does it usually involve? What knowledge or skills are emphasized?

Table 5.3 (opposite page) shows an example of a curriculum overview, a 6th-grade ELA unit on mythology from EngageNY, 2014 (one of four Modules for the year; this Module is supposed to take about 45 days):

Engage NY ELA curriculum, Grade 6 Module 1 Overview.

Topic: Myths—Not Just Long Ago

In this module, students are involved in a deep study of mythology, its purposes, and elements. Students will read Rick Riordan's *The Lightning Thief* (780L), a high-interest novel about a sixth-grade boy on a hero's journey. Some students may be familiar with this popular fantasy book; in this module, students will read with a focus on the archetypal journey and close reading of the many mythical allusions. As they begin the novel, students also will read a complex informational text that explains the archetypal storyline of the hero's journey which has been repeated in literature throughout the centuries. Through the close reading of literary and informational texts, students will learn multiple strategies for acquiring and using academic vocabulary. Students will also build routines and expectations of discussion as they work in small groups. At the end of Unit 1, having read half of the novel, students will explain, with text-based evidence, how Percy is an archetypal hero. In Unit 2, students will continue reading *The Lightning Thief* (more independently): in class, they will focus on the novel's many allusions to classic myths; those allusions will serve as an entry point into a deeper study of Greek mythology. They also will continue to build their informational reading skills through the close reading of texts about the elements of myths. This will create a conceptual framework to support students' reading of mythology. As a whole class, students will closely read several complex Greek myths. They then will work in small groups to build expertise on one of those myths. In Unit 3, students shift their focus to narrative writing skills. This series of writing lessons will scaffold students to their final performance task in which they will apply their knowledge about the hero's journey and the elements of mythology to create their own hero's journey stories. This task centers on NYSP12 ELA Standards RL.6.3, W.6.3, W.6.4, W.6.5, W.6.6, W.611c, L.6.2, and L.6.3.

Table 5.3. Building Background Knowledge

Week	Instructional Focus	Long-Term Targets	Assessments
Unit 1: Building Background Knowledge: Percy Jackson and the Hero's Journey			
Weeks 1–3 (13 sessions)	• Begin *The Lightning Thief*. • Make inferences about character.	• I can cite text-based evidence to support an analysis of literary text. (RL.6.1) • I can describe how the characters change throughout a literary text. (RL.6.3)	
	• Read informational article about "the hero's journey." • Analyze the stages of the hero's journey.	• I can cite text-based evidence to support an analysis of literary text. (RL.6.1) • I can describe how the characters change through a literary text (RL.6.3)	• **Mid-Unit 1 Assessment:** Inferring about the Main Character in *The Lightning Thief* (RL.6.1 and RL.6.3)
	• Evaluate Percy as an archetypal hero.	• I can cite text-based evidence to support an analysis of literary text. (RL.6.1) • I can describe how the characters change through a literary text. (RL.6.3) • I can cite text-based evidence to support an analysis of informational text. (RL.6.1) • I can use evidence from a variety of grade-appropriate texts to support analysis, reflection, and research. (W.6.9)	• **End of Unit 1 Assessment:** Drawing Evidence from Text: Written Analysis of How Percy's Experiences Align with "The Hero's Journey" (RL.6.1, RL.6.3, RI.6.1, and W.6.9)

Source: www.nysed.gov/curriculum-instruction/engageny. CC BY-NC-SA 3.0.

WHAT'S HERE?

- Unit 1 should take about thirteen classes (whatever that means).
- Students will do "close reading" of the first half of *The Lightning Thief* (780L) along with some other "informational texts."
- Students will learn "academic vocabulary."
- Students will do "discussions as they work in small groups."
- Students will (later) finish reading *The Lightning Thief* independently.
- Your whole class will (later) read some "complex Greek myths" together.
- Unit 1 features mid- and end-of-unit assessments, including students writing "their own hero's journey stories."

WHAT WOULD BE ON YOUR TO-DO LIST IF SOMEONE HANDED YOU THIS CURRICULUM?

a. Find the day-by-day lesson plans, read them to get a sense for what you'd do with students throughout the Module. Related: does "thirteen classes" estimated for Unit 1 seem reasonable for your school and students? Do you need to adjust for short or long class periods?

b. Get a copy of *The Lightning Thief* (and the other texts), read them, and make decisions about whether these texts match your student's reading levels and interests—will everyone be able to read a 780 Lexile book? (Lexile is a measure of text complexity; you can check any text here: https://hub.lexile.com/analyzer.) Will everyone *want* to? If not—what will you do?

c. Find the assessments and complete them yourself. Consider: Do they provide convincing evidence that students have met the standards listed? Do you need to edit, add, or remove any?

d. Find the "academic vocabulary" that you'll need to teach. Do the materials highlight terms that are key to understanding texts or concepts? Do you need to teach more (or different) vocabulary than the materials suggest? How will vocabulary be taught, anyway?

e. Last, you'll need to start adapting the curriculum, wherever possible, to the context of your students and your classroom. Are some resources inappropriate? Do you need to supplement? Are there routines (like bell work or exit tickets) that you need to add in? Are there mechanisms your school requires (such as use of devices for sharing curriculum or students completing assignments) that will require preparation?

If you taught the EngageNY 6th-grade ELA Unit 1, you'd be doing "close reading" in class, students would be having discussions in small groups, and students would write narrative essays. Notice that the curriculum is driving not just *what* but *how* you teach. Which brings us to the last question you'll want to keep in mind as you review curriculum:

WHAT KIND OF TEACHING (PEDAGOGY) DOES THIS REQUIRE?

Curriculum shapes instruction. It can be hard to visualize how teaching will work just by looking through curriculum. Look for teacher edition textbooks (if they exist) and look over any provided lesson plans. Does the curriculum suggest a lot of direct instruction (providing information while students respond or take notes)? Does it require students to work independently, or with partners or groups? What classroom routines or activities are common?

A NOTE ON PEDAGOGY AND TEACHING STYLE

You probably have ideas about the kind of teacher you want to be. Engaging, energetic, inspiring? I hope so. No matter what kind of teacher you hope to become—I recommend teaching the provided curriculum *as it is* during your first year, even if it doesn't seem to match your preferred teaching style. Why? You're not trained in curriculum development. Have some faith in those that are. And you'll be new. It takes time to get to know what's effective. Your first year, you won't yet know whether your preferred teaching style will be what your students need. I see a lot of new teachers who want to do fun things in class (don't we all?), but I worry when fun activities come at the expense of instruction students need. You can't (or at least *shouldn't*) emphasize fun math games while ignoring that your students can't subtract. They'll-maybe-probably-learn-it-while-playing isn't pedagogy—it's hope. If your students can't subtract, you owe them explicit subtraction lessons. If you stick with the provided curriculum your first year, you'll gain a good understanding of the curriculum and how it works with your students—and can make informed decisions about what to adjust the following year.

HOW WELL DOES THIS MATCH WHAT YOUR STUDENTS NEED?

This can be difficult to know in your first year. The best way to find out is to ask other teachers who work with your students, or who had them last year. You can also track down assessment data (state assessments, benchmarking, or progress monitoring) to get a general sense for student achievement. Most curriculum materials are written at or near grade level and assume that students mastered the knowledge and skills required in prior grades. *You* can't make the same assumption. If you have reason to think your students will struggle to understand the provided curriculum, you may need to adapt materials. It's also worth finding out as much as you can about the kinds of lessons that have been effective with your students. What happened last year? What went well? Where did they struggle? The more you can learn before you start, the more prepared you'll be to provide needed supports on day one.

Two good sources for curriculum reviews not polluted by blatant publisher self-interest:

- U.S. Institute for Education Sciences, *What Works Clearinghouse*: https://ies.ed.gov/ncee/wwc

- EdReports (non-profit reviewer of published curriculum): https://edreports.org

ACADEMIC FREEDOM AND CURRICULUM

Teachers do have free speech rights *outside* the classroom. For example, in 1964, a high school science teacher named Marvin Pickering wrote a letter to his local newspaper criticizing a proposed tax increase that would have improved the high school football field. Pickering wrote: "To sod football fields on borrowed money and then not be able to pay teachers' salaries is getting the cart before the horse" (*Pickering v. Board of Education*, 391 U.S. 563 [1968]). The school board, upset by the criticism, fired Pickering. Pickering claimed his letter to the newspaper, done entirely outside his classroom, was protected speech. The U.S. Supreme Court agreed, and ordered Pickering reinstated, noting that his letter neither "impeded the teacher's proper performance of his daily duties in the classroom or [. . .] interfered with the regular operation of the schools generally."

Teachers have more restricted rights *inside* the classroom, especially concerning the materials used for instruction. We can't just say whatever we wish or teach using whatever materials we might like. Or . . . we *can*, but districts can then fire us. The *Pickering* standard from 1968 is the core standard we have today concerning what teachers can or cannot claim to be protected speech—whether in letters to the editor, or in the selection of academic materials. Do our words or actions harm "daily duties in the classroom"? Do they interfere with the "regular operation of the schools"? Racist speech is one example of speech *not* protected because it harms "daily duties" with students (see the ironically named *Brown v. Board*, 15-1857, 7th Cir., 2016). Also not protected: questioning whether the Holocaust happened (*Ali v. Woodbridge Township School District*, 19-2217, 3d. Cir. 2020), showing kids R-rated movies (*Fowler v. Board of Educ.*, 819 F.2d 657, 661, 6th Cir. 1987), showing kids pictures of naked teachers (*Pagani v. Meriden Board of Education*, U.S. Dist. 92267, D. Conn. 2006), and/or showing videos about creationism and "intelligent design" in science class after having been told not to (*Freshwater v. Mt. Vernon City School District*, 137 Ohio St. 3d. 469, 2013; Pearce, 2013).

It's unclear how far public school teachers in the United States can nudge curriculum when there's unease or objection. As the federal 4th Circuit noted, "School authorities, not the courts, are charged with the responsibility of deciding what speech is appropriate in the classroom" (*Wood v. Arnold*, No. 18-1430, 4th Cir. [2019]). Given that schools are local institutions, subject to the authority of states and territories, if we push curriculum beyond what we're given, and there are objections from students, parents, or school officials . . . what ultimately happens may depend on where we teach. Three recent examples:

HOW AND WHEN CAN PUBLIC SCHOOL TEACHERS DISCUSS THE EXISTENCE OF LGBTQ INDIVIDUALS?

Florida passed a so-called "Parental Rights in Education" law (Florida House of Representatives, 2022) that went into effect July 1, 2022. The law, commonly known as "Don't Say Gay," states: "Classroom instruction by school personnel or third parties on sexual orientation or gender identity may not occur in kindergarten through grade 3 or in a manner that is not age-appropriate or developmentally appropriate for students in accordance with state standards" (Florida HB 1557, 2022). The Florida law is explicitly anti-LGBTQ and deliberately vague. There's neither a convincing rationale for why entire classes of individuals are prohibited for discussion in grades K–3, nor a definition of "age-appropriate or developmentally appropriate" (Durkee, 2022). An entire generation of Florida teachers faces uncertainty around what's permissible in class. New York, by contrast, has a statewide Human Rights Law that specifies "gender," "sexual orientation" and "gender identity or expression" as protected classes (New York State, 2022). Teachers in New York can't be fired for teaching about human rights with young students. Teachers in Florida . . . maybe can.

WHAT BOOKS ARE APPROPRIATE FOR SCHOOL-AGE STUDENTS?

By 2023, state legislatures in twelve states had passed or were considering laws that would remove or restrict access to various books in public and school libraries or prevent their use in classroom instruction (Jensen, 2023; Meehan & Friedman, 2023; for an up-to-date list of the most-banned books, see PEN America's *Banned in the USA:* https://pen.org). These laws banned books with themes that focused on race, ethnicity, national origin, youth activism, teen pregnancy, mental health, suicide, and . . . teenagers having sex.[4] Like Florida's "Don't Say Gay" law—the main effect of these proposed bans may not be the bans themselves, which are rarely upheld by courts (see *Board of Education v. Pico*, 457 U.S. 853 [1982]). The main effect may be fear and uncertainty among teachers and librarians about what they're allowed to teach.

HOW AND WHEN CAN PUBLIC SCHOOL TEACHERS DISCUSS RACIAL JUSTICE IN CLASS?

By late 2021, nine states had passed legislation restricting teacher discussions of racial justice, including explicit bans on the use of the *1619 Project* (The 1619 Project, 2019; Ray & Gibbons, 2021). A year later, efforts were under way in seventeen states to *expand* education relating to race or racial justice (Stout & Wilburn, 2022). Schools (and teachers, and curriculum) have become central to national conversations—and political contests—about how and whether racial justice is an appropriate domain for instruction in P–12 classrooms. What materials teachers are able to use—and what kinds of discussions teachers can have with their students—varies substantially by place. A lesson about white privilege, for example, could be encouraged and supported in one school context, and rejected in another (Pendharkar, 2021).

Some of your most important work as a new teacher will be to understand the state or territorial standards for the classes you'll teach. Those define what your students should know and be able to do. Helping students meet standards is the job. Some standards you may be able to address in just a few lessons; others may take all year. Your district will adopt curriculum and make decisions about the materials you'll use to teach. And in most cases, you'll find that the adopted curriculum meets many of your most pressing needs—from day-to-day lesson plans and materials to supplemental resources for students who need extra support. You may or may not love everything about the provided curriculum. You'll probably need to adapt or supplement at least some of it, for some students. Take good notes, so you can keep doing that adaptation and improvement work in the years ahead.

How Will I Know What to Teach?

Your school district will tell you. You won't decide standards, nor pick curriculum (usually). You'll design or adapt lessons and activities based on how well you know your students, which takes time. And while you'll have some freedom in pedagogy—how you teach—that freedom will not be absolute, nor will the boundaries on your instruction be clear or universal.

SUPREME COURT CASE FOR DISCUSSION

Case: *González v. Douglas* 269 F. Supp. 3d 948 (D. Ariz. 2017)[5]
Link: https://casetext.com/case/gonzalez-v-douglas

In 1980, the federal 9th Circuit Court of Appeals found that Tucson Unified School District (TUSD) operated racially and ethnically segregated schools, and had done little to rectify the harms segregation was doing to students (*Mendoza v. United States*, 623 F.2d 1338 [9th Cir. 1980]). TUSD agreed to implement a court-supervised desegregation plan (a consent decree) over the years that followed. Starting in 1998–1999, the district offered an elective Mexican-American Studies (MAS) program that included "art, government, history, and literature courses at the kindergarten through 12th-grade levels, with each course focusing on historic and contemporary Mexican–American contributions" (*González v. Douglas*, 269 F. Supp. 3d 948 [D. Ariz. 2017], I, 951). The stated purpose of the MAS program was to help close historic achievement gaps between Mexican-American and white students in Tucson. The MAS program was open to all students. By the 2010–2011 school year:

- TUSD had 53,000 students, 60% of whom were Latino (*González v. Douglas*, I, 951).

- A total of 1,300 students enrolled in MAS classes, ~90% of whom were Latino (ibid., I, 951).

- A University of Arizona study had confirmed that "participation in MAS was positively related to increased academic achievement, and this generally increased the more classes students completed" (Cabrera et al., 2014, 1107).

All seemed to be going well with the MAS program in Tucson. Then . . . in 2010, the Arizona legislature passed a new law explicitly targeting the MAS program (Arizona Revised Statutes, 2022, §§ 15–112):

> A school district or charter school in this state shall not include in its program of instruction any courses or classes that include any of the following:
>
> 1. Promote the overthrow of the United States government.
>
> 2. Promote resentment toward a race or class of people.
>
> 3. Are designed primarily for pupils of a particular ethnic group.
>
> 4. Advocate ethnic solidarity instead of the treatment of pupils as individuals.

Arizona State Superintendent of Public Instruction Tom Horne immediately decided that TUSD and the MAS program were out of compliance with the law, asserting "the only way in which compliance can be effective within the next 60 days is by elimination of the Mexican American Studies program" (Horne, 2010, p. 2). Horne threatened to withhold state funding if TUSD didn't eliminate MAS. TUSD refused. The dispute continued throughout the 2010–2011 school year. New Arizona State Superintendent John Huppenthal (who replaced Tom Horne on January 1, 2011), objecting to some texts used by the MAS program, commented that "The Mexican-American Studies classes use the exact same technique that Hitler used in his rise to power." Later, Huppenthal added: "MAS = KKK in a different color" (*González v. Douglas,* I, 963).[6]

On January 6, 2012, Superintendent Huppenthal ordered the Arizona Department of Education to withhold 10% of TUSD's state funding. Students and parents in TUSD sued the Arizona State Board of Education and Superintendent Huppenthal, arguing that elimination of MAS violated the desegregation plan, and their First Amendment rights. As the dispute moved through court, Tucson Unified School District stopped offering the MAS program, and many of the teachers involved left the district.

Five years later, on August 22, 2017, the federal 9th Circuit Court of Appeals found that the Arizona State Board of Education and its Superintendent of Public Instruction were motivated by racial animus, and that the state law had been enacted and enforced with discriminatory purpose, therefore it was unconstitutional. The law was gone—but so too was the MAS program, the teachers, and any certainty about what should come next (Tucson News Now, 2018).

QUESTIONS

1. When (and with whom) would it be appropriate to use curriculum that emphasizes the "art, government, history, and literature" of specific racial or ethnic groups in public schools?

2. Would it be acceptable for a district schools to *require* Mexican-American Studies coursework for all students (for example, to graduate from high school)? Why, or why not?

3. How would you respond to the State Superintendent's claim that "MAS = KKK in a different color"?

4. When, if ever, would it be appropriate for a teacher to use a song (or song lyrics) with the F-word, such as the Rage Against the Machine song "Take the Power Back"? ("Bam! Here's the plan / Motherf—Uncle Sam")

FURTHER READINGS AND RESOURCES

Common Core State Standards (ELA & Math):
www.thecorestandards.org/read-the-standards

Research on curriculum effectiveness:
Institute for Education Sciences, What Works Clearinghouse. https://ies.ed.gov/ncee/wwc

Reviews of curriculum:
EdReports. www.edreports.org

Standards for student learning:
Find your department of education for the most up-to-date set of learning standards relevant to your teaching.

Text complexity tool:
Lexile Analyzer. https://hub.lexile.com/analyzer

NOTES

1. Try to avoid this. Here, I'm thinking of TPT (Teachers Pay Teachers) and other sources (like Chat GPT) many rookie teachers use for ideas. The materials may be good and may be terrible. Be advised: one-at-a-time lesson planning risks incoherence.

2. One example of "hidden curriculum" (in toys, not schools, but you'll get the idea) was Teen Talk Barbie, a doll with a voicebox, who famously wondered, "Will we ever have enough clothes?" and lamented "Math class is tough!" (Associated Press, 1992). Much angst ensued re: sexism. Charmingly, a protest group switched out Barbie's voicebox with one from Talking Duke G.I. Joe, whereafter Barbie declared: "Attack!" and "Vengeance is mine!" (Firestone, 1993).

3. OK, fine. Some curriculum is objectively terrible. For example, the 9th-grade textbook *Mississippi: Portrait of an American State* (McKee, 1995) had a chapter

about the Civil Rights Movement that listed seventeen "key figures students should know." The key figures? Twelve white men (a majority of them segregationists), four Black men, and one Black woman. The book later lamented the lynching of Emmett Till as having "painted a poor picture of white Mississippians to the rest of the nation" (Mannie, 2017).

4. It's not clear whether U.S. state legislators understand that preventing teenagers from *reading books* about sex is perhaps the least likely mechanism out there to prevent them from *having* sex.

5. This is a U.S. District Court case from Arizona, rather than a Supreme Court case. It highlights a battle over curriculum in the Tucson Unified School District and focuses on U.S. Constitutional principles. It is not binding nationwide. It is likely to inform decision making as current disputes over curriculum work their way through various courts.

6. The text drawing the most ire was a 1992 song by the band Rage Against the Machine, "Take the Power Back," which included the following lyrics: "Bam! Here's the plan / Motherf—Uncle Sam / Step back, I know who I am [. . .] The present curriculum / I put my fist in 'em / Eurocentric every last one of 'em / See right through the red, white, and blue disguise / With lecture I puncture the structure of lies [. . .] Holes in our spirit causin' tears and fears / One-sided stories for years and years and years / I'm inferior? Who's inferior? / Yeah, we need to check the interior / Of the system that cares about only one culture / And that is why / We gotta take the power back" (Grow, 2015; Morello et al., 1992).

6

Instruction
What Should I Do in Class My First Year?

Here's a depressing study: a team of researchers recently asked a nationally representative sample of high school students to describe how they felt at various times during the school day (Moeller et al., 2020). The top three feelings of students in class?

1. Tired
2. Stressed
3. Bored

Yikes. Whatever those teachers were doing, it did not produce educational bliss. We should probably aim higher. Maybe go for "engaged"? Or "interested"? "Challenged"?[1]

Also: the feelings students have about school differ from those teachers have. Why? We *chose* teaching as a career. Most of us had *good* experiences in school. This does not appear to hold true for many of the students we serve. We can't just replicate whatever we remember doing in school and assume it'll be fine.

The thing that's missing when students are tired, stressed, or bored is *engagement*. Engagement is a slippery concept, akin to Supreme Court Justice Potter Stewart's definition of pornography ("I know it when I see it," *Jacobellis v. Ohio*, 378 U.S. 184 [1964]). One useful definition suggests that engagement includes behaviors, emotions, and cognition (National Center for Safe Supportive Learning Environments, n.d.). When students are engaged, they participate in class and activities, they take interest and pleasure in schoolwork, and they make an effort to do well. There's evidence that student engagement depends on what teachers do in class (Fredricks et al., 2004). If we are interesting, if our classes promote enjoyment in learning, and if student efforts are rewarded (e.g., with improved academic self-concepts like, "Hey! I'm pretty good at this!"), we have a chance to engage students, and a better chance for them to succeed in school.

As you prepare for the first days of school, you'll need to make decisions about classroom layout, rules and routines, and your general approach to instruction. Each is discussed below, and each should be (mostly) decided before day one. But . . . not entirely. You haven't met your students yet! You'll need to adapt what you do to meet their needs. You'll make some early decisions, and you'll need to revisit each as you get to know your students better (see Rosemary and Harry Wong's *The First Days of School* [2018]). Decide. Stay flexible.

CLASSROOM LAYOUT

I'm going to assume you have your own classroom. Unless you don't. In which case . . .

TEACHING FROM A CART ("FLOATING")

If you don't have your own room, you have my sympathy. Many teachers in crowded schools or who teach specialized subjects "float," or move between classrooms during the day (or . . . ugh . . . between *schools*). If you're doing that, you can't entirely control the spaces where you teach. What you *can* do:

- Ask for dedicated space in each room. This can include wall or whiteboard space (for routines and rules, agendas, calendar, homework, etc.) and/or storage space (for materials, papers, electronics and cords, etc.). Storage could be a cabinet, shelf or file box somewhere. Gathering materials for multiple classrooms can be expensive (you don't need *one* box of pencils—you need five!). See what your school will provide; if you can't get everything at once, plan for slow accumulation.

- Assemble a cart-on-wheels (or rolling suitcase) with materials that you bring to each class. If you work in just one building, seek a sturdy cart with multiple shelves and good wheels; see Yoshida (2020) and Rogers (2021) for good cart tips. If you move between schools, you'll need something smaller—more like airline luggage. You may need to scout elevators and ramps so you can roll between each room. Things to consider in your cart:

- Technology: laptop, charger, any cables needed to charge and connect to document cameras, screens, or projectors.

- Always-needed supplies: pens, pencils, paper, markers, clips, post-its, etc. All teachers have a cache; yours must be portable. Consider: sanitizer, paper towels, tissues, and a sweater or fleece for variable temperatures. Many teachers stock emergency snacks (for themselves and/or students). Maybe also lunch?

- Lesson-specific supplies: handouts, plans, demo materials, books, etc. for the day. Consider accordion folders (one for each class) or a file box with hanging folders. Central here is *paper flow*. For each class—what will you hand out, and what will you collect? Where will it all fit and be organized?

• Be a good guest. When you float, you'll be in shared spaces. You'll need good communication and relationships with everyone. Introduce yourself, thank them for sharing space, clean up after yourself always, avoid sprawl. Sometimes leave others chocolate.

ORGANIZING CLASSROOM SPACE

There's no such thing as a "perfect" classroom. Don't hope for that. The good news is that you can engage and inspire in any space, even when you've got ugly paint and mismatched furniture. Some classrooms are better than others, of course. Desirable features:

- Floor space, lots
- Windows (even if they don't open)
- Counters or other horizontal surface area
- Cabinets or other teacher storage space (ideally locking)
- Comfortable seats (and *enough* seats)
- Hooks, cubbies, or other student storage space
- Walls with whiteboards
- Screens or presentation technology (that functions)
- Outlets, like everywhere
- HVAC systems that heat, cool, and aren't smelly or loud
- No obvious safety issues

Primary goals for any classroom space are safety and comfort. You need to ensure students won't get hurt or sick simply because they come to class. Look for broken windows, peeling paint, exposed wiring, mold or mildew, unsecured chemicals or lab equipment, broken furniture. When you walk through your room, assume that anything students *can* hurt themselves with, they eventually *will*. Anything you're worried about, fix, remove, or bring to your principal's attention immediately.

Physical comfort, like safety, is really not optional, and I don't mean *it'd be nice if we all got foot massages*. You and your students will spend most waking hours every weekday at school. No one can be uncomfortable all day and teach or learn. Can you make the temperature and lighting reasonable? Are there comfortable places to sit and do classroom routines? Does everyone have a bit of personal space? Can you and your students put stuff away when not in use? What you're doing is addressing basic needs so you can teach and students can learn. One way to think about meeting human needs was developed by psychologist Abraham Maslow in "A Theory of Human Motivation" (1943). Maslow suggested that humans have five kinds of motivation. These motivations are universal, and each must be addressed *in order*. For example, Maslow described physiological motivation as the most basic: "For the man who is extremely and dangerously hungry, no other interests exist but food. He dreams food, he remembers food, he thinks about food, he emotes only about food, he perceives only food, and he wants only food" (1943, 374). Summary: hungry students don't learn algebra.[2]

Figure 6.1. Maslow's hierarchy of motivation. *Source:* Created by user Factoryjoe, CC BY-SA 3.0.

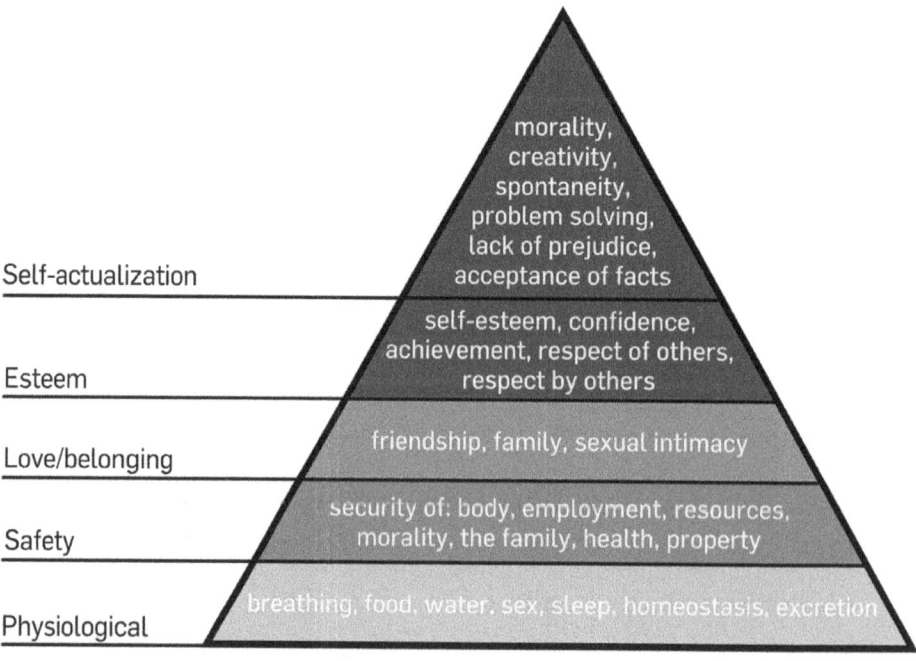

Figure 6.1 offers one visualization of Maslow's ideas (sometimes called "Maslow's hierarchy"). What to notice here? At the bottom of the pyramid are the most basic motivations, what Maslow calls physiological. They come before all others. Things like hunger, thirst, sleep, excretion. If you really need to pee, it's kind of impossible to read or think or contribute to vibrant class discussions. Once physiological motivations are met, then safety concerns come to the fore. If bullying in class is ignored or allowed, for example, students (targets *and* observers) will feel threatened and won't learn. Next: love and belonging. Does your classroom have a sense of community? Do any of your students face rejection from you, from other adults, from peers? You get the idea. Maslow's theory has been helpful for classroom teachers in thinking about how to prioritize their work—including classroom setup.

Beyond safety and comfort, a good goal for your room is ease of use. If you can't find your materials because your class is disorganized, or if students can't see what you write on the board, learning suffers. Naturally a kindergarten and a chemistry classroom will look different. Here's a general checklist:

STUDENTS NEED:

- To enter/exit the room quickly and safely.
- To see the teacher and boards or screens at all times.
- To get into partner groups quickly and easily.
- Individual/independent, comfortable workspace.
- Space for their stuff.

TEACHERS NEED:

- To see every student at all times.[3]
- To move next to and behind every student in class.
- To write or project things to a board, screen or devices.
- A spot in the room (usually up front) for regular direct instruction.
- Space for instructional materials (handouts, collected work, supplies for the day).
- A comfortable place to sit down and work.

It's common to have grade- or subject-specific uses unique to your room (maybe you do labs or demos up front, maybe you run reading groups, maybe you have a sand table or a Class Pet of Mysterious Provenance, etc.). Take what you know about the various activities you and students will need to do in your room and try to make sure they're doable with minimal fuss. One truth when considering classroom space: *transitions eat time*. A transition is any time students switch from one activity to another (for example, from whole-class notetaking to small-group discussion). The easier it is to transition between tasks, the more time you'll preserve for teaching and learning.

Early in your career, you may need to live with a less-than-ideal setup. You can make it work. No counters or storage space? Find some rolling cabinets or inexpensive/used furniture. No whiteboards? Order some, or make your own for cheap (LifeProjX, 2019). No working technology? Teach all-paper, find low-tech workarounds until it's fixed. Just chip away at whatever it is. They gave you the keys, make it yours.

LAYOUT

Your classroom is likely to have student desks, tables and chairs, or . . . ugh . . . chairdesks. Chairdesks are the worst. They're awkward, hard to move around, and they don't fit everyone. And chairdesks with angled tops can't be pushed together to make a big flat surface for groups. Get rid of any chairdesks as soon as you possibly can.

I digress. What's the best way to lay out your room? I'm a fan of two base formats, which you can adapt to meet your needs. First is for younger students, second is for older students. Both allow you to be able to reach every student at all times. Although you may frequently teach from a single spot (e.g., at the front of the room), most teachers spend a good amount of time working with students individually. If it's a pain to circulate you won't do it, and learning will suffer.

YOUNGER STUDENTS

Classrooms for younger students usually have two distinct areas. At the front: a rug or carpet where students can sit for things like story time or direct instruction. Each student is assigned their own square, letter, or whatever's on the carpet. Separately: clustered desks or tables for groups to work—often for rotating stations. Figure 6.2 (opposite page) illustrates an example.

Figure 6.2. Elementary classroom with stations, Sally Ride Elementary School, Orlando, Florida. *Source:* Photo by John Jernigan. Used with permission.

Notice a few things in Figure 6.2:

1. The carpet up front is for whole-class instruction, near the board. Each student is assigned a personal square where they sit.

2. Stations are for small group instruction and independent work.

3. Stations are for 3–4 students each (more is hard to manage).

4. The layout provides space for movement of teachers and students alike.

5. One station (at the back of the photo above, near the black cabinet) has a comfortable adult chair for small-group teacher-led instruction.

6. A typical routine is for students to rotate through multiple different stations during a session (for example, a literacy block). Students move from station to station in one direction (e.g., clockwise).

In the room above there are five stations. If students spent 10 minutes at each station, a full rotation would take 50 minutes (plus minor transition time). During those 50 minutes, each student would get 10 minutes of teacher-led instruction, and 40 minutes of independent work at different stations.

OLDER STUDENTS

Classrooms for older students generally drop the carpet and shift to individual student desks or tables. There's no hard and fast rule about when; often teachers switch to desks in 3rd or 4th grade. In higher grades, class sizes are often larger, so you may not have space for separate areas in your room even if desired. Older students have longer attention spans, so you can shift away from multiple short-duration tasks (as in stations) toward fewer, more sustained activities (often done whole-class or in pairs or groups). Figure 6.3 is a classic (flawed) layout for older students.

This layout (Figure 6.3) does some good things—there's a focal point for instruction, an individual flat workspace for each student, a projector, and boards. It's OK. There's no storage space, and there doesn't appear to be a natural place for students to collect handouts or turn papers in. I'm guessing there's maybe two electrical outlets in the entire room, which will annoy everyone. Also: imagine this room full of teenagers and all of their stuff. Where are all those backpacks and jackets and laptops and

Figure 6.3. Shuyukan High School classroom, Fukuoka, Japan. *Source:* Photo by user Kenta Odajima, CC BY-SA 4.0.

books going to go? On the floor? I'm betting this teacher spends 99% of each class up front. When moving around is awkward, you don't. Figure 6.4 shows a modest improvement.

Figure 6.4. Takanawadai Elementary school, Tokyo, Japan. *Source:* Photo by user scarletgreen, CC BY 2.0.

Windows! Counter space and storage! The major improvement here (Figure 6.4) is arranging desks in paired columns, which provides circulation aisles for you and a natural partner for each student. Notice the split-open tennis balls on the foot of each chair so they slide easily, without noise. In this setup, if students are too chatty, you can revert to the classic single-column-and-row, pushing desks together when there's partner work. Figure 6.5 (next page) illustrates another good layout.

I love the setup in Figure 6.5 (I'm a science teacher). There are windows with nature outside. There's all kinds of counter and cabinet space (and I suspect many cabinets lock). There's space for the teacher to circulate throughout the room, including the back and sides. There's a natural direction for students to face without twisting (the front). There's a table up front for handouts and demos (bottom right). The setup suggests regular use of partners.[4] The tables move, so you can shove them off to the side or change layouts for various lessons. You can see a projector installed (hanging from the ceiling), aiming at a board (off screen to the right). And hey: *sinks and science equipment and industrial-strength lab tables!* So much the better for doing stuff. No carpets that catch spills and get mildewy. Love it. Possible flaws: students are *always* paired up. It's

Figure 6.5. Skyline High School science classroom, Lake Frederick, Virginia. *Source:* Photo by user Reeveskd, CC BY-SA 4.0.

hard to tell if there's room for students to gather anywhere (e.g., for a demonstration up front). And ugh, those chairs. Those are the industrial-strength, steel-and-ceramic chairs that last for decades but stay comfy for maybe two minutes. Something should be done about those chairs. But the layout gets a near-perfect score in my book.

There are other good layouts, of course, mostly variations on a theme. Try to tailor your room to the students you have and the kinds of instruction you want to do. Figures 6.6 (below) and 6.7 (opposite page) are examples of what *not* to do.

Figure 6.6. Reading at Bardon Infant's School, Queensland, Australia, April 1951. *Source:* Queensland State Archives. Public domain.

Big circle? No. Everyone's eye gaze goes to the middle and across. Not to the teacher or the board. But everyone sure will notice that fidgety kid across the circle. Can you imagine this teacher getting up to work with anyone individually? Also: I count twenty-six students in this photo. There's no such thing as a "discussion circle" with twenty-six students. You just get sequential speeches at that point. Put the kids in smaller groups if you want them to discuss. Big circles (or squares, or dodecahedrons, or whatever) are good for demonstrations (so everyone can see The Thing) but otherwise should be avoided. Figure 6.7 shows a bad layout with good intentions:

Figure 6.7. Elementary classroom, Alaska. *Source:* Photo by user Liz, CC-BY-2.0.

These are permanent table groups. This layout looks like stations for younger students, without the alphabet carpet at the front. What's wrong? An alphabet carpet lets you quickly arrange students in a forward-facing position with all eyes on you and the instructional materials. Here, the tables are it. Students are *in groups permanently*. Consider what that means for eye gaze, comfort, and classroom management. Humans have their eyes at the front of their skulls (we are not horses). It is easiest for us to look straight ahead. In this layout, I see only two chairs directly facing the board. All students are permanently facing different directions. No matter where you (the teacher) are, somewhere between one quarter and one half of your students are facing elsewhere and will have to crane their necks. Ever tried to crane your neck all day? This setup is a chiropractic nightmare. Worse, it forces students to face each other all the time—not you, not the board. Your introverts will hate it. And it makes direct instruction harder. When students face each other, they chat. Like: constantly. This layout can doom you to frustrating battles of "Hey! Everyone! Listen to me! Hey!" One star, not recommended.

Don't despair if you're in a truly awful space—a corner of the gym, the cafeteria, a converted storage room. Kids can learn in all of them. What will make your year successful isn't so much about the room or how you set up desks—it's about how well you connect with your students, and the choices you make in your instruction.

THE FIRST DAYS OF SCHOOL

Before school starts, you'll need to make decisions about rules and routines. Keep in mind two basic principles:

- Rules and routines should save time. A major currency in teaching is time. If you use time well, your students will learn a lot. If you waste time (e.g., making students wait around while you pass stuff out or yell at that one kid for being out of his seat . . . again . . .), your students will learn less. John Goodlad's classic study *A Place Called School* (2004) reported that, on average, only about three-quarters of classroom time was spent on instructional activities. The rest was wasted. Rules and routines absolutely have social purposes we care about (*No stabbing!*). But the major point isn't control—it's saving time so students learn more.

- Think: 180 days. Rules and routines should last an entire year. Predictability saves time and cognitive bandwidth. Any routine you choose, you'll need to do over and over again (180 times at least). Any rule you establish needs to be one you are willing to enforce every day for every student.

RULES: SOME BACKGROUND

A note about the word "rules." Many of us understand rules as restrictions—stuff we can't do. Rules can also *teach*. If done well, rules explain how to be successful. This may sound odd, but it's comforting (not mean) to tell students what you want. When rules are unclear, enforcement is a surprise. Unclear rules may operate like moods (lax one day, harsh the next). The alternative to clear rules isn't chaos, it's arbitrary and unfair treatment. Getting the rules right means being clear and fair with everyone.

Bad Rules

Here's a bad rule that I spent all kinds of time trying to enforce my first year teaching at Greenwood High School in Mississippi: "No gum in class." I didn't pick the rule—it was schoolwide. Almost every class, someone would chew gum, I'd tell them to go spit it out, and they'd mostly do so. Sometimes, though—and I'm not proud of this—I'd see students with little gum lumps in their cheeks and I'd say something like, "Hey, I see you have gum, spit it out" . . . and they would occasionally respond, "I don't have any gum." On bad days this would make me mad, like, "Oh yes, you DO have gum! Now you are BEING DISRESPECTFUL! Now we have MORE PROBLEMS!!!"

Writing about it now, these conflicts were obviously silly and unnecessary. "No gum in class" was a bad rule because it wasted everyone's time, and occasionally caused bad feelings. I'm sure the school had reasons for "No gum in class." Probably something like: "Scraping gum off desks at the end of the year is horrible. Let's not." Which I understand. But those reasons did not, on balance, merit so much wasted class time and energy. A far better rule, if gum-scraping was to be avoided, would have been something like: "Throw out your gum after chewing."

Fortunately, you won't need to create rules from scratch. Your district will have a code of student conduct with rules for most of the big things (dress, speech, privacy, technology, bullying, academic honesty, disruption and threats, etc.). The code of conduct will also outline how violations should be handled. You won't need extra rules in your classroom about theft or vandalism or fisticuffs—you'll just need to enforce the code of conduct that already exists. For example, if you worked in the Rochester City School District (NY), you'd need to enforce these three "Student Rights and Responsibilities" in your classroom (there are several more; RCSD, 2021, 4):

Table 6.1. Excerpt from "Student Rights and Responsibilities," Rochester City School District *Code of Conduct* (2021)

RIGHTS	RESPONSIBILITIES
To be respected as an individual and treated courteously, fairly, and respectfully by other students and school staff	To respect everyone in the school community and to treat others courteously, fairly, and respectfully
To express one's opinion verbally or in writing	To express opinions and ideas in a respectful manner so as not to offend, slander, or restrict the rights and privileges of others
To dress in such a way as to express one's identity and personality	To dress appropriately in accordance with the dress code

Clearly these are big domains: respect, expressing opinions, dress. One challenge is that they're not terribly specific. It isn't obvious what they mean. What does the responsibility to "treat others courteously" require? What if a student's opinion *does* offend someone else in class? Where's the dress code, anyway? Almost all rules are going to present interpretive challenges. You can't expect to handle all possible classroom scenarios just by citing a code of conduct. Learning what's there is necessary but not nearly sufficient.[5]

Schools often have building-specific rules as well. Here are a few examples from Austin Steward School No. 46 (Rochester City School District, 2023):

- Please refrain from sending in soda or sweetened drinks. Also, no glass containers are allowed.

- Home cooked/baked foods cannot be served to students in school.

- Cell phones must remain in students' book bags while they are in the school building.

If you teach at School No. 46: no soda, no homemade cookies, no phones in use. No matter where you teach, there will be lots of rules in place, and you'll need to enforce them.

Most teachers also have their own classroom-specific rules. For example, many math teachers want students to write in pencil and to show their work. A classroom-specific rule like "Use a pencil, show your work" can make sense for math—but may be irrelevant elsewhere. Bilingual classrooms may have rules about language use; PE classrooms may have rules about equipment and safety. You get the idea.

What rules should your classroom have? The internet can provide you with forty million examples, but . . . be cautious. You can't just borrow someone else's rules and expect them to work flawlessly. Why not?

Consider rules within families: there's a lot of variation. *No biting. Brush your teeth before bed. No screen time after 9 p.m. Don't get anyone pregnant.* Family rules emerge from context. How old are the kids? How do family background and culture shape the rules? What personalities are involved? Most of us have known very strict and very loose families—and we understand that all kinds of approaches can be successful. There's no one right way. It's also true that some children thrive *despite* the rules their families enforced rather than *because* of the rules. It's the same in classrooms. Unless you're starting from scratch, your school will have a history, culture, and expectations for rules established long before you arrive. Whatever rules you pick will have to work within that history and culture to be successful.

Here's a frustrating truth: it's almost impossible to link specific classroom rules to improved student learning. Classroom rules are nested in school and community cultures, and in your teacher identity. You may need different rules than the teacher next door. Why? Because you are not the teacher next door. And because rules are, in part, about what you and your students need to function well. An example: kids who write in pencil will need to sharpen them. They'll want to sharpen them immediately when they break or get dull, which will happen every twelve seconds. If you get grumpy when your students sharpen pencils in the middle of class (which is noisy), you should consider a rule about sharpening pencils (perhaps: "Bring two sharp pencils to class" or "Trade dull pencils at the Cup of Sharp Pencils"). Why is that worth a rule? Because grumpy teachers are less effective than happy ones (Banerjee et al., 2017; Blazar, 2018). Your rules should make your classroom work better. Here's a summary of research from Peter Alter and Todd Haydon (2017) regarding classroom rules:

1. Teach the rules to students.

2. Tie rules to positive and/or negative consequences.

That's it. A bit obvious, perhaps? That's the extent of our knowledge base. There's no research showing that "No gum in class" helps kids read better. Nor research showing that "Co-create rules with your students" helps them subtract. The effectiveness of rules depends on context and on you. Teach your kids the rules, have positive and negative consequences, move along.

RULES: SOME GUIDANCE

- Fit within district and schoolwide rules. You don't need redundant rules like "No biting" (unless your class is full of bitey children) because biting is already a clear violation of any code of conduct. Before you develop classroom rules, find out what your district and school already require.

- State rules in affirmative language. Your rules should tell students what behaviors you expect—what to do (affirmatively) rather than what's forbidden. This is the difference between "Bring two sharp pencils to class" (affirmative) and "No sharpening pencils in class" (restrictive). Tell students what's expected.

- Promote learning. Good rules shape classroom behaviors that promote learning. Safety, of course—but also things like speaking and listening, task completion, organization and transitions. "Be on time with a pencil" is better than "No hats."

- Be specific. Teachers violate this all the time. Lots of classrooms have variations on "Show respect for others." The sentiment is good, but as a classroom rule it's pretty useless. "Show respect" doesn't tell you what to do (*Show respect how? In what contexts? What if our thinking about respect isn't the same?*). Vague rules leave interpretation up to teachers or whoever gets mad. Students often experience vague rules like "Show respect" as arbitrary. Think hard: What kinds of respect do you mean? What kinds of violations need prevention? What do you want students to *do*?

- Start with three to five rules. More, and they'll be difficult for everyone to remember. More, and you'll have a hard time with enforcement. You don't need a hundred rules; you're not trying to prevent your kids from being kids. If you see a bad behavior repeatedly not fixed by occasional reminders, OK—add a rule. It's easier to supplement three rules than thirteen.

- Enforce every rule. If you can't or won't enforce a rule, it's worthless. Consider: "Use a pencil, show your work." If you have this rule, you *must must must* be willing to enforce pencil use and showing work every time. What happens when students turn in work done in ink? Do they get a zero? Do you hand it back with a note that says "redo"? You must enforce each rule, every time. Rule enforcement should not be optional, or something you ponder before doing. Kids immediately pick up on arbitrary rule enforcement and consider it deeply unfair. They're right. Don't enforce by mood. If you don't love the idea of enforcing each of your rules with specific consequences every time, they're not the right rules.

- You decide. Some teachers develop rules "with" their students as a means for developing buy-in, or because they have a philosophical belief in a democratic classroom. That can work. And yet . . . I don't love the illusion of rule co-creation, because there's such a tiny range of what's acceptable. We can't accept suggestions like "When we're good, we get movie Friday!" because that compromises learning. Nor "Punch Bob when he's mean!" because, well, no. The risk of doing not-really-democratic exercises with students is that students wonder if we're just pretending to accept ideas when we've already decided things. That won't improve buy-in. Classroom rules—which need to be thoughtful, tailored to your classroom, and enforced by you daily—should come from you. Just write them, teach them, and be prepared to enforce them.

ROUTINES

All teachers rely on routines. The goal of routines is efficiency and predictability. You want to preserve time, and you want students to focus on learning rather than logistics. You'll need to explain, model, and practice classroom routines until they are habits done quickly and automatically.

The major question with routines is: *what do we do all the time?* You don't need routines for occasional or special things. Routines are for things that happen constantly. Students come to class. Class gets started. Teachers hand stuff out. Teachers put kids in groups. Students need to go to the bathroom. Everyone's going to lunch. Etc. You can identify areas needing a good routine by noticing when you (or others) are waiting. *Are you waiting for students to sit down and find something to write with? Is everyone waiting while you pass out papers? Are we all waiting to log in, for the video to load?* If you find yourself or students waiting around, you're probably wasting learning time and may be able to improve with a good routine.

> **How Much Should You Worry About a Minute Wasted Here and There?**
>
> Quite a lot, actually. Losing a minute every day adds up. Most public school teachers have around 180 days of instruction each year. Losing a minute per day means losing 180 minutes for the year—*three hours of learning, gone*. Three (or more) lessons you can't teach. Lose two minutes per day, you'll lose twice as many lessons. And so on. You can buy yourself a lot of learning time by getting routines right. The best are easy, automatic, and fast.

Good routines can take substantial planning. For example: students entering the classroom. Seems simple, right? A surprising amount of decisions are involved:

- Where will you be? (Many teachers stand in the hallway and greet students by name as they enter.)

- Where will students go when they enter? (Just . . . wherever, until you come in? To their cubbies to take jackets and boots off? To their desks?)

- What will you expect students to do by the time class starts? (Sit at their [assigned?] seats? Have specific materials out? Hand in homework, or have it out on their desks? Should they have pencils sharpened, the bathroom visited, laptops open and logged in? Are backpacks sprawling all over the floor, tucked under desks? Etc.)

- How will you signal that class is starting? (Walk in with the bell, and say something like "Hello class, it's Wednesday and I'm glad to see you" . . . or say nothing, because students will be completing do-nows or bell work?)

- When and how will you take attendance? (How long does that take? Do you need students working or seated?)

- How will you handle late arrivals or student questions at the beginning of class? (There will *always* be late arrivals . . . do they need a pass? Do you need to edit your attendance? What happens when students were absent yesterday, and show up today?)

- What will you do when students *don't* do the routine? (Don't turn in homework, don't sit down at their desk, don't bring materials to class, don't get started on the do-now?) What does enforcement of routines mean?

A good way to determine exactly what you want from each routine is to *do* the routine by yourself. Be the student entering class. Walk in . . . what comes next? Where do you go first and what's in your hand or at your seat? The beginning of class is particularly important for a strong routine because it's also the first time students see you that day. Any questions they've been waiting to ask, anything big or exciting they want to share, any uncertainty or anxiety they're feeling—they are usually hoping to share immediately. If you're busy repeating *"Sit down! Sit down! Get out your pencils! Bob, come on man—sit down!"* you're going to miss what they need. Effective routines:

- Save time.

- Repeat the same things daily (or Tuesdays or B days, etc.).

- Are simple and fast.

- Avoid physical bottlenecks (e.g., at the laptop cart, the sink, etc.).

- Minimize student movement (four students moving is better than twenty).

- Begin academic work as quickly as possible.

- Can be easily summarized for substitutes.

Students should be able to manage most routines without repeated explanations. If you're re-explaining, your routine is too complex or needs practice. I recommend thinking through routines for your classroom in these areas before your first day:

- Entering and leaving the classroom
- The first five and last five minutes of each class
- Distributing papers or materials to students
- Handing in papers or returning materials from students
- Accessing needed materials from storage (laptops, paper, pencils)
- Managing electronics (charging, logging into systems, storage)
- Accessing tissues, the garbage, sanitizer, or the pencil sharpener
- Going to the bathroom (including multiple simultaneous requests)
- Getting in groups for activities or instruction
- Rotating to stations or between areas in the classroom
- Transitioning to a next class (or lunch, dismissal, etc.)
- Making up work following absences (including in-school-but-missing for things like counseling or music lessons)

PEDAGOGY (HOW WE TEACH)

In most schools, pedagogy is left to teachers. This means you'll be able to try different approaches to instruction, see how well students learn, and adjust. You can also shift pedagogy *within* lessons multiple times. For example, one common lesson approach informally known as "I do, we do, you do" moves from demonstration to whole-class practice to independent practice in a single lesson. Below, I'll summarize briefly what we know about pedagogy and some major approaches to it—but keep in mind two cautions as you read:

1. Research on pedagogy is generally weak.

2. Pedagogy is complex.

Why our research base on pedagogy is weak is a topic for other books. What's important is that without a strong research base, U.S. schools have not developed universal standards for teaching practice. Teachers are doing all kinds of different things in their classrooms with no clear evidence they're the right things to do. If you ask five teachers in the same grade or subject area some basic questions about teaching practices (*How much time do students spend reading in your class? How much do you lecture? How do students take notes? Do you assign homework?*), you're likely to get five different answers, possibly quite opinionated ones. And it would be hard to know if any of them are right.

Teaching is complex. You will always juggle competing priorities when deciding how to teach. Every day, you'll need to account for what your students find interesting, what resources are available (including time), what state and district standards are at stake, what students already know and can do, and your own experience and skillset. *You* will know your classroom best.

I encourage you to question broad claims that specific kinds of pedagogy are engaging or motivating (which many well-meaning teachers will tell you). Hands-on pedagogy is not intrinsically motivating if it's pointless (*Cut out the cell parts . . . now cut out the labels . . . now glue them together . . .*). Lectures are not intrinsically boring.[6] No pedagogy is, of its own accord, engaging or motivating. Much more relevant is whether you've chosen pedagogy that matches who and what you're trying to teach. Effective teachers vary what they do for specific purposes. The key thing is to choose pedagogy that promotes learning the relevant standards with your specific students.

How can we know if our pedagogy promotes learning? Shaun Allison and Andy Tharby's excellent book about pedagogy, *Making Every Lesson Count* (2015), suggests we need to account for six major principles when we decide how to teach:

1. Challenge, so students have high expectations for what they can achieve.

2. Explanation, so students acquire new knowledge and skills.

3. Modeling, so students learn how to apply knowledge and skills.

4. Practice, so students become independent and remember new learning.

5. Questioning, so students are made to think hard with breadth, depth and accuracy.

6. Feedback, so students think about and further develop their knowledge and skills.

We don't need to cram every principle into every lesson. In fact, we probably can't. Some lessons will focus on explanation, others on practice. Over the course of a week, a unit, a year, we should ensure there are chances for students to encounter each.

Table 6.2 (which starts on the next page) outlines ten major approaches to instruction. It's not all the possible pedagogy in the universe. But if you learn how to do each, and provide students practice with several, you should be well along the way toward accomplishing Allison and Tharby's six principles in your classroom. A note before you look at Table 6.2: you'll see the term *differentiation*, and it's important for you to know what that term means.

Differentiation: A Cautionary Tale

Differentiation, or differentiated instruction, lacks a commonly accepted definition. Here's one, from Sarah Sparks at *Education Week* (2015):

> Differentiation: The process of identifying students' individual learning strengths, needs, and interests and adapting lessons to match them.

Almost everyone in teacher education discusses differentiation as an unreservedly good thing. We all have diverse classrooms, goes the thinking, so we should all adapt lessons to meet student needs. Right? But . . . adapt lessons how? What's a need? What if students can't do fractions . . . and are in algebra class? Should we . . . do algebra, just maybe not anything that's algebra-with-fractions? I've seen math teachers who claim to be differentiating or adapting lessons for students by requiring them to do less work (e.g., telling students to "just do every other problem"). I've seen reading teachers who claim to be differentiating that merely provide easier readings—and no additional reading instruction. Neither is differentiation. The first *reduces practice*. The second *reduces explanation*. Both also *reduce learning* and are therefore harmful. A far better approach for students in algebra who haven't mastered fractions would be for the math teacher to *teach fractions*. The reading teacher should *teach reading*.

While I absolutely agree that we should adapt lessons to meet student needs, I would caution that tailoring lessons to "learning strengths, needs and interests" may harm as easily as it helps. As in much of teaching, it matters how you do it.

Table 6.2. Ten Common P–12 Approaches to Instruction

	What It Is	Strengths and Limitations
Centers	Teacher sets up multiple centers (often tables) with separate tasks. Students split into small groups (2–4 students) and go to a center to complete tasks. Common for early grades. Example: A literacy class rotating through four centers, spending 15 minutes at each.	*Strengths:* Emphasizes practice or skills reinforcement. *Limitations:* Relies on student independence and strong routines. Limited chance for explanation, modeling, questioning, and feedback.
Competition or game	Students (individuals or groups) compete for points during a lesson. Common in PE classes, and for review or practice. Example: A whole-class *Jeopardy* game to prepare for an upcoming test.	*Strengths:* Competitions often focus on challenge and feedback. *Limitations:* Generally missing explanation and modeling, usually intended to reinforce instruction rather than new learning. Difficult to differentiate. May emphasize language skills or processing speed.
Creation	Teacher provides a prompt and materials; students create. Common in arts and creative writing classes. Example: A teacher sets up a still life in the middle of the room; students draw it.	*Strengths:* Excellent for challenge, practice, and feedback. Often simple to differentiate. *Limitations:* Relies on prior explanation and modeling.
Demonstration	Teacher shows students something; students watch. Common in science and career and technical education (CTE) classes. Example: A teacher demonstrates how to use a piece of equipment.	*Strengths:* Provides explanation and modeling, and the opportunity for students to ask questions. *Limitations:* Limited challenge, practice or feedback for students.
Discussion	Teacher provides a question or prompt; students respond at length. Common in English Language Arts (ELA) and social studies classes. Example: A teacher asks students to discuss a current Supreme Court case.	*Strengths:* Provides extended opportunity for practice, questioning, and feedback. *Limitations:* Discussions are unpredictable; explanation and modeling may vary in quality and outcome. May emphasize language skills or processing speed.
Hands-on	Teacher provides materials and a procedure or rules. Common in science, PE, and CTE classes. Example: Procedural labs in most science classes.	*Strengths:* Emphasizes modeling, practice, and feedback. Usually provides opportunity for questions while students work. *Limitations:* May lack challenge as many hands-on lessons are recipes (follow the directions, replicate a known result).

	What It Is	Strengths and Limitations
Independent practice	Students read or complete assigned tasks independently or in groups. Common in ELA, social studies, math and CTE classes. Example: A teacher tells students to read Chapter 5 while thinking about questions on the board.	*Strengths:* Emphasizes practice, especially in reading, writing, math or technical skills. Easy to differentiate. *Limitations:* Relies on student independence and strong routines. Limited chance for explanation, modeling, questioning and feedback.
Inquiry / problem-solving	Teacher provides materials and an open-ended question; students use the materials to test answers. Example: A science lab where students test paper airplane designs for flight distances.	*Strengths:* Emphasizes modeling, practice, questions, and feedback. May provide challenge. Can be differentiated for groups or individuals. *Limitations:* Provides little explanation—so presents the risk of students failing to solve or answer the problem or drawing the wrong conclusions.
Lecture / direct instruction	Teacher tells students information, usually at the front of the room. Example: A teacher explaining the many causes of World War I with slides.	*Strengths:* Efficient way to provide explanation; usually also provides opportunities for questions. *Limitations:* Unclear challenge, no opportunity for modeling, practice, or feedback. Difficult to differentiate.
Play	Teacher sets up the classroom with materials, often by theme ("kitchen" or "blocks" or "trains"). Students choose where and with whom they play while teacher rotates and monitors. Example: A teacher has daily "free choice" time for 15 minutes after lunch.	*Strengths:* Excellent for practice and feedback. *Limitations:* May lack challenge, especially as students return to preferred play areas repeatedly.

NOT SURE HOW TO TEACH? START WITH BACKWARD DESIGN

What are the goals for instruction? First and foremost, that your students meet standards for the grade level or content area you teach. In the previous chapter, we considered this standard for 6th-grade ELA (NYSED, 2017, 75): "6W1a: Introduce a precise claim, acknowledge and distinguish the claim from a counterclaim, and organize the reasons and evidence logically."

How can you help students meet a standard like 6W1a? One of the most systematic ways is called backward design, an approach popularized by Jay McTighe and Grant Wiggins in *Understanding by Design* (ACSD, 2005, 18). You start with the standard, and work your way back to pedagogy and lesson plans. Backward design is one of the most common and useful approaches P–12 teachers take to planning instruction. Here's how it works:

STAGE 1: IDENTIFY DESIRED RESULTS.

- Identify the standard(s). This is what students should know or be able to do.

- Review curriculum and timeframe. You may be required to use specific materials or emphasize specific standards. You'll need to account for what students already know or don't know. And you'll have limited time. Up front, you'll need to prioritize what to teach, and how much time to spend on each standard. A 6th-grade teacher could reasonably spend a week (or more) on standard 6W1a.

STAGE 2: DETERMINE ACCEPTABLE EVIDENCE.

- Pick assessments. What evidence will you collect from each student? Since standards can take many lessons to teach, you might collect many different pieces of evidence (classwork, homework, quizzes, essays, etc.). For standard 6W1a, for example, you might collect a three-paragraph essay responding to the prompt "Is Lying Ever Justified?"

- Define performance levels. How will you decide whether student performance on the assessment(s) meets the standard? Most teachers use answer keys and rubrics (e.g., X points for the claim, Y points for each bit of evidence, Z points for counterclaims, etc.). Let's say your rubric assigns up to ten points . . . what performance level meets (or indicates proficiency with) standard 6W1a? Eight points? Six? Why?

STAGE 3: PLAN LEARNING EXPERIENCES AND INSTRUCTION.

- Identify objectives. Standards are often big—they can take weeks or months to cover. Most teachers need to break standards down into parts, often called "objectives" or "student learning objectives." For 6W1a, examples of student learning objectives might include:

- *Students will be able to*
    - define the terms "precise," "vague," "claim," "counterclaim," and "evidence,"
    - distinguish precise and vague claims in provided essays,
    - identify claims and counterclaims in provided essays,
    - generate a precise claim of their own,
    - provide three sources of evidence in support of their claim,
    - acknowledge a counterclaim and explain why it is not convincing, and
    - assess the relevance of evidence in support of a claim.
- Choose pedagogy. How will you teach so that students can master the objectives you just wrote? Your pedagogy should be selected based on the work students will do to master the learning objectives in class. If you want students to learn how to pole vault, for example, they may need some basic Pole Vault Theory in the classroom (speed = height?) . . . but at some point they're going to have to go outside and vault. Pole vaulting requires some very specific pedagogical content knowledge (a teacher who knows how to show students things like how to hold the pole, where to start running, how to plant the pole and swing both feet up, how to not panic). Learning tennis would require different pedagogy. As would conversational French, phonics, or stoichiometry.
- Identify materials, resources and adjustments. What will you use in the lesson? You'll want to consider how you'll differentiate each of the lessons to meet various student needs, including alternate or enriched materials.
- Write lesson plans. Finally, write out a lesson plan for each day. How will class start? What will students do, and for how long? What materials will they have? What questions will you ask along the way? What accommodations will you provide? How will class end?

That's backward planning 101: start with the end in mind, and work your way back to pedagogy and planning.

STUDENT ENGAGEMENT AND COGNITION

This chapter opened with the claim that a necessary condition for learning is *engagement*. If your students are awake, interested, and working, they're engaged. If they're asleep, they're not. Although engagement can be a vague concept, a close-enough definition probably includes "paying attention" plus "thinking about the lesson" plus maybe "trying." Engagement is good. Engaged students learn. How can you engage most of your students most of the time?

No simple answer here, I'm afraid. What engages one student may not engage another. Some of your students who *love love love* reading may look forward to a schoolwide Read the Day Away, while others may prefer Grade Four Robot War.[7] You're going to have to try a variety of learning activities and see how they go. When do most of your students pay attention? What makes them think and try?

Below you're going to see a summary of an entire field—cognitive psychology—applied to teaching in a few paragraphs. My summary certainly doesn't do the field justice. If you want to know more, find Daniel Willingham's book *Why Don't Students Like School?* (2021). It's an engaging read, full of stories, and will make you a better teacher. Overall, Willingham presents ten principles to consider when thinking about instruction:[8]

1. People are naturally curious, but they are not naturally good thinkers.
2. Factual knowledge precedes skill.
3. Memory is the residue of thought.
4. We understand new things in the context of things we already know.
5. Proficiency requires practice.
6. Cognition is fundamentally different early and late in training.
7. Children are more alike than different in terms of learning.
8. Intelligence can be changed through sustained hard work.
9. Technology changes everything . . . but not the way you think.
10. Teaching, like any complex cognitive skill, must be practiced to be improved.

Without getting too lost in the weeds, I'll highlight the first three because they are immediately important for new teachers.

Principle 1. *People are naturally curious, but we are not naturally good thinkers.* Good news / bad news here. Your students *will* naturally get interested in things, especially if *you* are interested in them. You can engage them quickly by asking a good question, presenting an interesting fact, or showing a cool picture. But thinking for a long time is hard. Students should have to think hard enough to feel meaningful challenge and reward (*Hey! I thought about a real question, and I came up with a good answer!*), but not so hard that they get frustrated and quit. You've probably seen this truth yourself when doing a crossword or trying to solve a riddle. Challenging but doable, or we give up quickly.

Principle 2. *Factual knowledge precedes skill.* Facts are really important. Knowing facts is foundational for learning. It turns out that students who don't know facts (who lack background knowledge) struggle to read, struggle to learn new things, and struggle to think. It's false that students don't need to know things that they can Google. Known facts, in memory, are foundational for thinking and learning.

Principle 3. *Memory is the residue of thought.* We remember what we think about the most. Thought is practice for remembering. When we prepare lesson plans, we should pay attention to what students will be *thinking* during the lesson as much as what they'll be *doing*—because the thinking is what they'll remember. Here's an example Willingham shares from a chat with his daughter Rebecca, then in 6th grade (85):

DAD: What did you do in school today?

REBECCA: We had a guest in science. He taught us about chemicals.

DAD: Oh, yeah? What did you learn about chemicals?

REBECCA: He had this glass? That looked like water? But when he put this little metal thingy in it, it boiled. It was so cool. We all screamed.

DAD: Uh-huh. Why did he show you that?

REBECCA: I don't know.

Oops. The learning goal was probably not metal thingies or screaming. But that's what the students thought about and remembered. Fail. Note

> ### "Learning Styles" Theory Is Wrong
>
> You may have heard that students have various "learning styles"—ways in which they learn most effectively, and thus ways in which teachers should teach. This myth is pervasive in teacher preparation. A recent paper found that 95% of pre-service teachers believe it (Newton & Salvi, 2020). One popular version of "learning styles" theory suggests that there are visual, auditory, and kinesthetic learners. A so-called "visual learner" learns best by seeing new information. A so-called "auditory learner" learns best by hearing new information. And so on—there are dozens of different hypothesized "learning styles."
>
> They're all wrong.
>
> How do we know? "Learning Styles" theory suggests a testable approach: if true, then teaching in ways that matched preferred learning styles should yield measurable differences in learning. After decades of trying, psychologists have *never* found this to be the case. Matching students' so-called "learning style" . . . simply doesn't promote learning (see Willingham, 2021, 173–179).
>
> Why not? Because when we learn, we store information in memory. Most of what's stored in memory is *meaning*, not the sensory input involved during learning. Meaning "has a life of its own, independent of sensory details" (Willingham, 2021, 175).

what's *not* in Willingham's list, or in the above discussion of pedagogy: there's nothing about teaching in ways that match students' so-called "learning styles." Why not? Because the theory of "learning styles" is wrong, and has been shown to be so over and over.

One last thought from cognitive psychology, re: hard work. You may have heard the popular claim that it takes ten thousand hours to achieve expertise (from Malcolm Gladwell's *Outliers: The Story of Success*, 2008). Whether or not the specific claim about ten thousand hours is true, the idea that learning takes hard work is assuredly, definitely, absolutely true. Don't let anyone fool you into thinking good teachers make learning easy. Engaging? Yes. Fun? Sure, when possible. Easy? No. Easy means students are not being challenged. The point of school is learning. Your students need to do hard work. In your classroom, you'll see that this sometimes means they won't have fun, will be confused, and will want to do something else. Convincing a classroom of students to persevere through challenge often sounds a lot more like "Hang in there, y'all, this is worth it" than it does "Holy smokes, that was fun!"

One of the best teacher skills you can develop is the ability to motivate students to do difficult things. You can start by planning lessons that engage students and help them think about meaning (e.g., chemistry concepts—not metal thingies and screaming). Your work will always be complex; you'll be navigating standards, adopted curriculum, routines and rules, and relationships with students who have a wide range of individual and collective needs. The best evidence of engagement and learning is not the amount of *ooohs* and *aaaahs* during class but what happens on assessments. Did your students meet standards? Just remember: one of the best parts of teaching is you'll get a chance to try again tomorrow.

What Should I Do in Class My First Year?

Plan your physical space. Decide classroom rules and routines. Clarify goals—what you want students to know or be able to do—before you plan lessons. Challenge your students with engaging work (not necessarily fun-all-the-time work). And be willing to reflect, so you can do better next week, next month, next year.

SUPREME COURT CASE FOR DISCUSSION

Case: *Hendrick Hudson Central School District v. Amy Rowley* 458 U.S. 176 (1982).
Link: www.loc.gov/item/usrep458176

In 1975, the United States Congress passed Public Law 94-142 (later reauthorized as the Individuals with Disabilities Education Act [IDEA]; U.S. Department of Education, 1975). The law said that all students in U.S. public schools had the right to a "free appropriate public education" in the "least restrictive environment." The law required school districts to offer an Individualized Education Program (IEP) to any student with a disability who needed specially designed instruction. Parents who disagreed with an IEP could sue for relief.

In fall 1978, Amy Rowley started 1st grade at Furnace Woods Elementary School in the Hendrick Hudson Central School District (Cortlandt, New York). Amy was Deaf and used American Sign Language (ASL) to communicate, including with her parents Clifford and Nancy Rowley, both of whom were also Deaf. The Rowleys requested that Amy's school district provide an ASL interpreter in class. The district instead offered to provide a tutor for one hour daily, plus three hours of speech services each week. Part of the district's rationale for tutoring and speech was that Amy was "talented at lip reading."[9] Amy's parents didn't want speech services, or for her to rely on lip reading. They pointed out that Amy was Deaf, and couldn't access what the teacher or classmates said in class. In response, the district said they had met their obligations under the law because (a) they offered Amy *some* services, even if not everything her family wanted, and (b) Amy had passed kindergarten the previous year, so she was doing just fine without an interpreter.

Four years later, Amy's case wound up before the Supreme Court. One of the major questions the court needed to decide was what the word "appropriate" meant in Public Law 94-142.

The Court decided that the district didn't need to provide an interpreter because a "free appropriate public education" meant only that students must be provided "meaningful benefit" from an IEP (*Hudson v. Rowley,* 458 U.S. 176, 1982). The Court explicitly rejected the idea that IEPs were required to accomplish comparable outcomes among students with and without disabilities, explaining: "The Act does not require a State to maximize the potential of each handicapped child commensurate with the opportunity provided nonhandicapped children" (176). For the next thirty years, this was the standard for "appropriate": if a student with a disability could derive "meaningful benefit" from an IEP, the school district had met their burden under the law.[10]

QUESTIONS

1. Hendrick Hudson Central School District decided not to provide Amy Rowley with an ASL interpreter, in part because she'd passed the previous grade without one. To what extent is this logic convincing?

2. How should school districts decide whether special education services requested by a family are appropriate or not? (What if Amy Rowley's family requested that the school district provide weekly visual arts instruction rather than speech [because Amy loved drawing]?)

3. The Supreme Court rejected a standard for "appropriate" services that would have required districts to show they achieved comparable *outcomes* among students with and without disabilities. What are the pros and cons of holding schools to a "comparable outcomes" standard when making decisions about services?

4. As of 2020–2021, 15% of students in public schools had IEPs (National Center for Education Statistics, 2022). School districts often (correctly) point out that providing special education is expensive. They note that money spent on special education reduces money available for other school functions. When (if ever) are "limited resources" a valid excuse for not providing services?

FURTHER READINGS AND RESOURCES

Cognitive science and instruction:
Willingham, D. (2021). *Why don't students like school?: A cognitive scientist answers questions about how the mind works and what it means for the classroom* (2nd ed.). New York: Jossey-Bass.

Getting ready for your first day:
Wong, H., & Wong, R. (2018). *The first days of school: How to be an effective teacher.* Mountain View, CA: Harry K. Wong Publications. www.effective-teaching.com

Pedagogy:
Allison, S., & Tharby, A. (2015). *Making every lesson count: Six principles to support great teaching and learning.* Carmarthen, UK: Crown House.

Student engagement:
National Center for Safe Supportive Learning Environments. https://safesupportivelearning.ed.gov/topic-research/engagement

NOTES

1. I know, I know: high school kids don't always know what's good for them. They might all prefer to study *How to Drive Faster and Have More Sex*. But . . . is "tired, stressed, and bored" unavoidable?

2. Also, I'm not sure exactly what emoting only about food involves—but it can't be good.

3. Some classrooms are L-shaped. Check sightlines. Don't put desks or workspaces where you can't see them. A secret reading nook sounds cozy and awesome right up until something bad happens that you didn't see. Which it will.

4. You might be noticing just one chair at two of the front tables. Not sure why. Maybe this lucky teacher only has twenty-two students?

5. In the Rochester City School District (New York), the dress code is part of an eighty-four-page student Code of Conduct (Rochester City School District, 2021). Here's where expectations get more concrete: "*When on school property or at a school function, a person's dress, grooming and appearance, including jewelry, make-up and nails, must:*

- *Cover buttocks, stomach/midriff and chest.*
- *Not include clothing, headgear, or jewelry that is associated with or identifiable as a symbol of gang membership.*
- *Be void of abusive, suggestive, or profane language; symbols of illegal substances; or any other words, symbols, or slogans that disrupt the learning environment or deny dignity or respect to others.*
- *Include shoes, which are to be worn at all times for health and safety reasons.*" (58)

So: wear shoes and cover your belly button.

6. Go watch Randy Pausch deliver "The Last Lecture" (2007). If you still think lectures are boring, the Robot Overlords have already won.

7. Quoting Cornell University professor Ephrahim Garcia: *"There is nothing more purifying than robotic combat"* (Cornell Engineering, 2013).

8. Willingham, 2021, Table C1, 275. Permission to reprint from Wiley/Jossey-Bass.

9. "Lip reading" is more properly described as "lip guessing." English has a huge number of homophenes (words that look visually similar when spoken), and a small number of visemes (words that look distinct when spoken). Average lip readers can access about 12% of spoken words; the most talented can access about 30% (Altieri, 2011).

10. As it turns out, Amy Rowley was a brilliant kid with awesome parents, who after the Supreme Court decision moved to New Jersey to attend a school for the Deaf (Rowley, 2008). Amy graduated, went to college, earned a PhD, and became a professor at California State University. Not every kid with an IEP has the parents or supports Amy did.

7

Classroom Management
How Should I Manage My Classroom?

Classroom management is a common concern among new teachers. It's also a skill every school wants when hiring new teachers. Just keep in mind: *classroom management is not the goal*. The goal is *learning*. Classroom management is a *means*. If you can't manage your classroom, no one learns. If you can't manage your classroom, you'll waste a bunch of learning time and won't enjoy teaching very much.

Classroom management is difficult to learn by observation alone. Why? Because good classroom management means anticipating and preventing problems . . . and problems that don't happen are mostly invisible. When we observe skilled teachers, what they do often doesn't look like "classroom management" at all. It may look like they're not doing anything special. Class just . . . runs. (Look at how *good* these kids are . . .) The teacher *is* managing the class, though. They've learned students' strengths and weaknesses, they know how to structure engaging lessons, how to pace activities, and so on. What they're *not* doing is reacting to misbehavior or disruptions; they're structuring class in ways that avoid them in the first place.

Still, no students or classrooms are perfect. It's helpful to reflect when class doesn't go smoothly. Consider the following:

First-grade classroom, right before lunch. MS. CAROL, *halfway through her first year, is at the front of the classroom in a large rocking chair reading* Dragons Love Tacos *(Rubin & Salmieri, 2012) out loud to her seventeen students. Her students are (mostly) seated on an alphabet rug, each student on one letter, legs crisscross, except for one student (*BYRON*) who is lying down across three letters at the back.* MS. CAROL *looks at the clock and sees it's time for students to go to lunch.*

MS. CAROL: OK class, it's just about time for lunch. We can finish our book after. When I say line up, we're going to stand up, form a line at the door, and head down to lunch. Is everyone ready?

MS. CAROL *looks at her students for confirmation. Many students nod.*

MS. CAROL: Line up!

MS. CAROL *stands up and walks over to her desk to get her phone and keys. As she does, most students stand up and walk quickly over to the door. Those who sat closest to the door get there first and stand at the front of the line. Those who sat farther away wind up at the end of the line.* BYRON, *who stood up last, pushes his way to the front of the line, in front of* CARTER.

CARTER (*to* BYRON): Hey! You can't cut!

BYRON (*to* CARTER): I was here!

CARTER (*pushing* BYRON *out of line*): No, you weren't! You should be at the end!

BYRON (*pushing* CARTER, *getting back in line*): No shoving!

MANY STUDENTS: Ms. Carol, they're shoving!

Ah, kids. Kids kids kids. Are they terribly different from that guy at the airport demanding priority boarding? They are not. The good news is that teachers like Ms. Carol (and you, and me) have it easier than gate agents: we get to be in charge of our classrooms. You may have noticed one failure in the scene above. Although Ms. Carol did a nice job of telling students what was about to happen ("We're going to stand up, form a line at the door, and head down to lunch")—she clearly didn't explain or have a routine for how the line should form. Is it a mass-start race (hint: bad idea)? Are there designated line leaders? Should students line up by carpet letter (A, B, C . . .), or maybe one by one as the teacher dismisses them? Ms. Carol could have prevented the Byron/Carter shoving match by having a clear routine for forming a line. Although it's easy for Ms.

Carol to just get mad at Byron, and think, *Sheesh, Byron, why can't you just get in line like everyone else?? We're. Just. Going. To. Lunch.*—it's also risky to get mad at your students. When you do, everyone stops learning, including you. A more productive way for Ms. Carol to think about the shoving match: *Wait . . . why didn't that go the way I hoped? Where was I unclear, and how can I prevent line-shoving tomorrow?*

One truth about classroom management: students cannot read your mind. Students are most comfortable and learn the most when they know what's expected. Effective teachers tell students what's expected all the time. Not in iambic pentameter, not at *Moby-Dick* length. Briefly, clearly, frequently.

One tricky part about classroom management is that there are so many ways to fail, even when you get most things right. Analogy: when you drive a car, dozens of things are working (fuel, electric, engine, brakes, signals, computers, etc.). When any one thing breaks—you may not get where you're going. So too with classrooms. Dozens of things must work (attendance, routines, lesson structure, activities, group dynamics, materials, etc.) for class to function smoothly. One challenge is that when a lesson goes badly, it won't always be clear what's wrong. Hiccups won't mean that you're bad at *classroom management* (generally). They will mean that you'll need to figure out the thing that didn't work. Of course you won't get everything perfect your first year (or any year). Of course students won't always do what you want. Be patient. Student behavior is communication. A big part of classroom management is figuring out what's being communicated and how to respond. Here's what I mean by "classroom management":

Classroom management: What teachers do to make class safe, joyful and focused on learning.

Good classroom management looks different in different rooms with different students. Figure 7.1 (next page) shows what it looked like one April day in Sivunga (Savoonga), Alaska. See those kids? Every single one is smiling and paying close attention. They're focused. In the center is U.S. Coast Guard Lt. Tom Pauser, visiting school to teach a lesson about cold water safety. Lt. Pauser is clearly engaging, though from his expression it's not clear he knows this. Check out the student way at the back, tipped over with her head on the desk: even way back there, she's rapt. The teacher is there at the back, ready to help but letting the lesson take center stage.

The next image (Figure 7.2, next page) shows one September day in Shenzen (Guangdong), China:

Figure 7.1. Students at Hogarth Kingeekuk Sr. Memorial School, Sivunga (Savoonga), Alaska. *Source:* Photo by Grant DeVuyst, U.S. Coast Guard, 2012. Public domain.

Figure 7.2. Students at Nanyou Primary School at the end of class, Shenzen (Guangdong), China. *Source:* Photo by user WabbitWanderer, 2010, CC BY-SA 2.0.

Figure 7.2 happens some days. It's a good thing. Remember joy? Who knows, maybe the kids are joyful *because* it's the end of class.[1] You can't fake those expressions; you'll only see smiles like that among students who trust their teacher. Kids are kids—they'll be up and down throughout the year. It's important to embrace the ups—the joy—whenever you can, even if it's a little noisy or blurry on occasion.

Perspectives on classroom management vary. I'm not going to discuss philosophies or theoretical work here, as I'm not sure they're helpful for new teachers. Nor do I find it terribly useful to discuss big-picture or "holistic" classroom management, as some sort of hyper-complicated interplay between child psychology, social dynamics, teacher knowledge and skills, and the capricious gods of fate and chance. It *is*, of course (Sabortnie & Espelage, 2023). Yet large-scale pontificating risks overwhelming, and begs the question: what am I supposed to do tomorrow?

Classrooms are complicated. There's a lot going on all at once. You'll need to make management decisions anyway. You'll need to make your classroom safe *and* understand that it's developmentally appropriate for children to take risks and make mistakes. You'll need to know and support students as individuals *and* you'll need to lead them in groups. You'll need to structure challenging learning tasks *and* you'll need to account for when students aren't ready to learn, or your plans are just . . . bad. And you'll find yourself at the center of questions every student navigates: Am I learning anything in this classroom? Do I like it here? What's worth my effort? The good news is that classroom management isn't magic; it's work like any other aspect of teaching. You can improve through practice and reflection.

It's worth considering what "good" (effective) classroom management looks like. Above, I defined classroom management as what teachers do to make class safe, joyful, and focused on learning. Avoid the (obviously bad) extremes of chaos (no safety, no learning) and prison (no joy). I appreciate Zaretta Hammond's (2014) description of teachers who are "warm demanders": "Personal warmth and authentic concern exhibited by the teacher earns her the right to demand engagement and effort. Here is where the power of the teacher as ally in the learning partnership is realized. The culturally responsive teacher willingly develops the skills, tools, and techniques to help students rise to the occasion" (98). I like the idea that classroom management emerges from a teacher's "personal warmth and authentic concern," which in turn promotes engagement and effort. I do also worry that there's sometimes little distinction between classroom management practices and personality traits of teachers. There's no single personality type among teachers who are talented at classroom management. You can be you. (Unless you're that guy who yells at kids all the time—then no, don't be you.) Below, I'll outline ten guidelines to help you reach the goals of safety, joy, and learning.

TEN GUIDELINES FOR CLASSROOM MANAGEMENT

1. Safety first. Take care of your physical space. Do a walk-through and physically check everything. Communicate repairs needed to your principal immediately. Be sure you can see all students from all parts of the room. Your district will have safety protocols they expect you to follow (fire and lockdown drills, students bleeding, etc.)—learn them and follow them. You can find useful checklists at the U.S. Centers for Disease Control and Prevention (2004) and Healthy Childcare Colorado (2019).

2. The goal is learning. Not "order" or whatever. Management is a means, not an end. Don't confuse "quiet and compliant" with "actually learning stuff." Movement and noise and discussion are perfectly fine when in service to planned learning activities.

3. Include everyone. And keep them in class. Every student has the right to be in your class. Your job is teaching; the students' job is learning. Anyone you exclude from class misses learning. Any classroom management approach that removes students from class is a failure. It is your job to *teach* students, not get rid of them.

4. Behavior is communication. Sometimes students give you direct feedback ("This is boring!"), sometimes indirect (running around stabbing each other with pencils). Don't get mad at behavior. Figure out what the behavior communicates. Lead with questions: *Why is this happening? What needs does it serve? What came just before? Do I see any patterns?* And importantly: *What can I change?* Sometimes it's easiest to change a symptom (Hide the pencils! Switch to tablets!). You still need to know the cause. Why are kids running around stabbing each other with pencils? Fix that. Otherwise, next you'll be fixing kids whacking each other with the tablets you just handed out.

5. Take responsibility. Virtually all classroom management issues in your first years will be your fault. I'm not trying

to make you feel bad. Just take responsibility. You will feel tempted to blame your students. You'll be in class, they won't do what you're asking, and you'll think: "Sheesh, these kids! I wish they were different!" No. It's you. Next time you look at your teacher mirror, repeat these words: "Classroom management is *my* job. My kids are who they are. I will figure this out." When you take responsibility for your class, you have a chance to earn respect and trust among students.

6. Develop good relationships. Cliché alert: Students don't care how much you know until they know how much you care. I'm not saying you should spend all kinds of class time on Getting to Know Me worksheets or requiring group hugs. Instead, do meaningful work together. Why do sports teams and theater kids develop strong relationships? Because they're doing meaningful things together.

    a. Be positive. Students need us to be upbeat and optimistic. If we're doing our jobs, we're asking them to do difficult things for much of the day. Yes, teachers have bad days and private struggles. But I'm telling you: kids need positive people in their lives. You can be your grumpy, my-car-broke-down self after school.

    b. No yelling at kids. When was the last time someone yelled at you? Did that make you want to do better? Clarification: Yes, sometimes your class will be noisy, and yes, sometimes you'll have to raise your voice to get attention (e.g., "*Y'all! Switch groups!*"). That's OK—though it's better to have visual / silent cues since adding noise to a noisy environment isn't a great option. Just don't yell at kids or your class because you're upset. It shames them and damages relationships.

7. Lesson plan. This is foundational. One teaching cliché that carries truth: "The best classroom management plan is a good lesson plan." Another: "Fail to plan? Plan to fail." You are not an experienced teacher who can scribble notes on a post-it and have things go well. If you're disorganized or unprepared, you'll have management issues. If a lesson ends earlier than anticipated and you have ten (painful) minutes of nothing planned, guess what? Your students will find stuff to do. You will not love their ideas. Plan better.

8. Praise publicly, correct in private. When students do awesome things, point them out in public (aloud, in writing, whatever). You're communicating not only to the student(s) who did the awesome thing, you're communicating to everyone: *This* is what we're trying to do. When students do non-awesome things, reprimanding them with an audience causes shame or anger. Shame and anger are the worst; both interfere with learning. Correct or redirect privately whenever possible. Also: it's OK to wait before addressing behaviors, as long as there's no safety issue. (Pencil-stabbing problems? Go confiscate the stabby pencil immediately, you can figure out what to do about it later.) Waiting is often a good strategy. Classroom behaviors can be frustrating. Teachers feel emotions. Wait-and-deal-later can be a good way for you to get reflection time and emotional space. Ten minutes, the end of class, the end of the day . . . you may do better work later than right now.

9. Communicate. With administrators, counselors, parents, coaches, fellow teachers. Students typically see multiple adults daily (especially in middle and high school). Some of your best troubleshooting can be with others who know the same student(s) well. We often get limited windows into our students during class; it can help to get the bigger picture. What motivates them? Why are they doing things? Why are they *not* doing things? Share what you see. Ask others.

10. You'll get better. What's true elsewhere is true for classroom management: practice makes perfect (or *better,* anyway). When you start teaching, you'll have limited experience anticipating, preventing, and responding to management issues. Every time something goes wrong, you'll learn. Try to be patient, especially with yourself. You won't be perfect on the first day. You won't be perfect on the last. No doubt you'll get better over time.

Students don't always do what we expect. They're human. They have bad days, bad moments, conflicts with each other and with you. They get tired and cranky and don't always translate big emotions into good choices. *What to do?* Below I'll discuss two classroom management areas to emphasize during your first year: lesson planning and conflict de-escalation.

LESSON PLANNING

Use time well. This means maximizing time students spend with curriculum, working towards learning goals. It requires lots of preparation from your end, and good routines that minimize time loss on things like transitions, distributing materials, line leader conflicts, etc.

Give clear directions. What's clear in your head may dissolve when you try to explain it to students. Directions are worth writing down and practicing. For example, when students finish a quiz, what should they do? Identify the superior directions (hint: the last one):

- When you finish, wait until everyone else finishes.

- When you finish, read a book.

- When you finish, turn your paper over and start reading *We Came, We Saw, We Left*, Chapter 2 (p. 19).

- When you finish, turn your paper over and start reading *We Came, We Saw, We Left*, Chapter 2 (p. 19). I'll collect your papers at 2 p.m.[2]

One confusing thing we tell students to do all the time is to "work with a partner" or "work in your group." What does that mean? Work independently and trade papers for corrections? Elect a leader, a timekeeper, and a spokesperson? Make sure everyone's handwriting appears on the worksheet? Students do what we model and explain. We need to teach them what we expect them to do with partners or groups. Pro tip: if we aren't clear in our expectations for partners or groups, the student who cares the most does all the work. It's like the Seventh Law of Thermodynamics.

Establish momentum. This is about challenge and pacing (Shindler, 2009). You'll know when you get them wrong. Lessons that require students to copy text line after line, or perform the same math procedure over and over (looking at you, Worksheet Champion) is too simple. Students need to feel that they're *learning*, not just occupying time. Are students bored or want to move on? They'll disengage. Are tasks confusing and frustrating? Your lesson will grind to a halt while you explain and regroup. You'll want to plan lessons that most students find interesting and doable but not overly simple.

Require participation. Every student should have a task for most of each lesson. It doesn't necessarily matter *what* the task is, just that they're doing *something*. Participating. I'll note that "listen to the teacher being brilliant" is not much of a task. In small doses, it's fine—lectures can be efficient, and you need to explain things sometimes. I will note that everyone has a tolerance limit for sitting there and listening—and it's easy for teachers to forget that school is six and a half hours long. What else could your students do beyond just listening? If you're not sure, at the very least have students take notes (teach them how) and set a timer every few minutes so you stop and ask lots of questions. One of my favorite standing-the-test-of-time studies is Evertson et al. (1980), who described an effective junior high math teacher this way: "The more effective teachers were active, well organized, and strongly academically oriented. They tended to emphasize whole-class instruction, but with some time also devoted to seatwork. They managed their classes efficiently, and tended to 'nip trouble in the bud,' stopping a disturbance before it could seriously disrupt the class. They asked many questions during class discussions. Most were 'lower order' product questions, but 'higher order' process questions were also fairly common" (58). When in doubt, ask your students questions. We all need to find out what students have learned before moving along. Ask!

Avoid groupwork. Ick. I hate groupwork (or "cooperative learning," as it is often called). Remember that the goal of teaching isn't that *groups* learn, it's that *each student* learns. Groupwork can be useful for young students learning social skills, and for language class practice. Those are fine. Here's where groups go wrong: many teachers use groups as a way to require participation. For example, groups may have assigned roles, like "scribes" who write stuff down, "timekeepers" who watch the clock, "reporters" who share findings, etc. My question: do you really think an important learning goal is "be able to watch the clock?" Usually not. Usually that's busywork. Require participation on learning goals that matter.

Require effort. Learning takes effort. Learning *can* be fun, but sometimes isn't. Why not? Because learning is *hard*. Have you ever tried to learn how to juggle? Or memorize the digits of pi? See how long your tolerance is for new learning. My bold prediction: less than 6.5 hours (the length of a typical school day). Maybe 6.5 minutes? You should expect that class won't always be fun. Sometimes students won't want to do hard things—whether juggling, learning the digits of pi, or reading *Dragons Love Tacos*. One way to be a terrible teacher is to lower expectations to the point where effort is no longer required, and no one learns anything. A constant goal will be to find out how much effort you can get from students in service of learning. More effort? They'll learn more.

Require accuracy. As Doug Lemov points out, "right is right" (2021, 153). Don't be afraid to notice and correct errors—students need the knowledge and skills you are teaching. No shame in that. And *you owe them useful feedback.* One of the most powerful tools you have to shape learning is feedback. Your feedback should be specific and provided as soon as possible. What's right? What's not? How can they improve?

Prepare some extras. No lessons go precisely as planned. Some wrap up early; others take longer than expected. Nor do students work at the same speed. It's good to have some extras prepared that you can lean on as needed, including:

- *Individual work (enrichment) students can choose and complete independently.* This is for when students complete something early (and classmates are still working). You don't want students rushing through stuff, and then . . . just sitting there. Extra time means a good opportunity to provide cool / interesting / challenging work for students who work faster (or who want to do more, perhaps over lunch, free time, or after school). You can prepare Enrichment Folders or Challenge Bins at the back of your room or in an electronic folder, updated weekly or for each unit. Enrichment can include readings, videos, problems, etc., and should require student response. Assign some sort of modest credit (*+2 on the next unit test . . . collect 3, earn a homework pass, etc.*). If you stock five different options each week, you'll have enough for one each day.

- *A regular whole-class activity that takes 5–15 minutes.* It should be regular so you don't need to explain it after the first few times. ELA teachers like independent reading of chosen books. Review games like Around the World are a good option at any level. It just needs to be something you can pull out whenever class is done early (or scuffling)—and also something that's not critical if you don't get to it.

- *A backup lesson when you have an unexpected absence, or when your lesson fails.* You need something useful for your students to do (and learn) when your original plans fail or you have to miss class unexpectedly. I'd recommend a whole-class activity for each unit that students can largely complete on their own (because you might need someone else running class). Shoot for something like thirty minutes—substantial enough to replace a bad lesson, also brief enough that someone else can help them do the lesson without getting bogged down. It can feel like a lot of work to prepare a backup lesson in addition to all your daily lessons. It will also help you sleep at night knowing it exists.

At the end of this chapter, you'll find a sample lesson template. It's detailed. The intent isn't to waste time filling in blanks but to provide prompts for you to *think and plan through* so that you're prepared for each aspect of class. The amount of things you'll need to fill in will taper over the months and years to come. This template is adapted from one I use at SUNY Brockport, and includes the idea of "double planning" (Lemov, 2021). It's a flexible template; adapt to meet your needs, but try to keep the whole thing on a single page so you can refer to it during class without shuffling or scrolling. "Double planning" means planning for what *students* and also the *teacher* will be doing throughout the lesson. There should be a complete plan for both. Lots of blank space in the student column? Fix that.

CONFLICT DE-ESCALATION

A common classroom management mistake is making not-great things worse. You'll make things worse if you allow speed or emotion to take over decision-making. The goal isn't resolving conflicts or arguments within three seconds. The goal is resolving conflicts or arguments successfully, in ways that promote learning. One structural challenge of teaching is that we often juggle dozens of details simultaneously, and conflicts or arguments can catch us by surprise. You'll be in the middle of noticing Serenity staring at something in the ceiling (*What's up there? Is she just . . . zoning out?*) when WHAMMO Lillian will start crying because Darius just destroyed her origami finger claws.[3] And because you are human, you'll have some emotions (*Darius! Why?!? THIS IS WHY WE CAN'T HAVE NICE THINGS!!*). When students refuse to do what you're asking, or don't follow the rules, or laugh in the face of your efforts . . . it's natural and human to feel frustration, anger, embarrassment, etc. The best thing you can do with those emotions, though, is *avoid acting on them in the moment*. Feel the emotions, of course, but don't make decisions about how to respond while angry or embarrassed. You'll make things worse. A key aspect of de-escalation is separating behaviors, emotions, and responses by inserting a time delay.

De-escalation: Choose Your Own Adventure

In an earlier chapter, I mentioned a schoolwide "No gum in class" rule at my first teaching job. I wanted to follow school rules, so I'd monitor my students for gum throughout the day. Most of the time, this meant I'd say, "Hey, no gum" and they'd go spit it out in the garbage. But at least once a day I'd say, "Hey, no gum" and a student would respond: "I don't have any gum."

[Dramatic pause while teacher thinks]

Of *course* they had gum. They were *actively chewing on it*. It was bright blue, and I could see it, and it smelled like Sour Patch Kids. Were we living in separate realities? No. The kid just didn't want to spit out their gum. Which approach de-escalates?

APPROACH A

> ME (publicly): Oh yes, you DO have gum. I saw it, now go spit it out.
>
> STUDENT: I don't have any gum.
>
> ME: You do! It's right there! Quit being intransigent!
>
> STUDENT: Being what?
>
> ME: You've got to spit out your gum or go to detention at lunch.
>
> STUDENT: That's not fair!
>
> ME: What's not fair is you wasting class time! Make a decision: gum or detention!
>
> STUDENT: F--- that.
>
> ME: Okay, now I'm going to have to call the office. You've made some poor decisions today, etc. etc.

or

APPROACH B

> ME (privately): No gum, OK . . . and yet I feel a strange urge to visit the Sour Patch.
>
> STUDENT: Umm . . .
>
> ME: Let's check in when we do reading groups, OK?
>
> STUDENT: Why?
>
> ME: I'd like to chat. And I want to go over your essay from yesterday—you did a nice job summarizing the plot, but I think you could sharpen your thesis. OK?
>
> STUDENT: Umm . . . OK, I guess . . .

Obviously, approach A is a teacher failure. We went from chewing gum to cursing the teacher in roughly twelve seconds. I applied Approach A way too many times my first year. Approach A was wrong for a number of reasons:

- I criticized in public. Oops. Situational awareness, Wilkens.

- I had the wrong priority. The goal—my job—was student learning. This interaction removed a student from class. Hard to learn when you're not in class.

- I didn't take responsibility. Sure, there was a rule, and the kid broke it. But I didn't give the student a way to fix the violation that preserved dignity. They made two bad choices (chew gum, curse teacher)—but the cursing was on me because I backed them into a corner.

- I didn't value the relationship. I argued, prioritized the noncompliance, and called the kid intransigent. What did I expect?

- I failed to de-escalate. In Approach A, I argued and pushed on the noncompliance until it blew up. Which it did.

With Approach B . . . no, the gum didn't come out. But four good things happened:

- I did my job—stating the rule, monitoring for compliance. I also made the reasoned decision that noncompliance (gum chewing) was neither a safety concern nor an impediment to learning, and therefore not a crisis.

- The student stayed in class.

- Humor lowered the stakes of the correction.[4]

- We quickly refocused on academic work and learning.

Effective teachers buy time before making decisions about how to handle conflicts or arguments. They use time as a major de-escalation strategy. Consider: Do you have to resolve this right now? Can you state expectations without demanding immediate compliance or behavior change? Can you let the student(s) take thirty seconds to save face, to transition, to re-engage? A lot of de-escalation may look like doing . . . nothing, at least in the moment. It isn't doing nothing, of course. It's choosing to insert time between behavior and consequence. Any time you're not quite sure what to do about a conflict or argument (which may be often), maybe don't do anything yet. Just restate the rule or expectation and set a time to revisit. You'll be able to think, you'll be less angry or frustrated, and the same will be true for your students.

Another way to de-escalate is to listen. One mistake I make, even now, is moving too quickly to resolve a conflict or argument based on what I think I know (but . . . often get wrong). That too can make things worse. Students can move from frustration about something that happened, to greater frustration with a teacher who does not listen or understand. Remember: behavior is communication. Part of your work is figuring out what student behaviors communicate. Often, you'll know *what* a student did or said—but not *why*. And if you don't know why something happened, it's impossible to respond appropriately, or to prevent recurrence. So listen to what your students tell you during or after conflicts.

Listening has a side benefit: it can de-escalate on its own, without you doing anything else. When students feel big emotions, they may not know what to do . . . so they do things like ignore, refuse, or argue. Sometimes students just need to figure out what they're feeling and how it's impacting them. A student who refuses to spit out gum may be chewing gum because they're hungry. A student with their head down may be sleepy. Take time to meet privately with students, and listen. Your goal isn't "they'll say some stuff, then I'll figure out a punishment"—it's "they'll say some stuff, and I'll learn something." You can figure out next steps later, maybe on your own, maybe with a colleague or an administrator or a member of the student's family.

BULLYING AND HARASSMENT

The goal of classroom management is to make class safe, joyful, and focused on learning. Your class isn't any of those things if students bully or harass each other. Here are four guidelines to keep in mind (see also www.stopbullying.gov):

- Intervene quickly. If you think you heard it, you heard it. Kids are aware that they're not supposed to tease or be mean to each other—so they try to *hide* their behaviors. And victims won't often ask for help—because doing so puts them at additional risk. Intervening quickly, clearly, and consistently is the goal. For example: "X, I heard you making fun of Y's name. Stop. It's not OK, and it's against school rules. This is a warning. Next time we will have this conversation with the principal."

- Bullying isn't usually clear-cut (Big Scary Kid picking on Small Adorable Kid). It's often two-way, and can involve shifts in power. The power at stake isn't always physical; it can be *social* power that produces shame or humiliation (Bazleton, 2013). Nor is bullying usually a single experience—it's often multifaceted, and may include things like taunting, exclusion from a lunch table, or shaming online. Some victims retaliate (and, shame on us, victims are often the ones who get noticed and reprimanded). Some "bullies" and "targets" may be better understood as *rivals* or *adversaries* even if someone (a parent, for example) uses the language of "bullying."

- A rush to punish may do more harm than good. One defining trait of young people is that their frontal lobes are underdeveloped. They're pretty terrible at understanding consequences (Jensen & Nutt, 2015). Some of our best work isn't *punishing*, it's *teaching*. We can always tell and show students what we expect. For example: "In this class, we have assigned partners for lab work. One of our class rules is showing respect. It's not respectful to complain about a lab partner. We can all learn from working with different people."

- Report bullying and harassment. Bullying and harassment aren't often contained to a single setting. They may happen in hallways, classrooms, the cafeteria, or over group texts. Any one teacher is unlikely to have a complete picture. That picture may be clear only to administrators, who field reports from multiple teachers over time. Any teacher who witnesses bullying or harassment, however unclear, can help stop it by reporting what they've seen. Find out how to report bullying and harassment at your school and do so in writing every time you witness (or *think maybe* you witness) it.

WHEN TO CALL THE OFFICE FOR HELP

Good classroom management promotes *learning*. Your goal should never be to remove students from class. Don't buy into the thought process that "Sophia is disrupting the learning of others—she needs to go." That's a corruption of your responsibilities as a teacher. Try to keep every student in class every day, even on the bad days. Students are in your class to learn; you're there to teach them. If their behavior is disruptive—you should work with them on behavior. Find out what's going on. Make lesson adjustments, clarify expectations, improve routines, etc. Follow school procedures, of course; your school may expect specific behaviors to result in office referrals. But take responsibility. Keeping students in class, even when they're difficult or loud or disrespectful, demonstrates responsibility to and authority within your class. If you call the office every time your class gets spicy, students rapidly learn you're not in charge. The office is. And that's a problem, because the office isn't in your room all day. Ceding authority to others will just make classroom management even more difficult. When you show students that you're willing to do the hard work—to keep students who are having bad days, to work through arguments and conflicts without kicking them out—they come to see you as the one in charge. You'll need that respect and trust over the days and weeks ahead.

Sometimes, of course, you won't know what to do and will need some help. That's OK. Below I'll outline several areas where I'd recommend seeking help (and from whom). Two basic concepts apply here: First: never ask others to manage your classroom. Your classroom is your responsibility. Second: no fair asking for the permanent removal of any students from your classroom. Assume you'll have every student all year and need to find ways to make it work. The overall goal of asking for help isn't to offload problems onto others, it's to figure out how *you* can do better in your classroom, with your students. Here are areas where I'd recommend asking for help:

- Report bullying and harassment (to administrators). Teachers are mandated reporters. This is required by all districts. What you report doesn't need to seem major or huge, and you don't need to judge it by impact on the victim(s). Bullying and harassment thrives when no one reports seemingly minor things. Just report what you saw or heard. Your report gives administrators a chance to identify patterns and work on solutions (often with teachers and families).

- Report threats of harm (to administrators). Again: required. If a student threatens to physically harm another student, you, or themselves—report it. Sometimes threats are explicit ("I will f— you up"), sometimes indirect ("I know where you live"). Some threats are about self-harm. It can be hard to judge whether students are making threats they intend or have the means to carry out. You are not a mind reader. If you're not sure about something you heard, report it. You don't need to make decisions about intent or means. If a student tells you anything that suggests they may be considering suicide (e.g., "I just want to disappear"), you *must* communicate that, even if they tell you not to share—and even if they try to reassure you that they're fine now. You must also make sure the student remains under supervision until they are in the custody of family, an administrator, or law enforcement (call 911 if you can't find anyone else).

- Report suspected abuse or neglect (to administrators). Also required. Each state or territory will require you to be trained in how (and to whom) you should report suspected abuse or neglect to agencies responsible for investigations. It's not your job to decide if abuse or neglect is actually happening. You can't really know that most of the time. It's your job to report what you see or hear. For example, students who fall asleep in class all the time because (they say) they've been up all night gaming . . . is that neglect? Not your call. Just report what you see and what students tell you.

- Seek help when you're worried about a student (talk to other teachers, a counselor, the school support team, or an administrator). This is some of your best communication. When your students struggle with academics, social skills, or behaviors—there are often others in your school who know them and can help you think through options. A school support team may be able to arrange tutoring or counseling. A coach or fellow teacher may be able to offer insights from other contexts or last year. And if you're worried about the impacts of things outside school (e.g., a student tells you their family may get evicted), your school may have a social worker who can help, or connections to community-based resources useful for your families. You can ask for help with seemingly small things too. For example, if a student shows up late and misses school breakfast—can you call the office or cafeteria and find something for them to eat?

- Seek help when you're frustrated with a student or class (talk to fellow teachers, especially of those same students, the school support team, or an administrator). This happens. The goal is never to remove students from class but to better manage your frustration and solve problems in positive ways. During my first year, my nemesis was sixth-period biology, right after lunch. Everyone was sleepy, including me, and there was a mix of personalities in the class that just did not work. I dreaded sixth period.[5] When you dread things, you're not good at them. You're waiting for badness, which is not the way to develop good relationships or promote joy. One thing you can do is communicate with fellow teachers, who have all been there. They may know the students in your class, or may have worked their way through similar issues. And if you just need someone to listen to you process, there's no one better than a fellow teacher. I'm not telling you to go down to the teacher workroom and vent without end. No one needs negativity. But we can all use partners in finding perspective and ideas.

In general, seek help in person, face to face. Having a conversation enables others to ask you questions and get a clear sense for what's happening. Unless you're a novelist, you can't do teaching scenarios justice over text or email (nor does anyone want to read that three-page email). After you've met, follow up in writing, using forms your school requires (e.g., to report bullying or harassment, or to make a referral to the student support team) or email. A simple "Thanks for meeting, here's what we discussed . . ." can be a good summary and reminder of next steps.

CLASSROOM MANAGEMENT: A CODA

This chapter has been about classroom management, which includes all the work we do to make class safe, joyful, and focused on learning. Along with skilled instruction, classroom management lies at the heart of our work. Here's a final scene (Figure 7.3), which makes me smile:

Figure 7.3. Abe Wheeler, forester, visits Buckman Elementary School in Portland, Oregon, 2017. *Source:* Photo by U.S. Bureau of Land Management. Public domain.

This is a classroom at Buckman Elementary School in Portland, Oregon. You can see a few familiar things: a table in the foreground with a flower in an Erlenmeyer flask, a carpet where students are sitting, some colorful bins and posters and supplies. It looks, frankly, pretty awesome as a place to learn. In the helmet is Oregon state forester Abe Wheeler. Abe Wheeler, bless his heart, is visiting class, no doubt intending to inspire a few young people to become our next generation of state foresters. What makes me smile is that Abe Wheeler is turned *away* from his students, drawing something on a giant notepad. Check out where his students are facing. Abe Wheeler: is anyone paying attention?[6]

I love the details we can see. There are some crafty trees on the table in the foreground. All the students are gathered closely together on the carpet. The state forester is there, talking to Portland kids about forestry. All of this seems entirely right to me. There's a chance here: for safety, for joy, for learning. Although in this moment, we're not entirely sure what the students are looking at . . . it's entirely possible Abe Wheeler is going to turn around in another three seconds and be like: "Hey kids! I just drew a life-sized banana slug!" And the kids will be like: "Ew! Cool!" . . . I don't really know. But there's magic in these small moments, I think.

I want to leave you with some encouragement. Classroom management is hard. You can get nine things right, and the tenth may still pull your class sideways. It'll be frustrating. Just don't forget to be proud of the times in class when everything *does* work, when you're anticipating needs, when everyone's engaged, when the day ends with students understanding new things. In classroom management, as in the rest of your teaching life: be patient and forgiving. You and your students will always make mistakes. Just don't forget to identify the nine things you all did right, and then work on that tenth thing that needs fixing together.

How Should I Handle Classroom Management?

Good classroom management makes classes safe, joyful, and focused on learning. You'll need to get to know your students well, you'll need good relationships with them, and you'll need good lesson plans. Some days will be rough anyway. Be patient. Forgive yourself and your students. And keep trying to get better tomorrow.

SUPREME COURT CASE FOR DISCUSSION

Case: *Morse v. Frederick*, 551 U.S. 393 (2007).
Link: www.loc.gov/item/usrep551393

In 2002, runners carried the Olympic torch through forty-six states leading up to the winter games in Salt Lake City, Utah. The torch relay went through Juneau, Alaska, on a school day (January 24, 2002). The route took runners down Glacier Highway, past Juneau-Douglas High School: Yadaa.at Kalé (JDHS). High school principal Deborah Morse allowed students and staff to go outside to see the relay as a school-sanctioned event. The relay was newsworthy, with local TV and radio stations out to capture the scene.

High school senior Joseph Frederick, who hadn't yet reported to school that day, showed up on Glacier Highway across from JDHS with a fourteen-foot-long banner on which he had written (in duct tape): "BONG HiTS 4 JESUS." A bunch of Frederick's friends helped him unfurl and hold the banner while the torch relay and camera crews passed by.

Principal Morse saw the banner, walked across Glacier Highway, and told the students to take it down. All complied except Frederick, who claimed the banner was protected speech under the First Amendment. Morse then confiscated the banner and suspended Frederick for ten days. Morse explained that the suspension was appropriate because "she thought [the banner] encouraged illegal drug use, in violation of established school policy." Frederick disagreed, claiming that his free speech rights had been violated, that there was no intent to encourage illegal drug use, and "that the words were just nonsense meant to attract television cameras." Frederick appealed his suspension to the superintendent, who rejected the appeal. The case eventually wound up at the U.S. Supreme Court.

BACKGROUND

The landmark Supreme Court case concerning free speech at school was *Tinker v. Des Moines* (393 U.S. 503, [1969]). In *Tinker*, students wore black armbands to school to protest the Vietnam War. They were suspended, fought back in court, and the Supreme Court found in their favor, establishing two major legal tenets:

> Neither students nor teachers "shed their constitutional rights to freedom of speech or expression at the schoolhouse gate" (506) . . . and speech "cannot be prohibited unless it 'materially

and substantially interfere[s] with the requirements of appropriate discipline in the operation of the school'" (505).

The Supreme Court clarified student speech rights and restrictions in two subsequent cases, *Bethel v. Fraser* (478 US 675 [1986]) and *Hazlewood v. Kuhlmeier* (484 U.S. 260, [1988]):

"First Amendment rights of students in the public schools are not automatically the same as rights of adults in other settings" (*Hazlewood*, 260).

Schools need not "tolerate student speech that is inconsistent with its basic educational mission" (*Hazlewood*, 260).

Public schools may "prohibit the use of vulgar and offensive terms in public discourse" (*Bethel*, 676).

Prior to BONG HiTS, the Supreme Court hadn't considered whether free speech rights extended to student speech concerning drug use. Ultimately, the court rejected Frederick's claim that his banner was nonsense, and decided that "school officials in this case did not violate the First Amendment by confiscating the pro-drug banner and suspending Frederick" (393).

QUESTIONS

1. *Tinker v. Des Moines* (1969) established that student speech could be prohibited if it "materially and substantially interfered with the requirements of appropriate discipline in the operation of school." What kinds of disruption do you think meet the *Tinker* test?

2. In *Morse v. Frederick* (2007), the Court concluded that schools can prohibit "speech that can reasonably be regarded as encouraging illegal drug use." They reasoned that pro-drug speech is "inconsistent with [schools'] basic educational mission." What other categories of speech might violate the "basic educational mission" of public schools, even if those have not yet made it to the Supreme Court?

3. The Court's decision in *Morse v. Frederick* (2007) was split, 5-4. Justice John Paul Stevens, dissenting from the majority

opinion, wondered whether the Court had correctly set the right boundaries for student speech:

> Under the Court's reasoning, must the First Amendment give way whenever a school seeks to punish a student for any speech mentioning beer, or indeed anything else that might be deemed risky to teenagers? While I find it hard to believe the Court would support punishing Frederick for flying a "WINE SiPS 4 JESUS" banner—which could quite reasonably be construed either as a protected religious message or as a pro-alcohol message—the breathtaking sweep of its opinion suggests it would. (446)

Do you think a banner reading "WINE SiPS 4 JESUS" would be protected speech at school? What about "DRiVING TOO FAST 4 JESUS"? Why, or why not?

FURTHER READINGS AND RESOURCES

Bullying and harassment:
U.S. Department of Health & Human Services resources for educators. www.stopbullying.gov

Classroom management 101:
Sabornie, E., & Espelage, D., Eds. (2023). *Handbook of classroom management.* London: Routledge.

Classroom management strategies:
Lemov, D. (2021). *Teach like a champion 3.0: 63 Techniques that put students on the path to college.* San Francisco: Jossey-Bass. https://teachlikeachampion.org

Effective teaching with culturally and linguistically diverse students:
Hammond, Z. (2014). *Culturally responsive teaching and the brain: Promoting authentic engagement and rigor among culturally and linguistically diverse students.* Thousand Oaks, CA: Corwin.

NOTES

1. Aside: check out the expression of the student at the bottom left. Like: *Really? Is this necessary?* We love you, Slightly Grumpy Kid.

2. Lots of directions all at once, right? Many students would struggle to remember all of them, especially since they describe what to do *after* a quiz, which they have not yet completed. Good idea: write the main points on the board so students have a reference when they finish the quiz.

3. Finger claws 101: www.youtube.com/watch?v=Qzeaw7UXscw. *Wait . . . was Lillian making those during math . . . ?*

4. Humor in the classroom: love it. Humor can make class joyful and reinforce relationships. Be cautious with sarcasm, though. Sarcasm can confuse students (who may think you're serious). Avoid sarcasm until you have secure positive relationships with your students. And don't use sarcasm that could cause shame if misinterpreted. YES: "Socks and sandals, which I am modeling now, are the *pinnacle* of fashion." NO: "Way to go, Natasha-who-just-spilled-water-all-over-the-place" (*rolls eyes*) . . .

5. And because this is some sort of Law of Teaching—*no one was ever absent* from sixth period. I pretty much guarantee the same for you. Whichever class or students you find most difficult (ahem: whoever "*challenges you to become a better teacher*") will always, always be in class.

6. I'm teasing. Abe Wheeler may have just told everyone, "Hey! Look out the window, see if you can spot the tree I'm drawing!" There's another great photograph on the Oregon BLM's Flickr page wherein Abe Wheeler is laughing and *every single student* is rapt. Abe Wheeler has skills.

Lesson plan (template)*

Grade/subject/period:

Lesson (title or number or essential question):

Standard(s) (state or local):

Student learning objectives (SLOs):

Assessment(s) linked to SLOs:

Resources / materials needed:

Differentiation / adaptations / modifications:

Lesson timeline

Students		*Teacher*	
Entry	Pick up do-now, be in seat with pencil before bell.	Entry	Greet students in hallway. Enter room at bell.
0.00-3.00	Place homework @ top right desk corner, complete do-now.	0.00-3.00	Circulate, check HW for completion, take attendance.
3:00-8:00	Check HW answers @ front, ask questions as needed.	3:00-8:00	Respond to questions @ front, model #4 with edited numbers.
Etc.		Etc.	

*Adapt as needed. Try to keep the "Lesson Timeline" on a single page so you can refer to it during class without shuffling/scrolling.

8

Assessment

How Will I Know If Students Are Learning What They Should?

Figure 8.1. Cartoon illustration. *Source:* Illustration by P. C. Vey. Used with permission.

"*This may burn a little.*"

You're the doctor, the patient is your student, the giant magnifying glass is an assessment. Obviously, this will be unpleasant.

Why is this funny? Part of it is the deadpan delivery, I think. The equipment is massive, the risk insufficiently described—and, well, surely there are other ways of finding out whatever it is we're trying to find out?

Many teachers and students feel the same way about assessment: that it's intrusive, that it's painful, that it may not be worth whatever information it provides. My goal in this chapter is to help you understand why we assess—and to help you understand the various tools we can use in so doing. As I hope you'll see, you won't always need the giant magnifying glass.

Public schools assess students frequently. The most widely known assessments are end-of-year standardized tests. Just so we're clear up front: "standardized" doesn't mean "bad"; it means "administered and scored in a consistent way so we can compare data." Standardized tests are widely criticized—but as you'll see, they're not the only kind of tests, and they're not in themselves problematic. More problematic is what schools and teachers *do* in the name of such tests.

Since 2005–2006, all U.S. states and territories have given standardized tests at the end of each year to students in grades 3–8, and then again at least once in high school (Every Student Succeeds Act, 2015; 34 C.F.R. § 200.2). These tests are intended to tell us whether students have mastered grade level standards. Many teachers hate these tests, which I think is misguided. An end-of-year test linked to grade level standards makes sense if we care about what students know and can do. What's more justifiably hated is that many states and territories have tried to use tests as leverage to somehow force school improvement. Rather than investing resources in ways that help students *learn more* (hence earn better test scores), we have done bananas things like *teach less* (cutting art and music and science and social studies, or restricting what's taught to just focus on tested standards) and *threaten more* (cutting budgets or positions if scores don't improve). It turns out that teaching less and threatening more doesn't improve student achievement (Koretz, 2017; Schneider & Hutt, 2023).

Testing—and the broader concept of assessment—is neither good nor bad on its own. It's *necessary* if you want to be an effective teacher. If you teach in ways that fail to regularly assess student knowledge and skills, you're going to be missing vital information for instruction—and your students will learn less because of it. The point of this chapter in four words:

Assessment enables good teaching.

We don't actually need to care (much) about test scores on their own. We *do* need to care about what individual students know and can do. We care because it is our job to help students learn. But we can't read minds. All we can do is observe behaviors—things like what students write down, or what students do when we ask them to perform a task (Koretz, 2008). How can we know if a student understands a lesson or concept? Well . . . we have to ask them, via class work, homework, a quiz or test. And we may find ourselves asking them very specific, sometimes seemingly minor things, like the immediate cause of World War I.

[*The assassination of Archduke Francis Ferdinand!* I just wrote that *without* Google! (Thanks, middle school social studies!) Wait. Why did it matter that he got assassinated? Um . . . ah, shoot. Wikipedia tells me . . . he was actually "Franz" and had this super-long name that doesn't ring any bells: *Archduke Franz Ferdinand Carl Ludwig Joseph Maria of Austria* (Wikipedia, n.d.). And wow, he had an epic mustache . . .]

Why this particular digression? Because there's something important going on here from an assessment standpoint. We often ask students to recall specific facts or procedures on assessments. A common criticism of asking students to recall facts is that the internet is invariably better at recall, calculation, and translation than any human. That's true. Another criticism of asking students to recall specific facts is that those facts may be unimportant (e.g., in the "real world," whatever might be meant by the term). It's true that I don't really need to know Franz Ferdinand's full name now, as an adult. But . . . back in middle school, I needed to learn facts and figures in social studies class, including about Franz Ferdinand, in order to understand broader concepts of geopolitical alliances and the forces that have shaped modern Europe. De-emphasizing facts can do long-term damage to students. There's no path to conceptual understanding that avoids specific knowledge. There is no understanding war (generally) without learning about specific wars.

We can't ask everything on assessments, of course: the domain of knowledge and skills that we care about is just too vast. Most teachers are well aware of this. We can't ask students to do "all subtraction problems ever" or to read "all possible 7th-grade books." We need to decide, at some point, if a student has done *enough* subtraction *well enough* to move on . . . or if they need still more instruction and practice. There's a lot of judgment involved in assessment (and, eventually, the instruction that follows).

Further complicating our lives, knowledge and skills rarely exist in isolation. Figure 8.2, an item from a recent 8th-grade New York State science test, shows how a single test question can require a wide range of knowledge and skills for a student to respond correctly (New York State Education Department, 2022):

Figure 8.2. New York State Grade 8 Intermediate-Level Science Test (June, 2022).
Source: Written Test, Released Item #8. New York State Education Department (2022, 5). Public domain.

> 8 The photograph below shows four different dogs. All four dogs belong to the same species. 
>
> The significant differences between these four dogs were caused by humans. These differences are best explained by the process of
>
> A biological adaptation
> B selective breeding
> C metamorphosis
> D regulation

What do students need to know and be able to do to respond correctly? Turns out, lots:

- Read in English

- Identify what's being asked (*maybe you noticed there's no question mark?*)

- Recognize that A–D are responses (of which one should be chosen)

- Recognize "significant" differences between the dogs (you probably noticed size differences between the dogs . . . does fluffiness count as a "significant" difference? Color? Tongues sticking out?)

- Recall vocabulary, including "species," "biological," "adaptation," "selective," "breeding," "metamorphosis" and "regulation"

- Decide which vocabulary "best explain[s]" the differences between the dogs

- Identify a correct choice (or eliminate the three item distractors)

- Respond on a separate answer sheet in the right place

Complicated, right? Be advised: we often assess a lot of knowledge and skill in addition to what we intend. That's neither good nor bad—it just is. The problem is unavoidable: what we want students to know and be able to do is vast, and classroom and assessment time is limited. Before moving into details, here's some key assessment vocabulary:

Assessment Vocabulary

We build assessments by *sampling* from broad *domains* of knowledge and skills. We present sets of *items* to students that allow us to draw *inferences* about mastery.

- Sampling: selecting representative parts of a domain to include on an assessment (for example, a subtraction assessment that includes number lines, base 10 blocks, expanded notation, and the U.S. standard algorithm)

- Domain: the broad range of knowledge and skills we want students to master (for example, "single- and double-digit subtraction")

- Items: prompts or questions to which students respond during an assessment (for example, "Show twelve minus seven on a number line")

- Inference: use of student performance on assessment items to make estimates about mastery of the domain (for example, "they got 100% on the quiz, therefore they have mastered single- and double-digit subtraction using various methods")

On the opposite page, Figure 8.3 shows a biologist is examining some rockweed on an intertidal flat in the Gulf of Alaska. Everything in the intertidal flat is the biologist's *domain:* the rockweed, the snails, the barnacles, the adorable hermit crabs, etc. Within that plastic rectangle (a quadrat), the biologist is counting various species. Once everything in the quadrat is counted, the biologist will pick it up, move down the shoreline, and count everything again. He's *sampling* repeatedly from the domain. Later, he'll use all those samples to draw *inferences* about what lives in the broader intertidal ecosystem. Notice that there's a lot of shoreline (domain) that the biologist won't examine. And there are a lot of other ecosystems (beyond the domain) the biologist won't examine. See the ocean in the background? That hillside, the snow-capped mountain? Those are different ecosystems—different domains—and they are not being sampled. They'll remain unknown. We do similar things in education. We can't assess everything. We choose a domain we care about, and we sample from it. We learn about things in the sample. We do not learn about things not in the sample.

Figure 8.3. A biologist examining a sample of brown algae (Fucus spp.), Gulf of Alaska. *Source:* Photo by Jim Pfeiffenberger, National Park Service. Public domain.

Sampling is easy to mess up. I learned this early in my high school teaching life because I hate grading and wanted not to do it ever. Especially essays. Those took *forever* to grade. So one year I decided to assign fewer essays. Problem solved! No piles of writing to grade! Except, of course, that the "problem" wasn't solved at all—I had just stopped sampling from parts of the domain that remained important. My students still needed to know how to write, but now I had no idea if any of them could.[1] When we assess, whatever's in the sample is the only thing we learn about. How many quadrats does that biologist need to examine to draw reasonable inferences about life in the intertidal flat? I have no idea. More than one? Less than a million? Most likely something like: "as many as he can get done during the two weeks on site the grant will cover"?

Drawing inferences about student knowledge and skills needs to be done carefully. The inferences we draw must be justified by the sample. The biologist above could reasonably draw an inference like "Rockweed was common in Gulf of Alaska intertidal flats on this date, also it's super slippery"—because those things were part of the sample. The biologist above could *not* reasonably draw an inference about the ocean, the hillside, the mountaintop, or Floridian beaches—because those were not part of the sample. It's the same in education: when I stopped assigning essays, I stopped being able to draw conclusions about student writing skills.

WHY WE ASSESS

It's worth considering why we assess. You probably remember taking tests or quizzes in school and then being assigned grades. Assessments *can* be connected to grading—but that's not their only or most important purpose. Below I'll outline several useful purposes for assessment:

- To guide instruction. This is the most important reason to assess students. Remember: *Assessment enables good teaching*. Because we can't read minds, we need to assess to find out what students know and can do. Whatever students don't know, we should teach. You should hold this purpose close to your teaching heart at all times. What do you need to know to plan tomorrow's lessons?

- To provide feedback. This is another central purpose for assessment. By "feedback," I mean more than just a number or letter. Ideally, teachers should provide feedback linked to learning standards. How does the student's work compare to the standard? Does it meet or exceed the standard? If not, why not? The most effective feedback tells students what to do next to improve (Griffiths et al., 2023).

- To describe learning. Learning = growth. Measuring it requires multiple assessments over time (and subtraction). A student scoring eleventy-seven on a first assessment and eleventy-twelve on a second gained five points' worth of knowledge or skill. Is that a lot of learning? It depends. What's being assessed? How much time elapsed? What learning standards are involved? Describing learning in classrooms usually involves giving a "pre-assessment," teaching, and then giving a "post-assessment." The terminology is awkward; they're both assessments. More accurate would be "Assessment before instruction about something" and "Assessment after instruction about something." Voilà, learning described.

- To characterize achievement. Often the main purpose of unit tests, final exams, and state tests. Achievement tests are usually linked to standards. Achievement tests can have a score (or range of scores) that suggest a student "meets standards" or is "proficient." A common secondary use of achievement testing is to compare the achievement of different students (or classes, schools, districts, etc.). For example, we can compare the performance of our students on end-of-year assessments to state- or territory-wide averages, potentially directing supports toward those who struggle.

- To establish placement. Common when students enter school or begin new academic programs. Students may complete an assessment in reading, for example, to determine their instructional level or grouping. This has also become routine in published ELA and mathematics curricula at the elementary level, particularly for programs that include personalized or adaptive interventions for students who struggle or are behind.

- To screen for disabilities or English language skills. In most districts, universal screening for disabilities is offered to all students entering kindergarten (or 1st grade) as a means to identify students who may require specialized supports. English language screening is also typically offered to students in any grade identified as living in a home that uses a language other than English. Usually a specialist does these screenings, not classroom teachers.

- To identify specific learning needs. These focused assessments follow screenings that raise concerns, or referrals from a parent or teacher. These are typically given by specialists like school psychologists, and may include I.Q. tests, achievement tests, or assessments of language, behavior, hearing, vision, motor, social, functional, and/or vocational skills. Teachers or parents may complete checklists or surveys as part of the process.

A last note before we get into details about how to assess in your classroom: good assessment is properly about *individuals*. Not groups. All the purposes of assessment listed above—guiding instruction, providing feedback, describing learning, and others—function at the individual level. You need to know how each student is doing to plan for tomorrow. Each student is going to take individual achievement tests. Each student deserves individual feedback on their work, and may need individual academic supports or extensions.

It's fine to have students work together when learning goals rely on students working together. For example, young students may need to develop turn-taking conversational routines, rather than monologuing about their dog and their baby sister and Sonic the Hedgehog and did you ever get anything lost in your nose because my uncle did? You can certainly put students in groups to practice turn-taking, but remember: *you still need to assess learning individually.* Did each student make progress on turn-taking? Don't try to assess ephemeral groups like "Sienna and Leon as a dyad." You need to assess Sienna. And you need to assess Leon. Avoid the temptation to consider groupwork a meaningful assessment. Yes, reviewing groupwork may be easier or faster than reviewing individual work. But . . . unless you can read minds (you cannot), it's impossible to figure out what each individual student learned from groupwork. Some teachers have students submit "individual contribution" statements to groupwork. That's a modest improvement . . . but requires avoidable gymnastics. If students are doing something worthwhile, why can't every student do it? *Teach* with groups as you wish, *assess* individuals.

THE ASSESSMENT CYCLE

How and what you assess will vary by grade level and subject area—but there are core practices for all teachers, whether you're teaching "how to hold a pencil" or "statistics." Remember life cycles in biology? Frogs lay eggs, which develop into tadpoles, which develop into adult frogs who lay eggs, etc. Assessment and instruction is . . . well, not precisely like the life of a frog but operates in similar fashion. It's a cycle. We identify standards, write objectives, develop assessments, teach, assess . . . and then use assessment data to guide our next set of objectives. Here's the cycle:

Identify the state or local standard. Standards are often complex and can take days, weeks, or months for students to master. How much time to spend on a standard depends on the standard, and what students already know and can do. For example, a standard like "Makes good cookies" could be mastered in a few lessons if your students already knew how to bake and just needed some practice with cookies specifically. For students who have never read recipes or cracked eggs, "Makes good cookies" could take much longer. Almost all standards, including "Makes good cookies," require skills or knowledge that aren't stated but are necessary. For example, "Makes good cookies" probably includes skills like reading recipes, following multi-step directions, using measuring cups and spoons, mixing dough and forming cookies, operating an oven, cleaning up, and making judgments about "goodness" of various cookies. All of those skills may need to be taught and assessed. For most standards, you'll want students to have multiple attempts so you have clear evidence they have met the standard. Consider "Makes good cookies." Let's say your student makes excellent chocolate chip cookies one Friday. Have we accomplished "Makes good cookies?" Was that beginner's luck? Can they make frosted sugar cookies? Chocolate crinkles? Are they wise enough to never put raisins in any cookies ever?

Write student learning objectives (for each lesson). Good student learning objectives are observable behaviors—speaking, writing, doing, etc. What are the observable behaviors that would convince you a student has mastered part or all of a standard? For example, if the standard "Makes good cookies" suggests that cookies should not include little bits of eggshell (*ew*), then a reasonable student learning objective might be:

> Students will crack an egg into a bowl using Egg Farmers of Canada technique ("Crack on a flat surface, not the edge of your bowl"; eggs.ca).

You can't have a dozen student learning objectives in each lesson. I'd recommend *one* student learning objective per lesson. Maybe two. Any more, and you're going to struggle to assess all of your students during or immediately following the lesson. And if you don't quickly assess, you'll have no basis to adjust instruction tomorrow.

Develop assessments. These should emerge from the student learning objectives. *Assess every objective, every student.* Why? If you don't assess everyone, you're just guessing about who learned anything. Try to assess quickly, either during instruction or immediately following (via student work during class, at the end of the lesson, or on homework). Good homework has a lot of potential for reinforcing learning (Bempechat, 2019; Cooper, 2006; Canadian Council on Learning, 2009); bad homework wastes everyone's time (Wexler, 2019). One problem with using homework as an assessment is that the *timing* is tricky for adjusting instruction. If you assign homework Monday and collect it Tuesday . . . you just missed your chance to adjust Tuesday's lesson. I'd mostly avoid homework as an assessment, at least during your first few years (give homework for other reasons). Your assessments do not need to be complicated. An obvious assessment for egg-cracking would be . . . students cracking eggs while you rate technique (egg-cracking could also be peer-rated or self-rated—provide a rubric, collect results).

Write a lesson plan. Include standards, objectives, and assessments in your plan.

Teach the lesson. Do your plan.

Assess. Ideally, during the lesson or shortly after.

Analyze data. As quickly as possible. You don't need in-depth statistics. Try to review data before the next day, because you may need to adjust your plans. Where were students successful? Where did they struggle? Do they need more practice, different practice, re-teaching?

What supports will you provide students who didn't master one or more objectives?[2]

Adjust instruction. This is the goal of most assessment. Ideally, the day after an assessment would start with whatever instruction students needed. A different teaching approach? More practice? You may need to revisit some or all of the same student learning objective(s) as the day prior.

And . . . *repeat*, until each objective or standard has been mastered. Here's the process in graphic format:

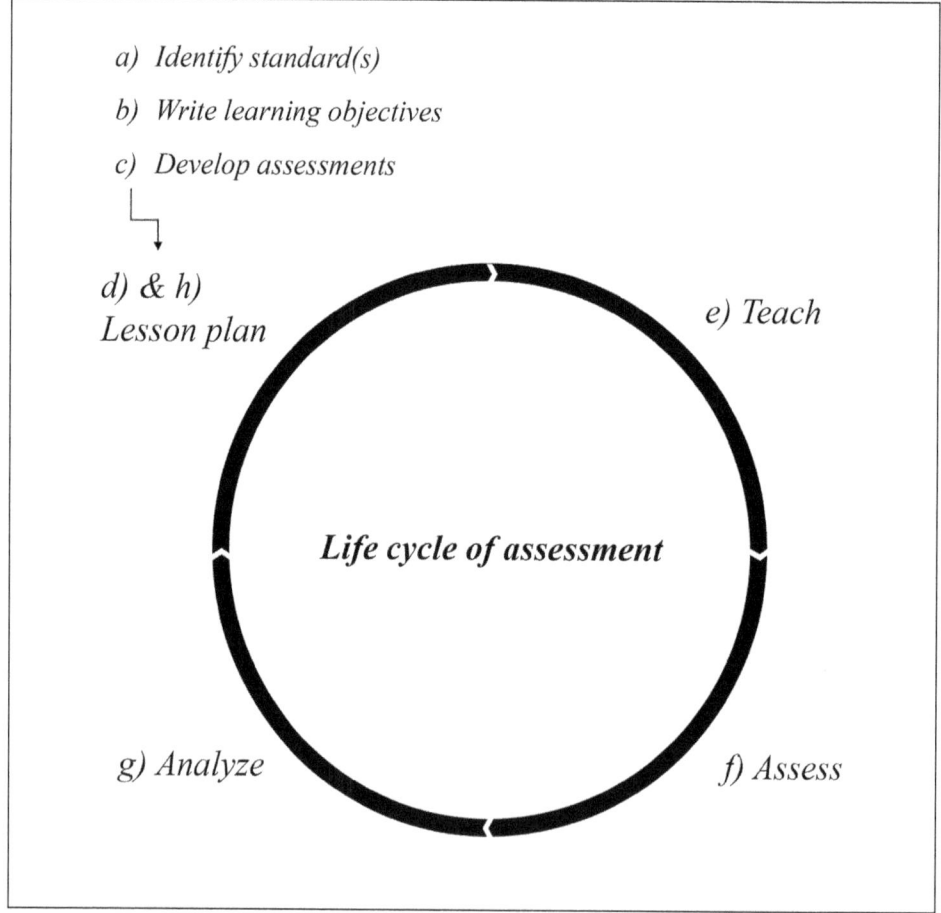

Figure 8.4. Life cycle of assessment. *Source:* Created by the author.

Whatever students need to learn, you should assess—and then you should use data to guide what and how you teach next. Be advised: you won't do all of this perfectly your first year. It can feel overwhelming just keeping up with planning day by day. Just don't be that teacher who plows through curriculum—student learning be damned—because you're following a predetermined curriculum calendar. We assess to guide our instruction. If we're just going to ignore the results, why bother assessing in the first place?

RESPONSE TO INTERVENTION (RTI) AND MULTI-TIERED SYSTEMS OF SUPPORT (MTSS)

Many school districts have formal processes for collecting and using assessment data. Two common models in U.S. public schools are "Response to Intervention (RTI)" and "Multi-Tiered System(s) of Support (MTSS)." RTI/MTSS models are intended to identify students who struggle with academics or other areas such as social or behavioral skills, and to provide them with supports ("interventions") that vary by intensity. The most developed RTI/MTSS models are in elementary grades ELA and mathematics. As far as I know, no one's doing RTI/MTSS models for 4th-grade science or U.S. History. Be advised: RTI/MTSS models aren't any single thing; there's substantial variation by district. Nor is it entirely clear whether RTI/MTSS models are effective. One of the better-designed studies of RTI systems for early literacy (Balu et al., 2015) found that placing students in Tier II or Tier III interventions (which theoretically *support* students) either *harmed* learning or had no impact. Bad RTI/MTSS models might simply be segregating struggling students from others in the name of "intervention." RTI/MTSS models are common, however, so you should at least recognize the terminology involved.

RTI AND MTSS TIERS (ADAPTED FROM UNDERSTOOD FOR ALL, N.D.)

Tier I: The whole class. Also known as "general education." Where most students spend the most time.

Tier II: Small group interventions. The first level of intervention for students who struggle (15–20% of students; Bailey, 2020). Usually, small groups of students in Tier II will work with a teacher *in addition to* receiving Tier I instruction. Many schools adjust schedules to provide regular "intervention" times for teachers to lead Tier II groups.

Tier III: Intensive interventions. The most involved level of intervention, for students who struggle despite Tier I and Tier II supports (3–5% of students; ibid.). Tier III may be delivered in separate classroom settings, like resource rooms, and may be delivered by teachers or other specialists.

RTI and MTSS Model Components

- Universal screening. Every student at school is screened in an area of interest. Most U.S. public schools screen students for hearing and vision problems. RTI/MTSS models usually also screen for early literacy and numeracy, speech, social and behavioral skills, fine and gross motor skills, and other areas of interest (such as communication at home).

- Benchmark testing. Common in elementary and middle grades ELA and mathematics, typically three times per year (fall, winter, and spring). Not common in other academic or non-academic areas. Benchmark assessments are often linked to grade-level standards and can help schools identify students who are behind. Benchmark assessments are typically computer administered (e.g., NWEA MAP, aimsweb+, and Renaissance Star). Benchmark testing usually establishes the tier for each student (see previous page).

- Progress monitoring. Regular assessment of students in areas of interest (e.g., reading fluency). Usually, progress monitoring is brief and done frequently (daily, weekly, or biweekly). The idea is to see whether students are making progress (growth or learning) over time, especially in response to interventions. Progress monitoring assessments are often included in commercial ELA and math curricula or can be purchased as a separate assessment suite (e.g., i-Ready, iXL).

- Growth modeling. Progress monitoring data can be charted to show how much students are growing (learning) over time. Teachers can see whether students are learning quickly (steep slope) or slowly (shallow slope). Students learning slowly (or not at all) may not be "responding" to the current instructional tier or intervention being provided. Growth models can help inform decisions to keep, adjust, or abandon instructional supports or interventions.

- Evidence-based interventions. "Interventions" = curriculum and instruction teachers do with students who struggle. In theory, interventions are "evidence-based" and are of modest duration, usually less than twelve weeks (National Center on Intensive Intervention, n.d.). Interventions are the most neglected component of RTI/MTSS models. There is little consensus among educators concerning what "evidence-based" may mean. Few districts have extensive catalogues of intervention materials or training for teachers to use them. Districts often provide intervention materials in just two areas, early literacy and mathematics.

ASSESSMENT DURING CLASS

If you attended a U.S. public school, you likely completed lots of assessments. You might remember end-of-year state tests, the SATs, or Scary Unit Tests. You might not have noticed the most common assessments your teachers relied on: the work you did in or after class. As a rule, student work is the most useful means teachers have for determining what students are learning, for providing feedback, and for figuring out what to do tomorrow. Here are examples of useful assessments students may complete during class:

BELL WORK (AKA "DO NOW" OR OTHER ENTRY ROUTINE)

The primary goal of bell work is to transition students into class quickly while preparing for instruction. You can also use bell work to assess what students remember from prior lessons, or what they already know about a topic for future lessons. Keep bell work brief and tied to the lesson. I love images, maps, memes, and cartoons because they lend themselves to quick responses (see Medori, 2023). Figure 8.5 provides an example of useful bell work:

> *Why is this meme [fig. 8.5] funny? Explain in three sentences.* (Meme circulated following Russia's invasion of Ukraine that began February 24, 2022):

Figure 8.5. We need air support (meme)! *Source:* Starecat.com (2022). Public domain.

STUDENT WORK DURING CLASS

How do we figure out what students know? We ask questions. Two hundred years ago, teachers called on students one at a time (or had them respond at the board). We still do both. We can get some good information about student understanding by asking—but clearly we can't ask *every* student *every* possible question. There's not enough time, and trying to do so would be repetitive and boring. What to do? We can distribute questions throughout class, *randomizing* who responds. Randomizing gives all students a chance to respond, and prevents us from being misled about student knowledge by a few students (who may already know everything . . . or may know nothing). One way to randomize is to write every student's name on a popsicle stick, put the sticks in a cup, and pull one out each time you have a question. You can do the same electronically (e.g., Classpoint or ABCya).

Even better than calling on *one* student at a time is calling on the *entire class* at a time. You just need a way to see responses quickly. Options include:

1. Small whiteboards—my favorite. Students write or draw on a small whiteboard and when prompted hold up for teacher review. Good for spontaneous questions, also avoids (most) peer influence because responses are silent and aimed at you. Modest expense (mostly replacing markers).

2. Fingers—students close their eyes (to avoid peer influence) and hold out a hand with a response (thumbs up/sideways/down or 1–5). Works best with Y/N, agree/disagree, and multiple-choice items. Good for spontaneous questions. Free.

3. Movement—students move to a part of the room to indicate response. Also known as "four corners" if you ask a question and provide four possible answers ("Response A in the corner by my desk, Response B in the corner near Natalya, etc. . . ."). Subject to peer influence since students see each other moving. Particularly useful for opinion polls or sleepy classes. Free. Downsides include time loss (students moving around the classroom burns time) and potential management challenges.

4. Electronic responses—if your students have 1:1 devices or use their phones in class. Students can respond individually, and you can display individual or collective responses up front. Examples include Kahoot!, Google classroom polls,

and Quizizz. Requires administration—setting up accounts/access. Best for review, since these often rely on pre-planned questions. Usually requires more setup and management than lower-cost options.

Anything your students write or complete in class can be an assessment. Most often, teachers collect work and evaluate or provide written feedback after class. Be advised: grading and feedback take time. One key decision you'll need to make about any written work: *do I collect this?* Collecting work buys you time to review and provide feedback. Feedback is especially important in areas where additional work is needed for learning or improvement.

NOTES ON COLLECTED WORK

1. Give it back tomorrow. If the goal of collecting work is guiding instruction, you need to review it immediately, or it was pointless to collect. If a goal of collecting work is providing a score or feedback, students need that information as close to instruction as possible. There's a decay in relevancy the longer you wait.

2. Or don't give it back at all. Just because students did it doesn't mean they want it back. If you met instructional goals in class *and* you got useful assessment data—that can be enough. Give stuff back if it's graded or has feedback, and recycle the rest.

3. Answer keys and rubrics save time. Collected work is simple to evaluate when it's right or wrong; you just need an answer key (consider automated mechanisms like ZipGrade or PaperScorer). For work requiring judgment (essays, projects, multi-step problems, etc.) develop a rubric. A rubric forces you to decide what's important. A rubric also saves you from writing "Provide more evidence" or "Cite sources for this claim" a thousand times on a hundred papers. Just circle the appropriate box.

4. Pick and choose what gets detailed feedback. This may depend on your student numbers. Elementary teachers can ordinarily provide feedback on most work daily. Middle and high school teachers, who may teach five or six times as many students, often cannot. What can reasonably get done? Can you pick one assignment for detailed feedback each week?

Good news: not everything needs to be collected, or merits feedback or a grade. One major goal when looking at student work is finding out what students know, which you can often do by quickly looking at their work. Not collecting work buys you time to do all the other parts of your job. If you already know how they did and you're not going to write a bunch of feedback on it, you don't need to collect it. Here are three approaches to *not* collecting-and-returning student work; all require you to prepare a key or rubric that defines proficiency:

1. Teacher observation/checklist. Circulate during class with a clipboard or your laptop. Mark down whose work meets the objective and whose does not. Useful information for tomorrow, accomplished. This is super-efficient. But it's not a panacea. I've seen teachers over-rely on "teacher observation" as an assessment strategy, and it can be code for "not trying that hard." The key thing is that you need to observe the *work* (not the students). And the work has to be meaningful; it has to provide you evidence for meeting the student learning objective(s). If you just print out a crossword and wander around marking down who's done, you're not "assessing." You're "wasting everyone's time."

2. Self-score. Go over the work together as a class or provide a rubric or key for students to self-assess. You can provide colored pencils for notes and corrections. You can also prompt them to summarize strengths and weaknesses (which you can review quickly after class).

3. Trade papers. As above, but students trade with a peer. One advantage is that partners can review together after scoring. One challenge is that you don't want to embarrass students or ask them to assign grades. Pay attention to partners, and don't assign grades to traded work.

EXIT TICKETS (AKA "TICKET OUT THE DOOR")

The purpose of an exit ticket is to determine whether students mastered the learning objective(s) that day. These too can be brief. Figure 8.6 (opposite page) shows an example from a 9th-grade biology class. You can get good insights into what students learned during class via brief exit tickets, even for complex or involved lessons.

Figure 8.6. Item adapted from New York State Regents Living Environment Test (January, 2023), released Item #20. *Source:* New York State Education Department (2023, 5). Public domain.

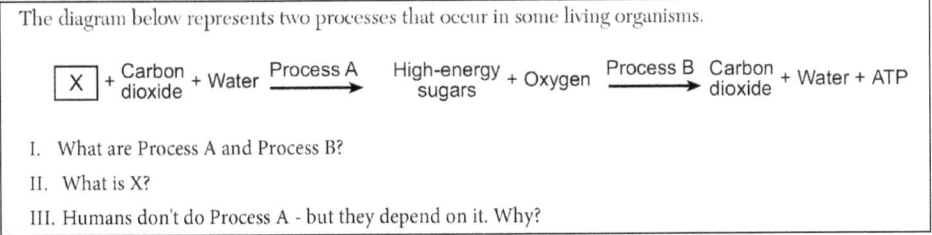

I. What are Process A and Process B?
II. What is X?
III. Humans don't do Process A - but they depend on it. Why?

Student work is the heart of classroom assessment because it gives you the information you need to adjust tomorrow's lesson. Other kinds of assessments, described below, are often less about adjusting instruction, and more about characterizing achievement or generating grades.

SUMMATIVE ASSESSMENTS

A summative assessment is intended to determine whether a student has mastered standards. Summative assessments are what most teachers think about in the context of assessments—things like quizzes, tests, papers, projects or performances. Summative assessments are often also used by teachers to assign grades. Here are three major types of summative assessments you'll want to consider using:

1. Performance (e.g., lab, competition, project or task). Students *do* something; the assessment focus is on skills. Elementary, art, P.E., language, science teachers and coaches of all kinds regularly give performance assessments where students do, say or listen to things. Can stretch over multiple days (part A on Thursday, part B on Friday, etc.). Often scored using a rubric. Can be logistically challenging, especially with high student numbers. If you can't have everyone do a performance task at once (because it involves equipment or 1:1 work), you can develop an assessment with multiple components—some performance, some written. Teachers often rotate students through stations to assess multiple performance skills. Some teachers have students do performance components at home (e.g., students can record themselves speaking French phrases) to preserve class time. Usually the most enjoyable type of summative assessment.

2. Constructed response.

   a. *Short answer.* Students write something brief; the assessment focus is on knowledge, perhaps incidentally writing or drawing or calculating, depending on content. A darling of ELA, math, social studies, science and math teachers everywhere. Can include drawings and diagrams—the basic idea is to ask a relatively focused question (e.g., "To what genus and species do groundhogs belong?") and provide a space for response. May be scored with a key or rubric. Be aware that short answer items often involve (hence require assessment of) skills beyond content knowledge alone, such as writing or drawing.

   b. *Essay or extended response.* Students produce an in-depth response, often written. Usually intended to assess knowledge, heavily influenced by response format. Essays invariably require and assess reading and writing skills along with knowledge. Other response formats (video or audio recording, drawing, lab reports, art portfolios, etc.) likewise assess skills specific to format. For example, if students must record video responses, you're also going to be assessing technical skills (like audio- and video-recording) in addition to the knowledge you care about. Usually involves open-ended prompts (e.g., "Why are groundhogs better than squirrels?"). Often scored with a rubric.

3. Selected response (Multiple choice, True/False, matching, etc.). Students choose a response from provided alternatives. Focused on assessing knowledge. Many different formats. Efficient to score. One issue is that selected response items encourage (and reward) guessing, which may impact reliability. Another issue is score compression; for example, on True/False (T/F) items, there are only two possible responses. Anyone can get a 50% on the "T/F Test of Brain Surgery"—so the interpretation of scores can be complex.[3]

Teachers often dismiss selected response as useless or brain-dead, because "the answer is just sitting there" or "they don't measure creativity." I'm not sure either critique merits abandoning selected response entirely. I like how efficient selected response items can be. Efficiency saves time—both student and teacher time. We only get about 180 days each year. Time spent on assessments is time we can't use for everything else. During the time students take to respond to one constructed response item, they might be able to respond to ten or twenty selected response items. More items can also mean better sampling from the domain.

The other thing I like about selected response items is that they can force us to be more objective than other item types (where we might score responses leniently or interpret student responses on the basis of prior student knowledge rather than evidence). Every day of your teaching life will require judgment (*How much time should we spend on this? Should I ask Thomas why he is licking his calculator?*) . . . but whether students have specific knowledge or skills should be reasonably clear. Of course multiple-choice tests won't tell us everything we want to know. Neither will essays or interpretive dances. You're going to have to use a variety of assessments all year.

THE MEANING OF GRADES (A CAUTIONARY TALE?)

The main purpose of grades is communication. Students (and families) have one overarching question about school: *how am I doing?* That's a big, complicated question.

Most schools report grades via report cards or student information systems. What gets reported varies, but letter grades (A–F) and number grades (0–100) are common. Grades in elementary schools are usually reported by subject (e.g., "Reading" or "Mathematics"); grades in middle and high schools are usually reported by class (e.g., "English 8" or "Chemistry in the Community").

What the letter or number *means* may be less clear than we think. Take Malia the Fictional Student's grade of, say, 85 for the first quarter of 8th-grade ELA (September—November). There may be a sharp divide between what Malia and her mom think an 85 means, and what it means to the teacher (see Figure 8.7):

Figure 8.7. Differing interpretations of a numerical grade. *Source:* Created by the author.

MALIA the FICTIONAL STUDENT	
Grade 8, English Language Arts, 1st quarter	
Assigned grade: 85 (out of 100)	
What Malia and her mom think the 85 means	*What the 85 means to the teacher*
<ul><li>Meeting 85% of whatever the 8th grade ELA standards are</li><li>Must be proficient at reading and writing</li><li>Doing pretty well; should be ready for high school…</li></ul>	<ul><li>Earned 85% of available points for attendance, participation, classwork, projects and papers, quizzes and tests</li><li>Doesn't turn in homework, is often on her phone during class</li><li>Is doing OK… not as well as many other students (more effort needed)</li><li>It's the beginning of the year, the work has been easy, progress may be a concern</li><li>No grade-level standards completed yet</li></ul>

See the difference? Students and families often assume grades indicate proficiency in a grade or subject. Malia's grade of 85 suggests she's on track to meet 85% of the 8th-grade standards for ELA . . . right? But that's not usually (or only) what grades mean for teachers. Few teachers assign grades based on standards mastery alone (Schinske & Tanner, 2017). At a minimum, for "grades" and "proficiency" to mean the same thing, teachers would need to:

1. teach every state and local standard for the grade or subject area during the year—and *only* at the assigned grade level,

2. assess each state and local standard in ways that provide convincing evidence of mastery for each student—again, *only* at the assigned grade level, and

3. assign grades *exclusively* on the basis of assessment evidence collected.

Few teachers assign grades this way. We pack a lot of other purposes besides standards mastery into our day-by-day grading. Assigned grades often include a mix of attendance, behavior, participation, and student work sometimes only indirectly connected to grade-level standards. What our grades mean, exactly, can vary substantially by teacher. Students and parents can be easily (if accidentally) misled about how they are doing if they don't understand what grades do (and do not) communicate.

In recent years, some districts have adopted "standards-based grading," which explicitly links grade reporting to mastery of grade-level (or subject area) academic standards (Matthews, 2022). For example, a kindergarten standard may be "Writes numbers 0–20." A standards-based grade report would include a space for kindergarten teachers to report whether the student has met that standard or not. The approach has promise for improved clarity around what, exactly, grades mean with respect to proficiency (Kramer et al., 2023). Many districts, especially at the elementary level, also ask teachers to separately report measures of effort, habits, or behavior.

Your school district will have policies concerning grades and grade reporting—and you'll need to live with whatever they might be. Just be advised that what *you* think grades communicate and what your *students and families* think may be quite different. The best guidance I can offer is honesty and clarity. Explain what your grades do and do not mean. And always, always be cautious about misleading. Most reasonable humans assume a passing grade means "proficient for the grade or subject." If your grade means something else—why? What else do your students and families need to know about how they're doing?

WHAT TO DO AFTER ASSESSMENT

Teach, of course. Assessment data should help you figure out what to teach. After you assess—whether it's work from class that day or a major unit test—ask yourself two questions:

1. What does this tell me about student knowledge or skills?

2. What should I do next?

Ideally, your assessment data will tell you whether students mastered the student learning objectives for the lesson or unit (which should also tell you something about standards mastery). You'll almost always have mixed results; some students will do well, others will struggle, and a third group will be absent or turn in incomplete work (*argh*). Your challenge will be to consider both individual and group data: Where were students generally successful? Where did they struggle? Who didn't do the assessment? Your analysis does not need to be complex. It needs you to make judgment calls about proficiency, and whether you are comfortable with the evidence each student has provided over time. I won't pretend to solve any of the specifics you'll face. Here's one (rough) way to approach "What does this tell me?" based on assessment data:

1. Most students (≥75%) mastered the objective(s). Awesome. Move class on to the next learning objective—while also finding a way to re-teach and re-assess the few individual students who did not.

2. Fewer than most students (<75%) mastered the objective(s). Not quite there. Re-teach, while finding a way to engage and enrich the learning of those who got it.

3. Very few students (<25%) mastered the objective(s). Ouch. Reflect. What happened? Why did so few students learn what you'd hoped? Did you miss key prior learning? Pick the wrong instructional approach? When few of your students learn something, you can't just shrug and move along in the curriculum. Plowing ahead without mastery damages learning. You may need to revisit key concepts, terms and skills. No matter what: change your approach. Re-teach differently, use different materials, or have students practice differently.[4]

Assessment data will almost always tell you that there are students who need individualized supports, groups of students who need common supports, and lessons that need re-thinking or a different approach. Hence most teachers need to approach instruction in ways flexible enough to meet variable student needs. How and when can you re-teach your whole class, or small groups of students who need it, or provide individual supports either in class or beyond?

TEST PREP

Many of you will teach classes that include an end-of-year test. Sometimes stakes are attached to these tests, such as high school credit. Because you are human, and because you are responsible for classroom learning, you'll want your students to do well. One question you may face: What kind of preparation for testing is appropriate and useful?

My recommendation: *do as little test prep as possible*.

Don't make testing a big deal, don't spend a month preparing. Why not? Here's an analogy: annual medical checkups. A checkup is an assessment of our general health. We step on scales, have our temperature and blood pressure measured, pee in a cup, and discuss eating, sleeping, substance use and other habits with our doctors. Some of us lie—maybe about food or sex or what hurts. We all want to "pass"—to be told we're healthy. But we also want our doctors to find out if anything's wrong and tell us what to do about it. If we lie or try to mislead (for example, by walking around in plastic wrap and losing ten pounds of water weight the day prior), we're not actually healthier. Our doctor may think we're fine ("I totally never drink alcohol!") while our liver rots and we miss a chance to get better.

Test prep is like trying to fudge an annual checkup. Maybe you can fool a test, but that doesn't mean you're healthier (or smarter). Remember basic testing theory—a test is a small sample of items that, in theory, represents a much broader domain of knowledge and skills that we actually care about. We care about what our students learn over the course of the entire year. We care about the *domain,* not the sample. We *may* care, within reason, about student performance on a single-day sample of items . . . but it's not the sample that's the big deal. It's the *domain*. Test prep gets this backwards; it emphasizes the sample while neglecting the domain.

Teachers sometimes spend huge chunks of class time on test prep rather than continued instruction—and may do so because that's what their schools expect. I've seen teachers in New York *stop teaching new things entirely* a month early so they can prepare for end-of-year Regents exams. That's a horror show. A month of test prep evaporates twenty days of instruction (11% of the year). What could you do with students if you had twenty extra days each year? My advice: skip the test prep and do those things instead. Your (smarter) students will thank you for it.

What about the argument that "good" test prep reviews and reinforces prior learning? There's an element of truth there—but the way to review and reinforce isn't at the end right before the test. It's all the way along as you go. Whatever's important in the domain will appear on the test—so just practice that knowledge and those skills throughout the year. Also recommended: Mixing prior knowledge and skills with new learning on assessments throughout the year. Second-quarter tests should include first-quarter material. Good assessment is cumulative. Why? Students with more practice remember things better (Willingham, 2021, "Is Drilling Worth It?").

There is one reason to do a small amount of test prep: unfamiliar formats. Often the format of the test itself is unfamiliar, or the items vary from how you typically assess in your classroom. If you always assign essays, but the test features a large number of multiple-choice items, students should practice doing some multiple-choice items. If the test features a specific constructed response format (for example, required use of evidence from multiple primary-source documents) or an interface they don't use in class, have students practice that. The proper focus for reasonable test prep isn't knowledge or skills; it's test and item format. You should be able to get that done by doing a single practice test before the real thing. Just one. And you can chop the practice test into parts and do them over time so you don't lose a full instructional day.

Don't overemphasize a single test. Remember the claim at the beginning of this chapter: *Assessment enables good teaching.* The bad news is that assessment can also enable bad teaching. One of the worst things we do in the name of testing is *domain restriction*. Rather than teaching the full range of knowledge and skills in a grade or subject area, teachers or schools may focus on a limited subset: whatever's on the test. No essay? *Don't worry about writing.* Nothing before the year 1400? *Skip ancient history.* No science, social studies, art or music? *Drop them; we need more time for literacy.* These actions are not the fault of evil people. They're *our* actions, often taken in good faith but resulting in real student harm. Daniel Koretz, professor of education at Harvard, summarizes:

> Ironically, our heavy-handed use of tests for accountability has also undermined precisely the function that testing is best designed to serve: providing trustworthy information about student achievement. [. . .] Standardized tests, *if properly used*, are a valuable and sometimes irreplaceable tool. They provide

us with important information that is not available from other sources. For example, we all know there is a troubling, large, and persistent gap in performance between white students and some minority students. How do we know that? Standardized tests. We've known for decades that American students don't perform as well in mathematics as students in many other countries. How do we know? Again, standardized tests. (2019, 18–20)

In the end, keep teaching central to how you think about assessment in the classroom. Assessment is a tool, one you'll use every day to find out what students know and can do. The best thing you can do is take that information seriously, and use it to prepare for tomorrow, and the next day, and the day after that. Do that, and the test at the end of the year will take care of itself.

How Will I Know If Students Are Learning What They Should?

You'll stay curious. You'll regularly give students tasks where they show you what they can do. You'll assess because you need to know what students know so you can teach better. You'll assess in lots of ways, including (*gasp!*) quizzes and tests. A worthy goal: assess every student on every standard every year. And please: avoid test prep.

SUPREME COURT CASE FOR DISCUSSION

Case: Students for Fair Admissions v. Harvard, 600 U.S. ___ (2023).
Link: www.supremecourt.gov/opinions/22pdf/20-1199_hgdj.pdf

Students for Fair Admissions (SFFA), a nonprofit legal activist group, filed suit against Harvard College (and the University of North Carolina) in 2014 over undergraduate admissions policies that included consideration of race. Here's how Harvard's process worked at that time:

> Every application is initially screened by a "first reader," who assigns scores in six categories: academic, extracurricular, athletic, school support, personal, and overall. [. . .] In the academic category, for example, a "1" signifies "near perfect standardized test scores and grades"; in the extracurricular category, it indicates "truly unusual achievement"; and in the personal category, it denotes "outstanding" attributes like maturity, integrity, leadership, kindness, and courage. [. . .] In assigning the overall rating, the first readers "can and do take an applicant's race into account." (*600 U.S. ___, 2*)

SFFA argued that this admissions process was unfair, particularly for Asian American students—because while they (on average) earned high standardized test scores, they were less likely than other racial groups to be offered admission (*Students for Fair Admissions v. Harvard*, 2023, 8). SFFA also argued that consideration of "personal" characteristics was unfair, because vague attributes like "leadership" or "kindness" could be used to discriminate against entire groups of students (such as Asian Americans). SFFA's core claim was that the inclusion of race as a factor violated the Equal Protection Clause of the Fourteenth Amendment: "No State shall make or enforce any law which shall abridge the privileges or immunities of citizens of the United States; nor shall any State deprive any person of life, liberty, or property, without due process of law; nor deny to any person within its jurisdiction the equal protection of the laws" (U.S. Const. amend. XIV, § 1). In a 6-3 decision, the U.S. Supreme Court agreed with SFFA (600 U.S. ___ [2023]). The Court noted that "Race is a determinative tip for" a significant percentage "of all admitted African American and Hispanic applicants" and that "Harvard's consideration of race has resulted in fewer admissions of Asian-American students" (ibid., 2–7).

The decision itself is important. But I want you to consider a side discussion that emerged during arguments. The Supreme Court asked SFFA to outline a process for selective college admissions that wouldn't involve race. SFFA suggested increased reliance on "objective" measures such as grades and standardized test scores (SFFA Petitioner brief, 2022). SFFA was not alone in suggesting the use of test scores. In 2022, the Pew Research Center found that 85% of Americans thought test scores should be a factor in college admissions (2022).

QUESTIONS

1. Why are test scores often considered more "objective" than high school grades?

2. To what extent is the inclusion of personal characteristics like "kindness" or "leadership" fair during selective admissions processes?

3. Standardized tests like the SAT have shown score gaps by race for generations (Reeves & Halikias, 2017). To what extent is the inclusion of standardized test scores fair during selective admissions processes?

4. When, if ever, do you think the use of race as a factor during college admissions is fair?

FURTHER READINGS AND RESOURCES

Assessment theory:
Koretz, D. (2008). *Measuring up: What educational testing really tells us.* Cambridge, MA: Harvard University Press.

Better classroom assessments:
Terada, Y. (2021). www.edutopia.org/article/how-design-better-tests-based-research

Giving feedback:
Brookhart, S. (2017). *How to give effective feedback to your students*, 2nd edition. Alexandria, VA: Association for Supervision & Curriculum Development.

Using assessments to guide instruction:
Bambrick-Santoyo, P. (2019). *Driven by data 2.0.* Hoboken, NJ: Wiley.

NOTES

1. Actually, I *did* know. They couldn't. That's why essays took *forever* to grade. I prioritized my preferences over their needs. Bad teacher.

2. Don't forget students who miss class! Anyone not in class (and not assessed) . . . didn't meet the objective(s). This may seem obvious, but attendance is a big deal. It is nearly impossible for us to help students learn when we can't figure out what they know. All the more reason for building good relationships, encouraging attendance, and developing remote-access tools so students can continue learning and assessment from anywhere, including home.

3. Re: score compression: on True/False assessments, the possible range of scores isn't 0–100%, it's 50–100%. Why? There are only two possible responses. Zero knowledge / random guessing produces an average score of 50%. Knowing everything should yield a score of 100%. So . . . someone scoring a 75% knows . . . half the stuff? Weird math, right? Multiple-choice items have similar compression issues; someone who knows nothing can score 25% via random guessing (if items all have four responses).

4. I hope it's clear these bins are arbitrary. Maybe for you it should be ≥90% = *most*, <90% = *not enough*, and <50% = *very few*.

9

Law and Ethics
How Can I Get Fired?

School law and ethics are complex—more so than speed limits or shoplifting. They can also be blunt instruments—sometimes too blunt to do a good job with the young people we teach. Here's an example: a school where I worked in rural Alaska provided free breakfast to every student every day. Breakfast was a big deal because most families in the community had limited incomes. The school district told schools to enforce a rule: *students must be at school at the beginning of the day in order to eat.* School started at 7:30 a.m. The intent of the rule, I think, was to encourage good attendance (and hence promote learning). But there were *always* students who got to school late and missed breakfast. A kindergartener who couldn't find their gloves. A 3rd-grader whose parents were still asleep. A couch-surfing high school student. One thing I loved about the principal at that school was that he'd bend the breakfast rule when it needed bending. I'd see kids show up late, and the principal would ask if they'd eaten and send them on to class. Then the principal would walk down to the gymneteria and scare up whatever he could.[1] If hot food was still out, he'd grab that. Otherwise he'd grab fruit and cereal, a box of milk, and bring it down to the student in class. Yes, there was a clear rule with a clear consequence: *students must be at school at the beginning of the day in order to eat.* But I always thought it was the ethical thing for the principal to find a way to feed hungry kids who came to school, even if they didn't make it by 7:30 a.m. precisely.

I tell this story because school law and ethics are fundamentally about working with people, especially young people. People are complex. Sometimes law and ethics can tell us clearly what to do: take attendance, use approved curriculum, report child abuse. Sometimes they tell us clearly what *not* to do: sell band instruments to buy drugs (Sturtz, 2014), sponsor middle school fight clubs (Sentendrey, 2023). Occasionally, they tell us nothing with clarity. The right thing to do may not be obvious. Overall, this chapter is less "do this and ye shall not be fired," and more "think about these things and ye shall (potentially) do more good than harm." Of course, you'll also want to avoid messing up and getting fired or sued. Or fired *and* sued. Let's start with peeing (Figure 9.1). Why not?

Figure 9.1. Inclusive restrooms. *Source:* Photo by Cuningham. Saint Paul Public Schools (MN), St. Anthony Park Elementary School. Used with permission.

LIABILITY AND NEGLIGENCE

Teachers are mammals. Contrary to lore, teachers lack infinite bladder capacity. At some point during the year you're going to need to pee (or worse!) during class. It happens. What to do? Can you just tell your students to behave, zip down the hall, and hurry back?

No. Nope. Don't.

One important legal concept for teachers is *liability.* You (teachers and the school generally) are responsible for the welfare of students at all times. You're *liable* for what happens to them. Being liable for students means that you are responsible for supervising and keeping them safe at all times. The school's liability starts when buses pick kids up in the morning and ends when they drop kids off in the afternoon—and includes all times in between. You can't supervise students when you run down to the bathroom.

And, well, they're children. Unsupervised children have long histories of poor decisionmaking. It's part of why schools make sure there are always adults around whenever students are in the building. We can't prevent every bad thing from happening while supervising. Kids faceplant on the playground, break a wrist in P.E., get scruffy with each other. Schools have some incredibly dangerous things in them (pools, labs, shops, those giant finger-chopping paper cutters with two-foot-long blades, etc.). What matters is that adults are there to supervise, enforce rules, and try to prevent the preventable.[2]

Liability among teachers includes students in our classes, and also includes students we don't teach when we're assigned supervision duties (e.g., in hallways, the bus loop, the cafeteria). When we supervise the hallway, we're responsible for every single student walking by. When we supervise in the cafeteria, we're responsible for every single student in the cafeteria. Liability exists wherever we are: we're supposed to enforce rules, watch the kids, and do what we can to ensure safety. Here's a teaching commandment: *do not ever skip assigned supervision*. Go. You don't have to love it. You don't have to be the Greatest Hall Monitor of All Time. But you have to be there, every time. You're liable.

A second (related) legal concept is *negligence*. What happens if we don't show up for class when we're supposed to, or skip lunch duty, or don't tell that kid running down the hallway with scissors to knock it off? We may be *negligent*. Negligence is "the failure to behave with the level of care that a reasonable person would have exercised under the same circumstances" (Cornell Law School, 2023). Negligence is about failing to act. In school settings, a "reasonable person" understands that children can't simply be left to their own devices in institutional settings.

Not all acts of negligence result in harm. You might leave your kids alone in class and have nothing bad happen. You might also leave your kids alone and have them try to figure out what the electric pencil sharpener can and cannot sharpen, and someone goes home with one less digit. There are varying degrees of negligence, too: a construction trades teacher leaving students alone to figure out circular saws is doing worse than an English teacher leaving students alone to figure out *The Absolutely True Diary of a Part-Time Indian* (Alexie, 2009).

Anyway: major concepts to keep in mind throughout the chapter:

- Liability = responsibility.

- Negligence = failure to do your job.

So . . . what should you do when you need to pee? You'll have to find another school employee to supervise your students. It might mean relying on a classroom aide, grabbing a custodian or security guard, calling the office, or asking a teacher next door to cover for you. You could bring your students over to another classroom for a few minutes. You've just got to do something reasonable for the circumstances, which may vary. For example, if your principal stops by with a parent who wants to speak with you—it's reasonable to ask your principal to watch your students for a few minutes while you talk to the parent. If one of your students seriously cuts themselves in class (e.g., on a giant paper cutter), a reasonable person would hustle them down to the nurse as quickly as possible. Reasonable in this second case might mean zipping down the hall with your student, knocking on other classroom doors as you go, calling out, "I AM GOING TO THE NURSE WITH DAVITTA PLEASE GRAB MY KIDDOS THANKS! BYE!"

A brief note on getting sued. Sometimes teachers worry that students or families might sue them. The worry goes something like this:

Kid gets hurt in class. → Angry parent sues teacher.

This is extremely rare. Parents *do* occasionally sue school districts when they're unhappy. But parents almost never sue teachers because it's *districts* that have resources. Not teachers. And as long as you're doing your job (and are not negligent or doing illegal things), you're covered by district insurance and legal support. My guidance? Don't worry about getting sued. Be where you're supposed to be. Do your best to keep kids safe (more on safety below).

WHAT DO SCHOOLS WANT FROM US? (ETHICS, IN SMALL FORM)

School law can be understood as a firm boundary—which if crossed can get us fired, sent to jail, or both. School law isn't the *only* boundary surrounding our work. Schools want more than just not-breaking-the-law. They want us to be good with children. They want us to be ethical.

What do words like "good" and "ethical" mean? They seem . . . squishy. Is a "good" teacher someone who maintains order and routines? Someone who knows a lot about their subject? Someone who inspires passion and creativity? (Maybe all of those?) Is an "ethical" teacher someone who will "nurture the intellectual, physical, emotional, social, and civic potential of each student" (New York State Education Department, n.d.)? Or at least someone who "[s]hall not intentionally expose [a] student to embarrassment or disparagement" (NEA, 2020)?

Some of the above, maybe all of the above? I can tell you that school districts *do* try to identify traits that add up to something like "goodness" when they hire teachers. Below, I'll list what I've heard over and over again from school leaders about the kinds of teachers they want. These aren't formal ethical principles, but they're visible in the work of good and ethical teachers:

- Teachers who work hard

- Teachers who are coachable

- Teachers who effectively collaborate

- Teachers who love kids

- Teachers who are low maintenance

- Teachers who accept responsibility for the learning of every student in class

Much of this may seem vague. One teacher's "work hard" can certainly look different from another's. You, however, should expect to work your butt off, visibly so, or your principal will wonder about your commitment. You will have some long days. You should not be hard to find. You are "coachable" when you seek feedback from supervisors and take action on it. How can a principal know you love kids? Think about the stories you tell. Teachers that love kids tell stories about kids. Teachers that love kids also tend to lead clubs or coach. "Low maintenance" teachers are not overly needy. They take care of their own issues when they can. New teachers naturally ask lots of questions. That's fine, just don't ask the same question twice. And: know that sometimes the best thing you can do is try, gain experience, and reflect. Teaching requires making something like 1,500 decisions per day (Klein, 2021). You can't lean on others for more than a tiny fraction of them or they will stab you with a fork.

One note on the last trait—being responsible for every student. Who could argue with that? Isn't that part of the job? Yes, of course. I've found the *idea* easier than the *doing*, though. I've been frustrated with students. I've thought of students as "difficult" or "challenging." I've kicked kids out of class because I didn't know what else to do. And I've wondered whether my students might do better in someone else's class . . . maybe because (I told myself) they needed more support than I could provide? I've definitely had daydreams that *someone else* would swoop in and take That One Kid off my hands. Such ethical lapses are obviously self-serving. All are failures. Every one of my students had the right to be in my class. I was responsible for everyone's learning. I just needed to figure it out.

Notice for a minute what's *not* on the list of what schools want. Nothing about GPAs or test scores or which university you attended. Why not? Grades and test scores and other pre-service experiences appear to be weak predictors of teaching effectiveness (Aloe & Becker, 2009; Barduch & Klassen, 2020; D'Agostino & Powers, 2009; McConnell et al., 2019). Schools appropriately worry more about finding people who will be good with kids and colleagues. Schools worry about the traits above—even the squishy ones—because they're aspects of good and ethical teaching.

Related note: I encourage you to examine the concept of "fairness" when you teach. I've seen teachers do some pretty terrible things to kids in the name of fairness. Fair does not mean "everyone gets the same thing." Every semester I tell my students the story of Callie Smartt to help them think though their own ideas about fairness. Here's her story:

> In 1996, Callie Smartt was a fifteen-year-old sophomore attending high school in Andrews, Texas. She was on the cheerleading team (*Go Mustangs!*). Andrews is in West Texas: serious high school football and cheerleading country. Callie had cerebral palsy, so she used a motorized wheelchair to get around. The year before, Callie had been on the freshman cheerleading squad. During freshman football games, Callie had dressed up in an Andrews High t-shirt and zipped back and forth along the sidelines waving pom-poms while the rest of the squad did splits and tumbles (Pressley, 1996). Fans were delighted. They called Callie "Hot Rod." And then . . . when Callie went out for varsity cheerleading as a sophomore, some parents of the other cheerleaders got upset. They were unhappy that Callie drew attention away from their kids, the ones doing splits and tumbles (Minor, 1996) . . . but that wasn't what they said out loud. Out loud, they said Callie might get hurt if she continued to cheer. Football players were large, they said—Callie might be in the way, and it just didn't seem *safe* for her to be out there zipping around on the sidelines. They said Callie shouldn't be cheerleading at all.
>
> What did the school do? They decided that to be fair, Callie would have to try out for the cheerleading team just like everyone else. Callie would need to do splits and tumbles and jumps—which for her were physically impossible. The school claimed they were being fair. Callie was *welcome* to try out. The expectations were *the same* for Callie and everyone else. Fair, right?

No. Obviously not. You can't tell a kid to do an impossible thing and call it fair. Those parents and school leaders and board members in Andrews, Texas, in 1996 were terribly wrong. Yes, you should be fair to your students. And no, treating every student the same isn't the same as being fair.

SCHOOL LAW: WHAT SCHOOLS MUST DO

You already met the concepts of *liability* and *negligence*. Below, I'll share four important things teachers should do under the law, tell a few stories . . . and talk about student fights (because everyone asks). The good news is that you don't need to memorize school law. You'll have resources that will help (district policies, a school handbook), and you'll work with people who will know the most important details. Whenever you're not sure about school law, just *ask* (your assistant principal, the school counselor, the social worker, etc.). You're not a lawyer. Your job is teaching.

KEEP STUDENTS SAFE

This is the most important responsibility of schools under the law. Because states and territories require school attendance of minor children (generally, those under age 18)—states and territories are responsible for them during school. The concept is called *in loco parentis* (literally "in the place of a parent"). Schools must prevent foreseeable bad things (no axe-throwing in PE!), must try to minimize accidents (no running in the halls!), and must always supervise. Safety drives a high percentage of policies and practices that will shape your experiences in teaching. Before we get into day-to-day policies and practices, it's worth discussing the worst thing that can happen in any school: a shooting or other violent act.

VIOLENCE IN SCHOOLS

It's OK to wonder about school shootings or other violence, including suicides, in schools. It's OK to wonder what might happen. Although news of violence in schools may break your heart (and *should* because we are supposed to keep children safe) I want you to be clear about the risks (to you and your students), even now. There are two very different risks, I think.

First is the actuarial risk, of being in a school where a violent event happens. This risk is very, very small. From 1992–1993 through 2019–2020, U.S. public schools have averaged about forty-five violent deaths at school each year (National Center for Education Statistics, 2023). Roughly fifty million students and three million teachers attend or work in U.S. public schools each year. The risk of violent death at school for students, staff, or anyone else is about . . . *math math math* . . . 0.085 per 100,000 people in a given year (the unit the Centers for Disease Control uses for standardized reporting). That's tiny. The risk *outside* schools is orders of magnitude higher, for us and for our students. In 2020, the United States recorded about fifteen suicides and 7.5 homicides per 100,000 people (Liu et al., 2023). Schools are among the safest places you and your students can be. If useful to know, we face far higher odds of death from heart disease and cancer, motor vehicle crashes, electrocution, and (not making this up) "hornet, wasp and bee stings" than we do from violence at school (Centers for Disease Control and Prevention, 2019). As we'll discuss below, schools have many layers of safety that don't exist elsewhere in homes or communities—controlled access, lots of supervision, safety equipment, trained personnel, etc. Schools are, on the whole, far safer places for students and staff to be than just about anywhere else.

The second risk is psychological risk, of worrying so much about shootings or other school violence that our health, our teaching, or our students suffer. Violence at school is among the worst acts we can imagine, and news about it can feel pervasive and burn into memory: Columbine, Red Lake, Sandy Hook, Parkland, Uvalde, far too many others. We *should* remember, of course—especially when our memories spark action (see the Sandy Hook Promise, for example: www.sandyhookpromise.org). Yet our memories and thinking about school violence can do ongoing harm if we are afraid to be at school, if we are afraid of our students, if we offload our fears onto students. We can't be afraid all the time and be the teachers we are supposed to be. If at any point you find it difficult to navigate thinking about school violence while teaching—take that difficulty seriously and seek supports. You are absolutely not alone. Yes, there are stories of unimaginable harm done in schools. No, those are not likely to become our stories. We need to be well in order to keep our best work front and center: getting to know our students, keeping them safe, and teaching freely, without fear.

How do schools keep students and teachers safe? Below are some examples of common school safety features:

BUILDING SAFETY

- Fences, locking doors, alarms, security cameras, security personnel

- Monitored traffic flow, especially near bus loops

- Restricted access to dangerous places like roofs, electrical systems, shops and laboratories

- Inspections and maintenance of dangerous things and safety equipment—buses, fire and alarm systems, cooking and food storage areas, etc.

- Testing for lead, mold, mildew, asbestos, radon or other hazards

- Internet restrictions or monitors

PEOPLE SAFETY

- Employee background checks

- Supervision of all students at all times by school employees

- Evacuation drills, lockdown drills, and drills for natural disasters

- Training for employees:
  o Child abuse and neglect recognition and reporting
  o CPR, lifesaving and/or injury reduction techniques
  o Mental health awareness and suicide prevention
  o Bullying and/or violence prevention

POLICY AND PROCEDURAL SAFETY

- Identifying and screening school visitors

- Responding to emergencies and threats of harm to self or others

- Keeping educational records private

- Health and wellness, including meals and snacks, recess and PE, and provision of services like social workers and counselors, etc.

There's a lot going on in schools to keep students and employees safe. There are policies and procedures for handling peanut allergies. Policies for students who walk and bike to school. Policies for whether and when drug-sniffing dogs can visit (or therapy dogs, or basic ordinary dog dogs). The absolutely worst thing a school can do is allow a student or employee to get hurt or killed. An overriding interest in safety will always shape your building, the people in it, and the policies you'll follow.

Before leaving safety, let's ponder a common question among new teachers: *what should I do when students fight?* I understand the question—and the anxiety that usually comes with it. Teacher candidates often know little about fighting. Many have never been *in* a fight themselves or have any idea what happens before, during, or after. (*Am I supposed to . . . break it up? What if I get hurt? If I don't intervene, will I get fired or sued?*). Fights in schools are rare. In 2019, 8% of high school students in the United States reported they had been in a fight at school during the last year (National Center for Education Statistics, 2021, Fig. 4). That doesn't mean 8% of your students are going to fight every year. Most schools have few or no fights; a fraction of struggling schools have multiple (National Center for Education Statistics, 2022). In my experience, fights in school are noisy, awkward, and brief with long tails of emotions before and after. They're not like MMA. More like yelling and stumbling and pulling hair and an emotional stew of frustration and anger and embarrassment. Kids don't want to fight any more than you do. Fights are scary, a last resort of the frustrated.

People fight for multiple reasons. Fights usually emerge from frustration or fear. Students fight to save face, to stop bullying, to be seen as not-to-be-messed-with. I'm not saying fights are ever justified, just pointing out that among students, fights can serve a meaningful social purpose (and a weird kind of relief) if begun and quickly stopped. Like: *See? I was willing to fight. Mr. Wilkens made us stop, though.* Try not to be mad at kids who fight. Often they don't know what else to do. You should worry more about relationships with students, about engaging instruction, and about useful assessment. Be prepared to respond, but don't teach afraid. See "What to Do about Fights" (next page) for more discussion.

It's hard when students fight. You worry about them. It's difficult to know how or when to intervene unless your kids are tiny and you can be gentle. If useful to know, when teachers intervene, we are (generally) covered by law and insurance as long as our actions are reasonable and we follow district training, policy, and procedures.

FOLLOW DISTRICT POLICIES AND PROCEDURES

Policies are decisions school districts make about how they will follow laws and regulations. And my goodness, public schools have many. The good news is that you don't need to be a lawyer to comply with school district policies, you just need to follow directions.

There are reasons behind every policy. For example, many districts prohibit teachers from driving students anywhere in their personal vehicles.

What to Do about Fights

1. Prevent them. The best approach, hands down. If you see something, say something. Warning signs like student arguments, body language, explicit threats, histories of aggression, or comments from students that a conflict is escalating should prompt you to intervene. Separate students in class, monitor them closely, share what you know with others (counselors, social workers, your principal).

2. Use your voice. Immediately tell students to stop, by name. This can work. Just be loud and clear: TAMIRA SMITH, STOP. TAMIRA, GO TO THE MAP CORNER NOW. GABBY ADAMS, STOP. GABBY, GO TO MY DESK. Etc.

3. Increase space. Move other students away so they don't get hurt or join in. Set a wide buffer. If fighting students are in your room and there's little space, move the rest of class out quickly (e.g., to the hall or room next door). Keep your door open. Once other students are safe, move furniture or other hazards in the room out of the way. (*Side note:* Removing spectators can remove energy and stop fights. Many conflicts are tangled with peer pressure.)

4. Call for help. Call the office, a security guard, or another teacher to help maintain space and supervision. If no adults or phones are around, send a trusted student down to the office to get help. You? Keep an eye on your students.

5. Minimize/avoid physical intervention. Are you trained in physical intervention? If not, don't. You are not ever required by law or policy to physically intervene. If you *do* decide it's safe and useful to physically intervene (e.g., to separate students), your actions must be reasonable. No one wants adults tackling kindergarteners. You're not Dwayne "The Rock" Johnson. (Though I'm 99% sure he'd be an awesome 3rd-grade teacher.)

Some districts require teachers to keep their classroom doors open whenever meeting with students individually. Both policies are intended to protect students. Both are also intended to protect teachers (from harm, or accusations of harm).

Teachers are usually provided training on policies when they start. The scope and quality of the training can vary widely. Pay attention, ask questions. Three good resources include:

- Written district policies themselves (these should be online; they're public documents)

- School handbooks (often written for parents and students)
- Your school principal

Wondering how to handle a situation? Find the policy, read the handbook, ask your principal. Simply following district policies will keep you on the right side of most school law.

ENSURE CONSTITUTIONAL AND CIVIL RIGHTS

Who has the right to an education in U.S. public schools?
U.S. citizens? Yes.
Non-citizens? Yes.
Undocumented students? Yes
Students who don't use English? Yes.
Students who are unhoused? Yes.
Students with disabilities? Yes.
(*Wait. What if they're really expensive and complicated to educate?* Yes.)
Students who are incarcerated? Yes.
Students who use drugs and alcohol? Yes.
Students with bad attitudes? Yes.
(*Really? Like even students who refuse to do stuff all the time?* Yes.)
(*But what if they skip school? Or don't try? Or don't seem to care?* Yes.)
Students with like four or five or all of the above? Yes and yes and yes.

You're picking up the pattern, I hope. All school-age students in the United States have the right to go to school (United States Department of Education, 2011). A district can refuse to educate a student for only two reasons:

- The student doesn't live in the district.
- The student is too young or too old.

Please don't spend time worrying about whether any of your students "should" be in your room. This is the main overarching student right in U.S. public schools: *they have the right to be there.*

It's fair to wonder whether student rights are different from adult rights. After all, some students eat crayons and cry when they don't get to be line leaders. What sorts of constitutional and civil rights could they have? Overall, student rights are similar to those of adults, and don't vary greatly in or out of school. Students have the right to equal opportunity, to free speech, to privacy, to nondiscrimination, to due process, and more (Essex, 2014; Hachiya, 2022). The U.S. Supreme Court, deciding a free speech case in 1969, summarized: "It can hardly be argued that either students or teachers shed their constitutional rights to freedom of speech or expression at the schoolhouse gate" (*Tinker v. Des Moines*, 393 U.S. 503 [1969]).

One topic my teacher candidates enjoy discussing is dress codes. It's fair to hate dress codes; they have been historically misogynistic, specifically anti-Black, and unfriendly to a range of students of color for generations (Pavlakis & Roegman, 2018; Perry, 2020). Schools clearly should not suppress student expression just because they feel like it. But . . . are *any* dress codes justifiable? What if a student wants to protest poor working conditions in fast-fashion factories? Could they . . . just go to school naked and sit there in math class without consequence? Probably not. The legal standard for student dress is whether it "materially and substantially interfere[s] with the requirements of appropriate discipline in the operation of the school" (*Tinker v. Des Moines*, 393 U.S. 503 [1969]). No-clothes-Monday probably interferes with school. "Wear clothes" is OK as a dress code. You can imagine that ideas about what interferes with "appropriate discipline" vary. Schools can probably ban t-shirts with pictures of penises or beer logos or obscenities (but the kids can usually get away with FCUK gear—thanks, French Connection UK!). It is less clear whether schools can ban t-shirts with confederate flags (probably), Donald Trump mugshots (probably not), or odious messages like "There Are Only Two Genders" (Papadopoulos, 2023) (probably yes).

Teachers enable the exercise of most student constitutional and civil rights simply by following district policies and procedures. For example: don't duct-tape kids to chairs (WSB-TV, 2023). Why not? Because it's against school policy everywhere. Also because it's unlawful imprisonment. For the most part, you won't need to worry much about violating student constitutional and civil rights, because your school will already have proper frameworks in place. There are, however, two areas where I've seen teachers (and schools) regularly fall short in ensuring that student rights are protected: disability rights and gender identity and expression:

DISABILITY RIGHTS

Disability rights are civil rights. Public schools are not allowed to discriminate against students (or employees) on the basis of disability. Who has a disability? Per the Americans with Disabilities Act, a disability is "a physical or mental impairment that substantially limits major life activities" (P.L. 101-336, 1990). It's a huge bin. The law does not list every possible disability but explicitly includes some non-obvious categories that can limit major life activities, such as cancer, depression, PTSD, and HIV+ status (United States Department of Justice, Civil Rights Division, n.d.). Be advised: students with mental health diagnoses like anxiety and depression are students with disabilities under civil rights law (ADA) and may also be eligible for special education services (under IDEA). Many public schools are surprised by this.

One of our major failings is what we expect of (and provide to) students with disabilities. Most schools understand that setting up an Advanced Math Class of Awesomeness for Boys Because Math is Hard for Girls would be illegal. Those same schools may not blink at statements like "Students with learning disabilities probably shouldn't take AP Calculus" or "Why would a Deaf student want to take French?" Schools often conflate "disability" with "lack of intelligence" or "inability to learn" (Hehir, 2002). They're wrong to do so.

Having a disability does not mean AP Calculus or French is impossible—or that it's weird that a student might be interested. Having a disability means having the right to a challenging, quality education—just like any other student. There's a depressing cycle at work in many U.S. public schools that I want you to notice and *not* replicate:

- A student struggles.
- The school labels the student "disabled."
- Because of the label, the school provides a mediocre-to-bad education.
- The student does worse.

This spiral of reduced expectations and lower-quality education for students with disabilities is common in schools. We can do better. Most students with disabilities attend general education classrooms most of the day. We just need to make creative accommodations, and teach engaging lessons built around the needs of individuals.

GENDER IDENTITY AND EXPRESSION

LGBTQ+ rights are civil rights. One key law you should know is Title IX (20 USC 1681, §1681.a, 1972), which prevents discrimination on the basis of sex. Title IX regulations have clarified that "sex" includes gender and gender expression. U.S. public schools have not, on the whole, done right by millions of LGBTQ+ students. Students who identify as LGBTQ+ report, on average, fewer school supports, more overt discrimination from teachers and peers, less engagement, more absences, worse grades, more bullying and violence, and more chronic sadness and suicidal ideation compared to non-transgender and straight peers (WestEd, 2021; United States Department of Health & Human Services, 2021; Sansone, 2019; GLSEN, 2022). Of course there are schools doing better than others. But they're not nearly common enough. It is the job of all public schools in the United States to provide a safe and supportive (and engaging and challenging) education to all students, including LGBTQ+ students. More on this in the last chapter. Get to know your students, keep them safe, and be useful when schools fail to meet their needs.

FOLLOW YOUR CONTRACT

After keeping students safe, following district policies, and ensuring student rights, this last general guidance—follow your contract—is foundational for keeping your job. Teacher contracts are legal agreements. When you sign a contract, most often for an academic year, you agree to do whatever work it describes, and the district agrees to pay you for it (including compensation like health insurance or retirement contributions). You teach, they pay. If you don't do the work described in the contract, you're in breach of contract, and they don't have to pay you or keep you on the job.

A majority of teachers in public schools work under collectively bargained contracts (National Council on Teacher Quality, 2019). A collectively bargained contract is the same for every teacher in the district, not specific to you individually. Teacher contracts can be long, complex, and include things you'll never do, because they have to cover every teaching job scenario. When you get a job offer, get a copy of the teacher contract before you sign it, and read it. The best source for contracts is the district human resources department. You may also be able to get a copy from the teacher union, or maybe online.[3] Do not sign a contract if you're not sure you can do every part of the job. And do not do the following:

Get job offer from District X *(Yay!)*

Sign a contract with District X *(Yay!)*

[Time passes]

Get another job offer, from District Y *(Yay . . . ?)*

[District Y is awesome. Like, way more awesome than District X.]

Try to break the contract with District X so you can work for District Y.

If you sign a contract with District X, do the job for District X. If you don't love it, change jobs next year. Although most districts will terminate a contract on good terms if you have an emergency that prevents you from fulfilling *any* contract, what counts as "good cause" is usually limited (think: medical emergencies or death). "Good cause" does not usually include wanting to teach somewhere else. Fulfilling legal commitments matters. One easy way to anger a school district is to break a contract you've signed, especially if it's near the start of the year. You'll never (ever) work for that district again. And in many states, districts can (and do) pursue sanctions for teachers who break contracts by reporting them to state or territorial education agencies, who may fine you or revoke your teaching certificate (FindLaw, 2016).

Teacher Unions and Tenure

A teacher union (also called an "association") is an organization whose purpose is to negotiate favorable contracts for teachers (good pay, good benefits). Teacher unions also usually do political advocacy, such as for increased school funding or the election of political candidates. Teacher unions often claim to be far more than this. The National Education Association (NEA), for example, claims that its purpose is "championing justice and excellence in public education" (National Education Association, 2023). The indirect claim appears to be "We fight for teachers, therefore we help kids." That hasn't always been my experience. The interests of teachers and students are not the same. I've seen unions fight to keep adults working in classrooms who had no business being there—directly hurting students. I think it's enough for unions to advocate for good pay without claiming they're somehow also "championing justice" or fighting for "excellence." Unions organize for adults. Teachers merit good pay and benefits. Full stop.

If you remain in a teaching position for years, you may earn tenure. The length of time it takes to earn tenure varies; most common in U.S. public schools is three years (Nittler, 2016). Tenure is the right to specific due process protections before removal from a job. If or when teachers struggle, districts typically need to tell them what they're doing badly, and give them time and training before firing them. Tenure doesn't mean a permanent job, exactly . . . but in some places the process to remove a tenured teacher can be so difficult or costly that administrators don't bother trying. Tenure is a good example of a benefit for adults that can harm students. I have tenure; I appreciate the job security. But tenure protects *me*. Not my students. If I do a poor job but am impossible to fire, my students are actively harmed (Moe, 2011).

An early question you'll face as a public school teacher is whether to join the union. I should clarify that in most collective bargaining contexts, all teachers are charged union dues, whether or not they are members of the union. Those dues cover the costs of negotiating your teacher contract, and you usually cannot opt out of paying them. So what *does* union membership mean? First, joining the union may, over time and indirectly, improve your pay, benefits, and/or job duties. A union with strong membership has greater leverage to negotiate a better contract with the district. Second, joining the union may provide you with additional individual benefits (e.g., access to vision or dental insurance), and will provide your union more money to spend on itself as an organization, or for policy or political advocacy. Joining a union means you'll pay an additional membership fee out of every paycheck. Fees for union membership are generally modest, and the benefits can be substantial. If something bad happens while you're teaching (someone gets hurt, someone accuses you of horrible actions, a supervisor or colleague does icky things), a union can support you. At the same time, it may bother you to be part of an organization that takes policy stances or actions with which you personally disagree. If you have an objection to being a union member, by all means follow your conscience; be advised that you may miss some useful benefits in not joining.

Now: ten ways to get yourself fired. It's not every way, of course. For example, if you write "F—the patriarchy" on your board and then use the N-word in class (as a high school Spanish teacher in Sacramento did), you're probably toast (Rutland, 2022). Same if you sleep with your students (Smith, 2023), steal a bunch of stuff from school (Hatch, 2023), or sell your kids marijuana (Betz, 2019).[4] I'm going to assume you understand that doing illegal stuff in school or with your kids will get you fired. Below are notes on the potentially less obvious.

TEN WAYS TO GET FIRED

NEGLECT OF DUTY

1. Fail to supervise students. This is Bathroom Emergency 101. If you fail to show up where you're supposed to be (the bus loop in the morning, your classroom during class, the hallway or lunchroom when assigned), you can't keep kids supervised and safe. Be where you're supposed to be.

2. Fail to keep kids safe. If you're a chemistry teacher, make the kids wear goggles. If you have baskets of scissors on your tables and Brent keeps trying to stab everyone—move the scissors or switch activities. *Don't* share your Advil with kids, *do* read the memo about peanut allergies, *do* let your principal know about Zappy the Exciting Electrical Outlet. You can fend off negligence claims by doing four things:

- Make reasonable attempts to anticipate dangerous circumstances.
- Take proper precautions.
- Warn students.
- Supervise.

3. Be late, leave early, or skip work. This one's easy to document, hence simple for termination. Your contract or handbook says when you're supposed to be at school. If you're not there, you violated your contract. Don't have anyone else sign you in or out. Follow procedures for requesting sick or personal leave. If you do have an emergency, communicate. Almost anything can be managed with good communication. And almost anything can be made worse with bad communication.

INSUBORDINATION

4. Don't follow district policies or supervisor directives. Policies and procedures emerge from law and regulation. Teachers must follow them or risk termination. And . . . teachers are employees within chains of command. Our supervisors—usually principals—have the authority to tell us what to do within the scope of instructional duties ("Turn in lesson plans by Friday at 3 p.m." = yes. "Go get me coffee" = no). Find and read district policies that impact your work, follow supervisor directives, and ask questions. Experienced teachers will be your best guide, along with your principal. How do you start a school club? How do you report absences? Can you sell cookies? How do you send a kid to the office? Etc.

5. Don't teach the curriculum. Or: *Teach stuff the district has prohibited.* Teaching unapproved curriculum is occasionally glorified in the news, with narratives like: "Plucky teacher fights for the right to expand students' worldviews against the wishes of stodgy Board members and a closed-minded community" (see, e.g., Hauser, 2023; Pendharkar, 2019; Schermele, 2023; Sonnenberg, 2023). Well, OK. If you want to go down fighting, you probably can. Keep in mind that your influence over student learning stops abruptly if you get fired. Also, you're about to be a *new* teacher. A rookie. You will not have immediate credibility. Unless you start your own school from scratch, you're going to teach in a place that has already decided how and what they want their students to be taught. They are unlikely to trust you enough to replace their judgment with yours. Even if you don't love the curriculum, you need to use it. Find ways to go beyond or adapt it if you can. But teach it. If you're still there during the next curriculum adoption, join the committee, help pick something better.

5a: Be partisan in class. Public school teachers are not supposed to do partisan advocacy in class. Don't tell your kids to vote for Candidate X or Y. Or that specific laws are bad and should be ignored. You can tell your kids that political action matters. You can discuss salient issues and histories and policies that impact them, their school, and their lives. You can teach about politics. You cannot advocate for your own specific policy or party beliefs.[5]

IMMORALITY

6. Demonstrate sketchy morals in school. Obviously, districts can fire you for breaking laws in school—pilfering yearbook funds, punching the art teacher, selling student information to hackers. Don't. Don't show up impaired, don't steal stuff, don't have wildly inappropriate and illegal relationships with students. You can also get fired for doing things at school that aren't exactly illegal but are clearly inappropriate. For example, teaching your kids:

- gambling (Edelstein, 2023),

- raunchy TikTok dances (Diaz, 2023),

- weird conspiracy theories (Gesualdi-Gilmore, 2021),

- Holocaust denials (Walsh, 2020), or

- white supremacy theories (Griffith, 2022).

Ew, no. And then there's weird stuff like asking your students to write a paper about what it would be like to die in twenty-four hours (Boey, 2023), or telling your kids to call pedophiles "Minor Attracted Persons" (Gordon, 2022). Be advised that the decider of what's acceptable in school isn't you. It's your school administration, and ultimately the school board. If your district can reasonably claim that you've lost the ability to be effective as a teacher, they can fire you. Remember that you work with minor students in a position of responsibility and trust. Err on the side of caution.

7. Demonstrate sketchy morals outside school. Districts can also fire you for doing sketchy things outside of school. Schools (and families) definitely don't want teachers who are convicted murderers. What about convicted drunk drivers? Domestic abusers? Those who fail to pay child support, or who use marijuana? Behavior outside school is a nebulous area of law that varies by act and jurisdiction. Teacher contracts sometimes include a "moral turpitude" clause, which allows termination when employees violate community standards for behavior (see www.law.cornell.edu/wex/moral_turpitude). The reasoning behind "moral turpitude" clauses is that adults who demonstrate poor judgment in their personal lives can't be trusted with kids. What's considered an act of "moral turpitude" isn't universal (Greenwalt, 2019). Right now, some of the least clear law concerns online behaviors—many of which are public (hence accessible to students and families). For example, an 8th-grade math teacher in Albuquerque was fired after her students found her in online pornographic videos (Knapp, 2021). Did her videos have anything to do with algebra? No. But the district successfully made the argument that family objections prevented her from teaching math effectively in the district after students found the videos. Some general guidance: before you apply for jobs, clean up your online footprint. Remove or delete anything you don't want students (or families) to see, including those posts from your angsty teenage years. Your kids will find them. Also: don't share your personal email or phone with students (I know this is common—it's still a bad idea); don't contact, friend, or follow students via any network outside school; don't game with students online. Students are *not* your friends. If your actions mimic those of friends, you incur risk.

8. Violate student rights. Students have constitutional and other legal rights at school. The good news is that teachers are rarely fired for violating student rights, unless we do bad things like whack kids with broomsticks (Hait, 2022). The major, huge, overarching student right is to not be discriminated against. You probably have no intention of discriminating against your future theoretical students. It doesn't really matter what you intend, though. It matters what effect you have. For example, you might not mean to discriminate against students with disabilities (*All are welcome here!*), but if you don't provide accommodations or makeup work when students miss class for therapy, guess what you're doing? Look for patterns. It's rare, but teachers can be liable for patterns of discrimination, especially in the domain of discipline—and your school and district most certainly can be held liable for the same (United States

Department of Education, 2023). Beyond nondiscrimination, pay attention to privacy rights. Privacy rights are commonly violated by teachers in these four ways (which are *bad*, which you *should not do*):

- Public posting of grades in class or in hallways. Grades are educational records, subject to the Family Educational Rights and Privacy Act (FERPA; 20 U.S.C. § 1232g). All educational records are supposed to be private. Things that should remain private: "grades, transcripts, class lists, student course schedules, health records [. . .] and student discipline files" (United States Department of Education, n.d.).

- Public sharing of photographs or videos. FERPA applies here too. Don't post images or videos of your students without explicit consent from your principal and from the family of every student involved. There are some limited exceptions, but always ask your administrator before you display or share anything.

- Providing student information to third parties. Still FERPA. Most often this happens when teachers use educational applications without thinking carefully about the information provided to vendors. For example, you might use a classroom management system like Class Dojo, or a learning management system like Google Classroom, or tell your kids to go practice French using Duolingo. They're all awesome (or they *were* back in 2024). But if you set up these applications with personally identifiable information (e.g., real student names, birthdates, email addresses, etc.), you may be violating privacy laws. Ask your administrator.

- Ignoring student gender identities. This may not seem like a privacy issue—but it is (also: basic human decency). Student names or pronouns, especially among transgender and gender expansive students, may not match educational records and may differ from those in use at home (Ryan et al., 2010). School may be the only place where students can be themselves and be safe. Students have a privacy right not to be outed by teachers (American Civil Liberties Union, 2023), including not being outed to their families.

INCOMPETENCY

9. Be ineffective. Maybe you're worried about this. Most new teachers are. Honestly, this is less of a firing offense than you might expect. Termination for poor instruction is quite rare—likely less than 1% of all teachers (Barnum, 2015; Kraft & Gilmour, 2017; TNTP, 2009). Andrew Saultz (2018) studied teacher dismissals in Georgia from 2011–2017 and concluded: "Teachers are largely dismissed due to professional obligations, not teacher evaluations. [. . .] Atlanta Public Schools provides clear support for the claims that if teachers keep their heads down and do not upset anyone, they will likely continue in their jobs." Although we may all agree that bad teachers should be fired, it's remarkably difficult to get consensus about what, specifically, makes a teacher "bad" or "so bad they can't improve and need to go." Bad at what? Bad at managing the classroom? Bad at sparking student interest? Bad at lesson planning or explaining stuff? Bad at giving directions, assigning homework, designing assessments, giving feedback, or supporting students? Bad at calling parents back? And how bad is *bad*, anyway? As with most aspects of our localized public school system, answers vary by context. What's "bad" in one school or district may not be seen as such elsewhere. Here's what seems to be "bad enough" that administrators take notice and action (hence *bad. Don't do this stuff*):

- Poor recordkeeping. You'll be expected to turn in lesson plans, grade papers, and keep on top of paper flow. You'll be expected to keep accurate records. Just like showing up every day by 7:15 a.m., this is very much under your control. Poor recordkeeping is easily documented, hence provides straightforward evidence a teacher is doing a bad job.

- Upsetting families. Your students spend way more time with you than anyone else. They'll talk about you with their families. If you upset your families—if they raise consistent concerns about you to your principal—their feedback must be taken seriously. If students or families regularly suggest you're not doing a good job, any school administrator is going to struggle to defend and keep you.

- Complaining. Principals want you to work hard, to solve as many problems as you can on your own, and to be successful. It's OK to let them know how you're doing. It's not OK to bring them a steady stream of complaints. Especially early in your career, you don't want a reputation as a complainer. Why? Teaching is hard. Running a school is hard. Everyone in your school will feel this. There is no such thing as a perfect school. It's easy for all of us to spot problems. It's harder, and more important, to identify solutions. Principals want teachers who solve classroom problems, who pitch in when there are challenges, and who improve. Also: no adult drama please.

It is your responsibility to get along with others and do your job. You do not have to love everyone. Be an adult at work, complain at home later.

- Poor communication. Stay on top of email, calls, and texts. Sometimes you'll fall behind. Prioritize what you read and respond to, first anything from your principal (or any administrator), then anything from a parent or guardian. Get to other messages later. Related: never surprise your principal. They want to know how things are going, especially if they're not going well and you need support. This can be hard and embarrassing. If you have a bad class and yell at your students—oops, you're human—let your principal know what happened, and what you plan to do about it. Walk down the hall and own it. You may be preparing them for a tough phone call from an upset parent later that day. Let your principal know if you're struggling to submit grades, to manage a student's behavior, to understand the curriculum. It's hard to share struggles. It's also the only way your principal (or others) will have a chance to help you improve.

- Rejecting constructive feedback. Principals are supposed to help teachers improve. They *want* you to. A better you means a better school. They will occasionally tell you things that can be difficult to hear ("Try to shriek less in class."). It's never easy to hear feedback that's mixed or negative. Criticism of our instruction can feel a lot like criticism of our selves. It's not. "You didn't see those hands raised at the back of the room, so you should circulate more" does not mean "You are a bad person." It means: "You should circulate more." Any time you get constructive feedback, don't argue. Say thank you, seek understanding, try to make changes. If you reject feedback, your principal will conclude that you are not going to improve. Take feedback for what it is: guidance on what your principal wants. Try to do those things. And follow up a few days or weeks later: *Hey, remember the Thing you suggested? I've been doing it, and here's how it's going . . .*

10. Be bad with kids. I'm including this as a reason teachers *should* be fired rather than one that frequently happens. Some teachers are just . . . mean. They don't care. They yell or belittle or embarrass kids. Why are they teaching? Because no one made them stop. Our best work is being good with every student: working hard, listening, showing respect, enabling joy. Sometimes this will be easy. Sometimes it will be hard. A truism in our profession is that students who are the most difficult to love probably need love the most. Some students come to school having been told over and over again just how worthless they are. They feel hurt, anger, neglect, and shame . . . and they bring those feelings to class. They may tell us we need to brush our teeth more, that our lessons are boring, that we don't know what we're doing. They can say deeply hurtful things to classmates. But we can't give any of that back. We owe them, each one of them, the best version of ourselves. The selves that are loving and optimistic. Why? Emotions mediate learning. When students feel bad, they don't learn; when students feel joy or curiosity, they do (Tyng et al., 2017; Valiente et al., 2012). So . . . it may look weird on paper like this, but I'm writing it anyway: some teachers need to be fired. If we can't be good with kids—if we can't keep our own emotions in check and support each and every student—we're simply not what they need.

You might have noticed that "Ten Ways to Get Fired" doesn't include a range of things you might be worried about. Let me reassure: you won't get fired for saying the wrong thing in class. You won't get fired because a student behaved badly and caught you by surprise. You won't get fired because you did the math wrong at the board, because your letter home to parents had spelling errors, or because you kind of lost your marbles with Serenity back there and told her she needed to sit in her chair and not touch anything or anyone else ever again forever. *You are going to make mistakes*. Every year. Maybe every day. The good news is that mistakes help us learn, as long as we're aware of them—and as long as we work to make things right. If you ever do get to a point in your teaching career where you think you're not making mistakes anymore: good news! You can retire! Because your self-awareness has clearly disappeared.

HOW TO FIX TEACHER MISTAKES

Figure 9.2 (opposite page) is you when you mess up.

Mistakes feel awful. They'll make you feel exposed and ashamed (maybe not . . . precisely as naked as Vidal's statue, but maybe you're catching the metaphor?). You can fix them, though:

1. Identify what you did wrong.

2. Directly apologize to those wronged. In person, if you can. Say, "I am sorry for X. I made a mistake."

3. Listen to what they tell you.

4. Don't make the same mistake again.

Figure 9.2. Cain, after killing his brother Abel. Statue by Henri Vidal, Paris. *Source:* Photo by user James Gose (2011), CC-BY-2.0.

That's honestly it. Just don't assume your mistakes will magically fix themselves. If you miss a deadline for turning in lesson plans, send an email that owns it. Apologize, and get them done as soon as you can. If you lose your marbles with Serenity, tell her, "I'm sorry I told you not to touch anything ever forever. I was frustrated. That was a mistake. What I should have said was: 'Wandering around class taking other students' pencils is disruptive. If you need another pencil, there's more in the cup on my desk. OK'?"

Good news: your principal and your school want you to succeed. They don't want to fire you. They want you to be good with kids and to do the job well. This chapter has discussed a lot of ways the job can go badly—negligence, poor ethics, bad teaching, irresponsible and illegal behavior. I want to reassure you that the job can go brilliantly, wonderfully well. Teaching is a lot of work. It's also totally worth it.

I opened this chapter with the claim that school law and ethics can't always provide precise instructions for what to do. I mentioned a principal who bent the rules to make sure every kid ate breakfast. If nothing else in this chapter sticks, I hope you understand that there are some absolute rules you must follow in your teaching life (don't leave kids unsupervised, don't do illegal things, follow your contract, etc.), but there are also a lot of judgment calls you'll need to make. You will make mistakes. I hope you'll own and learn from them. And I hope throughout that you'll seek goodness with kids no matter what.

> ### How Can I Get Fired?
>
> Wow, lots of ways. No one's actively *trying* to fire you. Your principal and school want things to work. You can *avoid* getting fired by prioritizing student safety and supervision. Always be in class and at assigned duties. Follow district policies and directives. Read and follow your contract. Protect your students' civil and constitutional rights. And when you make mistakes, own them, apologize, and learn.

SUPREME COURT CASE FOR DISCUSSION

Case: Mahanoy Area School Dist. v. B. L., 594 U.S. (2021).
Link: www.supremecourt.gov/opinions/20pdf/20-255_g3bi.pdf

In spring 2017, Brandi Levy was a fourteen-year-old, 9th-grade student at Mahanoy Area High School, a public school in Mahanoy City, Pennsylvania. Brandi tried out for the school's varsity cheerleading squad, and also for a private softball team. She did not make the varsity cheerleading team or get her preferred softball position, but she was offered a spot on the cheerleading squad's junior varsity team.

The weekend she learned of her non-selections, Brandi and a friend visited the Cocoa Hut, a local convenience store. There, Brandi used her smartphone to post photos on Snapchat, a social media application that allowed users to post photos and videos that disappeared after a set period of time. Brandi posted photos to her Snapchat "story," a feature that allowed any person in her friend group to view the images for twenty-four hours. The first image Brandi posted showed her and a friend with middle fingers raised and the caption: *"Fuck school fuck softball fuck cheer fuck everything."*

Over the next week, Brandi's post was shared beyond her friend group, including with the cheerleading coaches. The coaches decided that because the posts used profanity in connection with a school extracurricular activity, they violated team and school rules. As a result, the coaches suspended Brandi from the junior varsity cheerleading squad for the upcoming year. The school's athletic director, principal, superintendent, and school board all affirmed Brandi's suspension from the team. In response, Brandi, together with her parents, filed a lawsuit in Federal

District Court that argued school officials had no authority to punish students for speech that happened off campus. The case was heard by the U.S. Supreme Court in Fall 2020.

QUESTIONS

1. Explain when, if ever, teachers and schools should restrict student speech.

2. Would the school be more justified in punishing Brandi if her post had been made during class at school? Why, or why not?

3. Would the school be justified in punishing Brandi if her post had been more direct, for example "*f—Coach Smith*" or "*f—Grace Miller the 8th-grader who made varsity.*" Why, or why not?

4. Imagine you had Brandi Levy in your class. Her case was well known at school, and Brandi was now a subject of substantial chatter—maybe harassment—at school. What could you do as a teacher to protect Brandi from further harm?

FURTHER READINGS AND RESOURCES

Ethics (Generally; herein you can read more about Callie Smartt [the cheerleader] and other scenarios):
Sandel, M. (2010). *Justice: What's the right thing to do?* New York: Farrar, Straus and Giroux.

Fights:
Teaching Channel. (2018). How to manage school fights. Eagan, MN: Author. www.teachingchannel.com/k12-hub/blog/how-to-manage-school-fights

School Law:
Essex, N. (2021). *A teacher's pocket guide to school law*, 3rd ed. New York: Pearson. (If you can't find this pocket guide, go with another Essex book—Essex, N. [2012]. *The 200 Most frequently asked legal questions for educators.* New York: Skyhorse.)

Teacher Contracts:
EducatorFI. (n.d.) How to analyze your teacher contract. https://educatorfi.com/analyze-contract

Tenure:

Education Commission of the States. (2020). 50-state comparison: Teacher employment contract policies. Denver, CO: Author. www.ecs.org/50-state-comparison-teacher-employment-contract-policies

NOTES

1. In rural Alaska, many schools don't have separate gyms and cafeterias. Instead they have a big open gym/cafeteria with a kitchen next door, and a window between to serve food. Everyone eats at tables under the basketball nets, then folds up the tables and rolls them out of the way for gym class. Voilà: gymneteria.

2. I taught high school science in a room with Bunsen burners at every lab station. Fire is primordially awesome. I'd turn the supply line on, the kids would break out squeezy metal flint lighters, and you'd hear *scritch-scritch-scritch-WHOOSH!* all over the room. Fire! And there was always that one kid who would immediately try to melt his pen. Or shoe. Or lab partner. Part of my job was limiting the number of things set on fire in class.

3. In New York, a nonprofit (See Through NY) posts all public-sector contracts online, including teacher contracts: https://seethroughny.net/contracts. (They also post worker salaries. I work for SUNY—you can look up my pay if you're curious.)

4. This one, yikes. A middle school teacher "took [two] girls off-campus and taught them how to prepare and ingest drugs. [. . .] The girls had not previously used drugs" (Betz, 2019). Just so we are clear: *Don't take your kids off campus so you can teach them how to prepare and ingest drugs.*

5. Here's a no-no: a high school English teacher in Fort Worth, Texas, publicly posted messages to then President Trump in 2019 requesting that he (personally?) remove undocumented immigrant students: "Anything you can do to remove the illegals from Fort Worth would be greatly appreciated" (Victor, 2019). She was fired about two weeks later. To reiterate: public schools are required to educate every student living in their district. Immigration status does not change that requirement (see *Plyler v. Doe*, 457 U.S. 202, 1982).

10

What Comes Next

How Can I Make Things Better for Students?

Your first year will be hard.

My first year of teaching was at Greenwood High School in Greenwood, Mississippi (*Go Bulldogs!*). I taught high school biology. I was, I think, OK. Not fantastic. I remember trying for some reason to teach my kids a poem about frogs mating. And I remember trying really hard not to cry my first spring. It was science fair season. All my students had been doing experiments. They were set up all over my room—things like "Does salt harm germination?" and "Do fish swim faster in warm water?" and "What kind of music do plants prefer?"[1] . . . Anyway, I'd been eating lunch in the cafeteria one day, and while I was out of my room someone—students, I assumed—ruined several experiments. I don't remember the details. Did they tip over the radish seedlings? Dump all the fish food into the aquarium? I remember feeling angry, and ashamed, and that maybe whoever it was would not have wrecked the experiments if somehow they liked me or respected me more. I remember Mrs. Parham, a veteran teacher across the hall, pulling me into her room and telling me emphatically, "*You get yourself together before they come back.*" That was a hard day.

And then also, I remember Katrina, who wanted to be a nurse and had perfect handwriting. I remember Cory, who ran cross country (which I coached, not well), suggesting we take a day off any time it was over 90 degrees. (It was the Mississippi Delta in August and September and October. It was *always* over 90.) I remember Arthur and Jacob, who either got my nerdy jokes or who didn't mind pretending. And I remember Kendrick in sixth period. Kendrick, who was eighteen and still a freshman. Kendrick who was taking biology for probably the fourth time. Kendrick who would not listen or do the work or give me the time of day. I remember sixth period being so much easier when Kendrick wasn't there because I had no idea how to make class work when he was. I remember hoping he wouldn't show up, and feeling ashamed of that too.

Figure 10.1 is a picture of you, sometime in late October of your first year. Maybe late March:

Figure 10.1. Super tired teacher sitting at his desk, 1925. *Source:* Wikimedia Commons, CC-BY-SA-3.0.

Look at your *eyes*. You're wearing your teacher outfit, you've got a book and a chalkboard, and *damn* you're keeping it together on the outside. You are *tired*, though. On the inside, you're wondering: "What day is it?" and "Am I going to make it?" and "Did I pick the right work?"

Please listen: don't try to answer big questions about teaching or your career during your first year. Just meet each day as best you can. Be good—decent and understanding and caring—whenever you're with kids. And then forgive yourself for not getting done whatever your brain insists should have gotten done. The planning, the grading, those phone calls. Growing into teaching takes time. If you stay patient with yourself and curious about how to get better, you'll keep growing. The tired moments where the coffee does nothing will taper. You'll gain confidence. Maybe October will always feel long—but it'll get more doable. And at some point maybe you'll have time to rethink the vest and watch chain and checkered pants.

In Praise of Showing Up

New teachers often carry massive hopes into the work. They want to inspire, be hugged by crying grateful mothers, hear the orchestra swell as their students reluctantly leave class to go cure cancer. They want *magic*. The problem is that magic is an impossible standard. You can be an excellent teacher and feel . . . no magic. Teaching often just feels like hard work. You'll be planning lessons, making copies, rearranging seating charts, responding to emails, and enduring meetings. You'll need to stop at Walmart for stuff. And then go back because you forgot the other stuff. Some of our best work is preparing for class. Which is constant. And not magic.

Even in class, it's rare to feel like a lesson was perfect. Part of our job is paying attention to each student. We can teach an excellent lesson in all the right ways, and yet when one student has a tough day, that's what we remember. I worry that new teachers who expect magic will be disappointed. That they'll be harsh judges of themselves, of their work, of teaching generally. And I worry that they'll draw conclusions far too quickly. The best measures of whether you've made a difference as a teacher take *years* to emerge. Did your students do better in school the next year? Did they graduate? Did they get work, find love, live better lives than they would have otherwise? You can't know this stuff right away (if ever). The magic—if it exists—is in the lives your students lead long after they leave your room.

I'm telling you to be patient. You don't need to chase magic. You need to have a plan for what your students will learn today, and some materials at the ready. Same for the next day. Teaching is in a real sense cumulative. It matters that you show up, day after day after day. It matters that, over time, you try to structure more good learning experiences than bad ones. Your students are probably not going to remember specific lessons you teach (*do you, with your old teachers?*). They're going to remember *you*. They're going to remember who you were with them, whether you were optimistic or funny, whether class was interesting or difficult. And they're going to remember how they felt with you. You don't need magic for that. Just you, with a bunch of copies and a plan for the next forty-five minutes. And maybe some glue sticks.

If you stay, you'll get better.

One way you can make things better for students is to keep teaching. The longer you teach, the better you'll get. Not automatically, of course. As Tara Kini and Anne Podolsky (2016) point out: "the research does not indicate that the passage of time will make all teachers better or incompetent teachers effective" (1). I'm talking *averages*; new teachers generally improve substantially during their first three years and then continue to improve in the years following, albeit more gradually (Hanushek & Rivkin, 2010; Harris & Sass, 2011; Papay & Kraft, 2015; Rockoff, 2004). You're going to have to work hard to get better. Our profession is complex. You probably won't be the Best Teacher Ever on your first day, or by the end of your first year. You might get there a few years down the road. The point of this chapter in two sentences: *Your first year will be hard. Figure out where you need to improve.*

Making it through your first year of teaching upright is a win. There will be days you won't want to go to school. You'll have a tough day, then another one, then one morning your alarm clock will ring way before you're ready and you'll start wondering if you could maybe just not go be a teacher today. That's natural. You'll be fine. You do not have to love every minute of every day to be an awesome teacher. You just need to be there for your kids, and you need to put in the work to get better.

Your second year will be better than your first. Your second year will be about improvement. You'll have a base. You'll be less nervous, more prepared, better able to anticipate problems and solutions. You'll have a chance to fix some of the things you didn't love about your first year. Did you keep turning lesson plans in late? Did that unit on plant ecology put everyone to sleep? Did you not love how the end of classes just kind of dissolved into a random mess? Whatever gave you the hardest time in your first year, you'll have a chance to work on it, while preserving or tinkering with routines and lessons that worked.

Your third year you'll start to feel comfortable. You'll have more bandwidth. You'll be able to pay less attention to yourself and more attention to each student. You'll be able to meet students where they are and provide the supports and practice they need.

The rewards of teaching well over a period of years can be hard to describe. I'm not sure it's as simple as an accumulation of good days. Some days will bring humor and joy, others sadness—if not yours, that of your students. Some days will be sleepy. Others, usually in early October, will feature three fire drills. I suspect the most sustaining reward of teaching is *competence*. There's nothing quite like feeling capable of doing a good job in a meaningful profession.

Below are five areas where I think most of us can get better. They're areas where I think we can make real differences in the lives of our students. They're not necessarily issues that you need to tackle on your first day of class. They are long-term challenges, with long-term opportunities.

FIVE AREAS WHERE TEACHERS CAN GET BETTER

TEACH READING BETTER

This includes all of us—elementary and secondary teachers, math and PE and music teachers. Everyone. Learning to read is one of the primary purposes of schooling in the United States. A literate public is good for society and democracy, and literacy skills have strong associations with positive individual outcomes like graduating from high school, getting work, and not getting arrested (Fiester, 2013; Heckman et al., 2006; Lin et al., 2018; Parsons & Bynner, 2006; Ritchie & Bates, 2013; U.S. Department of Education, 2018). If I had to pick one major professional learning goal for all teachers, it would be that we learn to teach reading better.

We're not, collectively, good at teaching reading in the United States. Two-thirds of U.S. students in grades 4, 8, and 12 are not proficient readers (National Assessment of Educational Progress, 2022). It's been that way for decades. Go read that sentence again. *Two-thirds*. Translation: most of your students will need reading support every single year you teach. It doesn't matter what grade you teach. Reading is not just an elementary-grades issue. It's an all-grades issue. What's also true is that students who struggle to read in the early grades don't just magically disappear. They all carry on into the later grades. All these struggling readers will be in our classes. We're all responsible for teaching them to read. Can you imagine being a social studies teacher who avoids reading all year? Or a French teacher who skips print? I don't want my kids in those classes, with those teachers. Maybe you never expected to teach reading. Maybe you carry secret hopes that a phalanx of specialists will swoop in and teach all those struggling readers. I'm telling you: there's no way two-thirds of our students—*thirty million students*—will become better readers without each of us doing some of the work.

Go read *Language at the Speed of Sight* (Seidenberg, 2017). It will help you understand why two-thirds of our students are not skilled readers (spoiler: because we don't teach reading consistently well). The bad news is that reading instruction is rife with pseudoscience, unproven beliefs, and a lot of wishful thinking (Winter [2022] memorably called much reading instruction "vibes-based literacy"). Bad reading instruction has been with us for a long time. Horace Mann, a founding father of U.S. public education, thought *teaching the alphabet was a bad idea* because it was full of "skeleton-shaped, bloodless, ghostly apparitions" . . . by which he meant *letters* (see Mann, 1844, 82). Come *on*, Horace. While we do teach the alphabet these days (USA! USA!), we still have remarkable pockets of resistance to direct, explicit instruction in reading skills among teachers. Avoid magical thinking about reading. It's a skill we can and should teach. We've done a poor job with two-thirds of our students. We can learn to do better. Good resources:

- U.S. Department of Education, Institute for Education Sciences. *Practice Guides* in reading, writing and literacy and all grade levels: https://ies.ed.gov/ncee/wwc
- Florida Center for Reading Research. Broad collection of research, practice guides, and educator activities at all grade levels: https://fcrr.org

BE MORE INCLUSIVE

Some students you'll struggle to teach. If you see patterns, start there. Struggling to support students with reading challenges? Students with challenging behaviors? Boys? Focus on the students you find hardest to teach. Figure out what you're doing, what they need, and changes you can make to bring the two together. Then also: learn about the students *not yet* in your room. Where are they? Why aren't they there? Who said they shouldn't be?

Elsewhere in this book I've noted what a disappointing failure our systems of special education have been. I don't deny that for some students in some systems, special education has proven helpful. At scale and on average, however, students being provided special education do worse than their peers, and far worse when they're segregated into separate classrooms (Ballis & Heath, 2021; Butrymowicz & Mader, 2017; Schifter et al., 2019). That's not acceptable. It's not a stretch to wonder whether special education in U.S. public schools would more accurately be labeled "stuff we [schools] do, including lots of paperwork and segregation and lowered expectations, to students with disabilities, most of whom didn't actually have a disability until they [students] showed up at school and we [schools] gave them that label, when we [schools] haven't successfully educated them [students], and who for some totally mysterious reason happen to be disproportionately male."

The best way we know to improve outcomes among students with disabilities is for teachers to successfully include them in general education classes. Naturally, we can't just drop kids with needs into classes and hope it all works out. What we *can* do is learn how to do things we don't know how to do. How can you change your instruction or routines so that a student who struggles to sit still won't get kicked out of class all the time? How can you change your instruction for students with hearing impairments when your go-to pedagogy is talking and waving your arms a bunch? What equipment or training do you need to teach soccer or painting or geometry to students with visual impairments? I want us to avoid the assumption that because some students are not in our classrooms right now, they don't deserve to be, or can't be. I want us all curious. *Where is everyone??* If your classroom doesn't include at least 15% students with disabilities, why not? (15% = average enrollment, students with disabilities in U.S. public schools, 2021–2022; National Center for Education Statistics, 2023.) Where are they? Don't get hung up on superficially meritocratic worries like "they're not ready" or "they'll be overwhelmed and fail." Those self-fulfill. If we never include students who will grow us as teachers, we'll never grow as teachers. Is that what we want, professionally or personally? Good resources:

- Buttorff, D. (2021). 3 ways gen ed teachers can support students with disabilities. Portland, OR: NWEA. www.nwea.org/blog/2021/3-ways-gen-ed-teachers-can-support-students-with-disabilities

- Goodwin, B., & Rouleau, K. (2022). The new classroom instruction that works: The best research-based strategies for increasing student achievement. New York: ACSD.

- McCarthy, J. (2017). *So all can learn: A practical guide to differentiation.* New York: Rowman & Littlefield.

U.S. public schools also need to improve with LGBTQ+ students, especially transgender and gender expansive students. Students who identify as LGBTQ+ are at elevated risk of physical and educational harm in our schools, from bullying and harassment to physical assault and poor academic outcomes (U.S. Department of Education, 2023). Many LGBTQ+ students also face identity-based rejection by family or friends, especially in states or territories that have adopted laws and policies that discriminate on the basis of sex, gender, or gender expression.

When teachers take concrete steps to include and support LGBTQ+ students, we can reduce emotional distress, reduce violence and harassment, and reduce suicidal thoughts and behaviors. And—bonus—the steps we take to better include and support LGBTQ+ students are likely to improve outcomes among *all* young people. One good recent resource: the New York State Education Department's "Creating a Safe, Supportive, and Affirming School Environment for Transgender and Gender Expansive Students" (2023). Some tips:

- Interrupt bullying and harassment immediately. Set expectations for terminology, respect, and collaboration in your class. This makes a difference in all grades; students in middle schools have it worst (GLSEN, 2007).

- Use appropriate names and pronouns. Nonbinary and transgender students may have names that do not match official student records. Use preferred names and chosen pronouns.

- Be visibly supportive. Put up a safe space sticker, a poster, a flag in your room. Being visibly supportive is *especially* helpful for students navigating difficult family or school experiences. www.glsen.org/activity/glsen-safe-space-kit-solidarity-lgbtq-youth

- Start or help run a GSA in your school. A GSA, or Gender and Sexuality Alliance, is an extra-curricular student led club. You can help if there's one at your school, you can start one if there isn't: www.glsen.org/activity/10-steps-start-your-gsa

- Run inclusive clubs, sports, and activities. Maybe you can't fix the "boys" and "girls" soccer teams right now. But you probably *can* get cubing, animation, or *Dungeons & Dragons* clubs up and running inclusively. Avoid gendered participation expectations (no "boys" team or "girls" choir)—keep it inclusive.

- Teach using inclusive curriculum. LGBTQ+ students, like everyone, need to find themselves in curriculum. Who are the heroes and villains? What stories capture us all? Most big-publisher curriculum does a poor job. Roll up your sleeves, integrate material yourself. www.glsen.org/inclusive-curriculum

USE DATA

Not just any data. Seek data that characterize student *learning*, especially concerning grade level standards. Learning = growth, and requires multiple measurements over time. Seek data from assessments you did not create yourself. Why? You need comparisons. How are your students doing compared to others beyond your classroom?

Seek any of these:

- Common assessments created by teams of teachers in your school or district (tips here: www.edutopia.org/article/how-design-better-tests-based-research)

- Assessments provided as part of purchased curriculum
- Assessments your school uses as part of regular benchmarking or progress monitoring

Any or all of those can generate useful data. Just don't trust that whatever assessments you write yourself over the course of the year will be sufficient. They won't. You are not a trained psychometrician.

Also: no data from groups, or group work, or group projects. You need *individual data from each and every one of your students, connected to a standard*. You need to know what each student is learning. Regular assessment of each student on each standard is required. The good news: regular assessment of each student (quizzes, exit tickets, tests, etc.) is a technique that promotes learning and retention of its own accord. It provides retrieval practice. Quizzing students regularly helps them learn and retain information (Willingham, 2021, "Is Drilling Worth It?"). And regular data flow helps you see who's learning what—so you can re-teach, change how you teach, or provide immediate support to students who need it.

I'll acknowledge that anti-test sentiment is pervasive in teaching. I've met teachers who dismiss tests (and the data they generate) as worthless because (not making this up) . . . their students *keep failing them*. Sit with that for two seconds. If tests are "too hard," and students keep failing them . . . that's not a reason to get mad about *testing*. That's a reason to think hard about our *instruction*. When students struggle on tests, they need to learn more so they can do better. Resist any "I hate tests and data" attitudes you may encounter among your teaching peers. Try to learn what available assessment data can tell you (good overview in Boudett et al., 2013). Look into student strengths and weaknesses on a regular basis—and then (this is the key step): make instructional adjustments. Wherever students struggle, that's where they need different instruction, more practice, or both.

BELIEVE IN SCIENCE

Teachers should read and understand quality research. If during your teacher preparation program you never read an article with a standard deviation, a standard error, or an effect size—you should ask why. Do you know what "controlling" for something means? What are you missing? What are you doing that might be tradition but has no empirical justification?

A major problem in education is that teaching practices are rarely informed by research. It's a two-way problem. Education research is notoriously variable in rigor, often difficult to apply in classrooms, and published in journals most teachers never read. Teachers, in the absence of compelling and useful research, tend to embrace trends that have no basis in science. A classic example is "learning styles" theory, discussed in Chapter 6 on instruction. The theory emerged from work on cognition in the 1970s. The basic idea was that we all have preferred "learning styles" (such as auditory, visual, or kinesthetic); when teachers teach in ways that match our preferred "learning styles," we should learn more. The idea of "learning styles," or something like it, can *seem* almost obviously true. Don't we all have different talents and skills and preferences? Of course. The problem is that no evidence shows that this theory can improve student learning. Researchers have spent decades studying whether "learning styles" theory works. It does not. It's junk science. It should not inform teacher practice. And yet if you ask teachers right now whether they believe "learning styles" exist and are helping students learn, a huge majority of teachers will say yes (Furey, 2020; Papadatou-Pastou et al., 2017). That's a problem.

It can be tempting to seek one-stop shopping for research on education. Commonly cited in schools is the work of John Hattie, especially a text he wrote in 2008 called *Visible Learning* (which has since expanded into a network of similar products). What Hattie and colleagues have done effectively over the years is convince teachers and school leaders that their broad "meta-meta-analyses" (studies of studies of studies . . . of teaching and learning) of actual scientific work done by others can be trusted to guide educational practices. The paperback edition of Hattie's book says on the cover (not making this up): "Reveals teaching's Holy Grail!" (Hattie, 2009). One problem is that Hattie and others in the business of selling "meta-meta-analyses" don't actually do research. They're not responsible for making careful claims about what's known, what isn't, and how confident we can be that findings from one context can translate to another. They run stats on work done by others and make broad claims about "effect sizes" with easy-to-read color-coded dials. The more substantive problem with Hattie's claims is that they are, by and large, wrong (Slavin, 2016). Teaching doesn't have a Holy Grail. Teaching has complexity, uncertainty, and context that matters a great deal. You're going to make hundreds, perhaps thousands, of decisions each day in your life as a teacher. Good research can't possibly answer all of your questions in a book or series of books. Good research can help you answer questions, one at a time, and always with uncertainty. Should we start lessons with brainstorming? Does that help kids learn?[2] Maybe? The more you find yourself answering teaching questions with *it really depends*, the more I'm convinced you're on the right (scientific) track. Good resources:

- The U.S. Department of Education's Institute for Education Sciences What Works Clearinghouse: https://ies.ed.gov/ncee/wwc

- The U.S. Department of Education's ERIC (Education Resources Information Center): https://eric.ed.gov

SUPPORT MENTAL HEALTH

Abraham Maslow, the psychologist who wrote a "Theory of Human Motivation" (1943), appeared in an earlier chapter. Maslow's basic idea was that humans have different levels of motivation that are hierarchical in nature. If you can't breathe, for example, your primary motivation in that moment is breathing. If you fear for your safety, it's impossible to care about the Golgi apparatus. Concepts like "hungry kids don't learn" emerge from Maslow's theory.

Student mental health, like breathing or fear, directly impacts the experiences and motivations of the young people we teach. A recent estimate suggested that roughly 17% of children under the age of eighteen had at least one mental health disorder (such as anxiety or depression). That's one in six students. Less than half of those students received any services at school (National Center for Education Statistics, 2022, table 233.69a).

Mental health isn't a single thing. The Diagnostic and Statistical Manual of Mental Disorders (DSM) includes twenty-one chapters of disorder types, including nearly three hundred distinct mental illnesses (American Psychological Association, 2022). Student mental health can also be substantially context dependent. Supportive contexts (home, work, wind ensemble) may require little accommodation; others (U.S. history class, the cafeteria) may require substantially more. Figuring out appropriate and useful supports that keep students in class and learning is an ongoing, iterative process. What works Monday may not work Friday. I hope your school will have skilled mental health professionals—counselors, social workers, or psychologists—who can help. It may not.

What can you do? Get to know your students. Take their mental health seriously. Understand that behavior is communication—and that it might be indirect. I remember an ah-ha moment during my fourth year of teaching, at Juneau-Douglas Yadaa.at Kalé High School (*Go Crimson Bears!*). One of my students, who was awesome and talented and funny, had been missing school a lot. I started asking questions ("Where's Malachi? Did something happen?"). A fellow teacher told me Malachi had depression. My first reaction: *What? No, he doesn't. He's always laughing and smiling in class. He's a goof. He's not depressed.* My ah-ha moment was talking to the school counselor, who told me that depression often prevents students from getting out of bed, doing routines, going to school. That students with depression aren't necessarily moping around all the time being sad. That when they're at school, they may seem fine. And that when they're struggling, they're just . . . not there. We (teachers) sometimes don't *see* the depression. For Malachi, anyway, the math was: depression = absence, not depression = acting sad. For others, it might be different. We're in the early days of learning about mental health and how teachers can do better. The better we know our students, the more likely it is we'll be able to make school safe, positive, and learning-focused. Good resources:

- U.S. Substance Abuse and Mental Health Services Administration (SAMHSA): "What Educators Should Know." www.samhsa.gov/mental-health/how-to-talk/educators

- National Alliance on Mental Illness. www.nami.org

You may learn, from students or families or colleagues, that students have experienced serious trauma. No teacher can remove or fix the bad things that happen to students beyond our classes. We can, however, make our classrooms better places for students carrying heavy burdens. Our rooms can be places of understanding and sanctuary. You don't need to meditate with students or buy weird aromatherapy oils or anything. You do need to get to know your students and what they're experiencing. For example, a student may have experienced the death of a parent. If you're teaching the French vocabulary for "mother" or "father," *you* may be worried about pronunciation while *they* may be revisiting grief. If you know about their loss, you can mitigate impact (meet with the student before class, teach different vocabulary, adjust how and what you assess, change unit sequencing, etc.). If you don't know about their loss, you might just see a kid who puts their head on their desk in the middle of class or disappears to the bathroom for twenty minutes. See Korbey (2022) for good ways to learn more. I'm convinced that a good relationship with each and every student is central to good teaching and better experiences at school for all young people.

All teachers must recognize the warning signs of suicide. This includes elementary school teachers. Every teacher can learn to ask students directly: "Are you thinking of suicide?" and "Do you have a plan?" Every teacher can help students by connecting them with counselors, social workers, and the 988 Suicide and Crisis Lifeline. Only a small percentage of students with mental health disorders are at risk for suicide—but the stakes for any student are obviously vast. Two good resources:

- National Institute of Mental Health, "Warning Signs of Suicide." www.nimh.nih.gov/health/publications/warning-signs-of-suicide

- Suicide Prevention Resource Center, "Warning Signs for Suicide." https://sprc.org/warning-signs-for-suicide

That's a heavy place to close this book. Yet, there's an alignment, I think. We have the privilege of working with young people. Our best work is to keep them safe and whole. This chapter asks: "What comes next?" I hope the answer you're considering is something like: *make schools better.* You don't have to be superhuman to do so. Successful teachers don't zip into phone booths, don capes, and save the world. We help kids do this:

Figure 10.2. Three kids reading in a classroom. *Source:* U.S. Department of Education (2013). Public domain.

Two things I love about Figure 10.2. First, those kids are reading. Second, where's the teacher? Where are you? I have no idea. You're somewhere. But you're not the focus. The focus is those kids, comfortable and reading. Nice job, you. Thanks for joining the best work I know. It's hard work. It's *good* work. You'll do OK, and then you'll do better.

How Can I Make Things Better for Students?

You can make things better for students by being there for them, day by day. By showing up. You can make things better by being decent and understanding and caring, and by growing as a teacher over time (it will take years). You can become more inclusive. You can support students our schools don't yet serve well. And you can *keep teaching* over the years ahead, so that the better-and-better versions of you are there for the students you have yet to meet.

SUPREME COURT CASE FOR DISCUSSION

Note: This case is still being decided at the time of this writing by the Virginia Supreme Court. I'm including it because it revolves around actions taken by a single teacher—and because it touches on a chapter theme ("Be more inclusive"). However ultimately decided, I suspect the issues involved will remain salient for years.

Case: Vlaming v. West Point School Board et al. (E.D. Va. 2020).
Link: https://law.justia.com/cases/federal/district-courts/virginia/vaedce/3:2019cv00773/456658/37

From 2012 to 2018, Peter Vlaming taught high school French in West Point, Virginia—a small town about forty miles east of Richmond. Early in the 2018–2019 school year, Vlaming met with one of his students ("John Doe"), his student's parents, and the school guidance counselor. At the meeting, Doe and his parents disclosed that his gender expression had recently changed from female to male. Doe also disclosed his traditionally masculine chosen name, and that he/him pronouns were correct. Vlaming, like many high school language teachers in U.S. public schools, did not use English names with students in class, but instead used chosen French names. During class following the meeting, Vlaming used Doe's chosen French name but avoided using any pronouns. Outside of Doe's presence, Vlaming referred to Doe using she/her pronouns.

In late October 2018, Doe, his parents, and school administrators spoke with Vlaming about using pronouns that matched Doe's gender identity. The assistant principal, Suzanne Aunspach, followed up with Vlaming in writing, warning that his refusal to use Doe's correct pronouns was potentially a violation of federal law and a district policy that required teachers to use pronouns matching student gender identities. In the letter, Aunspach warned Vlaming "that he should use male pronouns or his job could be at risk" (*Vlaming v. West Point*, 3). Vlaming argued to Aunspach and Principal Johnathan Hochman that "his conscience and religious beliefs prohibited him from using pronouns that do not match a person's biological sex" (ibid., 3).

During a class exercise on October 31, 2018, Vlaming used female pronouns to refer to Doe. Following class, Doe withdrew from French. Principal Hochman immediately placed Vlaming on administrative leave. On November 6, Superintendent Laura Abel sent Vlaming a formal reprimand and final warning letter, noting that Vlaming's refusal to use Doe's correct pronouns was a violation of district policies against harassment and retaliation based on gender identity, and that he must use the proper pronouns. Vlaming told Abel he could not comply. At a public hearing on December 6, 2018, the West Point School Board fired Vlaming. In their letter of explanation (dated January 2, 2019), the Board explained to Vlaming that he was fired because he had violated district policies against discrimination and harassment, and because he had failed to follow the directives of the assistant principal, the principal, and the superintendent.

In September 2019, Vlaming filed a lawsuit against the West Point School Board, arguing that his termination violated his rights as a teacher, including:

- Freedom of speech,
- Free exercise of religion,
- Due process, and
- Freedom from "governmental discrimination."

Vlaming's suit is now under consideration by the Virginia Supreme Court.

QUESTIONS

1. When, if ever, should a teacher be able to ignore district policies on the basis of "freedom of speech" or "exercise of religion"?

2. Consider a district policy that requires teachers to use pronouns that correspond to biological sex rather than gender identity (as is the case in ten states, largely but not exclusively in the U.S. South at the time of this writing; Pendharkar, 2023). Should teachers be protected from termination for using correct pronouns, even when doing so violates district policy?

3. John Doe clearly had supportive parents in navigating French class with Peter Vlaming. Parent or guardian support is not universal for transgender and gender expansive students. How would you handle a request from a student like John Doe to use a chosen name and pronouns—if the student also asked you not to disclose either to their family?

FURTHER READINGS AND RESOURCES

Data Use: Boudett, K., City, E., & Murnane, R. (2013). *Data wise: A step-by-step guide to using assessment results to improve teaching and learning* (revised and expanded edition). Cambridge, MA: Harvard Education Press.

Education Science: What Works Clearinghouse (any practice guide). https://ies.ed.gov/ncee/wwc/practiceguides

Including LGBTQ+ Students: New York State Education Department. (2023). Creating a safe, supportive, and affirming school environment for transgender and gender expansive students: 2023 Legal update and best practices. Albany, NY: Author. www.p12.nysed.gov/sss

Including Students with Disabilities: McCarthy, J. (2017). *So all can learn: A practical guide to differentiation.* New York: Rowman & Littlefield.

Mental Health: Substance Abuse and Mental Health Services Administration (SAMHSA). (2023). How to talk about mental health, for educators. Washington, DC: Author. https://www.samhsa.gov/mental-health/how-to-talk/educators

Teaching Reading: Seidenberg, M. (2017). *Language at the speed of sight: How we read, why so many can't, and what can be done about it.* New York: Basic Books.

NOTES

1. At that time: Master P, "Make 'Em Say Uhh!" (1997). Plants these days may feel otherwise.

2. Um: maybe? Brainstorming can promote improved solutions where student tasks involve creative problem solving (Isaksen & Gaulin, 2005) . . . but would not promote learning when students face predefined tasks such as phonics practice. Please don't brainstorm ideas about phonics. Just teach the kids phonics. Oh, and be advised: brainstorming can inadvertently *suppress* creativity via cognitive inertia, wherein students just go along with whatever the group

says (Taylor et al., 1958). See what I'm telling you? Even a single small thing like brainstorming doesn't have a single *general* effect. The details matter. You have to read the research to understand the details. Recommended reads: Tullis (2023) and Willingham (2021).

Bibliography

The 1619 Project. (n.d.). *The 1619 Project: Education Materials Collection.* Washington, DC: Pulitzer Center. https://1619education.org

Action for Education Equity. (n.d.) How is the RCSD funded? Rochester, NY: Author. https://actionforeducationequity.org/understanding-education-inequity/rcsd-funding

Adams, C. (2020). What the research says about the best way to engage parents. *Hechinger Report*, February 28. New York: Teachers College Press. https://hechingerreport.org/what-the-research-says-about-the-best-way-to-engage-parents

Adams, D. (1995). *Education for extinction: American Indians and the boarding school experience, 1875–1928.* Lawrence: University Press of Kansas.

Alaska Department of Education & Early Development. (n.d.). State-Tribal education compacting. Juneau, AK: Author. https://education.alaska.gov/compacting

Alaska Department of Education & Early Development. (1998). Alaska standards for culturally responsive schools. Fairbanks: University of Alaska Fairbanks, Alaska Native Knowledge Network. https://uaf.edu/ankn/publications/guides/alaska-standards-for-cult

Alaska Department of Health. (n.d.) Get the facts about marijuana. Juneau, AK: Author. https://health.alaska.gov/dph/director/pages/marijuana/facts.aspx

Alber, R. (2017). Fire up your class with student-interest surveys. Nicasio, CA: Edutopia. www.edutopia.org/blog/fire-up-class-student-interest-surveys-rebecca-alber

Alexander v. Holmes County Board of Education, 396 U.S. 19 (1969). http://cdn.loc.gov/service/ll/usrep/usrep396/usrep396019/usrep396019.pdf

Alexie, S. (2009). The absolutely true diary of a part-time Indian. New York: Hachette.

Algar, S. (2019). Gym teacher fired for playing "Fortnite" with his students. *New York Post*, February 11. https://nypost.com/2019/02/11/gym-teacher-fired-for-playing-fortnite-with-his-students

Ali v. Woodbridge Township School District, 19-2217, 3d. Cir. (2020). https://law.justia.com/cases/federal/appellate-courts/ca3/19-2217/19-2217-2020-04-22.html

Allegretto, S., García, E., & Weiss, E. (2022). Public education funding in the U.S. needs an overhaul. Washington, DC: Economic Policy Institute. www.epi.org/publication/public-education-funding-in-the-us-needs-an-overhaul

Allison, S., & Tharby, A. (2015). *Making every lesson count: Six principles to support great teaching and learning.* Carmarthen, UK: Crown House.

Aloe, A., & Becker, B. (2009). Teacher verbal ability and school outcomes: Where is the evidence? *Educational Researcher*, *38*(8), 612–624. https://doi.org/10.3102/0013189X09353939

Alter, P., & Haydon, T. (2017). Characteristics of effective classroom rules: A review of the literature. *Teacher Education and Special Education, 40*(2), 114–127. https://doi.org/10.1177/0888406417700962

Altieri, N., Pisoni, D., & Townsend, J. (2011). "Some normative data on lip-reading skills." *Journal of the Acoustical Society of America, 130*(1): 1–4. https://doi.org/10.1121/1.3593376

American Civil Liberties Union. (2023). Trans students should be treated with dignity, not outed by their schools. January 26. www.aclu.org/news/lgbtq-rights/trans-students-should-be-treated-with-dignity-not-outed-by-their-schools

American Library Association. (n.d.) Frequently challenged books. Chicago: American Library Association, Office for Intellectual Freedom. www.ala.org/advocacy/bbooks/frequentlychallengedbooks

American Psychiatric Association. (2022). *Diagnostic and statistical manual of mental disorders (DSM-5-TR)*. Washington, DC: Author.

Americans with Disabilities Act of 1990, 42 U.S.C. § 12101 et seq. (1990). www.govinfo.gov/content/pkg/STATUTE-104/pdf/STATUTE-104-Pg327.pdf

Anderson, J. (1988). *The Education of Blacks in the South, 1860–1935*. Chapel Hill: University of North Carolina Press.

Anderson, L. (2008). *Carlisle vs. Army: Jim Thorpe, Dwight Eisenhower, Pop Warner, and the forgotten story of football's greatest battle*. New York: Random House.

Arellanes, J., Viramontez Anguaino, R. & Lohman, B. (2019). Bettering the educational attainment for Latino families: How families view the education of their children. *Journal of Latinos and Education, 18*(4), 349–362. https://doi.org/10.1080/15348431.2018.1426465

Arizona Revised Statutes. (2022). Ariz. Rev. Stat. § 15-112, Prohibited courses and classes; enforcement. https://casetext.com/statute/arizona-revised-statutes/title-15-education/chapter-1-general-provisions/article-1-general-provisions/section-15-112-prohibited-courses-and-classes-enforcement.

Aspen Institute. (2015). Roles and responsibilities of the state education agency. Washington, DC: Author. www.aspeninstitute.org/wp-content/uploads/2015/12/Aspen-SEA-Roles-Nov24-final.pdf

Associated Press. (1992). Company News: Mattel says it erred; Teen Talk Barbie turns silent on math. *The New York Times*, October 21. www.nytimes.com/1992/10/21/business/company-news-mattel-says-it-erred-teen-talk-barbie-turns-silent-on-math.html

Associated Press. (2023). 32 Mississippi school districts still under federal desegregation orders. *NBC News*, June 1. www.nbcnews.com/news/nbcblk/federal-government-orders-desegregation-32-mississippi-school-district-rcna87296

Autor, D., & Wasserman, M. (2013). *Wayward sons: The emerging gender gap in labor markets and education*. Washington, DC: Third Way. www.thirdway.org/report/wayward-sons-the-emerging-gender-gap-in-labor-markets-and-education

Autor, D., Figlio, D., Karbownik, K., Roth, J., & Wasserman, M. (2016). School quality and the gender gap in educational achievement. Cambridge, MA: MIT Department of Economics & National Bureau of Economic Research. Discussion paper #2016.01. https://blueprintcdn.com/wp-content/uploads/2016/05/

Blueprint-Labs-Discussion-Paper-2016.01-Autor-Figlio-Karbownik-Roth-Wasserman.pdf

Bailey, T. (2020). Is MTSS/RTI really that complicated? Let's get back to basics! Arlington, VA, Center on Multi-Tiered System of Supports. https://mtss4success.org/blog/mtssrti-really-complicated-lets-get-back-basics

Baker, S., Lesaux, N., Jayanthi, M., Dimino, J., Proctor, C. P., Morris, J., Gersten, R., Haymond, K., Kieffer, M., Linan-Thompson, S., & Newman-Gonchar, R. (2014). Teaching academic content and literacy to English learners in elementary and middle school (NCEE 2014-4012). Washington, DC: National Center for Education Evaluation and Regional Assistance (NCEE), Institute of Education Sciences. https://ies.ed.gov/ncee/wwc/Docs/PracticeGuide/english_learners_pg_040114.pdf

Ballis, B., & Heath, K. (2021). Special education: Beneficial to many, harmful to others. Washington, DC: Brookings. www.brookings.edu/blog/brown-center-chalkboard/2021/05/26/special-education-beneficial-to-some-harmful-to-others

Ballotpedia. (2022). Analysis of school district and board member characteristics, 2022. Middleton, WI: Author. https://ballotpedia.org/Analysis_of_school_district_and_board_member_characteristics,_2022

Balu, R., Zhu, P., Doolittle, F., Schiller, E., Jenkins, J., & Gersten, R. (2015). Evaluation of response to intervention practices for elementary school reading. Washington, DC: United States Department of Education, Institute of Education Sciences. m https://whatworks.ed.gov.

Bambrick-Santoyo, P. (2019). *Driven by data 2.0*. Hoboken, NJ: Wiley.

Banerjee, N., Stearns, E., Moller, S., & Mickelson, R. (2017). Teacher job satisfaction and student achievement: The roles of teacher professional community and teacher collaboration in schools. *American Journal of Education*, *123*(2). https://doi.org/10.1086/689932

Barabak, M. (1997). GOP bid to mend rift with Latinos still strained. August 31. www.languagepolicy.net/archives/LAT6.htm

Bardach, L., & Klassen, R. (2020). Smart teachers, successful students? A systematic review of the literature on teachers' cognitive abilities and teacher effectiveness. *Educational Research Review*, *30*. https://doi.org/10.1016/j.edurev.2020.100312

Barnum, M. (2022). As pandemic aid runs out, America is set to return to a broken school funding system. New York: Chalkbeat, August 25. www.chalkbeat.org/2022/8/25/23318969/school-funding-inequality-child-poverty-covid-relief.

Barnum, M. (2019). Critics of charter schools say they're hurting school districts. Are they right? *Chalkbeat*, June 11. www.chalkbeat.org/2019/6/11/21108318/critics-of-charter-schools-say-they-re-hurting-school-districts-are-they-right

Barnum, M. (2015). Fact-check: Just how many tenured teachers are fired each year anyway? (Hint: Not many). *The 74*, September 8. www.the74million.org/article/fact-check-just-how-many-tenured-teachers-are-fired-each-year-anyway-hint-not-many

Barshay, J. (2019). Inside the Reardon-Hanushek clash over 50 years of achievement gaps. Stanford scholars disagree about academic gaps between rich and poor students. *Hechinger Report*, May 27. New York: Teachers College. https://hechingerreport.org/inside-the-reardon-hanushek-clash-over-50-years-of-achievement-gaps

Barshay, J. (2021). Proof points: What research tells us about gifted education. *Hechinger Report*, October 18. https://hechingerreport.org/proof-points-what-research-tells-us-about-gifted-education.

Barshay, J. (2023). Proof points: Charter schools have improved in the past 15 years, but many still fail students, researchers say. *Hechinger Report*, June 12. https://hechingerreport.org/proof-points-charter-schools-have-improved-in-the-past-15-years-but-many-still-fail-students-researchers-say

Basu, T. (2016). So it seems New York is the most talkative state. *The Cut*, February 4. www.thecut.com/2016/02/it-seems-new-york-is-the-most-talkative-state.html

Batalova, J., & Zong, J. (2016). Language diversity and English proficiency in the United States. Washington, DC: Migration Policy Institute. www.migrationpolicy.org/article/language-diversity-and-english-proficiency-united-states-2015

Baugh, J. (2011). *The Detroit school busing case:* Milliken v. Bradley *and the controversy over desegregation*. Lawrence: University Press of Kansas.

Bazleton, E. (2013). *Sticks and stones: Defeating the culture of bullying and rediscovering the power of character and empathy*. New York: Random House.

Bempechat, J. (2019). The case for (quality) homework. *Education Next*, *19*(1). www.educationnext.org/case-for-quality-homework-improves-learning-how-parents-can-help

Berger, M., & Wilborn, L. (1976). Education. Texas State Historical Association. www.tshaonline.org/handbook/entries/education

Bergman, P., & McFarlin, I. (2018). Education for all? A nationwide audit study of schools of choice. Cambridge, MA: National Bureau of Economic Research. ERIC ED594347. https://eric.ed.gov/?id=ED594347

Bethel v. Fraser, 478 US 675 (1986). www.oyez.org/cases/1985/84-1667

Betz, B. (2019). Florida middle school teacher found guilty of selling drugs to students, court records say. Fox News, September 19. www.foxnews.com/us/florida-middle-school-teacher-found-guilty-of-selling-drugs-to-students-court-records-say

Beyer, D. (2021). Immigrants are vital to the U.S. economy. Washington, DC: U.S. Senate Joint Economic Committee. www.jec.senate.gov/public/_cache/files/6750b0f0-c851-4fee-9619-295582fd44e8/immigrants-are-vital-to-the-us-economy-final.pdf

Black, D. (2020a). America's founders recognized the need for public education. Democracy requires maintaining that commitment. *Time*, September 22. https://time.com/5891261/early-american-education-history

Black, D. (2020b). *Schoolhouse burning: Public education and the assault on American democracy*. New York: Public Affairs.

Blazar, D. (2018). Validating teacher effects on students' attitudes and behaviors: Evidence from random assignment of teachers to students. *Education Finance and Policy*, *13*(3), 281–309. https://doi.org/10.1162/edfp_a_00251

Board of Education v. Pico, 457 U.S. 853 (1982). https://caselaw.findlaw.com/us-supreme-court/457/853.html

Board of Education v. Rowley, 458 U.S. 176 (1982). www.law.cornell.edu/supremecourt/text/458/176

Boey, V. (2023). Florida teacher fired over "inappropriate" lesson: "I didn't do anything wrong." Fox 35 Orlando, April 5. www.fox35orlando.com/news/teacher-fired-over-inappropriate-lesson-says-he-was-trying-to-teach-students-how-to-stay-safe

Borman, G., & Dowling, M. (2010). Schools and inequality: A multilevel analysis of Coleman's equality of educational opportunity data. *Teachers College Record*, *112*(5), 1201–1246. https://doi.org/10.1177/016146811011200507

Boston Latin School. (n.d.) "BLS History." www.bls.org/apps/pages/index.jsp?uREC_ID=206116&type=d

Boudett, K., City, E., & Murnane, R. (2013). *Data wise: A step-by-step guide to using assessment results to improve teaching and learning* (revised and expanded edition). Cambridge, MA: Harvard Education Press.

Bramhall, E. (2021). Why does segregation between school districts matter for educational equity? Washington, DC: Urban Institute. https://housingmatters.urban.org/articles/why-does-segregation-between-school-districts-matter-educational-equity

Breiseth, L. (2021). Communicating with ELL families: 10 strategies for schools. Washington, DC: National Education Association. www.nea.org/professional-excellence/student-engagement/tools-tips/communicating-ell-families-10-strategies

Brenan, M. (2021). K–12 Parents remain largely satisfied with child's education. *Gallup*, August 26. https://news.gallup.com/poll/354083/parents-remain-largely-satisfied-child-education.aspx

Briston, T., Shirrell, M., & Britton, T. (2021). How does student-teacher matching affect suspensions for students of color? Washington, DC: Brookings, October 11. www.brookings.edu/articles/how-does-student-teacher-matching-affect-suspensions-for-students-of-color

Brookhart, S. (2017). *How to give effective feedback to your students*, 2nd ed. Alexandria, VA: Association for Supervision & Curriculum Development.

Brown v. Board of Education of Topeka, KS. 347 U.S. 483 (1954). https://supreme.justia.com/cases/federal/us/347/483

Brown v. Board of Education of Topeka, KS. 349 U.S. 294 (1955). https://supreme.justia.com/cases/federal/us/349/294

Brown v. Board, 15-1857, 7th Cir. (2016). https://law.justia.com/cases/federal/appellate-courts/ca7/15-1857/15-1857-2016-06-02.html

Buck v. Bell, 274 U.S. 200 (1927). www.law.cornell.edu/supremecourt/text/274/200.

Butrymowicz, S., & Mader, J. (2017). Low academic expectations and poor support for special education students are "hurting their future." *Hechinger*

Report, November 11. https://hechingerreport.org/low-academic-expectations-poor-support-special-education-students-hurting-future

Buttorff, D. (2021). 3 ways gen ed teachers can support students with disabilities. Portland, OR: NWEA. www.nwea.org/blog/2021/3-ways-gen-ed-teachers-can-support-students-with-disabilities

Cabrera, N., Milem, J., Jaquette, O., & Marx, R. (2014). Missing the (student achievement) forest for all the (political) trees: Empiricism and the Mexican American Studies controversy in Tucson. *American Educational Research Journal, 51*(6), 1084–1118. https://doi.org/10.3102/0002831214553705

Canadian Council on Learning. (2009). A systematic review of literature examining the impact of homework on academic achievement. Ottawa, ON: Author. https://edu.au.dk/fileadmin/edu/Udgivelser/SystematicReview_HomeworkApril27-2009.pdf

Carr, S. (2012). In Southern Towns, "Segregation Academies" Are Still Going Strong. *The Atlantic*, December 13. www.theatlantic.com/national/archive/2012/12/in-southern-towns-segregation-academies-are-still-going-strong/266207

Center for Research on Education Outcomes. (2023). *Study III: 2023 National Charter School Study*. Stanford, CA: Author. https://ncss3.stanford.edu

Centers for Disease Control and Prevention (2019). QuickStats: Number of deaths from hornet, wasp, and bee stings, among males and females—National Vital Statistics System, United States, 2000–2017. *Morbidity and Mortality Weekly Report,* 68(29), 649. http://dx.doi.org/10.15585/mmwr.mm6829a5

Chantrill, C. (n.d.). U.S. education spending history from 1900. *US Government Spending*. www.usgovernmentspending.com/education_spending

Chavira, G., Cooper, C. & Vasquez-Salgado, Y. (2016) Pathways to achievement: Career and educational aspirations and expectations of Latina/o immigrant parents and early adolescents. *Journal of Latinos and Education, 15*(3): 214–228. https://doi.org/10.1080/15348431.2015.1131693.

Cherng, H. (2017). If they think I can: Teacher bias and youth of color expectations and achievement. *Social Science Research,* 66, 170–186. https://doi.org/10.1016/j.ssresearch.2017.04.001.

Children's Literacy Initiative. (2020). Interest surveys: What, why and how. Philadelphia, PA: Author. https://cli.org/resources/session-2.

Churchill, W. (2008). *Kill the Indian, save the man.* San Francisco: City Lights.

City, E., Elmore, R., Fiarman, S., & Teitel, L. (2009). *Instructional rounds in education: A network approach to improving teaching and learning.* Cambridge, MA: Harvard Education Press.

City of Boston. (2018). Boston Latin School. www.boston.gov/departments/archaeology/boston-latin-school.

Civilization Fund Act. (1819). P.L. 15-85. https://govtrackus.s3.amazonaws.com/legislink/pdf/stat/3/STATUTE-3-Pg516b.pdf

Clarke, E. (1873). *Sex in education; or, A fair chance for the girls.* Boston: James R. Osgood and Company. https://dl.tufts.edu/pdfviewer/pz50h768t/h702qk13g

Clotfelter, C. (2011). *After Brown: The rise and retreat of school desegregation.* Princeton, NJ: Princeton University Press.

Coates, Ta-Nehisi. (2017). The first white president. *The Atlantic*, October. www.theatlantic.com/magazine/archive/2017/10/the-first-white-president-ta-nehisi-coates/537909

Codell, E. (2009). *Educating Esmé: Diary of a teacher's first year.* Chapel Hill, NC: Algonquin Books.

Coleman, J. (1966). Equality of Educational Opportunity. Inter-university Consortium for Political and Social Research. https://doi.org/10.3886/ICPSR06389.v3

Commonwealth of Massachusetts. (1780). *Massachusetts Constitution.* https://malegislature.gov/Laws/Constitution

Commonwealth of Massachusetts. (n.d.). Old Deluder Satan Law. Boston: Author. www.mass.gov/doc/old-deluder-satan-law/download.

Conron, K. (2020). LGBT Youth population in the United States. Los Angeles: UCLA School of Law, Williams Institute. https://williamsinstitute.law.ucla.edu/publications/lgbt-youth-pop-us

Cooley, A., Fleming, M., & Wade, G. (2011). The constitutional and contractual controversy of suspicionless drug testing of public school teachers. *Oklahoma Law Review*, *63*(3). https://digitalcommons.law.ou.edu/olr/vol63/iss3/1

Cooper, H., Robinson, J., & Patall, E. (2006). Does homework improve academic achievement? A synthesis of research, 1987–2003. *Review of Educational Research*, *76*(1), 1–62. http://www.jstor.org/stable/3700582

Cornell Law School. (2023). *Negligence.* Ithaca, NY: Legal Information Institute. www.law.cornell.edu/wex/negligence

Cornell University. (2002). *I will be heard! Abolitionism in America.* https://rmc.library.cornell.edu/abolitionism/narratives.htm

Cornell University. (2013). *Robot battles: Mechatronics class teaches students the culture of automation.* Ithaca, NY: Cornell Engineering. www.engineering.cornell.edu/magazine/features/robot-battles

Council of Chief State School Officers. (2022). Common Core State Standards. Washington, DC: Author. https://learning.ccsso.org/common-core-state-standards-initiative

Crawford, J., & Krashen, S. (2015). *English learners in American classrooms: 101 Questions, 101 Answers.* New York: Scholastic.

Cronin, A. (2016). Student-led conferences: Resources for educators. Nicasio, CA: Edutopia, July 8. www.edutopia.org/blog/student-led-conferences-resources-ashley-cronin

D'Agostino, J., & Powers, S. (2009). Predicting teacher performance with test scores and grade point average: A meta-analysis. *American Educational Research Journal*, *46*(1), 146–182. https://doi.org/10.3102/0002831208323280

Daugherity, B. (2016). *Keep on keeping on: The NAACP and the implementation of* Brown v. Board of Education *in Virginia.* Charlottesville: University of Virginia Press.

Dawes Act, Public Law 105-49 (1884). www.congress.gov/105/plaws/publ49/PLAW-105publ49.pdf

Dee, T. (2004). Teachers, race, and student achievement in a randomized experiment. *The Review of Economics and Statistics*, *86*(1), 195–210. https://doi.org/10.1162/003465304323023750

Defenbaugh, W., & W. Keesecker. (1935). *Compulsory school attendance laws and their administration* (Bulletin No. 4). Washington, DC: U.S. Government Printing Office. https://files.eric.ed.gov/fulltext/ED542358.pdf

Delmost, M. (2016). *Why busing failed: Race, media, and the national resistance to school desegregation*. Berkeley: University of California Press.

Dennis, A. (2021). Teacher Matthew Hawn, fired in critical race theory debate, fights to get his job back. *Knox News*, December 20. www.knoxnews.com/story/news/2021/12/20/sullivan-county-teacher-matthew-hawn-fired-critical-race-theory-sue/6508618001

Dewey, J. (1974 [1904]). The relation of theory to practice in education. In *John Dewey on education*, R. D. Archambault, ed., 313–338. Chicago: University of Chicago Press.

Diaz, A. (2023). Teacher fired for filming raunchy TikTok dances in classroom: Report. *New York Post*, May 12. https://nypost.com/2023/05/12/teacher-fired-for-filming-raunchy-tiktok-dances-in-classroom-report

Dorsey, D. (2020). Education is still (for now) not a fundamental right under the U.S. Constitution. Wichita: Kansas Policy Institute. https://kansaspolicy.org/education-is-still-for-now-not-a-fundamental-right-under-the-u-s-constitution

Douglas, D. (2005). *Jim Crow moves north: The battle over northern school segregation, 1865–1954*. Cambridge, UK: Cambridge University.

Dumont, H., & Ready, D. (2020). Do schools reduce or exacerbate inequality? How the associations between student achievement and achievement growth influence our understanding of the role of schooling. *American Educational Research Journal*, *57*(2), 728–774. https://doi.org/10.3102/0002831219868182

Dunbar-Ortiz, R. (2015). *An Indigenous peoples' history of the United States*. Boston: Beacon.

Duncan, G., & Murnane, R., eds. (2011). *Whither opportunity? Rising inequality, schools, and children's life chances*. New York: Russell Sage Foundation.

Durkee, A. (2022). 14 States claim Florida's "Don't Say Gay" law "does not discriminate" and want it to be upheld. *Forbes*, December 12. www.forbes.com/sites/alisondurkee/2022/12/12/14-states-claim-floridas-dont-say-gay-law-does-not-discriminate-and-want-it-to-be-upheld/?sh=21f83d7f3e25

EdBuild. (2019). *Dismissed: America's most divisive school district borders*. Jersey City, NJ: Author. https://edbuild.org/content/dismissed

Edelstein, J. (2023). Taylor Mathis got sacrificed at the altar of responsible gambling. *Sportshandle*, March 20. https://sportshandle.com/taylor-mathis-fired-superbook

Education Amendments Act of 1972, 20 U.S.C. §§1681–1688 (1972). https://uscode.house.gov/view.xhtml?req=20+USC+1681

Education Commission of the States. (2020). 50-state comparison: Teacher employment contract policies. Denver, CO: Author. www.ecs.org/50-state-comparison-teacher-employment-contract-policies

Education Commission of the States. (2021). 50-state comparison: Private school choice. Denver, CO: Author. www.ecs.org/50-state-comparison-private-school-choice

Education for all Handicapped Children Act, 90 Stat. 773 (Public Law 94-142) (1975).

Education Week. (2017). Single-gender public schools in 5 charts. Bethesda, MD: Author. www.edweek.org/teaching-learning/single-gender-public-schools-in-5-charts

EducatorFI. (n.d.) How to analyze your teacher contract. https://educatorfi.com/analyze-contract

Egg Farmers of Canada. (2023). How to crack an egg. www.eggs.ca/eggs101/view/19/how-to-crack-an-egg

EL Education. (n.d.). *Leaders of Their Own Learning.* "Student-Led Conferences." New York: Author. https://eleducation.org/resources/chapter-5-student-led-conferences

Essex, N. (2012). *The 200 Most frequently asked legal questions for educators.* New York: Skyhorse.

Essex, N. (2021). *A teacher's pocket guide to school law*, 3rd ed. New York: Pearson.

Evans-Marshall v. Board of Education, 624 F.3d 332 (6th Cir. 2010). https://caselaw.findlaw.com/us-6th-circuit/1541991.html

Evertson, C. M., Anderson, C. W., Anderson, L. M., & Brophy, J. E. (1980). Relationships between classroom behaviors and student outcomes in junior high mathematics and English classes. *American Educational Research Journal, 17*(1): 43–60. https://doi.org/10.2307/1162507

Every Student Succeeds Act, 20 U.S.C. § 6301 (2015). www.ed.gov/essa

Facing History. (2020). Stolen lives: The Indigenous peoples of Canada and the Indian residential schools. www.facinghistory.org/en-ca/resource-library/stolen-lives-indigenous-peoples-canada-indian-residential-schools

Fairlie, R., & Resch, A. (2002). Is there "white flight" into private schools? Evidence from the National Educational Longitudinal Survey. *The Review of Economics and Statistics, 84*(1): 21–33. www.jstor.org/stable/3211736

Family Educational Rights and Privacy Act, 20 U.S.C. § 1232g. www2.ed.gov/policy/gen/guid/fpco/ferpa/index.html

Farrell, W., & Gray, J. (2018). *The boy crisis: Why our boys are struggling and what we can do about it.* Dallas, TX: BenBella.

Felton, E. (2016). New York's upstate cities have some of the worst schools in the country. *The Hechinger Report*, August 3. https://hechingerreport.org/new-yorks-upstate-cities-worst-schools-country

Fenwick, L. (2022). *Jim Crow's pink slip: The untold story of Black principal and teacher leadership.* Cambridge, MA: Harvard Education Press.

Fiester, L. (2013). *Early warning confirmed: A research update on third-grade reading.* Baltimore, MD: Annie E. Casey Foundation. https://assets.aecf.org/m/resourcedoc/AECF-EarlyWarningConfirmed-2013.pdf

FindLaw. (2016). Teacher's rights: State and local laws. www.findlaw.com/education/teachers-rights/teachers-rights-state-and-local-laws.html

Finn, C., Manno, B., & Wright, B. (2016). *Charter schools at the crossroads: Predicaments, paradoxes, possibilities.* Cambridge, MA: Harvard Education Press.

Finnigan, K., & Stewart, T. (2009). Interdistrict choice as a policy solution: Examining Rochester's Urban-Suburban Interdistrict Transfer Program (USITP). Nashville, TN: National Center on School Choice, Vanderbilt University. https://eric.ed.gov/?id=ED513912

Firestone, D. (1993). While Barbie talks tough, G.I. Joe goes shopping. *New York Times*, December 31. www.nytimes.com/1993/12/31/us/while-barbie-talks-tough-g-i-joe-goes-shopping.html

Flatter, R. (1999). Thorpe preceded Deion, Bo. ESPN. www.espn.com/sportscentury/features/00016499.html

Florida House of Representatives. (2022). House Bill 1557, "An act relating to parental rights in education." www.flsenate.gov/Session/Bill/2022/1557/BillText/er/PDF

Florida Museum. (n.d.). The Nombre de Dios Mission Sites. www.floridamuseum.ufl.edu/histarch/research/st-augustine/menendez/nombre-de-dios

Ford, D., & King, R. (2014). No Blacks allowed: Segregated gifted education in the context of *Brown v. Board of Education*. *The Journal of Negro Education*, *83*(3), 300–310. https://doi.org/10.7709/jnegroeducation.83.3.0300

Formisano, R. (2004). *Boston against busing: Race, class, and ethnicity in the 1960s and 1970s.* Chapel Hill: University of North Carolina Press.

Fowler v. Board of Educ., 819 F.2d 657, 661. 6th Cir. (1987). https://casetext.com/case/fowler-v-board-of-educ-of-lincoln-county-ky

Frankenberg, E., Ee, J., Ayscue, J., & G. Orfield. (2019). *Harming our common future: America's segregated schools 65 years after Brown.* Los Angeles: University of California Los Angeles, Civil Rights Project / Proyecto Derechos Civiles. www.civilrightsproject.ucla.edu/research/k-12-education/integration-and-diversity/harming-our-common-future-americas-segregated-schools-65-years-after-brown/Brown-65-050919v4-final.pdf

Fredricks, J., Blumenfeld, P., & Paris, A. (2004). School engagement: Potential of the concept, state of the evidence. *Review of Educational Research*, *74*(1), 59–109. https://doi.org/10.3102/00346543074001059

French Connection UK. (n.d.). FCUK tees. https://usa.frenchconnection.com/collections/fcuk-tees

Freshwater v. Mt. Vernon City School District, 137 Ohio St. 3d. 469 (2013). www.supremecourt.ohio.gov/rod/docs/pdf/0/2013/2013-ohio-5000.pdf

Friedman, M. (1955). The role of government in education. In R. Solo (ed.), *Economics and the Public Interest*. New Brunswick, NJ: Trustees of Rutgers College.

Furey, W. (2020). The stubborn myth of "Learning Styles": State teacher-license prep materials peddle a debunked theory. *Education Next*, *20*(3). www.educationnext.org/stubborn-myth-learning-styles-state-teacher-license-prep-materials-debunked-theory

Gamson, D., & E. Hodge, Eds. (2018). *The shifting landscape of the American school district: Race, class, geography, and the perpetual reform of local control, 1935–2015.* New York: Peter Lang.

Garcetti v. Ceballos, 547 U.S. 410 (2006). https://www.oyez.org/cases/2005/04-473

García, D. (2018). *Strategies of segregation: Race, residence, and the struggle for educational Equality.* Berkeley: University of California Press.

García, E., & Weiss, E. (2017). Education inequalities at the school starting gate: Gaps, trends, and strategies to address them. Washington, DC: Economic Policy Institute. www.epi.org/publication/education-inequalities-at-the-school-starting-gate

Gary B. v. Whitmer, 957 F.3d 616. 6th Cir. (2020). www.opn.ca6.uscourts.gov/opinions.pdf/20a0124p-06.pdf

Gennetian, L., Conwell, J., & Daniels, B. (2021). How do low-income families spend their money? Medford, MA: Econofact, Tufts University. https://econofact.org/how-do-low-income-families-spend-their-money

Gentry, M., Gray, A., Whiting, G., Maeda, Y., & Pereira, N. (2019). *Access denied: Gifted education in the United States: Laws, access, equity and missingness across the country by locale, Title I school status, and race.* West Lafayette, IN: Purdue University. www.education.purdue.edu/geri/new-publications/gifted-education-in-the-united-states

Gershenson, S. (2020). Great expectations: The impact of rigorous grading practices on student achievement. Washington, DC: Fordham Institute, February 4. https://fordhaminstitute.org/national/research/great-expectations-impact-rigorous-grading-practices-student-achievement

Gershenson, S., Hart, C., Hyman, J., Lindsay, C., & Papageorge, N. (2022). The long-run impacts of same-race teachers. *American Economic Journal: Economic Policy, 14*(4), 300–342. https://doi.org/10.1257/pol.20190573

Gershenson, S., Holt, S., & Papageorge, N. (2016). Who believes in me? The effect of student–teacher demographic match on teacher expectations. *Economics of Education Review, 52.* https://doi.org/10.1016/j.econedurev.2016.03.002

Gesualdi-Gilmore, L. (2021). Taught a lesson: Teacher "FIRED after telling students Capitol rioters were paid Antifa members who dressed up like Trump supporters." *The U.S. Sun*, January 14. www.the-sun.com/news/2142713/teacher-fired-blaming-antifa-capitol-riots

Givens, J. (2021). *Fugitive pedagogy: Carter G. Woodson and the art of Black teaching.* Cambridge, MA: Harvard University Press.

Gladwell, M. (2008). *Outliers: The story of success.* New York: Hachette.

GLSEN. (2007). Research brief: The experiences of lesbian, gay, bisexual and transgender middle school students: Findings from the 2007 national school climate survey. www.glsen.org/sites/default/files/2020-01/The_Experiences_of_LGBT_Middle_School_Students_2007.pdf

GLSEN. (2022). *The 2021 national school climate survey.* www.glsen.org/research/2021-national-school-climate-survey

Goldhaber, D., & Theobald, R. (2022). Teacher attrition and mobility in the pandemic. *Educational Evaluation and Policy Analysis.* https://doi.org/10.3102%2F01623737221139285

Goldhaber, D., Kasman, M., Quince, V., Theobald, R., & Wolff, M. (2022). How did it get this way? Disentangling the sources of teacher quality gaps through agent-based modeling. CALDER Working Paper No. 259-0122. https://caldercenter.org/sites/default/files/CALDER%20WP%20259-0122.pdf

González v. Douglas, 269 F. Supp. 3d 948. D. Ariz. (2017). https://casetext.com/case/gonzalez-v-douglas

Gonzalez, G. (2013). *Chicano education in the era of segregation*. Denton, TX: University of North Texas Press.

Goodlad, J. (2004). *A place called school* (2nd ed.). New York: McGraw-Hill.

Goodwin, B., & Rouleau, K. (2022). *The new classroom instruction that works: The best research-based strategies for increasing student achievement*. New York: ACSD.

Gordon, J. (2022). Texas teacher who was FIRED for telling students "don't judge people for wanting to have sex with 5-year-olds" and asking them to call pedophiles "minor attracted persons" in disturbing classroom clip posted to TikTok. *Daily Mail*, September 11. www.dailymail.co.uk/news/article-11202311/Texas-teacher-Amber-Parker-fired-told-students-call-pedophiles-minor-attracted-persons.html

Government Accountability Office. (2010). K–12 education: Many challenges arise in educating students who change schools frequently. Washington, DC: Author. https://www.gao.gov/assets/gao-11-40.pdf

Graham, P. (2005). *Schooling America: How the public schools meet the nation's changing needs*. London: Oxford University Press.

Grant, L., Popp, P. & Stronge, J. (2018). Classrooms with revolving doors: Recommended practices for middle level and high school teachers of at-risk and highly mobile students. Brown's Summit, NC: National Center for Homeless Education, University of North Carolina. https://nche.ed.gov/wp-content/uploads/2018/11/eff_teach_mh.pdf

Greenwalt, K. (2019). Even when they aren't fired for being pregnant or gay, teachers face strict moral demands. *Michigan Advance*, October 24. https://michiganadvance.com/2019/10/24/column-even-when-they-arent-fired-for-being-pregnant-or-gay-teachers-face-strict-moral-demands

Gregory, A. (2017). Running free in Germany's outdoor preschools. *The New York Times*, May 18. www.nytimes.com/2017/05/18/t-magazine/germany-forest-kindergarten-outdoor-preschool-waldkitas.html

Griffith, J. (2022). Texas teacher who told Black students his race is "superior" is no longer employed. *NBC News*, November 14. www.nbcnews.com/news/us-news/teacher-fired-telling-black-students-race-superior-rcna57062

Griffiths, C., Murdock-Perriera, L., & Eberhardt, J. (2023). "Can you tell me more about this?": Agentic written feedback, teacher expectations, and student learning. *Contemporary Educational Psychology*, *73*. https://doi.org/10.1016/j.cedpsych.2022.102145

Grimm v. Gloucester County School Board, 19-1952 (4th Cir. 2020). https://law.justia.com/cases/federal/appellate-courts/ca4/19-1952/19-1952-2020-08-26.html

Grissom, J., & Redding, C. (2016). Discretion and disproportionality: Explaining the underrepresentation of high-achieving students of color in gifted programs. *AERA Open*, *2*(1). https://doi.org/10.1177/2332858415622175

Grissom, J., Redding, C., & Bleiberg, J. (2019). Money over merit? Socioeconomic gaps in receipt of gifted services. *Harvard Educational Review, 89*(3), 337–369. https://doi.org/10.17763/1943-5045-89.3.337

Grissom, J., Rodriguez, L., & Kern, E. (2017). Teacher and principal diversity and the representation of students of color in gifted programs: Evidence from national data. *The Elementary School Journal, 117*(3). https://doi.org/10.1086/690274

Grow, K. (2015). Rage against the Machine defy ethnic studies ban, says Arizona schools chief. *Rolling Stone*, January 5. www.rollingstone.com/culture/culture-news/rage-against-the-machine-defy-ethnic-studies-ban-says-arizona-schools-chief-179058

Hachiya, R. (2022). *The principal's quick-reference guide to school law* (revised). Thousand Oaks, CA: Corwin.

Hait, A. (2022). St. Lucie County teacher fired, arrested for hitting student with broomstick. *WPBF ABC News*, April 26. www.wpbf.com/article/teacher-fired-arrested-hitting-student-broomstick/39819312

Hammond, Z. (2014). *Culturally responsive teaching and the brain: Promoting authentic engagement and rigor among culturally and linguistically diverse students*. Thousand Oaks, CA: Corwin.

Hansen, M., & Quintero, D. (2018). How gender diversity among the teacher workforce affects student learning. Washington, DC: Brookings. www.brookings.edu/articles/how-gender-diversity-among-the-teacher-workforce-affects-student-learning

Hanushek, E., & Rivkin, S. (2010). Generalizations about using value-added measures of teacher quality. *American Economic Review: Papers & Proceedings, 100*: 267–271. www.aeaweb.org/articles.php?doi=10.1257/aer.100.2.267

Harris, B. (2020). "You can't help but to wonder": Crumbling schools, less money, and dismal outcomes in the county that was supposed to change everything for Black children in the South. *Hechinger Report*, February 10. https://hechingerreport.org/you-cant-help-but-to-wonder-crumbling-schools-less-money-and-dismal-outcomes-in-the-county-that-was-supposed-to-change-everything-for-black-children-in-the-south

Harris, B. (2019). Reckoning with Mississippi's "segregation academies." *Hechinger Report*, November 29. https://hechingerreport.org/reckoning-with-mississippis-segregation-academies

Harris, D., & Chen, F. (2023). The bigger picture of charter school results. *Education Next, 23*(3). www.educationnext.org/bigger-picture-charter-school-results-national-analysis-system-level-effects-test-scores-graduation-rates

Harris, D., & Sass, T. (2011). Teacher training, teacher quality and student achievement. *Journal of Public Economics, 95(7–8)*: 798–812. https://doi.org/10.1016/j.jpubeco.2010.11.009

Harris II, P. (2022). *The first five: A love letter to teachers*. Portsmouth, NH: Heinemann.

Hart, B., & Risley, T. (1995). *Meaningful differences in the everyday experience of young American children*. Baltimore, MD: Brookes.

Hatch, M. (2023). Fulton teacher stole over $13k from school and unregistered weapons found inside home. *LocalSYR.com*, February 7. www.localsyr.com/news/local-news/fulton-teacher-stole-over-13k-from-school-and-unregistered-weapons-found-inside-home

Hattie, J. (2009). *Visible learning: A synthesis of over 800 meta-analyses relating to achievement.* New York: Routledge.

Hazlewood v. Kuhlmeier, 484 U.S. 260 (1988). www.oyez.org/cases/1987/86-836

Healthy Childcare Colorado. (2019). Health and safety checklist. Denver, CO: Qualistar. https://healthychildcareco.org/wp-content/uploads/2019/01/HeathandSafetyChecklist-13.pdf

Heath, L. (1975). Education for confusion: A study of education in the Mariana Islands 1688–1941. *The Journal of Pacific History*, *10*(1): 20–37. www.jstor.org/stable/25168207

Heckman, J., Stixrud, J., & Urzua, S. (2006). The effects of cognitive and noncognitive abilities on labor market outcomes and social behavior. *Journal of Labor Economics*, *24*(3). https://doi.org/10.1086/504455

Hehir, T. (2002). Eliminating ableism in education. *Harvard Educational Review*, *72*(1), 1–32. https://doi.org/10.17763/haer.72.1.03866528702g2105

Hendrick Hudson Central School District v. Amy Rowley 458 U.S. 176 (1982). https://doi.org/10.1016/j.learninstruc.2019.101301

Hesse, H. (1925). *Siddhartha*. Translated by J. Delage. France: Grasset.

Hill, A., & Jones, D. (2021). Self-fulfilling prophecies in the classroom. *Journal of Human Capital*, *15*(3). https://scholarworks.montana.edu/xmlui/bitstream/handle/1/17176/hill-classroom-2021.pdf

Hopper, F. (2018). Yupik teen hunter receives death threats. *ICT*. Phoenix, AZ. https://ictnews.org/archive/yupik-teen-hunter-receives-death-threats

Horne, Thomas. (2010). Finding by the State Superintendent of Public Instruction of violation by Tucson Unified School District pursuant to § 15-112. https://studylib.net/doc/7524241/horne-s-conclusions-on-ethnic-studies

Hough, L. (2016). Mistakes were made. *Harvard Ed. Magazine.* Cambridge, MA: Harvard Graduate School of Education. www.gse.harvard.edu/news/ed/16/01/mistakes-were-made.

Houston, D., Peterson, P., & West, M. (2022). *Education Next* Survey of Public Opinion. Cambridge, MA: *Education Next*. www.educationnext.org/partisan-rifts-widen-perceptions-school-quality-decline-results-2022-education-next-survey-public-opinion

Huaser, C. (2023). Teacher is fired for reading book on gender identity in class. *The New York Times*, August 18. www.nytimes.com/2023/08/18/us/georgia-teacher-fired-gender-book.html

Human Rights Watch. (2016). "Like Walking Through a Hailstorm": Discrimination against LGBT Youth in US Schools. New York: Author. www.hrw.org/report/2016/12/08/walking-through-hailstorm/discrimination-against-lgbt-youth-us-schools

Hunter, T. (2022). Children are targets for ID theft. Here's what parents need to know. *The Washington Post*, June 14. www.washingtonpost.com/technology/2022/06/14/what-is-child-identity-theft

Immerwahr, D. (2020). *How to hide an empire: A history of the greater United States.* London: Picador.

Indian Reorganization Act, 25 U.S.C. 461 *et seq.* (1934). www.govinfo.gov/content/pkg/COMPS-5299/pdf/COMPS-5299.pdf

Indian Self-Determination and Education Assistance Act, P.L. 93-638 (1975). https://uscode.house.gov/view.xhtml?path=/prelim@title25/chapter46&edition=prelim

Individuals with Disabilities Education Act, 20 U.S.C. § 1400, *et. seq.* (1975). https://sites.ed.gov/idea/about-idea

Ingersoll, R., Merrill, E., Stuckey, D., & Collins, G. (2018). Seven trends: The transformation of the teaching force—Updated October 2018. Philadelphia, PA: University of Pennsylvania Press. https://repository.upenn.edu/entities/publication/f179131d-02df-47a7-b24d-0201ce0521e5

Isaksen, S., & Gaulin, J. (2005). A Reexamination of brainstorming research: Implications for research and practice. *Gifted Child Quarterly, 49*(4), 315–329. https://doi.org/10.1177/001698620504900405

Isenberg, E. (2007). What have we learned about homeschooling? *Peabody Journal of Education, 82*(2/3), 387–409. http://www.jstor.org/stable/25594749

Isenberg, E., Max, J., Gleason, P., & Deutsch, J. (2022). Do low-income students have equal access to effective teachers? *Educational Evaluation and Policy Analysis, 44*(2), 234–256. https://doi.org/10.3102/01623737211040511

Jacobellis v. Ohio, 378 U.S. 184 (1964). https://supreme.justia.com/cases/federal/us/378/184

Jason, Z. (2017). The battle over charter schools. *Harvard Ed. Magazine.* Cambridge, MA: Harvard Graduate School of Education. www.gse.harvard.edu/news/ed/17/05/battle-over-charter-schools.

Javelin. (2021). Child identity fraud: A web of deception and loss. *Escalent.* https://javelinstrategy.com/sites/default/files/files/reports/21-5012J-FM-2021%20Child%20Identity%20Fraud%20Study_1.pdf

Jensen, F., & Nutt, A. (2015). *The teenage brain: A neuroscientist's survival guide to raising adolescents and young adults.* New York: HarperCollins.

Jensen, K. (2023). Proposed legislation in several states to eliminate LGBTQ+, "obscene" books: Book censorship news, January 20. *Book Riot.* https://bookriot.com/book-ban-legislation-2023

Jim Crow Museum. (n.d.). Jim Crow Museum of Racist Imagery. Big Rapids, MI: Ferris State University. https://jimcrowmuseum.ferris.edu

Jones, L., Milligan, K., & Stabile, M. (2015). Child cash benefits and family expenditures: Evidence from the national child benefit. Cambridge, MA: National Bureau of Economic Research. Working Paper 21101. www.nber.org/papers/w21101

Juneau, D. (2018). The Bureau of Indian Education is broken. *Education Week*, February 6. www.edweek.org/leadership/opinion-the-bureau-of-indian-education-is-broken/2018/02

Jussim, L., & Harber, K. D. (2005). Teacher expectations and self-fulfilling prophecies: Knowns and unknowns, resolved and unresolved controversies. *Personality and Social Psychology Review, 9*(2), 131–155. https://doi.org/10.1207/s15327957pspr0902_3

Kahlenberg, K. (2007). Socioeconomic school integration. *North Carolina Law Review*, 1545. https://scholarship.law.unc.edu/nclr/vol85/iss5/9

Kane, T., Riegg, S., & Staiger, D. (2006). School quality, neighborhoods, and housing prices. *American Law and Economics Review*, 8(2): 183–212. https://doi.org/10.1093/aler/ahl007

Kauchak, D., & Eggen, P. (2014). *Introduction to Teaching: Becoming a Professional,* 5th ed. New York: Pearson.

Kennedy v. Bremerton School District, 597 U.S. (2022). www.supremecourt.gov/opinions/21pdf/21-418_i425.pdf

Kenyon, D., Paquin, B., & Munteanu, S. (2022). Public schools and the property tax: A comparison of education funding m9odels in three U.S. states. Cambridge, MA: Lincoln Land Institute. www.lincolninst.edu/publications/articles/2022-04-public-schools-property-tax-comparison-education-models

Kini, T., & Podolsky, A. (2016). Does teaching experience increase teacher effectiveness? A review of the research. New York: Learning Policy Institute, June 3. https://learningpolicyinstitute.org/product/does-teaching-experience-increase-teacher-effectiveness-review-research

Klein, A. (2021). 1,500 Decisions a day (at least!): How teachers cope with a dizzying array of questions. *Education Week*, December 6. www.edweek.org/teaching-learning/1-500-decisions-a-day-at-least-how-teachers-cope-with-a-dizzying-array-of-questions/2021/12

Klein, R. (2018). Schools that were segregation academies now ban pregnant and LGBTQ students. *Huffington Post*, December 14. www.huffpost.com/entry/segregation-academy-mississippi_n_5c12a7bee4b0449012f7f16d.

Kluger, R. (2004). *Simple justice: The history of* Brown v. Board of Education *and Black America's struggle for equality.* New York: Vintage.

Knapp, R. (2021). Albuquerque teacher fired after pornographic video surfaces. *KRQE News*, April 24. www.krqe.com/news/education/albuquerque-teacher-fired-after-pornographic-video-surfaces

Koretz, D. (2008). *Measuring up: What educational testing really tells us.* Cambridge, MA: Harvard University Press.

Koretz, D. (2019). *The testing charade: Pretending to make schools better.* Chicago: University of Chicago Press.

Korvey, H. (2022). What's the role of teachers in supporting student mental health? Nicasio, CA: Edutopia. www.edutopia.org/article/the-doctor-is-in-your-classroom

Kraft, M.A., & Gilmour, A.F. (2017). Revisiting the Widget Effect: Teacher evaluation reforms and the distribution of teacher effectiveness. *Educational Researcher, 46*(5), 234–249. https://doi.org/10.3102/0013189X1771879

Kramer, S., Posner, M., Lawrence, N., Browman, A., Krier, K., & Roemer, J. (2021). The impacts of a standards-based grading system emphasizing formative assessment, feedback, and re-assessment: A mixed methods, cluster randomized control trial in ninth grade mathematics classrooms. https://doi.org/10.35542/osf.io/pzc3f

Kruse, K. (2007). *White flight: Atlanta and the making of modern conservatism.* Princeton, NJ: Princeton University Press.

Kunzman, R., & Gaither, M. (2020). Homeschooling: An updated comprehensive survey of the research. *Other Education*, *9*(1). www.researchgate.net/publication/374195331_Homeschooling_An_Updated_Comprehensive_Survey_of_the_Research

Laertius, D. (1853). *The lives and opinions of eminent philosophers.* Translated by C.D. Yonge. New York: Gutenberg Project. www.gutenberg.org/files/57342/57342-h/57342-h.htm

Langenkamp, A. (2019). Latino/a immigrant parents' educational aspirations for their children. *Race Ethnicity and Education*, *22*(2): 231–249. https://doi.org/10.1080/13613324.2017.1365054

Laskey, M. (2014). The Great Dying: New England's Coastal Plague, 1616–1619. *CVLTNation.* https://cvltnation.com/the-great-dying-new-englands-coastal-plague-1616-1619

Lassiter, M., & Lewis, A., Eds. (1998). *The moderates' dilemma: Massive resistance to school desegregation in Virginia.* Charlottesville: University of Virginia Press.

Lau v. Nichols, 414 U.S. 563 (1974). https://supreme.justia.com/cases/federal/us/414/563

Learning for Justice. (n.d.). A glossary of terms. Montgomery, AL: Author. www.learningforjustice.org/magazine/publications/best-practices-for-serving-lgbtq-students/lgbtq-terms-definitions-the-acronym-and-beyond

Lee, J. (2023). Abbott wants to deny undocumented kids a public education. *Texas Observer*, March 2. www.texasobserver.org/abbott-wants-to-deny-undocumented-kids-a-public-education.

Lemon v. Kurtzman, 403 U.S. 602 (1971). www.loc.gov/item/usrep403602

Lemov, D. (2021). *Teach like a champion 3.0: 63 Techniques that put students on the path to college.* San Francisco: Jossey-Bass.

Lerner, M. (2022). Report: Homeownership rates surge but race and wealth gaps persist. *Washington Post*, March 10. www.washingtonpost.com/business/2022/03/10/report-homeownership-rates-surge-race-wealth-gaps-persist

Leslie, M. (2000). The vexing legacy of Lewis Terman. *Stanford Magazine.* Stanford, CA: Stanford Alumni Association. https://stanfordmag.org/contents/the-vexing-legacy-of-lewis-terman.

LifeProjX. (2019). DIY dry erase white board 4'x 8' for $20. www.youtube.com/watch?v=kaZsYoeYwSA

Lin, D., Lutter, R., & Ruhm, C. (2018). Cognitive performance and labour market outcomes. *Labour Economics*, *51*: 121–135. https://doi.org/10.1016/j.labeco.2017.12.008

Lindsay, C., & Hart, C. (2017). Exposure to same-race teachers and student disciplinary outcomes for Black students in North Carolina. *Educational Evaluation and Policy Analysis*, *39*(3), 485–510. https://doi.org/10.3102/0162373717693109

Liptak, A. (2023). Supreme Court rules for transgender girl in school sports dispute. *New York Times*, April 6. www.nytimes.com/2023/04/06/us/supreme-court-transgender-girl-school-sports.html

Liu, G., Nguyen, B., Lyons, B., Sheats, K., Wilson, R., Betz, C., & Fowler, K. (2023). Surveillance for violent deaths—National Violent Death Reporting System, 48 States, the District of Columbia, and Puerto Rico, 2020. *Morbidity and Mortality Weekly Report, Surveillance Summaries, 72*(5), 1–38. http://dx.doi.org/10.15585/mmwr.ss7205a1

Lord, L. (2021). *Design and deliver: Planning and teaching using Universal Design for Learning* (2nd ed). Baltimore, MD: Brookes.

Losen, D., Keith, M., Hodson, C., & Martinez, T. (2016). Charter schools, civil rights and school discipline: A comprehensive review. Los Angeles: University of California Los Angeles, Civil Rights Project / Proyecto Derechos Civiles. www.civilrightsproject.ucla.edu/resources/projects/center-for-civil-rights-remedies/school-to-prison-folder/federal-reports/charter-schools-civil-rights-and-school-discipline-a-comprehensive-review

Love, B. (2019). *We want to do more than survive: Abolitionist teaching and the pursuit of educational freedom.* New York: Penguin.

Lubienski, C., & Weitzel, P. (2010). *The charter school experiment: Expectations, evidence, and implications.* Cambridge, MA: Harvard Education Press.

Lujan, P. (1996). Role of education in the preservation of Guam's Indigenous language. *Guampedia.* www.guampedia.com/role-of-education-in-the-preservation-of-guams-indigenous-language

Lukes, D., & Cleveland, C. (2021). The lingering legacy of redlining on school funding, diversity, and performance. Annenberg: EdWorkingPapers. Providence, RI: Brown University. www.edworkingpapers.com/ai21-363

Lutz, M. (2017). The hidden cost of *Brown v. Board*: African American educators' resistance to desegregating schools. *Online Journal of Rural Research & Policy, 12*(4): 1–30. https://newprairiepress.org/ojrrp/vol12/iss4/2

Maciag, M. (2019). States that spend the most (and the least) on education 2017. Folsom, CA: Governing: The Future of States and Localities. www.governing.com/archive/gov-state-education-spending-revenue-data.html

Mahanoy Area School Dist. v. B. L., 594 U.S. (2021). www.supremecourt.gov/opinions/20pdf/20-255_g3bi.pdf

Maldonato, B. (2019). Eugenics on the farm: Lewis Terman. *The Stanford Daily*, November 6. https://stanforddaily.com/2019/11/06/eugenics-on-the-farm-lewis-terman

Mann, H. (1844). *Remarks on the Seventh Annual Report of the Hon. Horace Mann, Secretary of the Massachusetts Board of Education.* Boston: Charles C. Little and James Brown. https://tile.loc.gov/storage-services/public/gdcmassbookdig/remarksonseventh00asso/remarksonseventh00asso.pdf

Mann, H. (1853). *A few thoughts on the powers and duties of woman; Powers and duties of woman; two lectures.* Syracuse, NY: Hall, Mills. https://curiosity.lib.harvard.edu/women-working-1800-1930/catalog/45-990023415760203941

Mannie, S. (2017). Why students are ignorant about the Civil Rights Movement. *Hechinger Report*, October 1. https://hechingerreport.org/students-ignorant-civil-rights-movement

Markos, A., & Himmel, J. (2016). *Using sheltered instruction to support English learners.* Washington, DC: Center for Applied Linguistics. www.cal.org/siop/pdfs/briefs/using-sheltered-instruction-to-support-english-learners.pdf

Marr, J., & Cathey, J. (2010). New hypothesis for cause of epidemic among native Americans, New England, 1616–1619. *Emerging Infectious Diseases, 16*(2), 281–286. https://doi.org/10.3201/eid1602.090276

Maslow, A. (1943). A theory of human motivation. *Psychological Review, 50*(4), 370–396. https://doi.org/10.1037/h0054346

Mathews, J. (2022). Study provides rare control group review of standards-based grading craze. *Washington Post*, December 18. www.washingtonpost.com/education/2022/12/18/student-standards-based-grading.

Mayer v. Monroe Cty. Cmty. Sch. Corp. 474 F.3d 477. 7th Cir. (2007). https://caselaw.findlaw.com/us-7th-circuit/1233551.html

McBee, M., Peters, S., & Miller, E. (2016). The impact of the nomination stage on gifted program identification: A comprehensive psychometric analysis. *Gifted Child Quarterly, 60*(4), 258–278. https://doi.org/10.1177/0016986216656256

McCarthy, J. (2017). *So all can learn: A practical guide to differentiation.* New York: Rowman & Littlefield.

McConnell, J., Bruster, B., & Smith, V. (2019). Predicting teacher effectiveness based on various preservice factors: Implications for higher education and the evaluation of teacher preparation. *International Journal of Educational Reform, 28*(1), 63–78. https://doi.org/10.1177/1056787918824204

McKee, J. (1995). *Mississippi: A portrait of an American state.* Lilburn, GA: Clairmont Press.

McNeil, L. (2017). How a psychologist's work on race identity helped overturn school segregation in 1950s America. *Smithsonian.* www.smithsonianmag.com/science-nature/psychologist-work-racial-identity-helped-overturn-school-segregation-180966934

McTighe, J., & Wiggins, G. (2005). *Understanding by design* (2nd ed.) Washington, DC: ACSD.

Medina, E. (2023). Coach who won Supreme Court case over prayers on the field resigns. *The New York Times*, September 6. www.nytimes.com/2023/09/06/us/washington-coach-prayer-supreme-court-resigns.html

Medori, J. (2023). What are bell ringers aka do nows & how to use them (with examples). https://teachnthrive.com/teaching-ideas/bell-ringers

Meehan, K., & Friedman, J. (2023). Update on book bans in the 2022–2023 school year shows expanded censorship of themes centered on race, history, sexual orientation and gender. *PEN America*, April 20. https://pen.org/report/banned-in-the-usa-state-laws-supercharge-book-suppression-in-schools

Mendez v. Westminster, 64 F. Supp. 544. S.D. Cal. (1946). https://law.justia.com/cases/federal/district-courts/FSupp/64/544/1952972

Mendoza v. United States, 623 F.2d 1338. 9th Cir. (1980). https://casetext.com/case/mendoza-v-united-states-4#p1341

Mervosh, S. (2023). Who runs the best U.S. schools? It may be the Defense Department. *The New York Times*, October 12. www.nytimes.com/2023/10/10/us/schools-pandemic-defense-department.html

MI School Data. (2023). Student enrollment counts report: Wayne RSEA. Lansing, MI: Michigan Department of Education. www.mischooldata.org/student-enrollment-counts-report

Milligan, K., & Stabile, M. (2011). Do child tax benefits affect the well-being of children? Evidence from Canadian child benefit expansions. *American Economic Journal: Economic Policy*, *3*(3): 175–205. https://doi.org/10.1257/pol.3.3.175

Mills v. Board of Education, 348 F. Supp. 866 (D.D.C. 1972). https://law.justia.com/cases/federal/district-courts/FSupp/348/866/2010674

Minor, E. (1996). Three boos for cheerleader father. *The Spokesman-Review*, November 23. www.spokesman.com/stories/1996/nov/23/three-boos-for-cheerleader-father

Moeller, J., Brackett, M., Ivcevic, Z., & White, A. (2020). High school students' feelings: Discoveries from a large national survey and an experience sampling study. *Learning and Instruction*, *66*.

Monarrez, T., Kisida, B., & Chingos, M. (2019). Charter school effects on school segregation. Washington, DC: Urban Institute. www.urban.org/sites/default/files/publication/100689/charter_school_effects_on_school_segregation_0.pdf

Montana Historical Society. (2014). The right to procreate: The Montana State Board of Eugenics and body politics. Helena, MT: Montana Women's History. https://montanawomenshistory.org/the-right-to-procreate-the-montana-state-board-of-eugenics-and-body-politics

Moore, A. (2016). Who owns almost all America's land? Washington, DC: Institute for Policy Studies. https://inequality.org/research/owns-land

More, T. (2009). *Special interest: Teachers unions and America's public schools*. Washington, DC: Brookings.

Morello, T., Commerford, T., De La Rocha, Z., & Wilk, B. (1992). Take the power back. New York: Epic Records.

Morse v. Frederick, 551 U.S. 393 (2007). www.loc.gov/item/usrep551393

Movement Advancement Project. (2017). Talking about suicide & LGBT populations. Boulder, CO: Author. www.lgbtmap.org/file/talking-about-suicide-and-lgbt-populations-2nd-edition.pdf

Mun, R., Langley, S., Ware, S., Gubbins, E., Siegle, D., Callahan, C., McCoach, D., & Hamilton, R. (2016). Effective practices for identifying and serving English learners in gifted education: A systematic review of the literature. National Center for Research on Gifted Education. https://ncrge.uconn.edu/wp-content/uploads/sites/982/2016/01/NCRGE_EL_Lit-Review.pdf

Murnane, R., & Reardon, S. (2018). Long-term trends in private school enrollments by family income. *AERA Open*, *4*(1). https://doi.org/10.1177/2332858417751355

Murphy, J. (2018). Why are Rochester schools America's worst? Study Kodak Park School 41. *Democrat & Chronicle*, June 6. www.democratandchronicle.com/story/local/communities/time-to-educate/stories/2018/06/06/worst-public-schools-america-rochester-ny-rcsd-kodak-park-school-41/550929002

Murphy, J. (2022). *Your children are very greatly in danger: School segregation in Rochester, New York*. Ithaca, NY: Cornell University Press.

Nabi, S. (2022). Thirteen million US households have negative net worth. Will they ever move from debt to wealth? Washington, DC: Aspen Institute. www.aspeninstitute.org/blog-posts/thirteen-million-us-households-have-negative-net-worth-will-they-ever-move-from-debt-to-wealth

Nadworny, E., & Turner, C. (2019). This supreme court case made school district lines a tool for segregation. *National Public Radio*. www.npr.org/2019/07/25/739493839/this-supreme-court-case-made-school-district-lines-a-tool-for-segregation

Nagel, T. (1974). What is it like to be a bat? *Philosophical Review, 83*(4), 435–450. https://doi.org/10.2307/2183914

National Alliance for Public Charter Schools. (2022). *2022 Data digest: Charter schools overview*. Washington, DC: Author. https://data.publiccharters.org

National Assessment of Educational Progress. (2022). *Nation's Report Card: Student performance across subjects*. Washington, DC: United States Department of Education. www.nationsreportcard.gov

National Association of State Budget Officers. (2023). *State expenditure report*. Washington, DC: Author. https://higherlogicdownload.s3.amazonaws.com/NASBO/9d2d2db1-c943-4f1b-b750-0fca152d64c2/UploadedImages/SER%20Archive/2022_State_Expenditure_Report_-_S.pdf

National Center for Education Statistics. (2014). Mobility of public elementary and secondary teachers, by selected teacher and school characteristics: Selected years, 1987–88 through 2012–13. *Condition of Education*. Washington, DC: U.S. Department of Education, Institute of Education Sciences.
https://nces.ed.gov/programs/digest/d14/tables/dt14_210.30.asp

National Center for Education Statistics. (2015). Free or reduced price lunch: A proxy for poverty? *NCES Blog*, April 16. Washington, DC: U.S. Department of Education, Institute of Education Sciences. https://nces.ed.gov/blogs/nces/post/free-or-reduced-price-lunch-a-proxy-for-poverty.

National Center for Education Statistics. (2015). Teacher turnover: Stayers, movers, and leavers. *Condition of Education*. Washington, DC: U.S. Department of Education, Institute of Education Sciences. https://nces.ed.gov/programs/coe/indicator/slc/teacher-turnover

National Center for Education Statistics. (2017). Certification status and experience of U.S. public school teachers: Variations across student subgroups. Washington, DC: U.S. Department of Education, Institute of Education Sciences. https://nces.ed.gov/pubsearch/pubsinfo.asp?pubid=2017056

National Center for Education Statistics. (2018). A closer look at charter school characteristics. *NCES Blog*, September 20. Washington, DC: U.S. Department of Education, Institute of Education Sciences. https://nces.ed.gov/blogs/nces/post/a-closer-look-at-charter-school-characteristics

National Center for Education Statistics. (2018). Average and median age of public school teachers and percentage distribution of teachers by age category, sex, and state: 2017–18. Washington, DC: U.S. Department of Education, Institute of Education Sciences, National Teacher and Principal Survey (NTPS). https://nces.ed.gov/surveys/ntps/tables/ntps1718_fltable02_t1s.asp

National Center for Education Statistics. (2019). Fast facts: Public and private school comparison. Washington, DC: U.S. Department of Education. Institute of Education Sciences. https://nces.ed.gov/fastfacts/display.asp?id=55

National Center for Education Statistics. (2019). Number and percentage distribution of teachers in public elementary and secondary schools, by instructional level and selected teacher and school characteristics: 1999–2000 and 2017–18. *Condition of Education.* Washington, DC: U.S. Department of Education, Institute of Education Sciences. https://nces.ed.gov/programs/digest/d19/tables/dt19_209.22.asp

National Center for Education Statistics. (2019). Number, highest degree, and years of teaching experience of teachers in public and private elementary and secondary schools, by selected teacher characteristics: Selected years, 1999–2000 through 2017–18. *Digest of Education Statistics.* Washington, DC: U.S. Department of Education, Institute of Education Sciences. https://nces.ed.gov/programs/digest/d19/tables/dt19_209.20.asp

National Center for Education Statistics. (2019). Number of students receiving selected disciplinary actions in public elementary and secondary schools, by type of disciplinary action, disability status, sex, and race/ethnicity: 2013–14. *Digest of Education Statistics.* Washington, DC: U.S. Department of Education, Institute of Education Sciences. https://nces.ed.gov/programs/digest/d17/tables/dt17_233.27.asp

National Center for Education Statistics. (2019). Public high school 4-year adjusted cohort graduation rate (ACGR), by race/ethnicity and selected demographic characteristics for the United States, the 50 states, the District of Columbia, and Puerto Rico: School year 2018–19. *Common Core of Data.* Washington, DC: U.S. Department of Education, Institute of Education Sciences. https://nces.ed.gov/ccd/tables/acgr_re_and_characteristics_2018-19.asp

National Center for Education Statistics. (2019). School choice in the United States: 2019. Washington, DC: U.S. Department of Education, Institute of Education Sciences. https://nces.ed.gov/programs/schoolchoice/ind_03.asp

National Center for Education Statistics. (2020). Race and ethnicity of public school teachers and their students. *Data point.* Washington, DC: U.S. Department of Education, Institute of Education Sciences. https://nces.ed.gov/pubs2020/2020103/index.asp

National Center for Education Statistics. (2021). Number and percentage distribution of 14- through 21-year-old students served under Individuals with Disabilities Education Act (IDEA), Part B, who exited school, by exit reason, sex, race/ethnicity, age, and type of disability: 2018–19 and 2019–20. *Digest of Education Statistics.* Washington, DC: U.S. Department of Education, Institute of Education Sciences. https://nces.ed.gov/programs/digest/d21/tables/dt21_219.90.asp

National Center for Education Statistics. (2021). Number of public elementary and secondary schools, by school level, type, and charter, magnet, and virtual status: 2009–10 through 2019–20. *Condition of Education.* Washington, DC: U.S. Department of Education, Institute of Education Sciences. https://nces.ed.gov/programs/digest/d21/tables/dt21_216.10.asp

National Center for Education Statistics. (2021). Percentage of public school students enrolled in gifted and talented programs, by sex, race/ethnicity, and state: Selected years, 2004 through 2017–18. *Digest of Education Statistics.* Washington, DC: U.S. Department of Education, Institute of Education Sciences. https://nces.ed.gov/programs/digest/d21/tables/dt21_204.90.asp

National Center for Education Statistics. (2021). Public elementary and secondary school enrollment, number of schools, and other selected characteristics, by locale: Fall 2015 through fall 2019. *Condition of Education.* Washington, DC: U.S. Department of Education, Institute of Education Sciences. https://nces.ed.gov/programs/digest/d21/tables/dt21_214.40.asp

National Center for Education Statistics. (2021). Average base salary for full-time teachers in public elementary and secondary schools, by highest degree earned and years of teaching experience: Selected years, 1990–91 through 2017–18. *Condition of Education.* Washington, DC: U.S. Department of Education, Institute of Education Sciences. https://nces.ed.gov/programs/digest/d21/tables/dt21_211.20.asp

National Center for Education Statistics. (2021). Children 3 to 21 years old served under Individuals with Disabilities Education Act (IDEA), Part B, by age group and sex, race/ethnicity, and type of disability: 2020–21. *Digest of Education Statistics.* Washington, DC: U.S. Department of Education, Institute of Education Sciences. https://nces.ed.gov/programs/digest/d21/tables/dt21_204.50.asp

National Center for Education Statistics. (2021). English learner (EL) students enrolled in public elementary and secondary schools, by state: Selected years, fall 2000 through fall 2019. *Digest of Education Statistics.* Washington, DC: U.S. Department of Education, Institute of Education Sciences. https://nces.ed.gov/programs/digest/d21/tables/dt21_204.20.asp

National Center for Education Statistics. (2021). Enrollment, poverty, and federal funds for the 120 largest school districts, by enrollment size in 2019: 2018–19 and fiscal year 2021. *Digest of Education Statistics.* Washington, DC: U.S. Department of Education, Institute of Education Sciences. https://nces.ed.gov/programs/digest/d21/tables/dt21_215.30.asp

National Center for Education Statistics. (2021). Physical fights on school property and anywhere. *Condition of Education.* Washington, DC: U.S. Department of Education, Institute of Education Sciences. https://nces.ed.gov/programs/coe/indicator/a12

National Center for Education Statistics. (2022). Characteristics of elementary and secondary schools. *Condition of Education.* Washington, DC: U.S. Department of Education, Institute of Education Sciences. https://nces.ed.gov/programs/coe/indicator/cla

National Center for Education Statistics. (2022). Characteristics of public school teachers. *Condition of Education.* Washington, DC: U.S. Department of Education, Institute of Education Sciences. https://nces.ed.gov/programs/coe/indicator/clr

National Center for Education Statistics. (2022). *Condition of education: At a glance.* Washington, DC: U.S. Department of Education, Institute of Education Sciences. https://nces.ed.gov/pubs2022/2022144_AtAGlance.pdf

National Center for Education Statistics. (2022). Criminal incidents recorded by public schools and those reported to sworn law enforcement. *Condition of Education.* Washington, DC: U.S. Department of Education, Institute of Education Sciences. https://nces.ed.gov/programs/coe/indicator/a06

National Center for Education Statistics. (2022). Elementary / secondary information system (ElSi). Washington, DC: U.S. Department of Education, Institute of Education Sciences. https://nces.ed.gov/ccd/elsi

National Center for Education Statistics. (2022). Enrollment in public elementary and secondary schools, by level, grade, and race/ethnicity: Selected years, fall 1999 through fall 2021. *Digest of Education Statistics.* Washington, DC: U.S. Department of Education, Institute of Education Sciences. https://nces.ed.gov/programs/digest/d22/tables/dt22_203.65.asp

National Center for Education Statistics. (2022). Fast facts: Back-to-school statistics. *Condition of Education.* Washington, DC: U.S. Department of Education, Institute of Education Sciences. https://nces.ed.gov/fastfacts/display.asp?id=372#PK12-teachers

National Center for Education Statistics. (2022). Fast facts: Charter schools. Washington, DC: U.S. Department of Education, Institute of Education Sciences. https://nces.ed.gov/fastfacts/display.asp?id=30

National Center for Education Statistics. (2022). Fast facts: English Learners in public schools. Washington, DC: U.S. Department of Education, Institute of Education Sciences. https://nces.ed.gov/programs/coe/indicator/cgf

National Center for Education Statistics. (2022). Fast facts: Homeschooling. Washington, DC: U.S. Department of Education, Institute of Education Sciences. https://nces.ed.gov/fastfacts/display.asp?id=91

National Center for Education Statistics. (2022). Fast facts: Students with disabilities. Washington, DC: U.S. Department of Education, Institute of Education Sciences. https://nces.ed.gov/fastfacts/display.asp?id=64

National Center for Education Statistics. (2022). Homeschooled children and reasons for homeschooling. *Condition of Education.* Washington, DC: U.S. Department of Education, Institute of Education Sciences. https://nces.ed.gov/programs/coe/indicator/tgk/homeschooled-children?tid=300

National Center for Education Statistics. (2022). Number and percentage of public school students eligible for free or reduced-price lunch, by state: Selected years, 2000-01 through 2018–19. *Digest of Education Statistics.* Washington, DC: U.S. Department of Education, Institute of Education Sciences. https://nces.ed.gov/programs/digest/d20/tables/dt20_204.10.asp.

National Center for Education Statistics. (2022). Number of educational institutions, by level and control of institution: 2009–10 through 2019–20. *Digest of Education Statistics.* Washington, DC: U.S. Department of Education, Institute of Education Sciences. https://nces.ed.gov/programs/digest/d21/tables/dt21_105.50.asp

National Center for Education Statistics. (2022). Number of operating public schools and districts, student membership, teachers, and pupil/teacher ratio, by state or jurisdiction: School year 2020–21. *Common Core of Data*. Washington, DC: U.S. Department of Education, Institute of Education Sciences. https://nces.ed.gov/ccd/tables/202021_summary_2.asp

National Center for Education Statistics. (2022). Prevalence of mental health services provided by public schools and limitations in schools' efforts to provide mental health services. *Condition of Education*. U.S. Department of Education, Institute of Education Sciences. https://nces.ed.gov/programs/coe/indicator/a23

National Center for Education Statistics. (2022). Private school enrollment. *Condition of Education*. Washington, DC: U.S. Department of Education, Institute of Education Sciences. https://nces.ed.gov/programs/coe/indicator/cgc

National Center for Education Statistics. (2022). Racial/ethnic enrollment in public schools. *Condition of Education*. Washington, DC: U.S. Department of Education, Institute of Education Sciences. https://nces.ed.gov/programs/coe/indicator/cge

National Center for Education Statistics. (2022). School district boundaries, 2021–22 school year. Washington, DC: U.S. Department of Education, Institute of Education Sciences, Education Demographic and Geographic Estimates. https://nces.ed.gov/programs/edge/Geographic/DistrictBoundaries

National Center for Education Statistics. (2023). Fast facts: Charter schools. Washington, DC: U.S. Department of Education, Institute of Education Sciences. https://nces.ed.gov/fastfacts/display.asp?id=30

National Center for Education Statistics. (2023). Fast facts: Expenditures. Washington, DC: U.S. Department of Education, Institute of Education Sciences. https://nces.ed.gov/fastfacts/display.asp?id=66

National Center for Education Statistics. (2023). Fast facts: Students with disabilities, inclusion of. Washington, DC: U.S. Department of Education, Institute of Education Sciences. https://nces.ed.gov/fastfacts/display.asp?id=59

National Center for Education Statistics. (2023). Public charter school enrollment. *Condition of Education*. Washington, DC: U.S. Department of Education, Institute of Education Sciences. https://nces.ed.gov/programs/coe/indicator/cgb

National Center for Education Statistics. (2023). Public high school graduation rates. *Condition of Education*. Washington, DC: U.S. Department of Education, Institute of Education Sciences. https://nces.ed.gov/programs/coe/indicator/coi/high-school-graduation-rates?tid=4

National Center for Education Statistics. (2023). Public school expenditures. *Condition of Education*. Washington, DC: U.S. Department of Education Statistics, Institute of Education Sciences. https://nces.ed.gov/programs/coe/indicator/cmb/public-school-expenditure

National Center for Education Statistics. (2023). Students with disabilities. *Condition of Education*. Washington, DC: U.S. Department of Education, Institute of Education Sciences. https://nces.ed.gov/programs/coe/indicator/cgg/students-with-disabilities

National Center for Education Statistics. (2023). Violent deaths at school and away from school, school shootings, and active shooter incidents. *Condition of Education*. U.S. Department of Education, Institute of Education Sciences. https://nces.ed.gov/programs/coe/indicator/a01National Center for Homeless Education.

National Center for Homeless Education. (2022). Student homelessness in America: School years 2018–19 to 2020–21. Brown's Summit, NC: National Center for Homeless Education, University of North Carolina. https://nche.ed.gov/wp-content/uploads/2022/11/Student-Homelessness-in-America-2022.pdf

National Center for Safe Supportive Learning Environments. (n.d.). *Engagement*. https://safesupportivelearning.ed.gov/topic-research/engagement

National Center on Intensive Education. (n.d.). Academic intervention tools chart. Arlington, VA: Author. https://charts.intensiveintervention.org/aintervention

National Congress of American Indians. (2019). *Tribal Nations & the United States: An introduction*. Washington, DC: Author. www.ncai.org/about-tribes.

National Council on Teacher Quality. (2019). Collective bargaining laws. Washington, DC: Author. www.nctq.org/contract-database/collectiveBargaining

National Dropout Prevention Center. (n.d.) Economic impact of dropouts. Ballston Spa, NY: Author. https://dropoutprevention.org/resources/statistics/quick-facts/economic-impacts-of-dropouts

National Education Association. (2020). Code of ethics for educators. Washington, DC: Author. www.nea.org/resource-library/code-ethics-educators

National Education Association. (2023). Our mission, vision, and values. www.nea.org/about-nea/mission-vision-values

National Education Association. (2023). The state of educator pay in America. Washington, DC: Author. www.nea.org/resource-library/educator-pay-and-student-spending-how-does-your-state-rank

National Museum of the American Indian. (n.d.). *Native Knowledge 360°*. Washington, DC: Author. https://americanindian.si.edu/nk360

National Park Service. (n.d.). One camp, ten thousand lives; One camp, ten thousand stories. U.S. Department of the Interior, National Park Service. www.nps.gov/manz/index.htm.

National Park Service. (n.d.). The Little Rock Nine. www.nps.gov/people/the-little-rock-nine.htm

Neilson, K. (2013). *A disability history of the United States*. Boston: Beacon.

Newland, B. (2022). *Federal Indian boarding school initiative investigative report*. Washington, DC: U.S. Department of the Interior, Bureau of Indian Affairs. www.bia.gov/sites/default/files/dup/inline-files/bsi_investigative_report_may_2022_508.pdf

Newman, L., & Cornell, L. (2016). *Heather has two mommies*. Somerville, MA: Candlewick Press.

New Visions for Public Schools. (n.d.). *Living Environment Course Map*. New York City: Author. https://curriculum.newvisions.org/science/course/living-environment

New York City Department of Education. (2020). *New York City 9–12 Science Scope & Sequence*. New York: Author. www.weteachnyc.org/resources/collection/scope-and-sequence-science

New York State. (2022). *Laws of New York*, Article 15, Human Rights Law. www.nysenate.gov/legislation/laws/EXC/292

New York State Code, 8 C.R.R. § 83 (2021). Determination of good moral character. https://govt.westlaw.com/nycrr/Browse/Home/NewYork/NewYorkCodesRulesandRegulations?guid=If811fe70ab3811dd9e3f9b6a3be71c54

New York State Consolidated Laws, Education Law EDN § 915. (2022). www.p12.nysed.gov/sss/schoolhealth/schoolhealthservices/Article19Sections.html

New York State Education Department. (2017). *New York State Next Generation English Language Arts Learning Standards, Grade P–12*. Albany, NY: Author. www.nysed.gov/common/nysed/files/programs/curriculum-instruction/nys-next-generation-ela-standards.pdf

New York State Education Department. (2018). *Culturally Responsive-Sustaining Education Framework*. Albany, NY: Author. www.nysed.gov/common/nysed/files/programs/crs/culturally-responsive-sustaining-education-framework.pdf

New York State Education Department. (2020). New York State testing program, Next Generation Learning Standards, English Language Arts test: Performance level descriptions, Grade 6. Albany, NY: Author. www.nysed.gov/common/nysed/files/programs/state-assessment/6-nys-ela-plds-2020.pdf

New York State Education Department. (2021). Rochester City School District English language learners enrollment (2020–21). Albany, NY: Author. https://data.nysed.gov/ell.php?year=2021&instid=800000050065

New York State Education Department. (2022). Grade 8 Intermediate-level science test (June 6). Albany, NY: Author. www.nysedregents.org/Grade8/Science/622/ils62022-test.pdf

New York State Education Department. (2022). P–12 EngageNY—ELA, Grade 6. Albany, NY: Author. www.nysed.gov/curriculum-instruction/engageny

New York State Education Department. (2022). Sample score report, English Language Arts 2021–22 Grade 5 Test Results. Albany, NY: Author. www.nysed.gov/sites/default/files/programs/state-assessment/ela-3-8-score-report-english-2022.pdf

New York State Education Department. (2023). Creating a safe, supportive, and affirming school environment for transgender and gender expansive students: 2023 Legal update and best practices. Albany, NY: Author. www.nysed.gov/sites/default/files/programs/student-support-services/creating-a-safe-supportive-and-affirming-school-environment-for-transgender-and-gender-expansive-students.pdf

New York State Education Department. (2023). Public school enrollment, 2022–23. Albany, NY: New York State Education Department, Information and Reporting Services. www.p12.nysed.gov/irs/statistics/enroll-n-staff/home.html

New York State Education Department. (2023). Regents High School Examination: Living Environment (January 24). www.nysedregents.org/LivingEnvironment/123/lenv12023-exam.pdf

New York State Education Department. (2023). 2022–23 State aid handbook: Formula aids and entitlements for schools in New York State. Albany, NY: Author. https://stateaid.nysed.gov/publications/handbooks/handbook_2223.pdf

New York State Education Department. (n.d.). Glossary of terms—Enrollment data. Albany, NY: Author. https://data.nysed.gov/glossary.php?report=enrollment

New York State Education Department. (n.d.). History of New York State assessments. Albany, NY: Author. www.nysed.gov/state-assessment/history-new-york-state-assessments

(n.d.). New York State code of ethics for educators. Albany, NY: Author. www.highered.nysed.gov/tcert/pdf/codeofethics.pdf

New York State Education Department (n.d.). New York State data. Albany, NY: Author. https://data.nysed.gov

New York State Education Department. (n.d.). Timeline of New York State assessments. Albany, NY: Author. www.nysed.gov/state-assessment/timeline-new-york-state-assessments

New York State Education Law 2-d: Unauthorized release of personally identifiable information. (2015). www.nysenate.gov/legislation/laws/EDN/2-D

New York State Human Rights Law, § 291.2 (2019). www.nysenate.gov/legislation/laws/EXC/291

New York State Technical Assistance Center for Homeless Students. (2018). Meeting the unique learning needs of students exposed to trauma: How to apply trauma-sensitive strategies to improve academic outcomes for students in temporary housing. Albany, NY: Author. www.nysteachs.org/_files/ugd/10c789_99d34baaab9946bf9758af37b1236c7b.pdf

Newton, P. & Salvi, A. (2020). How common is belief in the learning styles neuromyth, and does it matter? A pragmatic systematic review. *Frontiers in education, 5*. https://doi.org/10.3389/feduc.2020.602451

Nilsson, J. (2010). Albert Einstein: "Imagination is more important than knowledge." *Saturday Evening Post*, March 20. www.saturdayeveningpost.com/2010/03/imagination-important-knowledge

Nittler, K. (2016). May 2016: Teacher tenure. Washington, DC: National Council on Teacher Quality. www.nctq.org/blog/May-2016:-Teacher-Tenure

Northwest Ordinance. (1787). Washington, DC: National Archives. www.archives.gov/milestone-documents/northwest-ordinance#transcript

O'Malley, J. (2017). The teenage whaler's tale: Internet death threats hound a young Alaskan after a successful hunt. *High Country News*, July 17. www.hcn.org/issues/49.12/tribal-affairs-a-teenage-whaler-pride-of-his-alaska-village-is-haunted-by-trolls

O'Sullivan, M. (2019). We worry about survival: American Indian women, sovereignty, and the right to bear and raise children in the 1970s. Unpublished dissertation. Chapel Hill, NC: University of North Carolina. https://cdr.lib.unc.edu/concern/dissertations/sx61dm783

Office of the New York State Comptroller. (2023). Real property tax levies, taxable full value and full value tax rates, 2022. Albany, NY: Author. www.

osc.state.ny.us/local-government/data/real-property-tax-levies-taxable-full-value-and-full-value-tax-rates

Ogletree, C. (2005). *All deliberate speed: Reflections on the first half-century of Brown v. Board of Education.* New York: Norton.

Opfer, V., Kaufman, J., & Thompson, L. (2016). Implementation of K–12 state standards for mathematics and English language arts and literacy: Findings from the American teacher panel. Santa Monica, CA: RAND Corporation. www.rand.org/pubs/research_reports/RR1529-1.html

Origami Ninja. (2014). How to make: Paper claws. www.youtube.com/watch?v=Qzeaw7UXscw

Ortiz Uribe, M. (2022). Students forced to bury "Mr. Spanish" look to make Blackwell School a historic site. *El Paso Times*, April 21. www.elpasotimes.com/in-depth/news/2022/04/21/marfa-texas-segregated-mexican-american-blackwell-school-nears-national-historic-site-designation/7157056001

Owens, A., Reardon, S., & Jencks, C. (2016). Income segregation between schools and school districts. *American Educational Research Journal, 53*(4), 1159–1197. https://doi.org/10.3102/0002831216652722

Owens, J. (2016). Early childhood behavior problems and the gender gap in educational attainment in the United States. *Sociology of Education, 89*(3): 236–258. https://doi.org/10.1177/0038040716650926

Padden, C., & Humphries, T. (2005). *Inside deaf culture.* Cambridge, MA: Harvard University Press.

Pagani v. Meriden Board of Education, U.S. Dist. 92267, D. Conn. (2006). https://casetext.com/case/pagani-v-meriden-board-of-education

Palardy, G.J. (2020). The impact of socioeconomic segregation in U.S. high schools on achievement, behavior, and attainment and the mediating effects of peers and school practices. In J. Hall, A. Lindorff, & P. Sammons, eds., *International Perspectives in Educational Effectiveness Research.* Cham, Switzerland: Springer. https://doi.org/10.1007/978-3-030-44810-3_11

Papadatou-Pastou, M., Haliou, E., & Vlachos, F. (2017). Brain knowledge and the prevalence of neuromyths among prospective teachers in Greece. *Frontiers in Psychology 8.* https://doi.org/10.3389/fpsyg.2017.00804

Papadopoulos, M. (2023). Middleborough boy asking Boston court to halt school's ban on "There are only two genders" shirt. *Boston 25 News*, June 1. www.boston25news.com/news/local/middleboro-boy-asking-boston-court-halt-schools-ban-there-are-only-two-genders-shirt/6LL4N2DLQVDXNL7ZDRCB7HXAQ4

Papageorge, N., Gershenson, S., & Kang, K. (2018). Teacher expectations matter. Cambridge, MA: National Bureau of Economic Research. Working Paper 25255. www.nber.org/papers/w25255

Papay, J., & Kraft, M. (2015). Productivity returns to experience in the teacher labor market: Methodological challenges and new evidence on long-term career improvement. *Journal of Public Economics, 130*: 105–119. https://doi.org/10.1016/j.jpubeco.2015.02.008

PARC v. Pennsylvania, 343 F. Supp. 279. E.D. Pa. (1972). https://law.justia.com/cases/federal/district-courts/FSupp/343/279/1691591

Parsons, S., & Bynner, J. (2006). Does numeracy matter more? London: National Research and Development Centre for Adult Literacy and Numeracy. https://discovery.ucl.ac.uk/id/eprint/1566244/1/parsons2006does.pdf

Patterson, J. (2002). *Brown v. Board of Education: A civil rights milestone and its troubled legacy.* London: Oxford University Press.

Paul, R. (1955). History of taxation in the United States. Williamsburg, VA: College of William & Mary Law School. https://scholarship.law.wm.edu/cgi/viewcontent.cgi?referer=&httpsredir=1&article=1659&context=tax

Pausch, R. (2017). Achieving your childhood dreams (The Last Lecture). September 18. www.youtube.com/watch?v=ji5_MqicxSo

Pavlakis, A., & Roegman, R. (2018). How dress codes criminalize males and sexualize females of color. *Kappan*, September 24. https://kappanonline.org/pavlakis-roegman-dress-codes-gender-race-discrimination

Pearce, M. (2013). Ohio court upholds firing of science teacher with classroom bible. *Los Angeles Times*, November 20. www.latimes.com/nation/nationnow/la-na-nn-ohio-teacher-bible-20131120-story.html

Pegoraro, L. (2015). Second-rate victims: the forced sterilization of Indigenous peoples in the USA and Canada. *Settler Colonial Studies*, *5*(2): 161–173. www.tandfonline.com/doi/abs/10.1080/2201473X.2014.955947

Pelsue, B. (2017). When it comes to education, the federal government is in charge of . . . Um, what? *Harvard Ed. Magazine.* Cambridge, MA: Harvard Graduate School of Education. www.gse.harvard.edu/news/ed/17/08/when-it-comes-education-federal-government-charge-um-what

PEN America. (2022). Banned in the USA: The growing movement to censor books in schools. Washington, DC: Author. https://pen.org/report/banned-usa-growing-movement-to-censor-books-in-schools

Pendharkar, E. (2021). Teacher fired for lesson on white privilege loses appeal. *EducationWeek*, October 16. www.edweek.org/teaching-learning/teacher-fired-for-lesson-on-white-privilege-loses-appeal/2021/10

Perry, A. (2020). Dress codes are the new "whites only" signs. *The Hechinger Report*, February 5. https://hechingerreport.org/dress-codes-are-the-new-whites-only-signs

Peters, S., & Carter, J. (2022). Predictors of access to gifted education: What makes for a successful school? *Exceptional Children*, *88*(4), 341–358. https://doi.org/10.1177/00144029221081092

Pew Charitable Trusts. (2016). Issue brief: Household expenditures and income. Philadelphia, PA: Author. www.pewtrusts.org/en/research-and-analysis/issue-briefs/2016/03/household-expenditures-and-income

Pew Research Center. (2022). About 5% of young adults in the U.S. say their gender is different from their sex assigned at birth. Washington, DC: Author. www.pewresearch.org/fact-tank/2022/06/07/about-5-of-young-adults-in-the-u-s-say-their-gender-is-different-from-their-sex-assigned-at-birth

Pew Research Center. (2022). As courts weigh affirmative action, grades and test scores seen as top factors in college admissions. Washington, DC: Author. www.pewresearch.org/short-reads/2022/04/26/u-s-public-continues-to-view-grades-test-scores-as-top-factors-in-college-admissions

Pickering v. Board of Education, 391 U.S. 563 (1968). https://caselaw.findlaw.com/us-supreme-court/391/563.html

Pirtle, W. (2019). The other segregation. *The Atlantic*, April 23. www.theatlantic.com/education/archive/2019/04/gifted-and-talented-programs-separate-students-race/587614

Pittsford Central School District. (2019). Report card information for parents. Pittsford, NY: Author. www.pittsfordschools.org/Page/23547

Pittsford Central School District. (2023). Pittsford Central School District policy manual index. Pittsford, NY: Author. www.pittsfordschools.org/cms/lib/NY02205365/Centricity/domain/32/policy%20manual/POLICY%20INDEX-%20CURRENT.pdf

Plyler v. Doe, 457 U.S. 202 (1982). www.law.cornell.edu/supremecourt/text/457/202

Popp, P., Grant, L., & Stronge, J. (2018). Classrooms with revolving doors: Recommended practices for elementary teachers of at-risk and highly mobile students. Brown's Summit, NC: National Center for Homeless Education, University of North Carolina. https://nche.ed.gov/wp-content/uploads/2018/11/eff_teach_elem.pdf

Porter, K., & Turner, L. (2020). Impact of the community eligibility provision of the Healthy, Hunger-Free Kids Act on student nutrition, behavior, and academic outcomes: 2011–2019. *American Journal of Public Health*, *110*, 1405–1410. https://doi.org/10.2105/AJPH.2020.305743Potter, H., & Nunberg, M. (2019). Scoring states on charter school integration. New York: The Century Foundation. https://tcf.org/content/report/scoring-states-charter-school-integration

Pressley, S. (1996). A "safety" blitz. *Washington Post*, November 12. www.washingtonpost.com/archive/politics/1996/11/12/a-safety-blitz/f7dd70dc-8f51-44fc-b293-e9afca9f9e12

Price, S. (2023). The little man has lost again: How a San Antonio lawsuit set back American education 50 years ago. *San Antonio Express-News*, March 21. www.expressnews.com/news/education/article/san-antonio-isd-rodriguez-50-17838148.php

Quintero, D., & Hansen, M. (2021). As we tackle school segregation, don't forget about English Learner students. Washington, DC: Brookings. www.brookings.edu/blog/brown-center-chalkboard/2021/01/14/as-we-tackle-school-segregation-dont-forget-about-english-learner-students

Quiocho, A., & Rios, F. (2000). The power of their presence: Minority group teachers and schooling. *Review of Educational Research*, *70*(4), 485–528. https://doi.org/10.3102/00346543070004485

Rademacher, T. (2017). *It won't be easy: An exceedingly honest (and slightly unprofessional) love letter to teaching*. Minneapolis: University of Minnesota Press.

Ravitch, D. (2016). *The death and life of the great American school system: How testing and choice are undermining education*. New York: Basic Books.

Rawick, G., Ed. (1972). *The American slave: A composite autobiography.* V.12, Georgia (II) 3, 78–79. Washington, DC: Smithsonian.

Ray, R., & Gibbons, A. (2021). Why are states banning critical race theory? Washington, DC: Brookings. www.brookings.edu/blog/fixgov/2021/07/02/why-are-states-banning-critical-race-theory

reardon, S., Fahle, E., Kalogrides, D., Podolsky, A., & Zárate, R. (2018). Gender achievement gaps in U.S. school districts. Palo Alto, CA: Stanford Center for Education Policy Analysis. https://cepa.stanford.edu/content/gender-achievement-gaps-us-school-districts

reardon, S., Weathers, E., Fahle, E., Jang, H., & D. Kalogrides. (2022). Is separate still unequal? New evidence on school segregation and racial academic achievement gaps. (CEPA Working Paper No. 19-06), Stanford Center for Education Policy Analysis: http://cepa.stanford.edu/wp19-06

Reber, S., & Gordon, N. (2023). A primer on elementary and secondary education in the United States: Who does what and how do we pay for it? Washington, DC: Brookings. www.brookings.edu/articles/a-primer-on-elementary-and-secondary-education-in-the-united-states

Reeves, R. (2022). *Of boys and men: Why the modern male is struggling, why it matters, and what to do about it.* Washington, DC: Brookings.

Reeves, R., & Halikias, D. (2017). Race gaps in SAT scores highlight inequality and hinder upward mobility. Washington, DC: Brookings, February 1. www.brookings.edu/articles/race-gaps-in-sat-scores-highlight-inequality-and-hinder-upward-mobility

Reeves, R., Guyot, K., & Krause, E. (2018). A dozen ways to be middle class. Washington, DC: Brookings, May 8. www.brookings.edu/interactives/a-dozen-ways-to-be-middle-class

Reeves, R., & Smith, E. (2021). The male college crisis is not just in enrollment, but completion. Washington, DC: Brookings, October 8. www.brookings.edu/blog/up-front/2021/10/08/the-male-college-crisis-is-not-just-in-enrollment-but-completion

Reeves, R., Buckner, E., & Smith, E. (2021). The unreported gender gap in high school graduation rates. Washington, DC: Brookings, January 12. www.brookings.edu/blog/up-front/2021/01/12/the-unreported-gender-gap-in-high-school-graduation-rates

Reyhner, J., & Eder, J. (2017). *American Indian education: A history* (2nd ed.). Norman: University of Oklahoma Press.

Richards, E. (2018). Lessons lost (series). *Milwaukee Journal Sentinel*, October 5. https://projects.jsonline.com/news/2018/10/5/high-student-turnover-in-milwaukee-stalls-achievement-despite-reforms.html

Richardson, J., Parnell, P., & Cole, H. (2015). *And Tango makes three.* New York: Simon & Schuster.

Riser-Kositsky, M. (2023). Education statistics: Facts about American Schools. *Education Week*, July 7. www.edweek.org/leadership/education-statistics-facts-about-american-schools/2019/01

Ritchie, S., & Bates, T. (2013). Enduring links from childhood mathematics and reading achievement to adult socioeconomic status. *Psychological Science*, 24(7), 1301–1308. https://doi.org/10.1177/0956797612466

Ritter, K. (2023). Nevada hands Tesla $330 million in tax breaks for a factory expansion that's supposed to create 3,000 jobs. *Fortune*, March 2. https://fortune.com/2023/03/02/tesla-tax-deal-nevada-expansion-tax-break

Robertson, K., & Ford, K. (n.d.). Language acquisition: An overview. Arlington, VA: Colorín Colorado. www.colorincolorado.org/article/language-acquisition-overview

Rochester City School District. (2021). *Code of conduct (2021): Plain language summary*. Rochester, NY: Author. www.rcsdk12.org/cms/lib/NY01001156/Centricity/Domain/16/COD_2021.pdf

Rochester City School District. (2023). *Austin Stewart School No. 46 Parent Handbook*. Rochester, NY: Author. www.rcsdk12.org/Page/10626

Rochester City School District. (n.d.). Bilingual education & world languages. Rochester, NY: Author. www.rcsdk12.org/domain/11868

Rockoff, J. E. (2004). The impact of individual teachers on student achievement: Evidence from panel data. *The American Economic Review*, *94*(2), 247–252. www.jstor.org/stable/3592891

Rogers, B. (2021). *Tips for teaching from a cart: Floating teachers and traveling teachers*. www.youtube.com/watch?app=desktop&v=1rrpw-JufPc

Rosenthal, R., & Jacobson, L. (1968). Pygmalion in the classroom. *The Urban Review*, *3*, 16–20. https://doi.org/10.1007/BF02322211

Rothstein, R. (2004). *Class and schools: Using social, economic, and educational reform to close the Black–white achievement gap*. Washington, DC: Economic Policy Institute.

Rothstein, R. (2017) *The color of law: A forgotten history of how our government segregated America*. New York: Liveright.

Rowley, A. (2008). "*Rowley* revisited: A personal narrative." *Journal of Law & Education*, *37*(3): 311–328.

Rubin, A., & Salmieri, D. (2012). *Dragons love tacos*. NY: Penguin Random House.

Rumberger, R. (2003). The causes and consequences of student mobility. *The Journal of Negro Education*, *72*(1), 6–21. https://doi.org/10.2307/3211287

Rutland, G. (2022). A white teacher said the N-word in a lesson. She was wrong—but shouldn't be fired. *Desert Sun*, April 4. www.desertsun.com/story/opinion/contributors/2022/04/04/white-california-teacher-who-used-n-word-lesson-should-not-fired/7272696001

Ryan, C., Russell, S., Huebner, D., Diaz, R., & Sanchez J. (2010). Family acceptance in adolescence and the health of LGBT young adults. *Journal of Child and Adolescent Psychiatric Nursing*, *23*(4), 205–213. https://doi.org/10.1111/j.1744-6171.2010.00246.x

Sabortnie, E., & Espelage, D., Eds. (2023). *Handbook of classroom management*. London: Routledge.

San Antonio v. Rodríguez, 411 U.S. 1 (1973). www.loc.gov/item/usrep411001

Sandel, M. (2010). *Justice: What's the right thing to do?* New York: Farrar, Straus and Giroux.

Sansone, D. (2019). LGBT students: New evidence on demographics and educational outcomes. *Economics of Education Review*, *73*. https://doi.org/10.1016/j.econedurev.2019.101933

Saultz, A. (2018). What does one do to get fired around here? An analysis of teacher dismissals in Georgia. *American Enterprise Institute*. www.aei.org/wp-content/uploads/2018/06/What-Does-One-Do-to-Get-Fired-Around-Here.pdf?x91208

Schaeffer, K. (2020). As schools shift to online learning amid pandemic, here's what we know about disabled students in the U.S. Washington, DC: Pew Research Center. www.pewresearch.org/fact-tank/2020/04/23/as-schools-shift-to-online-learning-amid-pandemic-heres-what-we-know-about-disabled-students-in-the-u-s

Schaeffer, K. (2022). 10 facts about today's college graduates. Washington, DC: Pew Research Center, April 12. www.pewresearch.org/short-reads/2022/04/12/10-facts-about-todays-college-graduates

Schafer, M., & Khan, S. (2016). Family economy, rural school choice, and flexischooling children with disabilities. *Rural sociology*, *82*(3): 524–547. https://doi.org/10.1111/ruso.12132

Schermele, Z. (2023). Texas teacher fired over Anne Frank graphic novel. The complaint? Sexual content. *USA Today*, September 20. www.usatoday.com/story/news/nation/2023/09/20/texas-teacher-fired-for-anne-frank-diary-lesson-that-included-sex/70911098007

Schifter, L., Grindal, T., Schwartz, G., & Hehir, T. (2019). Students from low-income families and special education. New York: The Century Foundation. https://tcf.org/content/report/students-low-income-families-special-education

Schinske, J., & Tanner, K. (2017). Teaching more by grading less (or differently). *CBE—Life Sciences Education*, *13*(2). https://doi.org/10.1187/cbe.cbe-14-03-0054

Schneider, J., & Hutt, E. (2023). *Off the mark: How grades, ratings and rankings undermine learning (but don't have to)*. Cambridge, MA: Harvard University Press.

Schultz, K. (2011). *Being wrong: Adventures in the margin of error*. New York: Ecco.

Schwartz, H. (2010). Housing policy is school policy: Economically integrative housing promotes academic success in Montgomery County, Maryland. New York: The Century Foundation, October 16. https://tcf.org/content/report/housing-policy-school-policy-economically-integrative-housing-promotes-academic-success-montgomery-county-maryland

Schwartz, K. (2016). *I wish my teacher knew: How one question can change everything for our kids*. Lebanon, IN: Da Capo Books.

Schwartzer, J., Ricci, L., & Melloni Jr., R. (2013). Prior fighting experience increases aggression in Syrian hamsters: Implications for a role of dopamine in the winner effect. *Aggressive Behavior*, *39*(4): 290–300. https://doi.org/10.1002/ab.21476

Section 504 of the Rehabilitation Act of 1973 (29 U.S.C. 701). (1973). www.law.cornell.edu/uscode/text/29/701

Seidenberg, M. (2017). *Language at the speed of sight: How we read, why so many can't, and what can be done about it*. New York: Basic Books.

Semege, J., & Kollar, M. (2022). Income in the United States: 2021. Washington, DC: United States Census Bureau. Report P60-276. www.census.gov/library/publications/2022/demo/p60-276.html

Sentendrey, D. (2023). Mesquite substitute teacher charged after allegedly encouraging student fights during class. Fox 4 News, April 17. www.fox4news.com/news/mesquite-substitute-teacher-charged-after-encouraging-student-fights-during-class

Shah, N. (2022). US school voucher programs have caught on—but are they funneling public dollars in private schools? *The Guardian*, September 7. www.theguardian.com/education/2022/sep/07/us-school-vouchers-covid-private-schools-parents-new-hampshire

Shindler, J. (2009). *Transformative classroom management*. San Francisco: Jossey-Bass.

Slavin, J. (2018). John Hattie is wrong. https://robertslavinsblog.wordpress.com/2018/06/21/john-hattie-is-wrong

Smith, S. (2023). Former "teacher of the year" arrested for allegedly having sex with 16-year-old: "There may be additional victims." *CBS News*, May 22. www.cbsnews.com/news/tracy-vanderhulst-arrested-former-teacher-of-the-year-sex-16-year-old-yucaipa-high-school

Solari, C., & Mare, R. (2012). Housing crowding effects on children's wellbeing. *Social Science Research*, *41*(2), 464–476. https://doi.org/10.1016/j.ssresearch.2011.09.012

Sonnenberg, R. (2023). Georgia teacher fired for reading children's book about acceptance in class. *Southern Poverty Law Center*, June 22. www.splcenter.org/news/2023/06/22/georgia-teacher-fired-reading-childrens-book-about-acceptance-class

South Dakota Department of Education. (2023). 2022–23 South Dakota School Districts (map). Pierre, SD: Author. https://doe.sd.gov/ofm/documents/schl-2223a.pdf

Spady, J. (2020). *Education and the racial dynamics of settler colonialism in early America: Georgia and South Carolina, ca. 1700–ca. 1820*. New York: Routledge.

Span, C. (2005). Learning in spite of opposition: African Americans and their history of educational exclusion in antebellum America. *Counterpoints*, *131*, 26–53. www.jstor.org/stable/42977282

Sparks, S. (2015). "Differentiated instruction: A primer." *Education Week*, January 28. www.edweek.org/teaching-learning/differentiated-instruction-a-primer/2015/01

Spencer, K. (2017). An examination of student mobility in U.S. public schools. (2017). PhD dissertation, University of Pennsylvania. https://repository.upenn.edu/edissertations/2591

Stark, J. (1987). The establishment of Wisconsin's income tax. *The Wisconsin Magazine of History*, *71*(1), 27–45. www.jstor.org/stable/4636094

State of California. (1866). Act to provide for a system of Common Schools. Statutes of California, Section 57. Sacramento, CA: Author. https://clerk.assembly.

ca.gov/sites/clerk.assembly.ca.gov/files/archive/Statutes/1865/1865_66. PDF#page=471

State of California. (1998). Proposition 227: English language in public schools. Sacramento, CA: Author. https://lao.ca.gov/ballot/1998/227_06_1998.htm

State of California. (2016). CA Education for a Global Economy initiative (Proposition 58). Sacramento, CA: Author. www.cde.ca.gov/sp/el/er/caedge.asp

State of Florida, House of Representatives. (2022). An act relating to parental rights in education, amending s. 1001.42, F.S. House Bill 1557. www.flsenate.gov/Session/Bill/2022/1557/BillText/er/PDF

Steen, B. (2022). Five Rs for Promoting Positive Family Engagement. Washington, DC: National Association for the Education of Young Children. www.naeyc.org/resources/pubs/tyc/winter2022/fiver-rs-family

Steinbuch, Y. (2022). NY school district sorry for homework calling Mexicans "ugly," Americans "pretty." *New York Post*, January 17. https://nypost.com/2022/01/17/ny-school-district-sorry-for-homework-calling-mexicans-ugly

Stolberg, S. (2006). The Decider. *New York Times*, December 24. www.nytimes.com/2006/12/24/weekinreview/the-decider.html

Stout, C., & Wilburn, T. (2022). CRT Map: Efforts to restrict teaching racism and bias have multiplied across the U.S. New York: *Chalkbeat*, February 1. www.chalkbeat.org/22525983/map-critical-race-theory-legislation-teaching-racism

Students for Fair Admissions v. Harvard, 600 U.S. ___ (2023).

Students for Fair Admissions. (2022). Petitioner brief, Students for Fair Admissions, Inc. v. President and Fellows of Harvard College. www.supremecourt.gov/DocketPDF/20/20-1199/222325/20220502145522418_20-1199 21-707 SFFA Brief to file final.pdf

Sturtz, K. (2014). Music teacher stole 50 instruments from school to buy drugs, state police say. Syracuse.com, March 19. www.syracuse.com/news/2014/03/music_teacher_stole_50_instruments_from_school_to_buy_drugs_state_police_say.html

Substance Abuse and Mental Health Services Administration (SAMHSA). (2023). How to talk about mental health, for educators. Washington, DC: Author. www.samhsa.gov/mental-health/how-to-talk/educators

Takanishi, R., & Le Menestrel, S., Eds. (2017). *Promoting the educational success of children and youth learning English*. Washington, DC: National Academies. https://nap.nationalacademies.org/catalog/24677/promoting-the-educational-success-of-children-and-youth-learning-english

Taylor, D., Berry, P., & Block, C. (1958). Does group participation when using brainstorming facilitate or inhibit creative thinking? *Administrative Science Quarterly*, *3*(1), 23–47. https://doi.org/10.2307/2390603

Teaching Channel. (2018). How to manage school fights. Eagan, MN: Author. www.teachingchannel.com/k12-hub/blog/how-to-manage-school-fights

Terada, Y. (2021). How to design better tests, based on the research. Nicasio, CA: Edutopia, October 15. www.edutopia.org/article/how-design-better-tests-based-research

Texas Declaration of Independence. (1836). https://avalon.law.yale.edu/19th_century/texdec.asp

Thieboult, C. (1956). A pure theory of local expenditures. *Journal of Political Economy*, *64*(5): 416–424. www.jstor.org/stable/1826343

Thomas, H. (2022). Indigenous knowledge is often overlooked in education. But it has a lot to teach us. *EdSurge*, January 13. www.edsurge.com/news/2022-01-13-indigenous-knowledge-is-often-overlooked-in-education-but-it-has-a-lot-to-teach-us

Thompson, K. (2017). English learners' time to reclassification: An analysis. *Educational Policy*, *31*(3), 330–363. https://doi.org/10.1177/0895904815598394

Thompson, O. (2019). School desegregation and Black teacher employment. Cambridge, MA: National Bureau of Education Research. Working paper 25990. www.nber.org/papers/w25990

Tillman, L. (2004). (Un)Intended consequences?: The impact of the *Brown v. Board of Education* decision on the employment status of Black educators. *Education and Urban Society*, *36*(3). https://doi.org/10.1177/0013124504264360

Tinker v. Des Moines. 393 U.S. 503, 506 (1969). www.law.cornell.edu/supremecourt/text/393/503

Title IX, Education Amendments of 1972. (1972). 20 U.S.C. §§ 1681–1688. www2.ed.gov/policy/rights/guid/ocr/sexoverview.html

TNTP. (2009). *The widget effect: Our national failure to acknowledge and act on differences in teacher effectiveness.* https://tntp.org/publications/view/the-widget-effect-failure-to-act-on-differences-in-teacher-effectiveness

Tobeluk v. Lind. (1976). Consent decree in the Superior Court for the State of Alaska, Third Judicial District, No. 72-2450. www.alaskool.org/native_ed/law/tobeluk.html

Trevor Project. (2022). 2022 National survey on LGBTQ youth mental health. West Hollywood, CA: Author. www.thetrevorproject.org/survey-2022.

Tucson News Now. (2018). TUSD board to talk reintroduction of Mexican-American Studies at meeting. Tucson, AZ: Author. www.kold.com/story/37270796/tusd-board-to-talk-reintroduction-of-mexican-american-studies-at-meeting

Tullis, J. (2023). 3 common myths about learning—and what teachers can do instead. Nicasio, CA: Edutopia, June 22. www.edutopia.org/article/common-myths-learning

Tutt, P. (2021). 20 Years of data shows what works for LGBTQ students. Nicasio, CA: Edutopia, November 19. www.edutopia.org/article/20-years-data-shows-what-works-lgbtq-students

Tyack, D. (1974). *The one best system: A history of American urban education.* Cambridge, MA: Harvard University Press.

Tyack, D., & Lowe, R. (1986). The constitutional moment: Reconstruction and Black education in the South. *American Journal of Education*, *94*(2), 236–256. www.jstor.org/stable/1084950

Tyack, D., & Hansot, E. (1988). Silence and policy talk: Historical puzzles about gender and education. *Educational Researcher*, *17*(3): 33–41. https://doi.org/10.2307/1174831

Tyng, C., Amin, H., Saad, M., & Malik, A. (2017). The influences of emotion on learning and memory. *Frontiers in Psychology*, *8*. https://doi.org/10.3389/fpsyg.2017.01454

Understood for All. (n.d.) 3 tiers of RTI support. New York: Author. www.understood.org/en/articles/3-tiers-of-rti-support

Underwood, J. (2019). Under the law: The legal balancing act over public school curriculum. *Phi Delta Kappan*, *100*(6), 74–75. https://journals.sagepub.com/doi/10.1177/0031721719834035h

University of Southern California. (2022). *The Segregation Index*. Los Angeles: USC Price School of Public Policy. https://segindex.org

Urban Institute. (2017). School funding: Do poor kids get their fair share? Washington, DC: Author. https://apps.urban.org/features/school-funding-do-poor-kids-get-fair-share

Urban Institute. (n.d.). State and local backgrounders: Property taxes. Washington, DC: Author. www.urban.org/policy-centers/cross-center-initiatives/state-and-local-finance-initiative/projects/state-and-local-backgrounders/property-taxes

U.S. Bureau of Labor Statistics (2015). People with a disability less likely to have completed a bachelor's degree. Washington, DC: Author. www.bls.gov/opub/ted/2015/people-with-a-disability-less-likely-to-have-completed-a-bachelors-degree.htm

U.S. Census Bureau. (2019). School enrollment in the United States: October 2018—Detailed tables. Washington, DC: Author. www.census.gov/data/tables/2018/demo/school-enrollment/2018-cps.html

U.S. Census Bureau. (2022). QuickFacts, United States. Washington, DC: Author. www.census.gov/quickfacts/fact/table/US/LFE046220

U.S. Census Bureau. (n.d.). About the Hispanic population and its origin. Washington, DC: Author. www.census.gov/topics/population/hispanic-origin/about.html

U.S. Census Bureau. (2022). School districts and associated counties. Washington, DC: Author. www.census.gov/programs-surveys/saipe/guidance-geographies/districts-counties.html

U.S. Census Bureau. (2022). Quick facts: Detroit city, Michigan. Washington, DC: Author. www.census.gov/quickfacts/fact/table/detroitcitymichigan,MI/PST045222

U.S. Centers for Disease Control and Prevention. (2004). General classroom conditions, Self-inspection checklist. Washington, DC: Author. www.cdc.gov/niosh/docs/2004-101/chklists/r1n05g~1.htm

U.S. Code, State responsibilities for assessment. 34 C.F.R. § 200.2 (2015). www.ecfr.gov/current/title-34/subtitle-B/chapter-II/part-200/subpart-A/subject-group-ECFR3da56646dfe7570/section-200.2

U.S. Code, Rules of construction. Title 20, Chap. 70, II Part C § 6692 (2002) www.law.cornell.edu/uscode/text/20/6692

U.S. Constitution. (1791). Amendment X. https://constitution.congress.gov/constitution/amendment-10

U.S. Constitution. (1868). Amendment XIV. https://constitution.congress.gov/browse/amendment-14

U.S. Department of Agriculture. (2022). Income eligibility guidelines. Washington, DC: Author. www.fns.usda.gov/cn/income-eligibility-guidelines

U.S. Department of Education. (2010). An overview of the U.S. Department of Education. Washington, DC: Author. www2.ed.gov/about/overview/focus/what.html

U.S. Department of Education. (2011). Fact sheet: Information on the rights of all children to enroll in school. Washington, DC: Author. www2.ed.gov/about/offices/list/ocr/docs/dcl-factsheet-201101.html

U.S. Department of Education. (2012). Equal access to education: Forty years of Title IX. Washington, DC: Author. www.justice.gov/sites/default/files/crt/legacy/2012/06/20/titleixreport.pdf

U.S. Department of Education. (2017). Every Student Succeeds Act high school graduation rate non-regulatory guidance. Washington, DC: Author. www2.ed.gov/policy/elsec/leg/essa/essagradrateguidance.pdf

U.S. Department of Education. (2017). Our nation's English learners: What are their characteristics? Washington, DC: Author. www2.ed.gov/datastory/el-characteristics/index.html

U.S. Department of Education. (2018). Ask a Regional Educational Laboratory: What does the research say about the relationship between reading proficiency by the end of third grade and academic achievement, college retention, college and career readiness, incarceration, and high school dropout? Washington, DC: U.S. Department of Education, Institute of Education Sciences, REL Midwest. https://ies.ed.gov/ncee/rel/Products/Region/midwest/Ask-A-REL/10268

U.S. Department of Education. (2022). What works clearinghouse version 5.0: Procedures and standards handbook. Washington, DC: U.S. Department of Education, Institute of Education Sciences. https://ies.ed.gov/ncee/wwc/Handbooks

U.S. Department of Education. (2022). Fact sheet: U.S. Department of Education's 2022 proposed amendments to its Title IX regulations. Washington, DC: Author. www2.ed.gov/about/offices/list/ocr/docs/t9nprm-factsheet.pdf

U.S. Department of Education. (2022). High school graduation rates for English Learners. Washington, DC: U.S. Department of Education, Office of English Language Acquisition. https://ncela.ed.gov/sites/default/files/2022-11/20200916-ELGraduationRatesFactSheet-508.pdf

U.S. Department of Education. (2023). Resource on confronting racial discrimination in student discipline. Washington, DC: U.S. Department of Education, Office for Civil Rights and U.S. Department of Justice, Civil Rights Division. www2.ed.gov/about/offices/list/ocr/docs/tvi-student-discipline-resource-202305.pdf

U.S. Department of Education. (2023). Toolkit for creating inclusive and nondiscriminatory school environments for LGBTQI+ students. Washington, DC: Author. www2.ed.gov/about/offices/list/ocr/docs/lgbtqi-student-resources-toolkit-062023.pdf

U.S. Department of Education. (n.d.). Improving basic programs operated by local educational agencies (Title I, Part A). Washington, DC: Author. www2.ed.gov/programs/titleiparta/index.html

U.S. Department of Education. (n.d.). National Assessment of Educational Progress. Washington, DC: Author. https://nces.ed.gov/nationsreportcard

U.S. Department of Education. (n.d.). What is an educational record? Washington, DC: Author. https://studentprivacy.ed.gov/faq/what-education-recordU.S. Department of Health and Human Services. (2023). HHS poverty guidelines for 2023. Washington, DC: Author. https://aspe.hhs.gov/topics/poverty-economic-mobility/poverty-guidelines

U.S. Department of Health and Human Services. (2021). Supporting LGBTQ+ youth. Atlanta, GA: Centers for Disease Control and Prevention. www.cdc.gov/healthyyouth/safe-supportive-environments/lgbtq_youth.htm

U.S. Department of Health and Human Services. (n.d.). stopbullying.gov. Washington, DC: Author. www.stopbullying.gov

U.S. Department of Housing and Urban Development. (n.d.). Housing choice vouchers fact sheet. Washington, DC: Author. www.hud.gov/topics/housing_choice_voucher_program_section_8

U.S. Department of the Interior. (2023). School directory. Washington, DC: Bureau of Indian Education. www.bie.edu/schools/directory

U.S. Department of Justice. (2015). Ensuring English Learner students can participate meaningfully and equally in educational programs. Washington, DC: Author. www2.ed.gov/about/offices/list/ocr/docs/dcl-factsheet-el-students-201501.pdf

U.S. Department of Justice. (n.d.). Introduction to the Americans with Disabilities Act. Washington, DC: Author. www.ada.gov/topics/intro-to-ada

U.S. Federal Reserve. (2022). Economic well-being of U.S. households (SHED). Washington, DC: Author. www.federalreserve.gov/publications/2022-economic-well-being-of-us-households-in-2021-dealing-with-unexpected-expenses.htm

U.S. Government Accountability Office. (2010). Many challenges arise in educating students who change schools frequently. Washington, DC: Author. www.gao.gov/assets/gao-11-40.pdf

U.S. Government Accountability Office. (2012). Charter schools: Additional federal attention needed to help protect access for students with disabilities. Washington, DC: Author. www.gao.gov/assets/gao-12-543.pdf

U.S. Government Accountability Office. (2022). K–12 Education: Student population has significantly diversified, but many schools remain divided along racial, ethnic, and economic lines. Washington, DC: Author. www.gao.gov/products/gao-22-104737

U.S. Government Accountability Office. (2022). Department of Education should help states address student testing issues and financial risks associated with virtual schools, particularly virtual charter schools. Washington, DC: Author. www.gao.gov/assets/gao-22-104444.pdf

U.S. House of Representatives, Committee on Public Lands. (1785). Land Ordinance of 1785. Washington, DC: National Archives. https://catalog.archives.gov/id/1943531U.S. Office of Personnel Management. (2018). Sizing up the Executive branch. Washington, DC: Author. www.opm.gov/policy-data-oversight/data-analysis-documentation/federal-employment-reports/reports-publications/sizing-up-the-executive-branch-2016.pdf

U.S. News & World Report. (2023). Best high schools in New York. www.usnews.com/education/best-high-schools/new-york

Usher, A. (2011). Public schools and the original federal land grant program: A background paper from the Center on Education Policy. Washington, DC: Center on Education Policy. https://files.eric.ed.gov/fulltext/ED518388.pdf

Valiente, C., Swanson J., & Eisenberg N. (2012). Linking students' emotions and academic achievement: When and why emotions matter. *Child Development Perspectives*, *6*(2), 129–135. https://doi.org/10.1111/j.1750-8606.2011.00192.x

Victor, D. (2019). Texas teacher fired over tweets asking Trump to "remove" immigrants. *The New York Times*, June 5. www.nytimes.com/2019/06/05/us/teacher-tweets-trump-georgia-clark.html

Vinovskis, M., & Bernard, R. (1978). Beyond Catharine Beecher: Female education in the antebellum period. *Signs*, *3*(4): 856–869. www.jstor.org/stable/3173119

Vlaming v. West Point School Board et al., 3 E.D. Va. (2020).

Walsh, M. (2020). Appeals court upholds teacher firing over Holocaust denial, 9/11 theories. *Education Week*, April 23. www.edweek.org/education/appeals-court-upholds-teacher-firing-over-holocaust-denial-9-11-theories/2020/04

Walsh, C. (2017). White backlash, the "taxpaying" public, and educational citizenship. *Critical Sociology*, *43*(2), 237–247. https://doi.org/10.1177/0896920516645657

Wang, K., Rathbun, A., & Musu, L. (2019). *School choice in the United States: 2019* (NCES 2019-106). Washington, DC: U.S. Department of Education, National Center for Education Statistics. https://nces.ed.gov/pubs2019/2019106.pdf

Washington, J. (2019). The untold story of wrestler Andrew Johnson's dreadlocks: How the high school athlete endured his infamous haircut. *Andscape*. https://andscape.com/features/the-untold-story-of-wrestler-andrew-johnsons-dreadlocks

Washington Office of Superintendent of Public Instruction. (n.d.). Types of Tribal Schools. Olympia, WA: Author. https://ospi.k12.wa.us/student-success/access-opportunity-education/native-education/types-tribal-schools

Wells, A., Fox, L., & Cordova-Cobo, D. (2016). How racially diverse schools and classrooms can benefit all students. New York: Century Foundation. https://tcf.org/content/report/how-racially-diverse-schools-and-classrooms-can-benefit-all-students

Welsh, R. (2017). School hopscotch: A comprehensive review of K–12 student mobility in the United States. *Review of Educational Research*, *87*(3), 475–511. www.jstor.org/stable/44667664

WestEd. (2021, February 25). Shedding light on the experiences of LGBTQ students: Sobering data and reasons for hope. San Francisco, CA: Author.

www.wested.org/wested-bulletin/insights-impact/shedding-light-on-the-experiences-of-lgbtq-students-sobering-data-and-reasons-for-hope

Wexler, N. (2019). Elementary education has gone terribly wrong. *The Atlantic*. www.theatlantic.com/magazine/archive/2019/08/the-radical-case-for-teaching-kids-stuff/592765

Wexler, N. (2019). Why homework doesn't seem to boost learning—and how it could. *Forbes*, January 3. www.forbes.com/sites/nataliewexler/2019/01/03/why-homework-doesnt-seem-to-boost-learning-and-how-it-could/?sh=62f38aa368ab

WHAM News. (2020). Gates Chili, Justice Dept. reach settlement on service dog lawsuit. https://13wham.com/news/local/gates-chili-justice-dept-reach-settlement-on-service-dog-lawsuit

Whitmire, R. (2011). *Why boys fail: Saving our sons from an educational system that's leaving them behind.* New York: Amacom.

Wikipedia. (n.d.). Archduke Franz Ferdinand of Austria. https://en.wikipedia.org/wiki/Archduke_Franz_Ferdinand_of_Austria

Willey, C. F. (1960). The three-decision multiple-choice test: A method of increasing the sensitivity of the multiple-choice item. *Psychological Reports*, 7(3), 475–477. https://doi.org/10.2466/pr0.1960.7.3.475

Williams, C. (2019, April 29). English learners and school choice: Helping charter schools serve multilingual families. New York: The Century Foundation. https://tcf.org/content/report/english-learners-school-choice-policies-delivering-charter-schools-equity-potential

Williams, H. (2005). *Self-taught: African American education in slavery and freedom.* Chapel Hill: University of North Carolina Press.

Williamson, V. (2017). *Read my lips: Why Americans are proud to pay taxes.* Princeton, NJ: Princeton University Press.

Willingham, D. (2021). *Why don't students like school?: A cognitive scientist answers questions about how the mind works and what it means for the classroom* (2nd ed.). New York: Jossey-Bass.

Willms, J. (2010). School composition and contextual effects on student outcomes. *Teachers College Record*, 112(4), 1008–1037. https://doi.org/10.1177/016146811011200408

Wilson, R. (2019). The new white flight. *Duke Journal of Constitutional Law & Public Policy*, 14(1). https://scholarship.law.duke.edu/djclpp/vol14/iss1/5

Winter, J. (2022). The rise and fall of vibes-based literacy. *The New Yorker*, September 1. www.newyorker.com/news/annals-of-education/the-rise-and-fall-of-vibes-based-literacy

Wong, A. (2018). The students suing for a constitutional right to education. *The Atlantic*, November 28. www.theatlantic.com/education/archive/2018/11/lawsuit-constitutional-right-education/576901

Wong, A. (2019). The U.S. teaching population is getting bigger, and more female. *The Atlantic*, February 20. www.theatlantic.com/education/archive/2019/02/the-explosion-of-women-teachers/582622

Wong, H., & Wong, R. (2018). *The first days of school: How to be an effective teacher.* Mountain View, CA: Harry K. Wong Publications.

Wood v. Arnold, No. 18-1430, 4th Cir. (2019). www.ca4.uscourts.gov/opinions/181430.P.pdf

Woods, A. (2020). The federal government gives Native students an inadequate education, and gets away with it. *ProPublica*, August 6. www.propublica.org/article/the-federal-government-gives-native-students-an-inadequate-education-and-gets-away-with-it

Woods, A., & Philip, A. (2021). The Bureau of Indian Education hasn't told the public how its schools are performing. So we did it instead. *ProPublica*, June 9. www.propublica.org/article/the-bureau-of-indian-information-hasnt-told-the-public-how-its-schools-are-performing

WSB-TV. (2023). Teacher accused of taping student to chair with duct tape for being "disruptive and not listening." Atlanta, GA: Cox Media Group, March 2. www.wsbtv.com/news/local/teacher-accused-taping-student-chair-with-duct-tape-being-disruptive-not-listening

Xu, Y. (2022). Where are charter schools located? Washington, DC: National Alliance for Public Charter Schools, December 6. https://data.publiccharters.org/digest/charter-school-data-digest/where-are-charter-schools-located

Yarrow, A. (2018). *Man out: Men on the sidelines of American life.* Washington, DC: Brookings.

Yoshida, H. (2020). Lessons à la cart: Teaching without a classroom. *Tools & tips*. Washington, DC: National Education Association. www.nea.org/professional-excellence/student-engagement/tools-tips/lessons-la-cart-teaching-without-classroom

Zero to Three. (2016). National parent survey report. Washington, DC: Author. www.zerotothree.org/resource/national-parent-survey-report

Zill, N. (2020). How do the children of immigrant parents perform in school? Charlottesville, VA: Institute for Family Studies, July 8. https://ifstudies.org/blog/how-do-the-children-of-immigrant-parents-perform-in-school

Zong, J., & Batalova, J. (2015). The limited English proficient population in the United States in 2013. Washington, DC: Migration Policy Institute, July 8. www.migrationpolicy.org/article/limited-english-proficient-population-united-states-2013

Index

Page numbers in italics refer to figures and tables.

1st Amendment (1791)
   students and, 99–101, 175–77, 218, 232–33
   teachers and, 17–19, 106–108, 116–18, 119–21, 121n4, 223, 248–50
   See also history of schools
10th Amendment (1791), 26–27, 53, 54–55, 65. *See also* governance (of schools); history of schools
14th Amendment (1868), 27–28, 53–54, 76n1, 99–101. *See also* history of schools; *San Antonio v. Rodríguez* (1973)

absences, preparing for, 141, 165, 178n5, 206n2
abuse (and/or neglect), child, 171–72
achievement (of students). *See* students, achievement of; National Assessment of Educational Progress (NAEP)
Alaska, 78–79, 104, *158*, 207, 234n1
Alexander v. Holmes Co. (1969), 31, 54
Americans with Disabilities Act (ADA) (1990), 219–20
anxiety (student). *See* mental health (student)
Apassingok, Chris Agragiiq (student), 93–95
assessment, 180–206, 242–43
   assessment/instruction cycle, 106, 145–47, 181–82, 186, 188–91, 201–202, 242–43
   classroom routines and, 111–12, 181, 194–97
   complexity of, 182, *183–84*, 194–95, 198–99, 206n3
   data analysis and, 186, 189–90, 201–202, 242–43
   definitions, 181, *184,* 184–85, *192*
   drawing inferences and, *184,* 184–85
   individual v. group, 164, 187, 242–43
   limitations of, 182, 194, 198–99
   MTSS/RTI systems and, 191–92, *192*
   National Assessment of Educational Progress (NAEP), 12, 12–13, 15–17, *16*, 239–40
   objections to, 181, 243
   preparation for ("test prep" or "teaching to the test"), 202–204
   purposes of, 150–51, 181–82, 186–88, 190–91, 203–204
   requirements for U.S. public schools, 181
   resources for, 206
   student work and, 111–12, 181–82, 193–97
   summative (standards-based), 114, 186–87, 188–91, 197–200, 242–43
   types of, 194–99
   standardized, 15–17, 181, *183–84,* 202–206
associations (teacher). *See* unions (teacher)
attendance, compulsory, 27, 99–101

295

background knowledge, importance of, 182
backward design, 145–47. *See also* assessment, assessment/instruction cycle
BONG HiTS 4 JESUS (*Morse v. Frederick* [2007]), 175–77
Boston Latin School, 21–22, 25, 27, 44
Brighton Central School District (NY), 35–36, *35*
Brown v. Board (1954), 9, 30–31, 34, 54, 76n1
Brown v. Board II (1955), 55
bullying (and harassment), 87–88, 126, 169–73, 177, 241–42

Carlisle Indian School (United States Indian Industrial School) (1879–1918), 37–38, *37*, 50n6. *See also* Indigenous students
carts (teaching from), 124–25
Central High School (Little Rock, AR), 30–31. *See also* desegregation (of schools)
charter schools, 46–47, 67–70, 77n8
　achievement of students in, 46, 68–70, 77n9
　criticism of, 46–47, 69–70, 77n10
　definition of, 68
　funding of, 67–70
　purposes of, 47, 67, 68, 69–70, 77n11
　segregation and, 46–47, 69
　Tribes and, *56*
　See also school choice
Clarke, Edward H. (physician), 44
classroom management, 155–78
　behavior as communication and, 160, 168–69
　challenges of, 134–39, 155–56
　code(s) of conduct, 135–37, *135*, 153n5
　definition of, 157
　guidelines for, 155, 159, 160–62, 166–69, *166–68*, 169–73

lesson planning and, 161, 163–66
resources for, 177
responsibility for, 160–61, 170–71, 211–13
seeking help with, 171–73
student learning and, 150–51, 156, 160
See also conflicts (in school); fights (responding to)
classrooms
　comfort and ease of use of, 125–28
　layouts of, 128–34, 153n3, 153n4, 174
　routines in, 111, 115, 129–30, 139–41, *139*, 155–56, 163–66
　rules for, 134–39, *135*, 153n5, *166–68*
　safety in, 126, 160, 162, 171–73, 209, 213–18, *217*, 234n2
college, graduation from (among parents), *12*, 12–13
communities, 78–102
　getting to know, 81, 93–96
　participation in, 83–85

conflicts (in school), 166–69, 216, *217*
　avoiding emotional responses, 166, *166–68*, 216
　identifying causes, 160
　responding to, 166, *166–68*, 168–69, 170–73, 178n3, 216, *217*, 233
　See also classroom management; fights (responding to); violence (in schools)
contracts (teacher), 58, 221, 233, 234n3
curriculum, 103–22
　adapting (for students with different needs), 95–96, 108–109, 115–16
　authority to adopt, 58, 103, 106–108, 116–18, 122n5, 224–25
　definition of, 103
　diverse, importance of, 95–96, 119–21

free speech and, 17–19, 106–108, 116–18, 119–21, 121n4, 223, 248–50
"hidden," 103, 121n2
materials from publishers or other teachers, using, 106, *107*, 109, 116, 121n1, 121–22n3
reviewing (for use with students), 108–16, *113*, 116–18
scope and sequence, 109–11, *110*, 112–15, *113*
See also teaching

d/Deaf students, 41–42, 50n7, 86, 151–52, 154n9, 154n10
depression (student). *See* mental health (student)
desegregation (of schools)
  Brown v. Board I (1954), 31–32, 34, 48
  Brown v. Board II (1955), 48
  busing and, 31–32, 48–49
  Detroit public schools and, 32, 48–49
  González v. Douglas (2017), 119–21
  "Massive resistance" and, 30–32, 34
  Milliken v. Bradley (1974), 32, 48–49, 62
  resistance to, 27–28, 30–32, 34, 47–49, 76n1
  Tucson Unified School District and, 119–21
  "white flight" and, 31–32, 34, 48–49
  See also history of schools; segregation (of students)
Dewey, John (philosopher), 1
differentiation, 112, 116, 143, 241
directions, giving, 163, 178n2
disabilities, students with (SWDs). *See* students with disabilities (SWDs)
dogs, service (in schools), 42–44, *43*

"Doll test" (1940s), 50n4. *See also* desegregation (of schools); segregation (of students)

Eckford, Elizabeth (student), 30–31. *See also* desegregation (of schools)
Einstein, Albert (scientist), 20n5
engagement (student), 15, 78–80, 115, 142, 148–51, 154n6, 163–66
  cognitive principles that support, *148*, 148–51
  definition of, 123–24, 148
English Language Learners (ELLs). *See* English learners (ELs)
English learners (ELs), 39–41, 82–83, 91–93
  assessment of, 187
  bilingual education and, 39–41, 92
  citizenship of, 40, 91, 218, 234n5
  families and, 40, 82–83, 91–93
  Proposition 227 (CA) and, 39–41, *39*
  right to public education, 40
  statistics describing, *12*, 13–14, 40, 91
  teaching guidelines for, 14, 40–41, 91–92
  translation (interpretation) and, 83, 92–93, 95
English as a New Language (ENL). *See* English learners (ELs)
English as a Second Language (ESL). *See* English learners (ELs)
Equal Protection Clause (14th Amendment [1868]), 27–28, 53–54, 76n1, 99–101
Escuela de Gramática, 22, 25
ethics (of teachers), 210–13, 223–30, 233
ethnicity (U.S. Census Bureau definition), 33
Evans-Marshall v. Board of Education (2010), 107–108
Every Student Succeeds Act (ESSA) (2015), 65

families, 78–85, 97–99, 228
  communication with, 82–83, 91–93, 228
  diversity of, 4, 93–96, 97–99
  experiences in school, 13, 78–85, 97–99, 228
  Family Educational Rights and Privacy Act (FERPA), 227
  relationships with, *12*, 12–13, 17, 78–85, 97–99, 102n3, 228
  using languages other than English, 39–40, 91–93
  See also homeschooling; relationships; school choice
Family Educational Rights and Privacy Act (FERPA), 227
federal government (role in schools), 26–27, 52–55, 65–66. *See also* 10th Amendment (1791); governance (of schools); history of schools
feedback (to students), 186, 195–96
fights (responding to), 216, *217*, 233. *See also* classroom management; conflicts (in school); violence (in schools)
finance (of schools), 34–36, 52, 62–67
  revenue sources, 34–36, 55, 59, 62–67, *64*
  spending, 36, 57, 66–67, *66*
  See also *San Antonio v. Rodríguez* (1973); taxes (that fund public schools)
fired (reasons teachers get), 223–30, 234n4, 234n5
  being bad with kids, 229–30
  contract violations, 224
  illegal actions, 223, 225, 226–27, 234n4, 234n5
  immorality, 223, 225–26
  incompetency, 227–29
  insubordination, 107–108, 116–18, 224–25
  neglect of duty, 223–24
  principal decisionmaking and, 59, *60*
  See also ethics (of teachers); teachers (roles and responsibilities of)
first day of school (preparation for), 124, 134, 140–41
first year teaching
  challenges of, *107*, 109, 208–12, 235–38, *236*
  expectations v. reality, *237*
  self-forgiveness and, 162, 174, 236–37
floating (between classrooms), 124–25
foundations of education (scholarly discipline), 1–2
Free Appropriate Public Education (FAPE), 151–52. *See also* students with disabilities (SWDs); Individuals with Disabilities Education Act (IDEA)
Free and reduced price meals (eligibility), *12,* 13, 101–102n1, 207. *See also* poverty, students and
free speech. *See* 1st Amendment (1791)
Friedman, Milton (economist), 72
funding (of schools). *See* finance (of schools)

Gates-Chili Central School District (NY), 42–44
gender expansive students, *10*, 45–46, 248–50. *See also* sex and gender (in schools)
"giftedness" (high ability) (of students), 88, 102n4
González v. Douglas (2017), 119–21
governance (of schools), 36, 48–49, 52–77
  definition of, 52
  district responsibilities and, 57–62, *60*, 76n4, 218
  federal government and, 26–27, 52–54, 55, 65–66

models for, 55, *60, 61*, 61–62
state, territorial and Tribal governments and, 22–23, 36, 37–38, 48–49, 52–54, 55–57, 59, 76n2–3, 119–21
Tribal schools and, 38, 55–56, *56–57*
See also 10th Amendment (1791); 14th Amendment (1868)
grades and grading, 199–200, *199*, 227
graduation rates (of students), *12*, 12, 14–15

harassment (and bullying), 87–88, 126, 169–73, 177, 241–42
Hattie, John (researcher), 244
Hawai'i Department of Education, 25, 50n2, *61*
Hendrick Hudson Central School District v. Amy Rowley (1982), 151–52
high mobility students, 89–91, 97
Hilton Central School District (NY), 42–44
history of schools, 21–51
   Boston Latin School (1635), 21–22, 25, 44
   Civilization Fund Act (1819), 27
   coeducation of sexes, 44
   Escuela de Gramática (1513), 22, 25
   establishment of first schools, 21–24, 25–26, 27, 55
   funding and, 62–66, *64*
   Indigenous peoples and, 21–24, 26, 27, 37, 42, *56–57*
   Jim Crow laws and, 26, 76n1, 121–22n3
   Manzanar Relocation Center (1942–45), *38*, 38–39
   Northwest Ordinances, 26–27
   Old Deluder Satan Act (MA, 1647), 25, 50n3
   Proposition 227 (CA), 39–41, *39*

slavery and, 23–24, 26, 27–28
U.S. Constitution and, 18–19, 26–27, 53–54
See also 10th Amendment (1791); 14th Amendment (1868); desegregation (of schools); local control (of public schools); segregation (of students)
homelessness (of students), 89–91, 97. See also poverty, students and
homeschooling, 6, 67, 70–71. See also school choice
homework, 112, 189

in loco parentis ("in the place of a parent"), 213
Indian Self-Determination and Education Assistance Act (1975), *56–57*. See also Indigenous students
Indigenous students, 21–24, 27–28, 37–38, 78–79
   Alaska Native students, *56–57*, 78–79, 93–95
   boarding (residential) schools and, 27–28, 37–38, *37*, 55–56, *56–57*
   Carlisle Indian School (United States Indian Industrial School) (1879–1918), 37–38, *37*, 50n6
   Civilization Fund Act (1819), 27
   Hawai'ian schools and, 22–23, 50n2
   Indian Self-Determination and Education Assistance Act (1975), *56–57*
   removal and, 23, 50n1
   sterilization and, 42
   Tribes and, 37–38, *37*, 55–56, *56–57*
Individualized Education Programs (IEPs), 11, 151–52. See also students with disabilities (SWDs); Individuals with Disabilities Education Act (1975)

Individuals with Disabilities Education Act (IDEA), 11, 15, 42–44, 65, 151–52. *See also* students with disabilities (SWDs)
instruction. *See* teaching
interest inventory (for students), *81*

Jefferson, Thomas (president), 26
Jim Crow laws, 28, 76n1, 121–22n3

Kamehameha III (king), 22
Kennedy v. Bremerton School District (2022), 18–19
Koretz, Daniel (psychometrician), 203–204

law (and P-12 schools), 207–34
   constitutional rights (of students), 99–101, 175–77, 218–21
   constitutional rights (of teachers), 17–19, 106–108, 116–18, 119–21, 121n4, 223, 248–50
   contracts (teacher), 58, 221, 233, 234n3
   lawsuits (and teachers), 210
   liability, 43–44, 208–10, 223–24
   negligence, 208–10, 224
   policies and procedures (responsibility to follow), 53, 55, 57, 213, 215
   resources for, 233
   See also fired (reasons teachers get)
learning (of students) 150–51, 155–74, 164, 186. *See also* assessment; objectives (student learning); standards (student learning); teaching
"Learning Styles" theory, *150*, 244
Least Restrictive Environment (LRE), 15. *See also* Individuals with Disabilities Education Act (IDEA); students with disabilities (SWDs)
lesson planning, 104, 145–47, 150–51, 163–66, *179*. *See also* assessment; curriculum; objectives (student learning); standards (student learning)
Lexile (measure of text complexity), 114
LGBTQ+ students, 87–88, 91, 116–17, 220–21, 227, 241–42, 248–50
   statistics describing, 87
   teaching guidelines for, 88, 91, 227, 241–42, 250
   See also bullying (and harassment); mental health (student); sex and gender expression (in schools)
liability, 43–44, 208–10, 223–24. *See also* law (and P-12 schools)
"lip reading," 151–52, 154n9
local control (of public schools), 25–29, *29*, 57–66, *73*
   district variability and, 17, 44, 58, *61*, 61–66, 89
   political interests and, 62, 119–21
   segregation and, 27–28, *29*, 31–36, 48–49, 119–21
   student mobility and, 72–73, 89–91
   See also governance (of schools); history of schools

Mahanoy Area School Dist. v. B.L. (2021), 232–33
Mann, Horace (lawyer), 44, 239–40
Manzanar Relocation Center (1942–45), *38*, 38–39
Marshall, Thurgood (U.S. Supreme Court justice), 54
Maslow, Abraham (psychologist), 126–27, 245
"Massive resistance," 30–32, 34. *See also* desegregation (of schools)
McKinney-Vento Act, 89–91, 97. *See also* homelessness (of students)
mental health (student), 5, 171–73, 220, 245–47, 250
   suicide (risk and prevention), 171, 214, 246–47

See also bullying (and harassment); safety, school
Mexican-American Studies (MAS) program (Tucson, AZ), 119–21
Milliken v. Bradley (1974), 32, 48–49, 62. *See also* desegregation (of schools)
Montana State Training School (Montana Deaf and Dumb Asylum), 41–42
Morse v. Frederick (2007), 175–77
Multi-Tiered Systems of Support (MTSS), 191–93. *See also* assessment, assessment/instruction cycle

Nagel, Thomas (philosopher), 3, 20n1
National Assessment of Educational Progress (NAEP), *12*, 12–13, 15–17, *16*, 239–40. *See also* assessment
National Association for the Advancement of Colored People (NAACP), 49
National School Lunch Program, 12, 13, 66, 96, 101–102n1, 207. *See also* poverty, students and
negligence, 208–10, 224. *See also* law (and P-12 schools)
New York City Public Schools, *61*
nonbinary students, *10*, 45–46, 248–50. *See also* sex and gender (in schools)
North Slope Borough School District (AK), *61*
Northwest Ordinances, 26–27

Obama, Barack (president), *80*
objectives (student learning), *113,* 113–15, 145–47, 189
Old Deluder Satan Act (MA, 1647), 25, 50n3

pedagogy, 103, 115, 141–45, *144–45,* 148–51, 154n6, 154n7. *See also* teaching

Pereira, Devyn (student), 42–44, *43*
performance descriptors, 105–106, *105*. *See also* objectives (student learning); standards (student learning)
Pittsford Central School District (NY), 76n4
Pickering v. Board of Education (1968), 116–17
poverty, students and, *12*, 13, 20n3, 34–36, *35*, 45, 89–91, 96–99
free and reduced priced meals ("Free and Reduced Lunch"; "FRL") and, *12*, 13, 96, 101–102n1, 207
language exposure and (Hart & Risley study), 96–97
statistics describing, *12*, 13, 96
teaching guidelines for, 13, 20n3, 89–91, 96–98
See also segregation (of students) by wealth
prayer (in schools), 18–19. *See also* religion and schools; 1st Amendment (1791)
principals (roles and responsibilities), 58–59, *60*, 170–73, 207, 213
advice for working with, 59, 107–108, 116–18, 162, 210–11, 216–18, 224–25, 228–29
See also governance (of schools)
proficiency (student), 105–106, 199–200, *199*. *See also* assessment; standards (student learning)
Proposition 227 (CA), 39–41, *39*. *See also* English learners
Pygmalion Effect, 97

Rage Against the Machine (band), 121, 122n6
reading instruction (need to improve), 97, 239–40, 250, 250n2
relationships
development of (with students), 5, 11, 78–85, 95–96, 161

relationships *(continued)*
  development of (with families), 12–13, 59, 60, 80–85, 91–93, 97–99, 228
  importance of (for learning), 4, 78–80, 161
  interest inventory (for students), *81*
  See also communities; families; students
religion and schools, 18–19, 99–101, 175–77, 248–50. *See also* 1st Amendment (1791)
research (on teaching practices), 243–45, 250–51n2
Response to Intervention (RTI), 191–93. *See also* assessment, assessment/instruction cycle
right to education (fundamental), 53, 74. See also *San Antonio v. Rodríguez* (1973)
Rochester City School District (NY), 35–36, *35*, 70, 77n11
routines (classroom), 111, 115, 129–30, 139–41, *139*, 155–56, 163–66
rules (classroom), 134–39, *135*, 153n5, *166–68*

safety, school, 213–18, *217*
  building, 160, 162, 209, 214–15, 234n2
  people, 162, 209, 213–18, 215, *217*, 245–47
  policy and procedural, 160, 215, 216–18
  school shootings, 213–14
  suicide (risk and prevention), 171, 214, 246–47
  See also mental health (student); violence (in schools)
salaries (of teachers), *9*, 9–10, 55, 67, 79, 101–102n1
San Antonio v. Rodríguez (1973), 53, 73–75
school boards (Boards of Education), responsibilities of, 25, 58–62, *60*. *See also* governance (of schools)

school choice, 67–73
  charter schools and, 46–47, 68–70
  definition, 67, 68
  funding and, 67–70, 72
  homeschooling and, 6, 70–71
  private schools and, 6, 32, 67–68, 72
  segregation and, 32, 46–47
  student mobility and, 72–73
  vouchers and, 72–73
  wealth and, 67–68
  See also families
school districts, 57–62, *60, 61*, 76n4
  authority and responsibilities of, 57–62, 106–108, 116–18, 200, 218
  number and variability of, 25, 57, 58, *61*
  organizational chart of (sample), *60*
  segregation and, 7–8, 31–32, 34–36, *35*, 48–49
  unified school systems and, 25, 50n2, *61*
  See also governance (of schools); local control (of public schools)
school law. *See* law (and P-12 schools)
schools, public
  demographics and enrollment in (students), 6, 7, 17, 2
  finance of, 7, 26, 36, 62–66, *64*, 67
  purposes of, 20–21, 25–26, 50n3, 53, 69–70
  segregation of, *7*, 7–8, *24*, 27–28, 47–48, 54, 119–21
  statistics describing, 6, *7, 16*
  See also governance (of schools); history of schools; local control (of public schools); students; teachers
schools, private, 6, 32, 67–68, 72
segregation (of students)
  by "giftedness," 88
  by disability, 14–15, 29–30, 41–44, 46–47, 240–41
  by language, 14, 28–29, *29*, 39–41, *39*, 46–47, 119–21

by nationality, 28–29, *29*, 37–39, *37, 38*, 39–41, *39, 56–57*, 119–21
by race and ethnicity, 7–8, 20n2, 23–24, *24*, 28, 29–36, *33, 35*, 46–47, 48–49, 75, 119–21, 121–22n3
by school choice, 31, 46–47
by sex and gender expression, 27, 44–46
by wealth, 7–8, 34–36, *35*, 46, 73–75
family engagement and, 46–47
fear as a cause of, 47–48
geography and, 23–24, *24*, 34, 40, 48–49
housing and, 31–32, 34–36, *35*, 40, 48–49
immigration policy and, 40
local control and, 27–28, *29*, 32, *32, 33*, 34, 48–49, 62, 119–21
negative impacts of, 29, 34, 50n4
private schools and, 31, 46
"Segregation academies" and, 31, 46
student achievement and, 34–36, *35*, 119–21
See also desegregation (of schools); history of schools
sex and gender (in schools)
coeducation, timing of, 44
definitions, 45, 87–88
gender expansive and nonbinary students, *10*, 45–46, 248–50
girls, limited expectations of, 27, 44, 121n2
outcomes of students, by sex, 45–46
respectful language and, 88, 227, 248–50
segregation by, 27, 44–46
statistics describing, *10*, 87
teaching about, 87–88, 116–17
Title IX (1972), 45, 220–21
transgender students, 45–46, 54, 227

See also bullying (and harassment); LGBTQ+ students
Smartt, Callie (student), 213–14
standards (student learning), 103–106, 109–11, 188–91, 199–200, *199*, 242–43
authority to establish, 55, 103–104, 116–18
backward planning and, 145–47, 188–91
Common Core State Standards (CCSS), 105
definition of, 103–104
organization of, 104–105
performance descriptors and, 105–106, *105*
See also assessment; lesson planning; objectives (student learning); teaching
states, territories and Tribes (responsibilities for schools), 54–57, 76n1. *See also* governance (of schools)
students
achievement of, *12*, 12–13, 15–17, *16*, 45–46, 186–87, 239–40
demographics of, 6–8, *10*, 10–15, *12, 32, 33, 35*, 36
dropout and graduation rates of, *12*, 12, 14–15, 89
engagement of, 15, 78–80, 115, 142, 148–51, 154n6, 163–66
getting to know, 79–85, *81*, 93–96
mental health and, 5, 171–73, 220, 245–47, 250
parent educational attainment of, *12*, 12–13
poverty and, *12*, 13, 20n3, 34–36, *35*, 45, 89–91, 96–99
supervision of, 208–10, 223–24
struggles of, 4–5, 172, 229–30
statistics describing, 6, 7, 10–12, *12*, 13–14, 40, 87, 91, 96
See also communities; families; relationships; teaching

Students for Fair Admissions v. Harvard (2023), 204–205
students with disabilities (SWDs)
adaptations for, 86–87, 112, 212–13
Americans with Disabilities Act (ADA) and, 219–20
assessment of, 187
eugenics and, 41–42, *41*, 102n4
exclusion from schools and classrooms, 14–15, 41–44, 86, 160, 212–13, 220, 226–27, 240–41
inclusion of, 14, 42, 86, 240–41
Individualized Education Programs (IEPs) and, 11, 151–52
Least Restrictive Environment (LRE) and, 15
low expectations for, 152, 212–13, 220, 240–41
statistics describing, *12*, 13, 14–15, 42, 241
teaching guidelines for, 14, 86–87, 240–41, 250
See also Individuals with Disabilities Education Act (IDEA; 1975); Universal Design for Learning (UDL)
suicide (risk and prevention), 171, 214. *See also* mental health (student)
SUNY Brockport (State University of New York, Brockport), 78
superintendents, responsibilities of, 58–59, *60*, 76n5. *See also* governance (of schools)

taxes (that fund public schools), 25–26, 36, 55, 62–66, 67, 73–75
housing and, 34–36, 64–66
property taxes as main type, 64–66, *64*, 73–75
resistance to, 26, 62–63, 65, 76n6
segregation and, 32, 34–36, *35*
variability of, 63–67, *64*, 67

See also finance (of schools); *San Antonio v. Rodríguez* (1973)
teachers
academic freedom of, 103, 106–108, 116–18, 122n4
attrition of, *9*, 10, 80, 98, 237–39
background differences with students and, 10–11, 45, 79, 93–96, 118, 119–21, 123, 177 248–50
challenges faced by, 5–6, 17, 79, 208, 227–30, 235–37
contracts and, 58, 221, 233, 234n3
decisionmaking of, 1–2, 10, 57, 211, *237*, 244
demographics of, 9–11, *9*, *10*, 45
employment, supervision and 57, 223–30
ethics and, 210–13, 223–30, 233
fairness (with students) and, 14, 98, 134–39, 212–13
fears of, 17, 47–48, 79, 83, 85, 102n2, 118, 214, 216
improvement of, 48, 78–80, 87, 162, 229, 237–39, 239–47
mental health and, 5, 214, 216, 238
preparation of (teacher preparation programs), 1–2, 212
professional development (learning) of, 96, 155, 239–41
roles and responsibilities of, 14, 17, 60–61, *60*, 210–13, 218, 228–29, 239–47
salaries of, *9*, 9–10, 55, 67, 79, 101–102n1
statistics describing, 7–11, *9*, *10*, 79
tenure and, *222–23*, 233
unions and, *222–23*
See also teaching; relationships
teaching
anticipating student challenges, 78–79, 114–16, 155, 245–47
assessment and, 180–206, 242–43
backward design and, 145–47
classroom management and, 155–78

data use and, 242–43, 250
differentiation and, *143*
getting to know students and families, 79–85, 91–93, 97–99, 102n3, 155
lesson planning, guidelines for, 161, 163–66
mistakes and, 102n2, 203–31, *231*
pedagogy, principles for choosing, 78–79, 115, 142–43
preparation for, 104–15, 155, 163–66, 186, 212
reading, need to improve, 239–40
research on, 141–42, 148–51, 243–45
theory-practice divide and, 1
trauma-informed, 245–47
types of (examples), 103, 141–45, *144–45*
what it is like, 1–20, 57, 80, 109, 163–66, 211–12, 235–37, *237*
See also teachers; relationships

tenure (teacher), *222–23*
territories, U.S., 20n4, 25
testing. See assessment
Tinker v. Des Moines (1969), 175–77
Title IX (1972), 45, 220–21. See also LGBTQ+ students; sex and gender (in schools)
transgender (students), 45–46, 54, 227. See also LGBTQ+ students; sex and gender (in schools)
Tribes (Indigenous Nations), 37–38, *37*, 53. See also Indigenous students; governance (of schools)

unhoused students, 89–91, 97. See also poverty, students and

unions (teacher), 221, *222–23*
United States Indian Industrial School (Carlisle Indian School) (1879–1918), 37–38, *37*, 50n6
U.S. Bureau of Indian Education (BIE), 25, 38, *56*. See also Indigenous students
U.S. Congress of the Confederation (1781–1789), 26
U.S. Constitution, 26–27, 53, 218–21. See also 1st Amendment (1791); 10th Amendment (1791); 14th Amendment (1868); history of schools
U.S. Department of Agriculture, 66. See also poverty, students and
U.S. Department of Defense, 25
U.S. Department of Education, 52. See also governance (of schools)
Universal Design for Learning (UDL), 87

violence (in schools), 213–18, *217*. See also classroom management; conflicts (in school); fights (responding to)
vocabulary, academic, 112, 114
Vlaming v. West Point School Board et al. (2020), 248–50
vouchers, 72–73. See also school choice

Waldkindergarten, 76–77n7
"white flight," 31–32, 34, 48–49. See also desegregation (of schools)
Willingham, Daniel (psychologist), 111, 148–51, 243, 250–51n2
Wisconsin v. Yoder (1972), 99–101

www.ingramcontent.com/pod-product-compliance
Ingram Content Group UK Ltd.
Pitfield, Milton Keynes, MK11 3LW, UK
UKHW051851210426
5322IPUK00025B/667